AF867266

Head-to-Head and Heart-to-Heart

Head-to-Head and Heart-to-Heart

Contemporary Discourse on Deaf Mental Health

Edited by Cathy J. Chovaz

Gallaudet University Press
Washington, DC

Gallaudet University Press
gupress.gallaudet.edu

Gallaudet University Press is located on the
traditional territories of Nacotchtank and Piscataway.

© 2026 by Gallaudet University
All rights reserved. Published 2026
Printed in the United States of America

ISBN: 978-1-954622-73-9 (casebound)
ISBN: 978-1-954622-76-0 (ebook)

The Library of Congress's Cataloging-in-Publication data for this title can be found online at https://www.loc.gov.

∞ This paper meets the requirements of ANSI/NISO Z39.48–1992 (Permanence of Paper).

Cover description: Background is a light blueish green and at the top of the cover is a graphic with a stylized outline of a face with eyes closed and a gentle smile, and an outline of a hand with a heart in the palm. In the background of the outlined figure are several solid-colored shapes. Below the graphic the sans serif text reads: HEAD-TO-HEAD AND HEART-TO-HEART; CONTEMPORARY DISCOURSE ON DEAF MENTAL HEALTH; EDITED BY CATHY J. CHOVAZ.

Cover design by Michel Vrana.

While the authors have made every effort to provide accurate internet addresses and other contact information at the time of publication, neither the publisher nor the authors assume any responsibility for errors or changes that occur after publication. Further, the publisher does not have any control over and does not assume any responsibility for third-party websites or their content.

No part of this book may be used or reproduced in any manner for the purpose of training artificial intelligence technologies or systems unless explicit written permission has been given by Gallaudet University Press and the author(s) of the book or chapter.

Contents

Foreword

When I first read the title of this book, I stumbled a bit, as it seemed like quite a mouthful. As I started reading the introduction, however, the title made increasingly more sense, until I finally realized that it is a perfect fit. The title, *Head-to-Head and Heart-to-Heart: Contemporary Discourse on Deaf Mental Health*, covers the depth, breadth, and urgency of the work within—a comprehensive and compassionate exploration of mental health in deaf individuals across the lifespan and across a range of experiences.

This book is a treasure. It is a rare and timely contribution to a field that has long been underrepresented in both academic literature and clinical practice. It offers a thorough description of the mental health needs of deaf people, including those who are Deaf+, and it does so with a perfect balance of knowledge (i.e., head-to-head) and storytelling (i.e., heart-to-heart). Each chapter is written by experts in the field. Yet it is the lived experiences of deaf individuals throughout the book that truly captivated me. These stories do more than illustrate the facts; they touch us deeply, reminding us that behind every diagnosis, every policy, and every intervention is a person whose life is shaped by language, culture, and community.

I have had the privilege of knowing Dr. Cathy Chovaz for more than a decade. Her work has been a source of inspiration in my own research and clinical practice, and I refer to her publications often. I had hoped Cathy would be part of my dissertation committee—an honor that the COVID-19 pandemic and its traveling restrictions put a stop to. The pandemic did not, however, prevent me from following her career and benefitting from her knowledge and experience.

Cathy's background as both a nurse and a clinical psychologist gives her a rare dual perspective—one that is grounded in both care and clinical precision. Her personal journey from hearing to Deaf, and her embracing American Sign Language and the Deaf community, adds a layer of authenticity and insight that few can offer. Cathy stands at the intersection of insider and outsider, clinician and client, researcher and storyteller. This allows her to create a collection that is not only academically robust but also deeply human.

Her investment in this work is evident in every chapter. Cathy is an active participant in the international field of mental health and deaf people, and her network of collaborators—many of whom contributed to this volume—reflects the global relevance and reach of her work. The book draws on diverse voices and perspectives, offering knowledge that spans clinical practice, education, justice, and end-of-life care.

What makes this book particularly vital is its relevance today. Despite the growing body of research in recent years, there continues to be a dearth of updated and accessible resources that address the mental health needs of deaf individuals in a holistic and culturally competent way. This book fills that gap. It offers new perspectives, summarizes recent research and provides a historical overview that helps readers understand how far we have come—and especially how far we still need to go. Most importantly, it emphasizes the vital role of language in addressing mental health issues, including the devastating consequences of language deprivation.

Each chapter is a call to action. The authors do not merely describe problems—they offer solutions that are grounded in research, clinical experience, and community engagement. They advocate for systemic change, for better training of professionals, for inclusive policies, and for the recognition of Deaf culture as a source of strength and resilience. The book is easy to read, yet it does not shy away from complexity. It invites readers to think critically, feel deeply, and act responsibly.

As someone who has worked in this field for many years, I found myself nodding in recognition, pausing to reflect, and at times moved to tears. The stories reminded me of the children, families, and colleagues I have met—each navigating a world that too often misunderstands or overlooks them. The theoretical insights confirmed what I have seen in practice, and the recommendations offer new pathways for advocacy and change.

I am deeply honored and grateful to have been asked to write this foreword. It has been a privilege to read this remarkable book, and I extend my deepest gratitude to Cathy and her collaborators for the opportunity. I hope that every reader—whether clinician, researcher, educator, policymaker, or family member—will find the same inspiration and insight in these pages as I did.

This book is more than a resource. It is proof of the power of language, community, and compassion. It reminds us that mental health care must be inclusive, culturally competent, and rooted in the lived experiences of those we serve. It also challenges us to do better—not just for deaf individuals, but for all who have been marginalized by systems that fail to see their full humanity.

To borrow a phrase from the book: "A story is nothing if not told." This book tells many stories. May they be heard, understood, and acted upon.

Chris Margaret Aanondsen
Clinical Psychologist
St. Olav's University Hospital
Trondheim, Norway
October 1, 2025

Introduction

Head-to-Head and Heart-to-Heart: Contemporary Discourse on Deaf Mental Health

Cathy J. Chovaz

This is a book of stories. It is also a book about stories.

Herein, the reader will find stories about advocates as well as those being supported: stories about clinicians, stories about deaf individuals, and stories about clinicians and deaf people, all describing and endeavoring to understand the mental health of people who are deaf and hard of hearing (DHH). Stories, especially those that provide insights into an individual's lived experiences, serve as a site for understanding the discourses surrounding mental health in a deaf context.

Prior to the 1960–70s, much of the literature on deaf people and mental health was written from a medical perspective. Deafness was categorized almost exclusively as an impairment resulting in a functional disability and even cognitive deficits. According to this medical model, individuals who were deaf needed medical interventions such as (re)habilitative services and assistive devices to be restored to [a healthy, abled] society. This pathologization extended to deaf people's mental health (Du Feu & Chovaz, 2014).

In 1975, the First National Symposium on Mental Health Needs of Deaf Adults and Children, held in Chicago, Illinois, was a turning point toward a more balanced view of deafness as not just a disability, but also a way of being in and experiencing the world. Stein et al. (1981) subsequently published their conference proceedings in *Deafness and Mental Health,* which included expanded and updated papers from the 1975 National Symposium on Mental Health Needs. In this seminal text, authors such as Kathryn P. Meadow summarized studies of behavior problems of deaf children, Laszlo Stein and Theresa Jabaley wrote about the importance of early identification and parent counseling, Fred Levin addressed insight-oriented psychotherapy with the deaf, Larry Stewart discussed counseling the deaf, and William Stokoe and Robbin Battison wrote about societal issues such as sign language, mental health, and satisfactory interaction. In the decades to come, these clinicians and scholars leveraged their theories and stories to [re]shape the general perception of deaf individuals as people in their own right, rather than as defective bodies.

During this time, texts filled with case studies and stories, such as Eugene Mindel and McCay Vernon's (1971) *They Grow in Silence: The Deaf Child and His Family,* Hilde Schlesinger and Kathryn Meadow-Orlans's (1972) *Sound and Sign: Childhood Deafness and Mental Health,* and John Denmark's (1974) *Deafness and Mental Health*, as well as Allen Sussman and Larry Stewart's (1971) *Counselling with Deaf People,* all had significant influences on mental health care for (and with) deaf people. These books serve to reframe discourses on deafness and mental health by describing deaf people as having their own perspectives and goals, and not as impaired ears to be remedied within the constraints of available diagnoses and treatment plans.

The following decade, Michael Harvey's textbook (1989) *Psychotherapy with Deaf and Hard of Hearing Persons: A Systemic Model* was published, followed by *Listen with the Heart: Relationships and Hearing Loss* (2001) and *Odyssey of Hearing Loss: Tales of Triumph* (2004). In these books, Harvey shares stories from his psychotherapy practice with individuals, couples, and families. The literature in mental health and deafness increasingly continues to provide readers with studies and descriptions of the lived experiences and well-being of deaf people (Duncan & O'Neill, 2022; Chovaz et al., 2022), stories of Deaf professionals regarding resilience and risk (Listman & Kurz, 2020), and many other deeply informative perspectives.[1]

As these studies demonstrate, it is critical to understand the lived experience of mental healthiness from those DHH people who have intimate knowledge of it rather than relying solely on clinical observations. That is, stories of deaf lived experiences should be a driving force behind not just texts and praxes, but also clinical practice.

The term "lived experiences," which I use throughout this introduction, derives from phenomenology—the study of lived experiences. It is a philosophical movement and research method developed at the turn of the 20th century by Austrian-German philosopher Edmund Husserl (Laverty, 2003), who contended that the focus of psychology should be seeking to understand an individual's consciousness and perceptions and not diagnosing a person based on criteria that might be informed by personal biases and perceptions. Husserl's coworker, Martin Heidegger, built on the original theory and coined what is now known as hermeneutic phenomenology. One of the key differences in these philosophies is Heidegger's call for self-reflection and acknowledgement of clinician biases/assumptions, which are "embedded and essential to interpretive process" (Laverty, 2003, p. 28), as opposed to Husserl's advocacy of "bracketing," or putting aside the clinician's own worldview entirely (Laverty, 2003). The authors in this collection are aligned in some ways with Husserl's theory—specifically, the belief that individuals should be understood on their own terms—and in other ways with Heidegger's theory—particularly the adoption of self-reflective practices.

Many informative descriptions of the lived experiences of DHH people stem from knowledge gained from the client's perspective, their identity, or their historicality.[2] This edited volume strives to go beyond individualistic descriptions, focusing on a variety of perspectives and experiences. This book of and about stories includes those DHH individuals who may be unable to articulate their own experiences, those DHH individuals who do not exhibit symptoms and behaviors as described in the *Diagnostic and Statistical Manual of Mental Disorders—Fifth Edition* (*DSM-5*) or the *International Classification of Diseases—11th Revision* (*ICD-11*) diagnoses yet are clearly suffering,[3] those family members and friends who may physically and emotionally walk beside the DHH individual even without a shared language, as well as those professionals who provide DHH individuals with mental health care, forensic services, palliative care, residential counseling, or educational curriculums.

To describe lived experiences in a deeper sense, I reflected on a way to organize and share these myriad perspectives as stories within and beyond theory and assumptions. One metaphor came to me: Phenomenologist theory is a trellis. While providing structure, a trellis is bare, perhaps

---

1. Throughout this volume, authors use "deaf" and "Deaf" inconsistently. The capital-D Deaf is generally used by culturally deaf individuals as an identity label, but the practice is not uniform throughout deaf communities.

2. Historicality, according to Heidegger, is "a person's history or background, includ[ing] what a culture gives a person from birth and is handed down, presenting ways of understanding the world" (quoted in Laverty, 2003, p. 28).

3. The *DSM-5* is produced by the American Psychiatric Association and used in the United States and Canada for clinical diagnoses of mental disorders. The *ICD-11* is produced by the World Health Organization and is used as a global standard for diagnostic health information.

even purposeless, without that which it supports. The trellis itself does not live; the interweaving vines of personal narratives are what flourishes. The clinician's work is not just maintaining the trellis, but also tending to the vines, learning and documenting the ways they grow. But the trellis analogy is insufficient on its own as a central theme; thus, further reflection was required. The thematic terms that resonated with me were "head-to-head" and "heart-to-heart," which led to the title of this book. For the unfamiliar reader, I will explain my intentions for the uses of these terms throughout this volume.

In clinical work, there are times when head-to-heads are necessary as we critically appraise symptoms for evidence-based meaning. These head-to-heads are often the clinical experiences of others described within the structure of theoretical paradigms. Head-to-head evokes the concept of learned conversations or academic discourse. Todd, author of *The Accidental Creative: How to Be Brilliant at a Moment's Notice* (2010), founded The Accidental Creative podcast in 2005. In his podcasts, Henry frames head-to-heads as a method of sharing new insights and resources to enrich each other's mental health and relationships. Similarly, the authors in this volume share new insights and resources through head-to-heads that ultimately strengthen, stretch, and grow the reader's awareness and knowledge on deafness and mental health.

As clinicians, practitioners, and academics, every author in this collection frames their work within some set of theoretical assumptions or guidelines. It may be that these theories work well; yet often in mental health and deafness, some of us find that traditional theory constrains us, tests our ability to utilize it in the way it was intended, or simply seems lacking. An example of this is language deprivation. This is not a new term, but was reconceptualized by child psychiatrist Sanjay Gulati as a syndrome experienced by some deaf individuals with delays and impoverishment in language development. Language deprivation syndrome has significant implications for cognitive, social, and emotional development. The reader is encouraged to read Glickman et al.'s (2020) journal article, "Language Deprivation Is a Game Changer for the Clinical Specialty of Deaf Mental Health," which is a head-to-head examination of language deprivation syndrome.

Currently, as a practicing clinician in Canada, I cannot diagnose language deprivation syndrome under the tenets of the *DSM-5*, as it does not exist as a diagnostic classification. However, it is clear to me that many of the DHH individuals whom I assess experience the life-long mental health sequalae of language deprivation. In these paradigms, then, it is essential that clinicians working with DHH clients understand the traditional system of diagnoses, yet also be aware of the age-old dilemma of forcing a square peg into a round hole. Sometimes it just does not fit. This is when head-to-head discourse between clinicians, between clinicians and clients, and between clinicians and their students supports and deepens our ever-growing understanding of the complexities inherent at the intersection of mental health and deafness.

There are also times when we as professionals engage in and appreciate the heart-to-hearts of those whom we serve. These are the stories they tell us in whatever way they can—through language, behavior, or the voices of others. And quite frequently, professionals may also share stories from their perspectives as caregivers. Stories often evoke emotion both in the storyteller and the story receiver. Stories can construct meanings, teach others about the world and its inhabitants, communicate innermost personal feelings, and build community. A story often allows two individuals to tend to each other through handshapes, tone, and expressions. In stories, we are not alone but rather part of something or someone else. These are heart-to-hearts.

Traditionally, the head-to-heads provide structure to the discussion and formation of diagnostic classifications. It is my hope that in the future, both head-to-heads and heart-to-hearts (such as in this volume) will be instrumental in the understanding and categorization of mental health diagnoses within the deaf population.

Reading a book is a head-to-head activity, yet some shared stories may also be a heart-to-heart between reader and author. The stories these authors tell are often rooted in stories they have been told by clients or, in some cases, stories that they themselves want to tell. The stories sometimes resonate with theory and sometimes push, or even break, the boundaries so that we understand more and can build better support structures. These head-to-heads and heart-to-hearts give the theory/trellis meaning. We, the authors of this book, are both the story holders and the storytellers, and this book is about the connections we are forging with the reader. Without the reader, there is no one to receive the story.

To better illustrate the rationale for this book, I begin with my own heart-to-heart.

I had an unremarkable birth (perhaps remarkable to my parents!) and grew up in a safe, loving, and privileged home. I had food, shelter, friends, education, and security. As a young adult, I was well poised to take flight into love, a career, and adulthood. At that point, everything changed. Everything I knew, everything I trusted, everything I understood, and everything I could predict changed. You might be asking how can that happen? And to the reader, I share that it indeed happened and became the story of my life.

I was born as a child who could hear into a family who could all hear, as could everybody I knew. I did not think about communicating; we just did it. Family dinner times were times to share—we told each other stories about our days, experiences, and feelings. We shared and created stories with our friends which helped shape who we were and better understand where we were headed. University was a wonderful culmination of stories on a whole different level—stories about topics that interested me and created excitement in me for a career.

And my career blossomed. I graduated with a degree in nursing and began employment in the neonatal intensive care unit in a large Canadian hospital. The science, skill set, technology, families, and above all, stories that my tiny premature baby patients told me through their courage and their fights for life profoundly changed me. I watched them struggle, was overcome with emotion when they thrived, held them as they died, and both celebrated and grieved with their families. The stories I was told by these babies, their families, and my medical peers inspired and energized me. I had found my niche in the art and science of helping others.

And then I became sick. I became so very sick so quickly and so seriously that everything was forced to stop and hang in the balance. I was eventually diagnosed with a very rare, potentially fatal autoimmune disorder characterized by encephalopathy, retinal vaso-occlusive disease, and hearing loss. The disorder attacked three areas of my body: my brain, my eyes, and my ears. The days I was sick became weeks which became months which became years. The treatment involved long-term medications to suppress my immune system, each with its own side effects.

I remember the night well that changed my life. I was in a step-down intensive care setting with a nurse assigned for my care. Each morning, my mother would phone to see how my night had been. That morning, as the nurse worked around my bedside, she handed me the phone (I did not hear it ring). I said hello but heard nothing and the nurse hung the phone up. A bit puzzled, she handed the phone to me again after it rang once more. I again said hello and heard nothing. This time, the nurse took the phone from me and spoke into it to my mother. I had essentially lost my hearing in the night from an inner ear vasculopathy, and my world had changed forevermore.

This is my heart-to-heart story that I share with you, and it is one where I traveled from sound to silence, joy to despair, understanding to not understanding, and being accepted to being isolated. I had many months of feeling hopeless, scared, and so sick, and my response was, at times, anger and, at times, to be withdrawn. Yet it is also a story of survival, as I eventually surrounded myself with deaf people. (Who knew deaf people even existed? Not I.) I was so fortunate that the Deaf community in the city where I lived at that time nurtured and supported me, and I was empowered by them. They told me their stories albeit sometimes only using gestures so I could understand, yet I began to learn their language and understand more. Whereas I thought I had understood the world before, they shared a totally new worldview with me, a different way of understanding what was around me, and a new level of self-acceptance. The medicine may have stopped the small blood vessels from causing me more neurological damage, but it was the Deaf community, as one part of my support network, that saved my life.

The shortest distance between two people may be a story. As I slowly put my life back together again and shifted my career toward psychology, I became acutely aware of the power that stories held. Theory was important, but it was the stories that made theory come alive. As a young deaf clinical psychologist (the first in Canada), I was not yet the storyteller, but a repository for these stories. Deaf children, deaf youth, deaf adults, hearing parents, and hearing families began to share their stories with me often of pain and significant mental health distress. And as I held their stories, healing happened—sometimes within me and sometimes within them. I did not have a magic wand to heal, but I did have theory and clinical tools. With these, I paid close attention to the storytellers. Over time, I began to see patterns.

Hearing parents shared their confusion and angst of not knowing how to parent a child who was so different from them, not knowing which language (spoken or sign) to implement at home, or even how to begin to communicate with their own child. The children shared their anger and frustration and loneliness at not feeling accepted and not fitting in with their peers. Grandparents and siblings shared their sadness and sometimes guilt for not really knowing or understanding their deaf grandchild or sibling. The teachers shared their frustration at not being able to reach their students. And I observed the medical professionals often trying to "fix" it all, often without really paying attention perhaps to the most important parts of the story. The application of the medical model to deaf individuals felt wrong to me even then, though I couldn't have articulated why. Now I recognize that I had not yet been well informed of the significant implications on one's mental health when a person is viewed as a deficient body to be "made whole" rather than as someone to be nurtured and celebrated on their own terms.

My experiences opened me to all the work that had gone before me. Spectacular, rigorous, ground-breaking work to which I had no exposure in any of my previous studies. I began to devour the literature, amazed at the scholarly work describing that which I was observing in my own life. I remember, as a graduate student, standing in the magnificent archives of the library, gazing at past issues of the *American Annals of the Deaf* and vowing one day to publish in it (and I did).

The last 25 years have seen an explosion of important textbook and journal articles regarding deaf people and mental health. Reading these fuelled my head-to-head awareness of important issues.[4] There is currently available a wealth of excellent information and resources regarding mental health with deaf adults. The literature is less robust for deaf children, especially regarding counseling strategies, but it is growing.

As authors were publishing their research on deaf people's mental health, world conferences focusing on the same began to convene. The first World Congress on Mental Health and Deafness

4. For some notable works that have shaped my personal and professional journey, please see the Further Reading section at the end of this introduction.

took place at Gallaudet University in Washington, DC, in 1998. The World Congress has been held in the intervening years in Copenhagen, Denmark (2000); Worcester, South Africa (2005); Brisbane, Australia (2009); Monterrey, Mexico (2012);[5] and the sixth and final World Congress was held in Belfast, Ireland (2014).

It was a professional and personal highlight for me to present a paper at the 2009 Brisbane world health congress, where I had the pleasure of meeting Dr. Margaret Du Feu from Ireland. Margaret and I (she using British Sign Language and me using American Sign Language—and both of us trying to meet in the middle!) began a long friendship there and later collaborated on our 2014 textbook *Mental Health and Deafness*. I was further honored to be asked to be a keynote presenter at the 2014 world congress in Belfast. That congress resulted in the important Belfast Statement on Mental Health and Deafness (https://esmhd.org/10-years-belfast-statement). The statement sets out the right to effective communication access in mental health settings for Deaf, late-deafened, hard of hearing, and Deafblind people of all ages. It is endorsed by the World Federation of the Deaf (WFD),[6] the European Society on Mental Health and Deafness, the British Deaf Association, Sense/Sense International, and the Northern Ireland Human Rights Commission.

The WFD hosts many events around the world, including conferences focused on mental health. In 2015, I was fortunate to be invited to be the keynote presenter of "Mental Health of Deaf Children and Adults" at the WFD conference in Istanbul, Turkey, and the following year, I was a keynote presenter of "Mental Health and Deaf People: What Are the Facts?" at the WFD Asia Conference in Singapore. In 2017, I was invited to give a keynote presentation ("Life Stories—Mental Health and Deafness") to the Deaf Cultural Festival in Bergen, Norway. For each of these presentations, I shared stories of deaf people I had worked with in my practice.

As I have developed in my skills as a clinician, author, and presenter at conferences, I have often turned to stories to illustrate my points. It has become clear to me that perhaps my strongest contribution can be the head-to-heads and the heart-to-hearts strongly framed within my professional area of expertise. The importance of clinical stories, on a heart-to-heart note, recently resulted in my first fiction book: *No, No, Bad Dogs*, published by Austin Macauley Publishers in 2023. This is a fictitious story based on three decades of holding stories for and with deaf people as well as examining my own heart and mind as a clinician and deaf person.

My 2014 textbook with Margaret Du Feu (*Mental Health and Deafness*) was largely written for mental health care professionals with limited knowledge of working with DHH clients. Recently, Austen and Holmes (2021) independently published *An Introductory Guide for Professionals Working with Deaf and Hard of Hearing Clients in Clinical, Legal, Educational and Social Care Settings* to raise awareness of important issues affecting DHH people and to facilitate the development of basic knowledge for professionals with little experience working with this population. Both these textbooks provide excellent basic yet invaluable information.

For this current volume, I build on that knowledge by gathering academic and clinical storytellers based on their significant and notable experiences working with deaf children, adolescents,

---

5. The interested reader may find thirteen papers from this congress published by Aranda et al. (2015).

6. The WFD is a global organization which works to ensure equal rights for deaf people around the world.

and adults. Being a clinical storyteller comes with certain obligations, such as protecting the confidentiality of the deaf client yet remaining truthful to the story intent and content. In a clinical context, the original storyteller—the deaf client—has the potential to be understood, often for the first time. The sharing then of these conversations or lived experiences has the power to teach others, the ability to reach people in meaningful places, and the potential for individuals to realize there may be shared life paradigms and that fundamentally none of us are quite alone.

All the authors in this volume are accomplished professionals, each with their own publication list and areas of research expertise, as you will see in their brief professional biographies below. Not all are used to being storytellers, yet all have stories to tell. The catalyst for this book was to invite these individuals to tell their stories and the stories of their clients, their patients, and those they have served. A collection, if you will, of heads-to-heads and hearts-to-hearts.

Kristin Snoddon, **Wyatte C. Hall**, and **Cathy J. Chovaz** begin the collection with an emphasis on the critical importance of language acquisition and development in deaf children. Given that language is one of the antecedents of mental health, this chapter serves as the foundation for the trellis upon which the stories in this collection weave themselves. Chapter 2, written by **Joanne C. Weber** and **Jennifer S. Thom**, is largely a head-to-head chapter that explores ways in which deaf children in particular are failed by educational institutions. They provide a thought-provoking dialogue on the ongoing, unresolved issues in deaf education, set within the context of the story of Carter Churchill, a profoundly deaf child whose parents, in 2022, won a human rights case against the Newfoundland and Labrador English School District for failure to provide an equitable and accessible education.

Justin Mulder and **Cathy J. Chovaz** build parallel tracks in Chapter 3, outlining the challenges of American Sign Language (ASL) translations and psychometric testing of existing assessment instruments, such as the Strengths and Difficulties Questionnaire. They emphasize the critical need for culturally and linguistically appropriate assessment tools and informed assessors when working with DHH individuals. Expanding on this, in Chapter 4, **Cathy J. Chovaz** seeks to better understand the complex clinical presentations clinicians may encounter. Through the narration of stories, which come directly from clinical work in Canadian schools for the Deaf, private practice, and a children's mental health agency for DHH and child of deaf adult (Coda) children and youth, Chovaz emphasizes the necessity of being aware of and often needing to recruit additional communication expertise in complex assessments. In the same vein, **Patrick Boudreault** and **Lori A. Day** describe best practices and recommendations in the assessment and treatment of DHH children. Through the stories of these children, the authors emphasize that language assessments should ideally be conducted by language specialists separate from the clinical assessor.

While the aforementioned chapters work toward building and stabilizing the trellis structure, as well as planting the seeds of stories, the stories flourish on the vines in Chapter 6, written by **Veronica Bickle** and **Cathy J. Chovaz**, which showcases the challenges of supporting DHH children and Codas with complex clinical presentations, including language delay/deprivation, trauma, family conflict, and mental health disorders, and in Chapter 7, written by **Meghan L. Fox** and **Mary K. Matchett**, who outline—through heart-to-heart stories which give "voice" to diverse deaf individuals, their families, and professionals—the research on the risks and protective factors associated with deaf adult mental health, as well as highlight the importance of resilience or positive meaning-making, often in the face of traumatic realities and experiences.

The trellis is further beautifully expanded by **Johannes Fellinger**, whose chapter describes the prevalence, etiologies, and specific developmental living conditions of individuals who are deaf or hard of hearing with intellectual disabilities. The specific stories of the individuals and their families for whom these therapeutic communities were developed in Austria provide a successful model of serving clientele effectively. **Debra Russell** and **Catriona J. Revell** weave a supportive thread through the trellis, exploring sign language interpreting services as one aspect of the provision of mental health and addiction support in Canada. The authors include a comparison of the Canadian and international policies and practices that have shaped interpreting services in mental health contexts, sharing the heart-to-heart stories of a survey of 107 Canadian interpreters and two targeted interviews.

In Chapter 10, **James C. MacDougall** tells the story of barriers and issues relative to equitable justice for DHH persons in a Canadian context. The most compelling stories of this chapter describe issues with the determination of fitness to stand trial for deaf individuals who, for a wide variety of reasons, do not use a standard sign language and do not have a mental disorder. Showcasing stories that focus on marginalized groups within the justice system, MacDougall highlights the intersections of constructs such as diversity among deaf people, language deprivation, communication assessments, and forensic assessments.

The final chapter of this collection, written by **Victor Maddalena** and **Myles K. Murphy**, explores the challenges that deaf people experience when accessing palliative, end-of-life, and bereavement care. Seven participants share their experiences with deafness, dying, and accessing health services at end of life in Newfoundland, Canada. It is a poignant end to the collection, as many of the issues regarding language acquisition as antecedents of mental health (outlined in Chapter 1) remain unfortunately salient at the end of life for many deaf individuals.

In closing, the heart-to-hearts and head-to-heads in these chapters describe the salient experiences of DHH individuals, their families, and those of us who work with them. As the editor of this book, I was privileged to request heartfelt sharing from the chapter authors, many of whom are world-renowned experts in their content area. Reading their work caused me to reflect again on my own heart-to-heart and head-to-head journey, leading me to where I am today. I realize now with conviction that we cannot—in fact, we must not—divorce head-to-heads from heart-to-hearts. The theoretical assumptions that we often base our work on as clinicians must be informed by, as well as honor, the heart-to-hearts.

An analogy recurs in this introduction of a trellis (theory) and the plants (clinical stories) it supports. Plants bloom tremendously in auspicious conditions and wither in adverse ones. The trellis is not a living entity, yet the plants most certainly are, responding to necessary constructs in our world of mental health and deafness such as the following:

- early and accessible language acquisition,
- thoughtful, constructive, and efficacious educational strategies,
- meaningful and inclusive family relationships, and
- community and social systems (mental health, forensics, interpreting, palliative) that competently reflect those they serve.

It is our collective hope as authors with diverse backgrounds, training, ways of being in the world, and experiences that we have given the reader a deeper understanding of the perspectives, insights, and discourse regarding DHH people and mental health. A story is nothing if not told.

Contributors

Chapter 1: Language Acquisition and Language Deprivation: Antecedents to Mental Health

Kristin Snoddon is a deaf scholar and associate professor with the School of Early Childhood Studies, Toronto Metropolitan University, Canada. Her research and professional experience include collaborative work with deaf communities in developing sign language and early literacy programming for young deaf children and their parents. Her longstanding program of research has focused on developing a parent ASL curriculum that is aligned with the Common European Framework of Reference for Languages. Additionally, she analyzes policy issues related to inclusive education, sign language rights, and acquisition planning for ASL. Her current research focuses on sign language ideologies and ideologies of understanding related to deaf interpreters.

Wyatte C. Hall is a Deaf scholar and an assistant professor of public health sciences, pediatrics, obstetrics & gynecology, and neurology at the University of Rochester Medical Center, USA. He is director of the Visual Language Access & Acquisition Lab, which explores the relationship between early childhood language experiences and quality-of-life outcomes across the lifespan. This includes a particular focus on the social epidemic of language deprivation and its impact on trauma and mental health.

Cathy J. Chovaz is a deaf scholar, author, and full professor in the Department of Psychology and director of the Centre of Deaf Education and Accessibility Forum, King's University College, Ontario, Canada, with a cross-appointment in the Department of Psychiatry, Schulich School of Medicine & Dentistry at Western University, Canada. She is the consulting clinical psychologist to PAH!, which is a mental health program for DHH children at the Bob Rumball Canadian Centre of Excellence for the Deaf. Dr. Chovaz teaches courses in clinical psychology, and her area of expertise is mental health and deafness.

Chapter 2: Deaf Education

Joanne C. Weber is a Deaf scholar, author, Canada research chair (tier 2) in deaf education, and an assistant professor in the faculty of education at the University of Alberta, Canada. Her research interests include language and literacy education, arts-based literacy interventions, arts-based research, arts education, posthumanism, applied linguistics, and sign language studies. Her lifelong passion is to improve the quality of education for deaf students. She is the artistic director of Deaf Crows Collective, which aims to provide opportunities for theater performance by deaf actors of all ages to celebrate Deaf culture, encourage self-expression, and foster relationships between hearing and Deaf communities.

Jennifer S. Thom is an associate professor of curriculum studies and mathematics education in the faculty of education at the University of Victoria, Canada, and the mother of a deaf child. In general, her work focuses on ecological, (em)bodied, and culturally responsive forms of teaching, learning, and research. Her current interests include DHH learners' mathematics abilities, education and the cultural commons, collective learning systems, theories of cognition, and STEM (science, technology, engineering, and mathematics).

Chapter 3: Psychological Assessment of Deaf and Hard of Hearing Individuals: Translating and Implementing the ASL Strengths and Difficulties Questionnaire

Justin Mulder is an addiction and mental health worker with the Canadian Mental Health Association Thames Valley Addiction and Mental Health Services. He is currently a graduate student in psychology at the University of Ottawa, Ontario, Canada.

See the Chapter 1 biography above for **Cathy J. Chovaz**'s professional designations.

Chapter 4: Mental Health of Deaf and Hard of Hearing Children and Youth

See the Chapter 1 biography above for **Cathy J. Chovaz**'s professional designations.

Chapter 5: Best Practices in Mental Health Assessment and Treatment of Deaf Children

Patrick Boudreault is a research scientist at Gallaudet University, specializing in sign language teaching and Deaf studies. A native of Quebec City, he is fluent in Langue des Signes Québécoise, ASL, English, and French. He holds a PhD in educational psychology, a MSc in communication sciences and disorders, and a BA in linguistics. With over 25 years of experience, Dr. Boudreault has made significant contributions in both Canada and the United States. His interdisciplinary work spans medicine, humanities, and technology, benefiting Deaf, Hard of Hearing, and Deafblind communities. As a principal or coinvestigator, he has been involved in federally and privately funded projects. Dr. Boudreault is a passionate advocate for sign language as the most accessible means of communication for the Deaf community.

Lori A. Day is a licensed psychologist and professor in the Department of Psychology in the School of Human Services and Sciences, Gallaudet University, Washington DC. She is the director of the Deaf and Hard of Hearing Child Resilience Center, which is a treatment center created to address the gap between DHH children who have experienced trauma and the mental health services they deserve.

Chapter 6: Stories About Challenges Supporting the Mental Health of Deaf and Hard of Hearing Children and Hearing Children of Deaf Families

Veronica Bickle is a registered social worker and the clinical lead at PAH!, a program within the Bob Rumball Canadian Centre of Excellence for the Deaf in Toronto, Ontario. PAH! is a children's mental health program for DHH children, youth, and families and hearing children of Deaf adults.

See the Chapter 1 biography above for **Cathy J. Chovaz**'s professional designations.

Chapter 7: Mental Health of Deaf and Hard of Hearing Adults

Meghan L. Fox is a licensed clinical psychologist in private practice in Rochester, NY, with a specialty in conducting licensed services with DHH persons and their families. Dr. Fox has been working with DHH persons and their families since 2008, including psychotherapy, psychological testing, program development and evaluation, conference presentations, workshops, and forensic evaluations. Dr. Fox has an appointment as a clinical instructor at the University of Rochester Medical Center and holds editorial positions with various national academic journals. She is a proud hearing sibling of a Deaf adult.

Mary K. Matchett is a Deaf social worker with a doctorate in executive leadership. She is currently assistant vice president for student and academic services at the National Technical Institute for the Deaf at Rochester Institute of Technology, Rochester, NY. Her professional passion is working with DHH students in higher education. She strives to create better services and opportunities to break down the barriers that DHH students may face.

Chapter 8: Unlocking the Potential of Deaf Adults with Multiple Disabilities

Johannes Fellinger is the head of the Institute for Neurology of Senses and Language, Hospital of St. John of God Linz and head of the Research Institute for Developmental Medicine, Johannes Kepler University Linz in Austria. He is a psychiatrist, a neuropediatrician, teaches developmental medicine, and has been the key initiator and developer of therapeutic living communities for adults who are deaf and have multiple disabilities in Austria. He is the son of a Deaf father.

Chapter 9: Mental Health Interpreting in Canada: A Call to Action

Debra Russell is an ASL/English interpreter, educator, researcher, and consultant. She has a PhD in educational psychology, and her research interests include legal interpreting, consecutive and simultaneous interpreting, interpreting in mediated educational environments, Deaf interpreters, conference interpreting, and power dynamics within teams of interpreters. She is the honorary president of the World Association of Sign Language Interpreters (WASLI).

Catriona J. Revell is an ASL/English Interpreter. She has a BA in psychology from the University of Pennsylvania and a MA in interpretation from Gallaudet University. She is currently working as a mental health interpreter in Toronto, Canada.

Chapter 10: Deaf and Hard of Hearing Persons in the Canadian Criminal Justice System: A Time for Action

James C. MacDougall is a retired associate professor of psychology at McGill University, Montreal, Canada. He is the senior consultant of mental health and research at the Bob Rumball Canadian Centre of Excellence for the Deaf and the president and CEO of the Canadian Deafness Research and Training Institute. In 2010, he became a member of the Order of Canada and in 2013 received the Queen Elizabeth II Diamond Jubilee Medal. Dr. MacDougall's research has been in the field of deafness, and he is a committed advocate for the needs and rights of all Canadians with disabilities. He grew up in a family with Deaf parents.

Chapter 11: Palliative and End-of-Life Care of Deaf and Hard of Hearing Adults

Victor Maddalena is an associate professor in health policy and health service delivery, faculty of medicine, Division of Community Health and Humanities, Memorial University of Newfoundland, Canada. He completed two postdoctoral fellowships in palliative and end-of-life care and currently teaches graduate-level courses in public health leadership and management and program development in public health. Dr. Maddalena's research interests are in the areas of assessing and serving the health needs of vulnerable populations, governance of health systems, palliative and end-of-life care, family caregiving, health human resources planning, and health policy.

Myles K. Murphy is the executive director and employment facilitator at the Newfoundland and Labrador Association of the Deaf, a nonprofit organization with the aim of protecting and promoting the rights, needs, and concerns of people who are Deaf/communicate in ASL within the province of Newfoundland and Labrador. Mr. Murphy is a member of and strong advocate for the Deaf community. In 2020, Mr. Murphy was awarded the civilian honor of the Order of Newfoundland and Labrador.

Further Reading

The following is an inexhaustive list of those works that have been notable in shaping my personal and professional journey:

- Altshuler's (1971) article, "Studies of the Deaf: Relevance to Psychiatric Theory," describes the author's observations over a 16-year period of mental health symptoms in individuals with profound deafness.
- Denmark's (1974) text, *Deafness and Mental Health*. Denmark was considered one of the world's leading psychiatrists in his work with deaf people. His writing describes the many problems deaf people face, specifically within the context of recognizing mental disorders.
- Vernon and Andrew's (1990) text, *The Psychology of Deafness: Understanding Deaf and Hard-of-Hearing People*, provides a very clear introduction to the psychology of deafness and has become a classic reference book.
- Pollard's (1996) article, "Professional Psychology and Deaf People: The Emergence of a Discipline," depicts the emergence of a field of professional psychology and specifically comments on the accessibility of the profession to deaf students and clinicians.
- Glickman and Harvey's (1996) text, *Culturally Affirmative Psychotherapy with Deaf Persons*, is one of the first works to exhaustively describe the implications of using a culturally affirmative model for understanding and counseling deaf people.
- Hindley and Kitson's (2000) text, *Mental Health and Deafness*, was written as an introductory text for care workers and mental health workers, both those familiar with deaf people but not with mental health and those familiar with mental health but not with deaf people.
- Gutman's (2002) edited collection, *Ethics in Mental Health and Deafness*, explores the many ethical issues specific to working with deaf clients.
- Vernon's (2006) article, "The APA and Deafness," outlines deaf people's access to mental health care in the United States following the 1990 American with Disabilities Act.
- Leigh's (2010) text, *Psychotherapy with Deaf Clients from Diverse Groups*, second edition, provides detailed information on ethical issues relevant to working with deaf clients as well as descriptions of the assessment and treatment of deaf clients from diverse groups, such as lesbian, gay, and bisexual deaf populations; CODAs; people with Usher syndrome; and Black, Indigenous, and people of color who are deaf.

- Estrada's (2011) text, *Mental Health and Some Sociocultural Issues in Deaf People*, outlines the psychological realities of deaf people, with a focus on depression and stress.
- Leigh and Pollard's (2011) chapter, "Mental Health and Deaf Adults" (in Marschark and Spencer's text, *Oxford Handbook of Deaf Studies, Language, and Education*), addresses many critical issues in providing mental health services to deaf adults in need. The results of public policy advocacy in the United States around the time of this book's publication are discussed as being influential in program development and administration.
- Fellinger, Holzinger and Pollard's (2012) article, "Mental Health of Deaf People," describes deafness as a heterogeneous condition with far-reaching effects on social, emotional, and cognitive development. There is an emphasis on the importance of the provision of specialist services with professionals trained to directly communicate with deaf people and with sign language interpreters.
- Glickman's (2013) edited collection, *Deaf Mental Health Care*, includes contributions from many of the leading clinicians, teachers, administrators, and researchers from the United States and Great Britain, who in their contributions address critical issues working within deaf mental health care.
- Pollard et al.'s (2014) article, "Integrating Primary Care and Behavioral Health with Four Special Populations: Children with Special Needs, People with Serious Mental Illness, Refugees, and Deaf People," focuses on four special populations: children with special needs, persons with severe and persistent mental illness, refugees, and deaf people who communicate via sign language. American primary care and behavioral health collaboration regarding each of these four populations are examined using a primary care/behavioral healthcare model of collaboration.
- Glickman's (2017) text, *Preparing Deaf and Hearing Persons with Language and Learning Challenges for CBT: A Pre-Therapy Workbook*, discusses relevant theories and approaches based on evidence-based best practices. Each chapter presents scenarios describing problems a mental health therapist might encounter when working with deaf people who don't read well or have trouble with abstract ideas, problem solving, reasoning, attention, and learning.
- Glickman and Hall's (2018) edited volume, *Language Deprivation and Deaf Mental Health*, explores the impact of the language deprivation that some deaf individuals experience due to a lack of fully accessible language exposure during childhood. Leading experts in Deaf mental health care discuss the implications of language deprivation for a person's development, communication, cognitive abilities, behavior, and mental health.
- Fellinger, Dall, and Holzinger's (2021) article, "Therapeutic Living Communities for Adults Who Are Deaf and Have Intellectual Disabilities: A Conceptual Model Linking Social Communication and Mental Health," describes a practical approach to supporting mental health implemented in the Austrian therapeutic living communities (known as Lebenswelt).
- Guthman, Lomas, Paris, and Martin's (2021) edited collection, *Deaf People in the Criminal Justice System: Selected Topics on Advocacy, Incarceration, and Social Justice*, addresses issues in the U.S. criminal justice system such as accessibility needs; gaps regarding data collection and the need for more research; additional training for attorneys, court personnel, and prison staff; the need for more qualified sign language interpreters, including certified Deaf interpreters who provide services in court, prison, and juvenile facilities; substance use disorders; the school-to-prison nexus; and the need for advocacy.

References

Altshuler, K. Z. (1971). Studies of the deaf: Relevance to psychiatric theory. *The American Journal of Psychiatry, 127*(11), 1521–1526. https://doi.org/10.1176/ajp.127.11.1521

American Psychiatric Association (APA). (2022). *Diagnostic and statistical manual of mental disorders* (5th ed., text rev.). https://doi.org/10.1176/appi.books.9780890425787

Austen, S., & Holmes, B. (2021). *An introductory guide for professionals working with deaf and hard of hearing clients in clinical, legal, educational and social care settings.* Self-published.

Chomsky, N. (1965). *Aspects of the theory of syntax.* MIT Press.

Chovaz, C. J. (2023). *No, No, Bad Dogs.* Austin Macauley.

Chovaz, C. J., Russell, D., & Daly, B. (2022). Lived experiences of deaf Canadians: What we want you to know! *Canadian Psychology / Psychologie canadienne, 63*(4), 651–666. https://doi.org/10.1037/cap0000313

Denmark, J. C. (1974). *Deafness and mental health.* Jessica Kingsley Publishers.

Du Feu, M., & Chovaz, C. (2014). *Mental health and deafness.* Oxford University Press.

Duncan, J., & O'Neill, R. (2022). The importance of the lived experience of deaf people. *Deafness & Education International, 24*(1), Article 1. https://doi.org/10.1080/14643154.2022.2035485

Estrada Aranda, B. D. (Ed.) (2011). *Mental health and some sociocultural issues in deaf people.* Nova Science Publishers.

Fellinger, J., Dall, M., & Holzinger, D. (2021). Therapeutic living communities for adults who are deaf and have intellectual disabilities: A conceptual model linking social communication and mental health. *International Journal of Developmental Disabilities, 67*(5), 391–396. https://doi.org/10.1080/20473869.2021.1953938

Fellinger, J., Holzinger, D., & Pollard, R. (2012). Mental health of deaf people. *The Lancet (British Edition), 379*(9820), 1037–1044. https://doi.org/10.1016/S0140-6736(11)61143-4

Glickman, N. S. (Ed.) (2013). *Deaf mental health care.* Taylor and Francis.

Glickman, N. S. (2016). *Preparing deaf and hearing persons with language and learning challenges for CBT: A pre-therapy workbook.* Routledge.

Glickman, N. S., Crump, C., & Hamerdinger, S. (2020). Language deprivation is a game changer for the clinical specialty of deaf mental health. *Journal of the American Deafness and Rehabilitation Association, 54*(1), 54–89.

Glickman, N. S., & Harvey, M. A. (Eds.) (1996). *Culturally affirmative psychotherapy with deaf persons.* Lawrence Erlbaum Associates.

Glickman, N. S., & Hall, W. C. (Eds.). (2018). *Language deprivation and deaf mental health* (1st ed.). Routledge.

Gutman, V. (Ed.) (2002). *Ethics in mental health and deafness.* Gallaudet University Press.

Guthmann, D., Lomas, G. I., Paris, D. G., & Martin, G. A. (Eds.). (2021). *Deaf people in the criminal justice system: Selected topics on advocacy, incarceration, and social justice.* Gallaudet University Press.

Harvey, M. (1989). *Psychotherapy with deaf and hard of hearing persons: A systemic model.* Erlbaum.

Harvey, M. A. (2001). *Listen with the heart: Relationships and hearing loss.* DawnSignPress.

Harvey, M. A. (2004). *Odyssey of hearing loss: Tales of triumph.* DawnSignPress.

Henry, T. (2010). *The accidental creative: How to be brilliant at a moment's notice.* Portfolio.

Hindley, P., & Kitson, N. (Eds.) (1999). *Mental health and deafness.* Wiley.

Laverty, S. M. (2003). Hermeneutic phenomenology and phenomenology: A comparison of historical and methodological considerations. *International Journal of Qualitative Methods, 2*(3), 21–35. https://doi.org/10.1177/160940690300200303

Leigh, I. W. (Ed.). (2010). *Psychotherapy with deaf clients from diverse groups* (2nd ed.). Gallaudet University Press.

Leigh, I. W., & Pollard, R. Q, Jr. (2011). Mental health and deaf adults. In M. Marschark & P. E. Spencer (Eds.) *Oxford handbook of deaf studies, language, and education* (2nd ed.) (pp. 214–226). Oxford University Press.

Listman, J. D., & Kurz, K. B. (2020). Lived experience: Deaf professionals' stories of resilience and risks. *Journal of Deaf Studies and Deaf Education, 25*(2), 239–249. https://doi.org/10.1093/deafed/enz045

Mindel, E. D., & Vernon, M. (Eds.). (1971). *They grow in silence: Understanding deaf children and adults.* National Association of the Deaf.

Pollard, R. Q, Jr. (1996). Professional psychology and deaf people: The emergence of a discipline. *American Psychologist, 51*(4), 389–396. https://doi.org/10.1037/0003-066X.51.4.389

Pollard, R. Q, Jr., Betts, W. R., Carroll, J. K., Waxmonsky, J. A., Barnett, S., de Gruy, F. V., III, Pickler, L. L., & Kellar-Guenther, Y. (2014). Integrating primary care and behavioral health with four special populations: Children with special needs, people with serious mental illness, refugees, and deaf people. *American Psychologist, 69*(4), 377–387. https://doi.org/10.1037/a0036220

Schlesinger, H. S., & Meadow-Orlans, K. P. (1972). *Sound and sign: Childhood deafness and mental health.* University of California Press.

Stein, L. K., Mindel, E. D., & Jabaley, T. (1981). *Deafness & mental health.* Grune & Stratton.

Sussman, A. E., & Stewart, L. G. (Eds.) (1971). *Counseling with deaf people.* Deafness Research and Training Center.

Vernon, M. (2006). The APA and deafness. *American Psychologist, 61*(8), 816–824. https://doi.org/10.1037/0003-066X.61.8.816

Vernon, M., & Andrews, J. F. (1990). *The psychology of deafness: Understanding deaf and hard-of-hearing people.* Longman.

World Health Organization. (2019/2021). *International classification of diseases—11th revision* (ICD-11). https://icd.who.int/browse11.

1

Language Acquisition and Language Deprivation

Antecedents to Mental Health

Kristin Snoddon, Wyatte C. Hall, and Cathy J. Chovaz

Construct

This chapter outlines language acquisition and its inverse, language deprivation, in young deaf and hard of hearing (DHH) children and their link to mental health. We start with a brief overview of language acquisition and language deprivation and then review research regarding language deprivation and mental health. We then describe strategies for supporting young DHH children and their families' American Sign Language (ASL) acquisition. DHH children and their families acquiring ASL have ongoing learning needs to support family communication and DHH children and youth's well-being.

Head-to-Head and Heart-to-Heart

The first part of this chapter includes a head-to-head review of clinical research in language acquisition and language deprivation. To incorporate a heart-to-heart perspective, findings are then shared from case studies of language deprivation in DHH children. In addition, the chapter describes a 9-month study of intensive parent ASL courses that were adapted and developed for online instruction to meet the second or additional ASL learning needs of parents of DHH children. This includes data regarding participating parents' learning processes and experiences.

Statements of Self-Reflexivity

First Author: Kristin Snoddon

I am a deaf applied linguist as well as a white settler cisgendered woman. I became deaf in early childhood and grew up in schools without signing access. I began learning ASL and International Sign when I was in my early twenties through participation in deaf clubs and working for deaf advocacy organizations. Reflecting my lived experience and commitment to bridging theory and practice, my research has focused on teaching ASL to parents of DHH children and studying how understanding is mediated by deaf interpreters.

Second Author: Wyatte C. Hall

I am a Deaf public health researcher and psychologist. I am a white male who was identified as deaf at 2 years old. I grew up in a public school with a large DHH program and used signed and spoken language, classroom interpreters, and hearing aids throughout my education. My primary work focuses on the relationship between early childhood language experiences and quality-of-life outcomes across the lifespan. Via my lived experiences and previous clinical work, I have a particular interest and focus on investigating language deprivation as a DHH population health crisis with sociocultural origins.

Third Author: Cathy J. Chovaz

I acknowledge my view as a deafened white female clinical psychologist. I was deafened as a young adult and grew up with spoken English as my first language and as such do not share the same early experiences of many of my patients. After becoming deaf, I learned ASL as a second language and culture. I identify with the tenets of hearing culture, as that was my first language and culture, yet also identify with and appreciate many of the tenets of a visual world and signed language. My reflection of the head-to-head information comes from decades of study in this area, and my appreciation of the heart-to-heart comes from intentional reflection of stories as they have been told to me by DHH patients and their families as well as my own life experience.

Recommendations

We conclude with recommendations for supporting the ASL learning needs of parents and young DHH children and for broad support from governments and service providers.

Head-to-Head: Language Acquisition

Language is a foundational component of human development and a fundamental aspect of communication and meaning-making. It occurs across different codes and modalities and connects individuals to diverse communities and environments. Multilingual, multimodal communication occurs in everyday life across societies and cultures. Even people who regard themselves as monolingual are often proficient in different dialects, modalities, and registers (Canagarajah, 2013). National sign languages, such as ASL, Langue des signes québécoise (LSQ), or other sign languages that make up the linguistic ecology of a community or region, are natural languages that evolve through everyday use by communities of deaf and hearing people. Natural sign languages have their own vocabulary, grammar, and social rules of use (Rowley et al., 2022), just like any spoken language. DHH children who acquire a sign language from birth do so on an identical maturational timeline as hearing children who acquire spoken languages (Petitto, 2000).

Language acquisition is a subconscious, instinctive process that is both amazingly simple and amazingly complex. The simplicity is that barring catastrophic events or genetic anomalies, all babies are born with brains hardwired and structured for language acquisition. The complexity is that this acquisition is very much dependent on the successful and necessary connections made between brain cells which are highly impacted by the language experiences provided by the child's environment. Furthermore, the linguistic experiential exposure needs to happen during a neurodevelopmentally critical time period. It is compelling that the young baby's brain is composed of such intricate systems that allow acquisition of any and all languages to which they are exposed (Kuhl, 2010) and that the baby (or language learner) is unaware of the process.

Effective language acquisition happens then when the child is fully exposed to a natural, fully accessible language or languages (often called their first or native languages) during their critical language-learning years, which is estimated to be between birth to approximately 5 years of age. It is through the ongoing and consistent process of fully accessible language exposure that the baby begins to make sense of their own experiences, eventually leading to a sophisticated inner voice (i.e., cognition and thinking) and an understanding of the world around them. Beyond most learning (language and spatial abilities), improved memory function (long and short term), better capacity for creative and critical thinking, and the understanding of social/emotional relationships, language acquisition is a foundational aspect of human development that permeates every moment of our everyday lives.

What Happens When Language Exposure Is Not Fully Accessible?

It is during the critical developmental years (birth to approx. 5) that the brain is most primed for language acquisition and after which the plasticity of the brain cells responsible for learning language begins to gradually decrease (Mayberry, 1993, 1994; Mayberry et al., 2011; Pénicaud et al., 2013; Cheng & Mayberry, 2019; Cheng et al., 2019; 2023). Generally, this appears to alter neurodevelopmental trajectories in ways that are permanently different from typical development paths and can lead to a much more difficult time mastering a completely fluent language foundation later in life. Complete and healthy language acquisition is so important that inconsistent access during the critical period can have a cascade effect on other developmental domains. For instance, this can include cognitive activities that rely on a first language such as literacy, memory organization, number manipulations (Humphries et al., 2012, Cheng et al., 2019), language abilities (Yoshinaga-Itano et al., 1998), other developmental delays and associated issues (Hall et al., 2018), and overall mental health (Glickman & Hall, 2018). Furthermore, delays in language acquisition affect development of other neurolinguistic brain structures. As Hall (2017) wrote, "Altogether, a fundamental and irreversible biological impact—on the brain and on healthy development—appears to occur when an accessible language is not provided by a certain early time period in brain development" (p. 962).

Language Policy in Early Intervention Service Systems for DHH Children

Supporting language acquisition in DHH children brings a new awareness of the importance of language that otherwise is often taken for granted. Language development is generally regarded as the primary area of need in early intervention and education for young DHH children, and public health and education services for this population are geared toward supporting language development. It is presented as the primary rationale for universal infant hearing screening and early intervention for DHH children (Snoddon & Paul, 2020), and for pediatric cochlear implantation. Cochlear implants, however, have an uneven and unpredictable rate of success in terms of supporting language development (e.g., Geers et al., 2017; Humphries et al., 2014, 2023; Kral et al., 2019; Niparko et al., 2010; Spellun and Kushalnagar, 2018), which can leave children who have cochlear implants without the full everyday access to language that is vital for ideal development. Parents and caregivers of young DHH children are often faced with artificially binary either/or choices regarding signed and spoken language development service options, and most DHH children receive auditory-verbal therapy (AVT) that restricts all visual language input, including sign language (Friedner, 2022; Mauldin, 2016; Snoddon, 2008; Snoddon & Paul, 2020).

Moreover, many parents and caregivers of DHH children are, at best, not informed of the benefits of sign language for supporting children's language acquisition and overall development, including supporting elaborated parent-child communication, and at worst, actively discouraged from using sign language. Rather, advice to parents "has been characterized by an overreliance on technology" (Humphries et al., 2023, p. 2). Technology, however, is not a cure for hearing loss, does not make deaf people become hearing people, and does not reliably provide unfettered access to language. The lack of information about sign language for parents and caregivers of DHH children can be traced to longstanding historical biases and prejudices against sign languages, leading to knowledge gaps among early intervention service providers, including audiologists and early intervention personnel who are often the first to inform parents about intervention strategies and language development services. Audiologists and other early intervention professionals are not required to have any knowledge about sign languages in their professional work; the same is true of family support workers (registered nurses or social workers) who counsel parents regarding service options under the Ontario Ministry of Children, Community and Social Services' Infant Hearing Program (IHP) (Snoddon, 2008; Snoddon & Paul, 2020).

By being presented with a dichotomous choice of language development service options, as with the IHP service guidelines, parents and caregivers of DHH children can experience undue pressure with decision-making and are limited in terms of their ability to access comprehensive, publicly funded support for their child's language development (Snoddon & Paul, 2020). For example, hearing parents may believe that ASL is important for their DHH children and wish to learn it themselves, but struggle to access resources supporting such choices in current early intervention systems (Lieberman et al., 2022). In Ontario, at the time of this writing, the guidelines state that parents may choose language development services in either a spoken language or signed language, but not both together, and children would need to stop receiving spoken language services to access sign language services (Ministry of Children and Youth Services, 2018; Snoddon and Paul, 2020). In August 2023, however, the IHP announced in a memo to associated agencies that it was removing the previous 6-month trial period when parents must decide on which language development service to receive for their child (Weber, S., personal communication, August 28, 2023). This suggests that Ontario families may now be able to receive both spoken and signed language services together. In comparison, the U.S. Joint Committee on Infant Hearing (2019) Position Statement indicates that early intervention services to support communication and linguistic competence in spoken language, sign language, or both should be provided. Furthermore, the American Academy of Pediatrics recently published clinical guidelines that noted all DHH children are naturally at risk for language deprivation, and providing bilingual (spoken and signed) language acquisition services may provide the necessary linguistic input to prevent language deprivation (Bower et al., 2023).

The rationale for the IHP's restrictions on sign language learning is the requirement for children who receive cochlear implants to enroll in AVT, whose practitioners may refuse to treat children who are learning sign language (Snoddon, 2008). Research, however, indicates that these types of explicit or operational policy restrictions on sign language learning leave DHH children vulnerable to the effects of language deprivation and communication neglect; this is because limiting or delaying exposure to sign language can significantly impede language development (see review in Humphries et al., 2023), and the developmental domains that depend on healthy language acquisition (Hall, 2017), if cochlear implants do not provide enough access to language.

Language Deprivation

Language deprivation occurs when a child experiences inconsistent exposure to a fully accessible language during the critical period of language development. This is rarely seen in hearing children, except in situations where a child has been reared in extreme social isolation and stimulus deprivation, such as so-called "feral" children who have been reportedly raised by wild animals or lived entirely alone in the wilderness. One example is the case of Genie in California, who was an adolescent girl subjected to severe social isolation and experiential deprivation (Fromkin et al., 1974). Reports indicate that following her rescue and despite a number of years of intentional language exposure/therapy, Genie's speech continued to exhibit the grammatically uninflected and telegraphic stages of a typical 2-year-old child, and that she showed limited cognitive abilities in addition to significant behavioral and emotional issues (Curtiss, 1981). Other examples of language deprivation in hearing children include Viktor, the wild boy of Aveyron; the Ukrainian girl named Oxana; and others summarized by Dombrowski et al. (2011), who all showed similar language and behavioral outcomes tied to early language deprivation and in some cases, severe lack of human contact.

Crucially, examples of language deprivation in hearing children are few and far between (highlighting how easily hearing children can passively access language in their everyday environments) and frequently are extreme situations; the examples also, in modern times at least, receive heightened attention from societal systems, including the police, developmental experts, and child protection services. This is in direct contrast to the everyday, unacknowledged occurrence that language deprivation can be for DHH children.

Various developmental domains are connected to and rely on language development; consequently, when DHH children lack effortless access to a language they fully understand, their overall development and health is impacted (Hall et al., 2018; Murray et al., 2019). The critical period for language acquisition is generally regarded as occurring during the first 3 to 5 years of life (W. C. Hall et al., 2017; Rowley et al., 2022). This critical period applies to signed as well as spoken language acquisition (i.e., the brain does not discriminate between language modalities as long as it receives natural language exposure). Assertions by opponents of the use of sign languages have tried to claim the critical period for language acquisition is modality-dependent, with the auditory critical period being shorter. Therefore, these sign language opponents claim, spoken language should be prioritized. These assertions are not in line with research evidence regarding the long-term, detrimental effects of late sign language acquisition (Pénicaud et al., 2013; Cheng et al., 2019; 2023; Mayberry, 1993; Mayberry & Eichen, 1991; Newport, 1990, 1991) which is evidence that the critical period is amodal (i.e., applicable to both visual and spoken languages). While many DHH children can and do acquire language and learn after this formative period, there remain long-term impacts on health, education, and well-being when there is a sustained lack of accessible language input in early childhood.

Language Deprivation and Mental Health

Consequences of language deprivation and communication neglect can manifest as general developmental delays and social and behavioral issues, such as attention deficit disorder and emotional dysregulation (Hall et al., 2018; Kushalnagar et al., 2020). Language deprivation also has impacts on cognitive development, such as executive function and theory of mind abilities that enable a child to recognize different mental states and perceptions in others, and on academic achievement and literacy (Humphries et al., 2014; Murray et al., 2019). Furthermore, language deprivation impacts DHH children's and adults' ability to access health services and leaves DHH individuals at heightened risk for abuse and neglect (Hall et al., 2023; Humphries et al., 2016).

Adverse childhood experiences (ACEs) are negative psychosocial experiences in early childhood and are generally considered to be a major public health concern. Preliminary work suggests there are DHH-specific factors that increase the risk of ACEs, including hearing loss status (i.e., being labeled as hard of hearing); type of school environment (i.e., with no sign language); and having a cochlear implant; what exactly these factors may mean in the context of ACEs risk requires further investigation (Hall et al., 2023). These experiences elevate the body's stress response system in a toxic manner and can lead to poor health outcomes in adulthood. In the case of DHH children, adverse childhood *communication* experiences relate to language deprivation, including lack of access to direct communication with caregivers and others in the DHH child's milieu, and communication neglect, which is ongoing exclusion from indirect communication and incidental learning (Kushalnagar et al., 2020). Being habitually excluded from communication in one's environment leads to psychological distress and gaps in world knowledge. Adverse childhood communicative experiences have been linked to higher risk of chronic disease, including diabetes, hypertension, heart and lung diseases, depression, and anxiety disorders (Kushalnagar et al., 2020). Other health disparities among DHH adults, such as sleep disturbances, are also emerging from research (Carr et al., 2022).

Language Deprivation in DHH Children

Language deprivation has been studied in tragic cases with hearing children as described above, and the research repeatedly supports the importance of early language learning in the critical developmental period. This same concept, however, is easily applied to DHH children, albeit for vastly different sociocultural reasons. It is critical to understand, however, that language deprivation in hearing children from extreme situations of abuse and/or neglect is usually qualitatively different from language deprivation in DHH children.

Causes of language deprivation, by definition, include language-impoverished early environments and may be related to a myriad of factors. The most severe examples of language deprivation mean that the DHH child was not exposed to consistent and accessible language in those early time-sensitive years. However, educators and clinicians who work with the DHH population typically see a spectrum of language dysfluency ranging from mild language deficits to full dysfluency (lack of fluency in a first language). Gulati (2018), however, clarifies that even mild language deficits may have serious consequences, and it is important to examine each person individually within their own context.

Why Does Language Deprivation Happen in DHH Children?

Unlike the circumstances described above with hearing children who suffer from abuse and neglect in their environments, it has been the experience of one of the authors of this chapter as a Deaf clinician (CC) that the majority of parents try to make the best decisions for their DHH child, including those involving language acquisition. DHH children are typically born to hearing parents who face many difficult decisions about how to raise their child. Du Feu and Chovaz (2014) describe this as what is often a grieving period for parents as they struggle to accept the reality of their child which is far different from their own, overlaid by pressing and often conflicting opinions of professionals about how best to parent their child, teach their child, bond with their child, play with their child, and communicate with their child.

Quitnner et al. (2010) concluded that context-specific measures of parenting stress were elevated in this population, reflecting the very unique challenges facing these families. Embedded in these stressors are the fact that many hearing professionals/systems strongly advocate for only spoken language, while other professionals (and the Deaf community) strongly advocate for the inclusion of sign language. This, however, is not a simple binary division of language preference, as these decisions tend to be heavily biased, loaded with inequitable assumptions, and often rooted in power differentials. Typically, hearing professionals (the larger majority) tend to advocate for only spoken language, while Deaf communities tend to advocate for DHH children's access to sign language in addition to spoken and written languages. In the field of linguistics, both signed and spoken languages are considered full languages (with phonology, morphology, syntax, etc.) that just use different forms of expression or modalities. A comprehensive review of the language politics in early intervention and deaf education is beyond the scope of this chapter, but it should be acknowledged that the polarization and either/or frame of spoken and signed languages that parents often experience in the discourse of early intervention professionals has been detrimental to the successful language development of many DHH children over the past few centuries and a leading cause of developmental consequences associated with language deprivation and communication neglect.

Effects of Language Deprivation in DHH Adults

It is important to emphasize again that language deprivation and its effects are on a spectrum, and its impact can present in highly individualized ways. This makes it difficult to concretely describe how language deprivation may present, and it also makes it difficult to measure and separate the consequences of language deprivation from other conditions that individuals may experience. Historical stigma and prejudices against DHH people can also lead people to confuse what they might believe to be unavoidable consequences of hearing loss with what are actually avoidable consequences of language deprivation. Currently, we only clearly see what is clinically judged as effects of language deprivation in broad system-level trends (such as poorer language scores and education achievement) and extreme individual cases within the DHH mental health system.

A DHH adult who is linguistically deprived may suffer many personal maladaptive effects (e.g., cognitive, emotional, and social implications) as does society, such as in terms of cost to medical systems and loss of potential productive participation in employment or recreation (Humphries et al., 2012). This is because the effects of language impoverishment suggest that "language subtly underlies wide aspects of brain function, including many skills traditionally classified as 'nonverbal' language" (Gulati, 2018). In addition, language deprivation may be associated with low levels of psychosocial functioning and independent living, poor emotional social regulation skills and behavioral problems (Glickman et al., 2020). W. C. Hall et al. (2017) note that psychiatric health is often affected by social factors such as poverty, discrimination, and social distress, and that language development (or the lack thereof) is essentially another social factor that contributes to mental health issues in the DHH population. Gulati (2018) has suggested that early language deprivation is a recognizable constellation of social, emotional, intellectual, and psychiatric consequences, proposing the term language deprivation syndrome. In this context, then, language deprivation syndrome is considered a neurodevelopmental disorder with sociocultural origins (W. C. Hall et al., 2017). Gulati (2018) has listed characteristics he has observed in his clinical work with DHH adults with language deprivation syndrome, including the following:

- may superficially appear to use sign language fluently, but on closer examinations shows characteristic linguistic deficits
- struggles with the concept of time
- struggles with cause-and-effect comprehension
- lacks awareness of a conversational partner's need for context and more generally lacks theory of mind abilities
- struggles with abstract concepts
- has difficulty learning
- struggles with emotional regulation
- struggles in relationships
- shows a reduced fund of information (worldly knowledge) but may be quite "streetwise"
- "acts feelings out"

These points also apply to DHH children, who are discussed in the next section.

Effects of Language Deprivation in DHH Children

The effects of language deprivation in DHH children comprise a spectrum from mild to severe, with the emergence of a similar pattern of cognitive and behavioral symptoms (Hecht, 2020). DHH children with language deprivation are at risk for the following, and more:

- cognitive delays from permanent brain changes (Cheng et al., 2019)
- mental health difficulties (Glickman et al., 2020)
- higher level of trauma and limited health literacy (W. C. Hall et al., 2017)
- difficulties with executive function (W. C. Hall et al., 2017)
- impulse control (Harris, 1978)
- difficulties with working memory (Marshall et al., 2015)
- lower quality of life (Kushalnagar et al., 2011)
- less-well-developed theory of mind (Marschark et al., 2019)

This cluster of symptoms makes it imperative that parents, health care professionals, and policymakers become diligent in ensuring that DHH children have adequate and consistent exposure to an accessible language during their early years. It is clear that evidence-based decisions are not a goal but a necessity, as the well-being of DHH children depends on them. The results of not making evidence-based decisions are evident in adulthood, and unfortunately the overall life trajectory for these individuals is generally worse than that of DHH individuals with full access to language from childhood onward.

Language acquisition is a process which needs to occur in very young children, albeit realizing that the children themselves are not cognitively or emotionally capable of reporting their own progress. It is therefore incumbent on the adults in the environment to ensure that language is developing properly through careful and comprehensive assessments, preferentially by a professional team well-versed in these issues. For example, a young child with a cochlear implant has a tool that may potentially be useful for the brain to acquire language. The question then becomes whether this tool is effective in facilitating language acquisition. Tools, however, are simply tools and are effective for specific tasks but perhaps not other tasks; that is, there may be nothing wrong with the hammer, but it certainly would be ineffective at inserting a screw.

The solution for the prevention of language deprivation is shockingly simple—ensure that all DHH babies/young children are provided with consistent and full exposure and effortless (on the part of the child) acquisition to a fully accessible language throughout their development. Generally, this can be guaranteed through a natural sign language (as the issue becomes one of practicality in finding enough fluent signers to form a language-rich environment) relative to technology avenues that attempt to remediate hearing to levels that still do not reach typical hearing. The treatment of the consequences of language deprivation is tragically not as simple. Although the acquisition of some functional language, learning, development, and general skills is possible beyond early childhood, we simply cannot recreate or reclaim the superb capacity of the early brain in terms of language acquisition potential. This is clearly an illustration of the "use it or lose it" paradigm. Losing out on access to language during the critical period can be devastating for the child's overall quality of life across their lifespan. Societal, educational, and medical systems need to be held accountable when they put families on paths which can result in these consequences.

Heart-to-Heart: Lived Experiences of Language Deprivation in DHH Children

The following short case studies from the clinical practice of one of the chapter authors (CC) in Ontario, Canada, are presented to highlight lived experiences of language deprivation in DHH children. All patient names are pseudonyms.

Heart-to-Heart Experiences #1

Olivia was a full-term baby born without complication, and the IHP screening identified her as having a congenital, bilateral, severe-to-profound sensorineural hearing loss. Her parents were told by their physician that the etiology was genetic, it was best for Olivia to have cochlear implants (CIs), and the earliest she could receive them was 12 months of age. For Olivia's first year, the parents felt unsure of how to interact with her and ended up treating her much like her three older, hearing siblings. They talked and sang and played with her but did little to really consider if Olivia was an active participant in the interactions.

At the age of 12 months, Olivia was reviewed again, but the parents were told that unfortunately there was a backlog in surgeries, and she would be put on the waiting list. The parents continued interacting with Olivia in the same way. At the age of 24 months, Olivia had unilateral (right-sided) CI surgery. The sound processor was activated 4 weeks later, and the parents and Olivia began attending aural rehabilitation therapy (listening therapy). By the age of 3 years, Olivia continued to babble but had yet to say a word. She began speech therapy to help her develop and understand spoken language. The CI team shared that in laboratory conditions, the CI was working well.

By age 3-1/2 years, the parents were feeling overwhelmed with the demands of life as Olivia's father had lost his job, one of the older siblings was having significant behavior problems, and the mother's parents had both recently died. Given the family pressures as well as the pressure of attending frequent rehabilitative appointments with Olivia, the parents decided to stop attending appointments. Their intention was to continue trying to develop Olivia's language at home.

By age 4 years, Olivia was described by the parents as a stubborn, spoiled child who had temper tantrums when they said no. Olivia did not appear to listen to what her parents said, did not interact positively with her siblings, and seemed to spend a lot of time crying and screaming. The parents were relieved to send her to junior kindergarten and have some quiet at home. At school, the teacher noted that Olivia did not follow the classroom rules, did not seem to play nicely, and did not interact like the other children did during story time. Olivia was using some speech, but the teacher noted that she preferred to repeat words she heard rather than come up with words on her own.

By age 5 years and in senior kindergarten, Olivia's parents were repeatedly notified by the school that Olivia's behavior was unacceptable. She was having temper tantrums, physically hitting the other children when she became frustrated, and her academic activities were behind. The parents noticed similar behaviors at home, to the point where the three older children avoided interacting with their younger sister.

By the age of 6 years and in grade 1, Olivia was suspended from school for stealing items from the desk of another child. Olivia did not appear to understand that what she had done was wrong and became angry and broke items in the classroom. The teachers recommended a psychological assessment, and Olivia was put on a waiting list. The assessment with the school psychologist (who had a considerable wait list) did not happen until the age of 8 years (grade 3), and the summary noted that Olivia had attention deficit hyperactivity disorder (ADHD), learning disorder (LD) and oppositional defiant disorder (ODD).

Head-to-Head Points to Consider

- The language and communication interactions with the parents were likely not accessible to Olivia for her first 2 years of life.
- The CI surgery was considered to technically be a success (e.g., in a laboratory situation); yet language acquisition and development was not assessed or monitored.
- Olivia likely has a language disorder related to not having accessible language exposure rather than (or possibly in addition to) ADHD, LD, and ODD.
- Olivia has language deprivation with corresponding emotional and behavioral sequalae.

Heart-to-Heart Experiences #2

Eric was a 17-year-old Deaf youth in a youth correctional facility who had been convicted on charges of burglary. Eric's lawyers struggled to communicate with him, even with a sign language interpreter. Eric seemed unable to comprehend the nature of his alleged crime, explain his actions, feel remorse, or participate in his rehabilitation.

Eric had been identified as DHH through the IHP, and his parents were told by the attending healthcare workers that bilateral hearing aids would enable Eric to speak. The parents had Eric fitted with bilateral hearing aids by 8 months of age. Eric was a mild-mannered little boy and continued to wear his hearing aids without difficulties. Yearly audiology appointments indicated the hearing aids were functioning well.

Eric was a shy, quiet boy and caused no issues at home or school. Although he was not doing well academically, the school kept passing him onto the next grade. Eric kept to himself, had few friends, and did not cause problems at home or in school. By age 10 and in grade 5, Eric had failed every aspect of his curriculum. The school suggested to the parents that Eric would fit better with DHH children who used ASL, and he was transferred to a residential school for the DHH.

Eric did not know any sign language and slowly learned some functional signs. As before, he did not cause any issues at school or in residence but continued to have few friends and to do poorly in academics. Eric eventually graduated from high school, and his parents wanted him to either go to college or get a job. As they applied pressure on Eric to complete applications and make choices, Eric's behavior became negative, and he frequently shut himself in his room for days at a time. When his father, handing him applications, insisted he apply for a job, Eric ripped them up and trashed his room. His mother said, "All those years of hearing aids were no help. Eric could/would not talk with us, and we never learned any sign language. I have no idea what he is thinking or feeling, and we have no idea why he behaves the way he does."

When Eric was 18 years of age, he was arrested and convicted for burglary. He had broken into his neighbor's house, as he wanted to use the computer that he could see through the window. The neighbor was an elderly woman who was home sleeping at the time and was terrified. Eric grabbed the computer and pushed the elderly woman out of his way; as a consequence, she fell and broke her hip.

The results of a court-ordered psychological assessment with a psychologist who was familiar with mental health and deafness indicated that Eric had little if any formal language in either spoken English or ASL. Eric had progressed through school without any formal evaluation of his language development or learning abilities. Without the structure and familiarity of school, Eric was lost upon graduation and reacted negatively through his actions and emotions. By the time he was convicted, Eric was diagnosed with depression and language deprivation. The psychologist noted that Eric seemed to have very little understanding of social relationships or society's laws of right and wrong. Eric did not have any friends and had little to no relationship with his family and a sense of hopelessness. His reading and writing abilities were at a grade 1 level.

Head-to-Head Points to Consider

- How and why did Eric graduate from school without ever being formally assessed regarding language and learning abilities?
- Eric's quiet demeanor as a child likely meant he did not bring attention to himself.
- Eric's language development was not assessed to ensure his hearing aids were facilitating the acquisition and development of language.
- The parents were informed by the professionals that the hearing aids were adequate.
- When he was considered to be a failure using his hearing aids, Eric was switched to sign language despite having never been exposed to it prior to age 10.
- Eric learned some functional signs but did not acquire any degree of fluency in ASL.
- Eric has experiences of language deprivation with corresponding emotional and behavioral sequalae.

Strategies for Supporting ASL Acquisition

Language expands our access to social worlds and possibilities for communication and meaning-making. In turn, our approaches to supporting language development should be expansive and geared toward opening multiple channels and opportunities for communication. Professionals, parents, and educators can work together to support children's access to multiple communicative resources. Like other minority languages, ASL and other national sign languages require resources and funding for qualified DHH teachers and mentors, curricular and programming resources, and community and early learning spaces. Importantly, service providers and parents and caregivers need to be adequately informed about the benefits of national sign languages and bimodal bilingualism in signed and spoken/written languages for supporting children's healthy development. Bimodal bilingualism in a national sign language and spoken/written languages protects children from the effects of language deprivation and poor mental health outcomes that are outlined above (Wilkinson & Morford, 2020).

The ongoing lack of support for bimodal bilingualism when children receive a CI and AVT is rooted in outmoded notions of language learning and bilingualism (Lieberman et al., 2022; Snoddon, 2008). According to this view, learning sign language is thought to interfere with the development of a "hearing brain" and normal speech in DHH children (Mauldin, 2016). This is another way of saying that sign language interferes with (or has no positive effect on) the development of spoken language (and that developing spoken language is necessary for learning how to read). However, these views and claims are not evidence-based. Instead, there is research showing that acquisition of sign language supports spoken and written language development in DHH children, including children with CIs (Caselli et al., 2021; Davidson et al., 2014; see review in Hall et al., 2019; Hassanzadeh, 2012; Hratinski & Wilbur, 2016). Critically, the failure to support sign language acquisition has detrimental effects on DHH children's health and increases the risks language deprivation and communication neglect.

All parents and caregivers of DHH infants and young children should be encouraged to make use of gesture and pointing to support parent-child interaction and language development (Rowley et al., 2022). Parents and caregivers should also be advised of the importance of establishing eye contact for supporting visual and joint attention; this is a central part of receptive and expressive language development. Eye contact and visual attention can be supported using animated facial expressions, waving hands for attention, and moving into babies' line of sight (Rowley et al., 2022).

For supporting parents' and children's learning of sign language, various resources are available, including resource teacher home visiting programs that are provided by some deaf schools, including bilingual schools for DHH students, and DHH mentor or ASL consultant programs that involve DHH professionals working with families (see, e.g., Sass-Lehrer, 2015). These programs can provide families with sign language models, strategies, and resources for learning sign language. However, the sign language tutoring provided to parents is typically less formal than structured courses (Snoddon, 2015). DHH professionals can also help families link with deaf communities and other families with DHH children and thereby support the development of social networks (Rowley et al., 2022). There are also various online resources, including online classes and sign language dictionaries, that can help support parents' sign language learning.

Deaf community initiatives such as the ASL Parent-Child Mother Goose Program introduce young children and parents to ASL rhymes and stories that support children's familiarity with narrative structure and visual and joint attention (Snoddon, 2012, 2020a). Sign language rhymes and stories also support children's development of phonological and phonemic awareness and working memory (Humphries et al., 2023). Sign language phonology involves handshapes, movements, and locations of signs as patterned units of sign languages. An ASL rhyme from the ASL Parent-Child Mother Goose Program involving rhythmic repetition of one ASL handshape in varying locations can be glimpsed in this video clip of "Jolly Bear": https://youtu.be/fUQ-COHFk90. This type of language play is linked to metalinguistic awareness, literacy, and reading development (Snoddon, 2012, 2020a; Rowley et al., 2022).

DHH professionals can also support families by teaching parents how to read children's books through sign language. Reading books through sign language supports and builds on eye contact and joint attention and also supports concept development and knowledge of narrative structure as well as children's familiarity with print (Snoddon, 2014; Rowley et al., 2022). Fingerspelling is another way to introduce infants and young children to printed words (Rowley et al., 2022).

Researchers have demonstrated the importance of specialized, intensive sign language courses for parents and caregivers of DHH children, and the success of these initiatives with supporting parents' communicative competence in sign language and children's well-being. These specialized courses emphasize grammar-focused instruction instead of only or mainly vocabulary learning. Many existing resources for teaching sign language to parents have focused on vocabulary only (Oyserman & de Geus, 2021). Additionally, because most sign language curricula are designed for sign language interpreting students, classes geared toward parents require a different curriculum. This is because parents and caregivers' communication with DHH children often takes place in a different domain and location, and for purposes that are different from interpreters' communication with who are typically DHH adult signers (Snoddon, 2015).

In the Netherlands, an ongoing, long-term study of intensive parent sign language courses provided in different regions of the country has shone a light on parents' sign language learning experiences and needs (Oyserman & de Geus, 2021). This research has also indicated that with an appropriate, formal curriculum developed following the Common European Framework of Reference for Languages (CEFR), parents and caregivers can achieve an independent level of competence to support elaborated communication with their children and other DHH individuals across the lifespan (Oyserman & de Geus, 2021; Snoddon & Madaparthi, 2023). The CEFR describes language proficiency following six levels, from basic user (A1–A2), to independent user (B1–B2), to proficient user (C1–C2). In Canada, there have also been ongoing studies of developing and field-testing a parent ASL curriculum aligned with the CEFR (Snoddon, 2015, 2016, 2020b). The CEFR is useful as a framework and guide for curriculum development because it explicitly describes what learners need to do with language (Piccardo & North, 2019). This research is important because it demonstrates how parents and caregivers of DHH children can be supported to become fluent signers.

Study of the Effectiveness of Intensive Parent ASL Courses

DHH children and their families acquiring ASL have ongoing learning needs to support family communication and DHH children and youth's well-being. In this section, findings are shared from a 9-month study of intensive parent ASL courses that were adapted and developed for online instruction to meet the second or additional ASL learning needs of parents and caregivers of DHH children. This includes questionnaire, interview, observations, and assessment data regarding participating parents' learning processes and experiences.

Since the beginning of the COVID-19 pandemic, DHH children and their families have faced greater educational inequities and service gaps (World Federation of the Deaf, 2021). During the pandemic, many resource teacher and ASL consultant home visiting programs were suspended or moved online. However, the pandemic also intensified the need for supporting parent-child communication due to school closures and increased isolation for both DHH children and their parents. This necessitated the development of an online delivery model for parent ASL courses (Snoddon & Madaparthi, 2023).

In September–October 2020, teaching materials developed through previous research were adapted for an online delivery format. This course was intended for parents of elementary school–aged children who had some previous experience with learning ASL and whose learning needs extended beyond the early intervention service delivery period. Therefore, this course was aligned with CEFR level A2 (pre-intermediate). This group of parents often lacks access to specialized public resources for learning ASL. This course ran for 14 weeks during October 2020–February 2021. In January–February 2021, planning meetings took place for developing a new, successive course for the same group of parent learners that was aligned with level B1 (intermediate). This course ran for 14 weeks during February–June 2021. The course materials included a teacher's guide with lesson plans for each class that included the class theme, ASL linguistic goals, and goals for parents to learn about deaf culture as related to DHH children's well-being. For example, in the teacher's guide for the first, A2-level course, deaf culture pedagogical goals for different classes included, but were not limited to, the following:

- teaching children how to order for themselves in restaurants (by pointing, writing, etc.)
- signing to children about money (e.g., tipping, the cost of items, saving money)
- explaining events to children with specific details before the events take place
- teaching children how to manage and resolve conflicts
- telling children where the parent is going when they leave a room

In this way, the parent courses were intended to support elaborated communication in ASL with DHH children and children's language development and world knowledge in addition to parents' signing skills. Homework assignments included asking parents to make and respond to short videos and participate in activities at home with their children.

The online courses met for approximately 1 hour each week, instead of the 2-1/2-hour format that was followed for in-person parent courses. This was due to the risk of Zoom fatigue among parents, who often worked remotely while supporting their children with their own online learning. However, because online classes were smaller than the in-person courses that were held before the pandemic, this format also enabled more one-to-one instruction and dialogue between participating parents and the instructor (Snoddon & Madaparthi, 2023). For the first time, the online courses also made use of the electronic European Language Portfolio (ELP) for sign languages to enable parents to record their learning goals and progress and reflect on their learning experiences (ProSign, 2019). The ELP includes the language passport, which provides an up-to-date record of learners' language competency levels; the language biography, which helps learners reflect on their learning processes and experiences; and the dossier, which is a collection of learner work. This use of the ELP is intended to help parents feel they are taken seriously as ASL learners and to clarify their learning goals. As shown by instructor assessments, participating parents achieved on-target proficiency levels for each course (Snoddon & Madaparthi, 2023). One parent participant wrote in her language biography that she was able to communicate and understand more complex ideas in ASL and help her child with their homework (Snoddon & Madaparthi, 2023). Several parents reported that their children were happy and excited that their parents were expanding their knowledge of ASL. Together, these findings demonstrate the success of intervention initiatives and illustrate the importance of ASL assessment in monitoring parents' learning outcomes.

Conclusion and Recommendations

Throughout this chapter, we have discussed head-to-head some key aspects of language development as a foundational part of healthy human development, and especially its context within DHH child development. The main take-home message from this chapter is this: Language deprivation and communication neglect of DHH children are 100% preventable. This is a social public health epidemic rooted in a long history of language politics centered around DHH children and the DHH community at large in preventing sign language exposure at the population level; such views, while dominant, are largely not evidence-based. If DHH children are given unfettered access to a fully accessible language as soon as possible after birth, there is no reason to expect them not to thrive. That so much energy is expended on unproductive dialogues centered on language modalities rather than on giving DHH children every possible option is an ongoing tragedy.

Cases of language deprivation in DHH children being educated in public school systems are beginning to receive more attention from legal systems and the media. In *Perez v. Sturgis Public Schools*, the U.S. Supreme Court ruled unanimously for a deaf student who sued his public school system for providing an inadequate education. Similarly, in Newfoundland, Canada the human rights complaint of *Carter Churchill v. the Newfoundland and Labrador English School District* was successfully adjourned in favor of the plaintiff, a young deaf student (VOCM, 2023). Both cases involved DHH students who did not have access to an education in ASL or to educators or paraprofessionals who were qualified to deliver this education. These cases signpost new directions in thinking about human rights for DHH children in early intervention and education, including the right to education and the right to health services that prevent further disabilities (Murray et al., 2019; Snoddon & Paul, 2020). This rights framework is outlined in the United Nations Convention on the Rights of Persons with Disabilities, the United Nations Sustainable Development Goals, and the 2021 World Report on Hearing (World Health Organization, 2021). These international agreements, however, lack the force of domestic policies and are subject to interpretation by domestic decision-makers. As we have seen in this chapter, often government and health officials may lack the required knowledge to implement successful early intervention and education systems for DHH children and their parents and caregivers. Thus, there continues to be a need to expand awareness of language deprivation and the benefits of a national sign language for DHH children and their families.

While efforts to create systemic change for better language access continue to move forward (i.e., with Language Equality and Acquisition for Deaf Kids, also known as LEAD-K legislative efforts in the United States [see ASHA, 2026]), from a heart-to-heart perspective, we also must support those who continue to experience, and have experienced, language deprivation. Cases where DHH children are clearly experiencing ongoing effects of language deprivation need the same remedy as if we were trying to prevent it in the first place: full immersion in a language-rich environment with a critical mass of fluent signers with a full range in ages from peers to adult language models. The best time to do this is as soon as a DHH child is identified (at birth or shortly thereafter); the next best time to do it is as soon as possible when language deprivation becomes an increasing concern.

Farther along, individuals who sadly become severely impacted by chronic, uninterrupted experiences of language deprivation typically need considerable extra social support and services. This impact can be evident on an individual level and is due to a combination of a lack of life skills, not understanding basic societal expectations and rules, being unable to live independently, and experiencing severe mental health issues. Often, these individuals will find their ways to treatment settings by running afoul of the law or somehow triggering systemic oversight of their situations. While technically, these individuals are not in mental health settings for reasons specific to mental health but rather due to underlying language dysfluency and subsequent issues, these settings remain the best available option for them. At this point, treatment likely will center on trying to build basic life skills that theoretically promote their eventual ability to live independently (often, they may end up remaining within inpatient settings and group homes indefinitely).

It is our combined hope as authors of this chapter that all levels of society will be educated about the devastating effects of language deprivation on DHH children and that individuals will collectively embrace the simple solution—the provision of fully accessible language(s) during the early developmental years.

References

American Speech-Language Hearing Association. (2026). Language Equality and Acquisition for Deaf Kids (LEAD-K). https://www.asha.org/advocacy/lead-k/?srsltid=AfmBOort3ZBDbSQo4GYWA5CVpqjlgzsXley3aa9j7vXsmqYuCXM-Elnb

Bower, C., Reilly, B. K., Richerson, J., & Hecht, J. L. (2023). Hearing assessment in infants, children, and adolescents: Recommendations beyond neonatal screening. *Pediatrics*, *152*(3), Article e2023063288. https://doi.org/10.1542/peds.2023-063288

Canagarajah, S. (2013). *Translingual practice: Global Englishes and cosmopolitan relations*. Routledge.

Carr, M., Yoo, A., Guardino, D., Hall, W. C., McIntosh, S., & Pigeon, W. R. (2022). Characterization of sleep among deaf individuals. *Sleep Health*, 9(2), 177–180. https://doi.org/10.1016/j.sleh.2022.10.011

Carter Churchill v. the Newfoundland and Labrador English School District. (2023). CanLII 16071 (NL HRC). https://www.carterchurchill.ca/board-of-inquiry-decision-2023.html#/.

Caselli, N., Pyers, J., & Lieberman, A. M. (2021). Deaf children of hearing parents have age-level vocabulary growth when exposed to ASL by six months. *The Journal of Pediatrics*, *232*(May 2021), 229–236. https://doi.org/10.1016/j.jpeds.2021.01.029

Cheng, Q., & Mayberry, R. I. (2019). Acquiring a first language in adolescence: the case of basic word order in American Sign Language. *Journal of Child Language*, *46*(2), 214–240. https://doi.org/10.1017%2FS0305000918000417

Cheng, Q., Roth, A., Halgren, E., Klein, D., Chen, J.-K., & Mayberry, R. I. (2023). Restricted language access during childhood affects adult brain structure in selective language regions. *Proceedings of the National Academy of Sciences*, *120*(7), Article e2215423120. https://doi.org/10.1073/pnas.2215423120

Cheng, Q., Roth, A., Halgren, E., & Mayberry, R. I. (2019). Effects of early language deprivation on brain connectivity: Language pathways in deaf native and late first-language learners of American Sign Language. *Frontiers in Human Neuroscience*, *13*, Article 320. https://doi.org/10.3389/fnhum.2019.00320

Curtiss, S. (1981). Dissociations between language and cognition: Cases and implications. *Journal of Autism and Developmental Disorders*, *11*, 15–30. https://doi.org/10.1007/BF01531338

Davidson, K., Lillo-Martin, D., & Chen Pichler, D. (2014). Spoken English language development among native signing children with cochlear implants. *Journal of Deaf Studies and Deaf Education, 19*(2), 238–250. https://doi.org/10.1093%2Fdeafed%2Fent045

Dombrowski, S. C., Gischlar, K. L., & Mrazik, M. (2011). *Assessing and treating low incidence/high severity psychological disorders of childhood.* Springer.

Du Feu, M., & Chovaz, C. (2014). *Mental health and deafness.* Oxford University Press.

Friedner, M. I. (2022). *Sensory futures: Deafness and cochlear implant infrastructures in India.* University of Minnesota Press.

Fromkin, V., Krashen, S., Curtiss, S., Rigler, D., & Rigler, M. (1974). The development of language in Genie: A case of language acquisition beyond the "critical period." *Brain and Language, 1*(1), 81–107. https://psycnet.apa.org/doi/10.1016/0093-934X(74)90027-3

Geers, A. E., Mitchell, C. M., Warner-Czyz, A., Wang, N.-Y., Eisenberg, L. S., & the CDaCI Investigative Team. (2017). Early sign language exposure and cochlear implantation benefits. *Pediatrics, 140*(1), Article e20163489. https://doi.org/10.1542/peds.2016-3489

Glickman, N. S., Crump, C., & Hamerdinger, S. (2020). Language deprivation is a game changer for the clinical specialty of deaf mental health. *JADARA, 54*(1), Article 54. https://nsuworks.nova.edu/jadara/vol54/iss1/4

Glickman, N. S., & Hall, W. C. (2018). Introduction: Culture and disability. In N. S. Glickman & W. C. Hall (Eds.), *Language deprivation and deaf mental health* (pp. 1–23). Routledge.

Gulati, S. (2018). Language deprivation syndrome. In N. S. Glickman & W. C. Hall (Eds.), *Language deprivation and deaf mental health* (pp. 24–53). Routledge.

Hall, M. L., Eigsti, I.-M., Bortfeld, H., & Lillo-Martin, D. (2017). Auditory deprivation does not impair executive function, but language deprivation might: Evidence from a parent-report measure in deaf native signing children. *Journal of Deaf Studies and Deaf Education, 22*(1), 9–21. https://doi.org/10.1093/deafed/enw054

Hall, M. L., Hall, W. C., & Caselli, N. K. (2019). Deaf children need language, not (just) speech. *First Language, 39*(4), 367–395. https://doi.org/10.1177/0142723719834102

Hall, W. C. (2017). What you don't know can hurt you: The risk of language deprivation by impairing sign language development in deaf children. *Maternal and Child Health Journal, 21*(5), 961–65. https://doi.org/10.1007/s10995-017-2287-y

Hall, W. C., Dye, T. D. V., & Siddiqi, S. (2023). Associations of childhood hearing loss and adverse childhood experiences in deaf adults. *PloS ONE, 18*(6), Article e0287024. https://doi.org/10.1371/journal.pone.0287024

Hall, W. C., Levin, L. L., & Anderson, M. L. (2017). Language deprivation syndrome: A possible neurodevelopmental disorder with sociocultural origins. *Social Psychiatry and Psychiatric Epidemiology, 52*, 761–776. https://doi.org/10.1007/s00127-017-1351-7

Hall, W. C., Li, D., & Dye, T. D. V. (2018). Influence of hearing loss on child behavioral and home experiences. *American Journal of Public Health, 108*(8), 1079–1081. https://doi.org/10.2105/ajph.2018.304498

Harris, R. I. (1978). The relationship of impulse control to parent hearing status, manual communication, and academic achievement in deaf children. *American Annals of the Deaf, 123*(1), 52–67.

Hassanzadeh, S. (2012). Outcomes of cochlear implantation in deaf children of deaf parents: Comparative study. *Journal of Laryngology & Otology, 126*(10), 989–994. https://doi.org/10.1017/s0022215112001909

Hecht J. L. (2020). Responsibility in the current epidemic of language deprivation (1990–Present). *Maternal and Child Health Journal, 24*(11), 1319–1322. https://doi.org/10.1007/s10995-020-02989-1

Hrastinski, I., & Wilbur, R. B. (2016) Academic achievement of deaf and hard-of-hearing students in an ASL/English bilingual program. *Journal of Deaf Studies and Deaf Education, 21*(2), 156–170. https://doi.org/10.1093/deafed/env072

Humphries, T., Kushalnagar, P., Mathur, G., Napoli, D. J., Padden, C., & Rathmann, C. (2014). Ensuring language acquisition for deaf children: What linguists can do. *Language, 90*(2), e31–e52. https://doi.org/10.1353/lan.2014.0036

Humphries, T., Kushalnagar, P., Mathur, G., Napoli, D. J., Padden, C., Rathmann, C., & Smith, S. (2016). Avoiding linguistic neglect of deaf children. *Social Service Review, 90*(4), 589–619. https://doi.org/10.1086/689543

Humphries, T., Kushalnagar, P., Mathur, G., Napoli, D. J., Padden, C., Rathmann, C., & Smith, S. R. (2012). Language acquisition for deaf children: Reducing the harms of zero tolerance to the use of alternative approaches. *Harm Reduction Journal, 9*(16), 1–9. https://doi.org/10.1186/1477-7517-9-16

Humphries, T., Mathur, G., Napoli, D. J., & Rathmann, C. (2023). Sign language and multimodality as indicators of health for deaf newborns and young children: Guidance for families and medical professionals. *Medical Research Archives, 11*(1), 1–23. https://doi.org/10.18103/mra.v11i1.3280

Joint Committee on Infant Hearing. (2019). Year 2019 position statement: Principles and guidelines for early hearing detection and intervention programs. *Journal of Early Hearing Detection and Intervention, 4*(2), 1–44. https://doi.org/10.15142/fptk-b748

Kral, A., Dorman, M. F., & Wilson, B. S. (2019). Neuronal development of hearing and language: Cochlear implants and critical periods. *Annual Review of Neuroscience, 42*, 47–65. https://doi.org/10.1146/annurev-neuro-080317-061513

Kuhl, P. K. (2010). Brain mechanisms in early language acquisition. *Neuron, 67*(5), 713–727. https://doi.org/10.1016/j.neuron.2010.08.038

Kushalnagar, P., Ryan, C., Paludneviciene, R., Spellun, A., & Gulati, S. (2020). Adverse childhood communication experiences associated with an increased risk of chronic diseases in adults who are deaf. *American Journal of Preventive Medicine, 59*(4), 548–54. https://doi.org/10.1016/j.amepre.2020.04.016

Kushalnagar, P., Topolski, T. D., Schick, B., Edwards, T. C., Skalicky, A. M., & Patrick, D. L. (2011). Mode of communication, perceived level of understanding, and perceived quality of life in youth who are deaf or hard of hearing. *Journal of Deaf Studies and Deaf Education, 16*(4), 512–523. https://doi.org/10.1093/deafed/enr015

Lieberman, A. M., Mitchiner, J., & Pontecorvo, E. (2022). Hearing parents learning American Sign Language with their deaf children: A mixed-methods study. *Applied Linguistics Review, 15*(1), 309–33. http://dx.doi.org/10.1515/applirev-2021-0120

Marschark, M., Edwards, L., Peterson, C., Crowe, K., & Walton, D. (2019). Understanding theory of mind in deaf and hearing college students. *Journal of Deaf Studies and Deaf Education, 24*(2), 104–118. https://doi.org/10.1093/deafed/eny039

Marshall, C., Jones, A., Denmark, T., Mason, K., Atkinson, J., Botting, N., & Morgan, G. (2015). Deaf children's non-verbal working memory is impacted by their language experience. *Frontiers in Psychology, 6*, Article 527. https://doi.org/10.3389/fpsyg.2015.00527

Mauldin, L. (2016). *Made to hear: Cochlear implants and raising deaf children*. University of Minnesota Press.

Mayberry, R. I. (1993). First-language acquisition after childhood differs from second-language acquisition: the case of American Sign Language. *Journal of Speech and Hearing Research, 36*(6), 1258–1270. https://doi.org/10.1044/jshr.3606.1258

Mayberry, R. I. (1994). The importance of childhood to language acquisition: Evidence from American Sign Language. In J. C. Goodman & H. C. Nusbaum (Eds.), *The development of speech perception: The transition from speech sounds to spoken words* (pp. 57–90). MIT Press.

Mayberry, R. I., Chen, J.-K., Witcher, P., & Klein, D. (2011). Age of acquisition effects on the functional organization of language in the adult brain. *Brain and Language, 119*(1), 16–29. https://doi.org/10.1016/j.bandl.2011.05.007

Mayberry, R. I., & Eichen, E. (1991). The long-lasting advantage of learning sign language in childhood: Another look at the critical period for language acquisition. *Journal of Memory and Language, 30*(4), 486–512. https://doi.org/10.1016/0749-596X(91)90018-F

Ministry of Children and Youth Services. (2018). *Language development services guidelines: Ontario Infant Hearing Program. Version 2018.2*. Ministry of Children and Youth Services. https://www.uwo.ca/nca/pdfs/clinical_protocols/IHP%20Language%20Development%20Services%20Guidelines_2018.01.pdf

Murray, J. J., Hall, W. C., & Snoddon, K. (2019). Education and health of children with hearing loss: The necessity of signed languages. *Bulletin of the World Health Organization, 97*(10), 711–716. https://www.doi.org/10.2471/BLT.19.229427

Newport, E. L. (1990). Maturational constraints on language learning. *Cognitive Science, 14*(1), 11–28. https://doi.org/10.1016/0364-0213(90)90024-Q.

Newport, E. L. (1991). Contrasting conceptions of the critical period for language. In S. Carey & R. Gelman (Eds.), *The epigenesis of mind: Essays on biology and cognition* (pp. 111–130). Lawrence Erlbaum.

Niparko, J. K., Tobey, E. A., Thal, D. J., Eisenberg, L. S., Wang, N. Y., Quittner, A. L., Fink, N. E., & the CDaCI Investigative Team. (2010). Spoken language development in children following cochlear implantation. *JAMA, 303*(15), 1498–1506. https://doi.org/10.1001/jama.2010.451

Oyserman, J., & de Geus, M. (2021). Implementing a new design in parent sign language teaching: The Common European Framework of Reference for Languages. In K. Snoddon, & J. C. Weber (Eds.), *Critical perspectives on plurilingualism in deaf education* (pp. 173–194). Multilingual Matters.

Pénicaud, S., Klein, D., Zatorre, R. J., Chen, J. K., Witcher, P., Hyde, K., & Mayberry, R. I. (2013). Structural brain changes linked to delayed first language acquisition in congenitally deaf individuals. *Neuroimage, 66*, 42–49. https://doi.org/10.1016/j.neuroimage.2012.09.076

Perez v. Sturgis Public Schools, 598 U.S. 142 (2023). https://supreme.justia.com/cases/federal/us/598/21-887/

Petitto, L. (2000). On the biological foundations of human language. In K. Emmorey & H. Lane (Eds.), *The signs of language revisited: An anthology in honor of Ursula Bellugi and Edward Klima* (pp. 447–471). Lawrence Erlbaum.

Piccardo, E., & North, B. (2019) *The action-oriented approach: A dynamic vision of language education*. Multilingual Matters.

ProSign. (2019). *The structure of an eELP for sign languages*. https://www.ecml.at/Portals/1/5MTP/Pro%20Sign%20II/documents/ProSign-structure-of-ELP-EN.pdf?ver=2019-11-30-165059-940

Quittner, A. L., Barker, D. H., Cruz, I., Snell, C., Grimley, M. E., Botteri, M., & the CDaCI Investigative Team (2010). Parenting stress among parents of deaf and hearing children: Associations with language delays and behavior problems. *Parenting: Science and Practice, 10*(2), 136–155. https://doi.org/10.1080/15295190903212851

Rowley, K., Snoddon, K., & O'Neill, R. (2022). Supporting families and young deaf children with a bimodal approach. *International Journal of Birth and Parent Education, 9*(3), 15–20.

Sass-Lehrer, M. (Ed.). (2015). *Early intervention for deaf and hard-of-hearing infants, toddlers, and their families: Interdisciplinary perspectives*. Oxford University Press.

Snoddon, K. (2008). American Sign Language and early intervention. *The Canadian Modern Language Review, 64*(4), 581–604. https://doi.org/10.3138/cmlr.64.4.581

Snoddon, K. (2012). *American Sign Language and early literacy: A model parent-child program*. Gallaudet University Press.

Snoddon, K. (2014). Ways of taking from books in ASL book sharing. *Sign Language Studies, 14*(3), 338–359. https://doi.org/10.1353/sls.2014.0010

Snoddon, K. (2015). Using the Common European Framework of Reference for Languages to teach sign language to parents of deaf children. *Canadian Modern Language Review, 71*(3), 270–287. http://dx.doi.org/10.3138/cmlr.2602

Snoddon, K. (2016). Whose ASL counts? Linguistic prescriptivism and challenges in the context of parent sign language curriculum development. *International Journal of Bilingual Education and Bilingualism, 21*(8), 1004–1015. https://doi.org/10.1080/13670050.2016.1228599

Snoddon, K. (2020a). ASL and early literacy: From ASL phonological awareness to print literacy. *Society for American Sign Language Journal, 4*(1), 24–35. https://tigerprints.clemson.edu/saslj/vol4/iss1/1/

Snoddon, K. (2020b). Teaching sign language to parents of deaf children in the name of the CEFR: Exploring tensions between plurilingual ideologies and ASL pedagogical ideologies. In A. Kusters, M. Green,

E. Moriarty Harrelson, & K. Snoddon (Eds.), *Sign language ideologies in practice* (pp. 145–164). Mouton de Gruyter. https://doi.org/10.1515/9781501510090-008

Snoddon, K., & Madaparthi, K. (2023). Conceptualizing the role of mediation in an online American Sign Language teaching model for parents of deaf children. *Deafness and Education International, 25*(1), 4–20. https://doi.org/10.1080/14643154.2022.2076010

Snoddon, K., & Paul, J. J. (2020). Framing sign language as a health need in Canadian and international policy. *Maternal and Child Health Journal, 24*, 1360–1364. https://doi.org/10.1007/s10995-020-02974-8

Spellun, A., & Kushalnagar, P. (2018). Sign language for deaf infants: A key intervention for a developmental emergency. *Clinical Pediatrics, 57*(14), 1613–1615. https://doi.org/10.1177/0009922818778041

VOCM. (2023, April 10). NLESD apology does not address gaps in school system: Churchill. https://vocm.com/2023/04/10/nlesd-apology-does-not-address-gaps-in-school-system-churchill/?fbclid=IwARohqYJvPLittoM54eEEVaaWugngnA1mqPUooIOf6kG3pGJkAUq-Bnjy1FA

Wilkinson, E., & Morford, J.P. (2020). How bilingualism contributes to healthy development in deaf children: A public health perspective. *Maternal and Child Health Journal, 24*, 1330–1338. https://doi.org/10.1007/s10995-020-02976-6

World Federation of the Deaf. (2021). *Position statement on educational rights for deaf learners during the COVID-19 pandemic and beyond.* https://wfdeaf.org/position-statement-educational-rights-for-deaf-learners-during-the-covid-19-pandemic-and-beyond/.

World Health Organization. (2021). *World report on hearing.* https://www.who.int/publications/i/item/9789240020481

Yoshinaga-Itano, C., Sedey, A. L., Coulter, D. K., & Mehl, A. L. (1998). Language of early- and later-identified children with hearing loss. *Pediatrics, 102*(5), 1161–71. https://doi.org/10.1542/peds.102.5.1161.

2

Deaf Education

Joanne C. Weber and Jennifer S. Thom

Construct

This chapter outlines the ongoing, unresolved issues in deaf education which are framed as wicked problems (Rittel & Webber, 1973) that continue to impact the lives of deaf children and youth in adverse ways. Wicked problems are highly complex problems commonly addressed by multiple stakeholders who hold different opinions, ideologies, and promote competing strategies. Often wicked problems are exacerbated by imposed simple "scientific" solutions without regard for the complex, competing, and layered approaches to the problem (Rittel & Webber, 1973).

Head-to-Head and Heart-to-Heart

In this head-to-head chapter, we start with a literature review of major trends in deaf education that are highly problematic and in need of radically different ways to move forward despite ongoing efforts at resolution. Drawing on the work of Bowers and Aoki (Bowers, 1997, 2005; Aoki, 2004a, 2004b, 2004c), we provide a discourse analysis of common statements which are found in everyday parlance used by stakeholders in deaf education and which were prevalent in the Newfoundland and Labrador Human Rights Commission Hearing concerning the discrimination of Carter Churchill in 2022.

The discourse analysis, at heart, reveals that instead of what appears to be dissenting voices among the stakeholder groups, a common set of root metaphors (Bowers, 1997, 2005) shapes and unifies their approaches to deaf education. Moreover, the application of root metaphors within research, pedagogy, and curriculum often renders the deaf child and youth invisible. In this sense, words do matter, and language thinks us as we think with, and in, language (Heidegger, 1962). As university academics specializing in educating teachers and as provincially certified teachers, we observe the impact of words on our own lives as a profoundly deaf adult fluent in ASL and English (Joanne) and as a hearing mother of a deaf child (Jennifer). We see the seemingly endless recycling of ideas, concepts, and actions that contribute to language deprivation. In this chapter, we draw on and connect our lived experiences, research interests, and professional work with deaf children to adopt creative and innovative approaches to educating deaf children within our home, schools, and communities—many of which often do not match easily with the standard provision of programs and services for deaf children.

Statements of Reflexivity

First Author: Joanne Weber

I was born profoundly deaf due to maternal rubella, a child of educators who took deaf education courses at Minot State College and espoused an oral approach to language development. I was able to develop oral language skills which enabled me to successfully navigate K–12 and acquire university degrees. At age 25, due to mental health difficulties, I took up American Sign Language (ASL) and became an active member of the deaf community. I am a veteran teacher of the deaf, having worked with deaf children who use ASL, communicate orally, embrace both deaf and hearing worlds, and identify solely with deaf culture. My experiences in working with deaf immigrants and BIPOC (Black, Indigenous People of Color) students, along with my own experiences in navigating the hearing world, lend themselves to the critical examination of discourses that often confound the delivery of deaf education services.

Second Author: Jennifer Thom

I live in the world as a hearing person. As a mainstream public schoolteacher and a teacher educator, I have experience teaching deaf learners. Yet, it was not until I found out my child was deaf that I really began to learn what it means to support and advocate for a deaf person as they make their way through school and life in a world that is neither distinctly hearing nor deaf but complexly both (and more!). The insight I gain from learning ASL, interacting with deaf communities, and collaborating with deaf educators and scholars like Joanne Weber continues to profoundly shape the work I do in mathematics education, STEM education, and curriculum studies—whether empirical, theoretical, or pedagogical.

Recommendations

Readers are now invited to consider how the root metaphors of universalism, mechanism, and progressive do not allow us to see the ways in which the wicked problems in deaf education could be addressed.

Frank Conversations About the Wickedness of Problems in Deaf Education

This chapter outlines the ongoing, unresolved issues in deaf education which are framed as wicked problems which continue to impact the lives of deaf children and youth in adverse ways. Despite our best efforts, there is no end in sight concerning the eradication of language deprivation. We are compelled to address these issues in the light of ongoing language deprivation which impedes neurolinguistic development, hampering social and emotional growth, and interferes with academic achievement. We recognize that our ways of thinking about deaf education are not producing the desired results in preventing or ameliorating language deprivation and therefore wish to explore alternative discourses. Instead of remaining trapped in polarizing positions, discourses, and philosophies concerning the provision of services to deaf children and youth, we need alternate discourses to allow for new, different, and emergent perspectives. We start with a literature review of major trends in deaf education that are highly problematic and in need of solutions despite ongoing efforts at resolution. Drawing on the work of curriculum scholars Chet A. Bowers and Ted T. Aoki (Aoki, 2004a, 2004b, 2004c; Bowers, 1997, 2005), we provide a discourse analysis of common statements found in everyday parlance used by stakeholders in deaf education, and which were prevalent in the Newfoundland and Labrador Human Rights Commission Hearing concerning the discrimination of Carter Churchill in 2022 (*Carter Churchill v. the Newfoundland and Labrador English School District*).

Carter Churchill was a 12-year-old deaf boy enrolled in Newfoundland and Labrador English School District, Canada, who received bilateral cochlear implants and oral/aural habilitation services, which did not produce the desired results for oral language acquisition. His parents requested intensive sign language therapy and programming within a congregated setting to maximize opportunities for sign language development. After several years of lobbying the school district, the parents then hired a lawyer, Kyle Rees, to advocate for their son through a Human Rights Commission hearing in Newfoundland in the fall of 2022. This included an intense period of examination of all parties, including school administrators, clinical professionals, teachers, educational assistants, and the parents of Carter. In 2023, the commission found that Carter Churchill was actively discriminated against in his early school years because he was not provided consistent exposure to sign language; nor was he placed in a congregated setting where he could interact with signing deaf peers and signing instructional staff.

In this chapter, we take a systemic ecological approach (e.g., G. Bateson, 1972, 1980; M. C. Bateson, 1996) to study language deprivation as it relates to mental health. Present systems often engender mental health states that impact cognitive functioning; emotional and social well-being; healthy relationships with peers, families, and professionals; and the sense of belonging to multiple communities. We propose that systemic approaches can easily override lower-level attempts to ameliorate mental crises, dilemmas, and ongoing issues by ignoring the root metaphors that currently guide thinking. We aim to contribute to an emerging deaf education research paradigm which focuses on linguistic dynamics among persons, biosocial (inter)relations, and vision as recursive (Skyer, 2023). In doing so, we examine core assumptions that discursively corral all stakeholders, including deaf children and their parents, into the same pen and effectively hold them there through iterations of assumptions ad infinitum. Such a cultural enclosure, as suggested by Bowers (2016), persists despite the commonly held belief that we are all free to think beyond cultural influences. It is in this manner that certain core or root assumptions perpetuate systematic, mechanistic, objectified, and prescriptive approaches (Bowers, 1996, 2016) to issues in deaf education (Skyer, 2023).

We do not intend to provide a historical overview or a contemporary description of available programs and services for deaf children and their families that contribute to the status quo as manifested in current polarizations regarding the use of aural/oral habilitation. Recognizing that the intent of this entire volume is to explore head-to-head knowledge and heart-to-heart experiences, we refer to the mental states, discourses, and emotional investments made by professionals who are grappling about the best ways to provide services to deaf children and their parents. Cognition and resulting discourses do contribute to mental health, and we want to open spaces for healthier and more robust dialogues.

In taking a systemic ecological perspective, we conceive cognition as a process of living whereby world, world view(s), and meaning are brought forth co-emergently with others from life as life (Maturana & Varela, 1992). Not objectified as a thing, cognition is understood as continuous activity wherein "[a]ll doing is knowing and all-knowing is doing" (Maturana & Varela 1992, p. 27). Thus, "to live is to know" (Maturana & Varela, 1992, p. 174).

Included here are our discursive ways of knowing and doing that we learn, embody, and linguistically (re)create through interacting with others (e.g., Bowers, 1997; Martusewicz et al., 2021). Further, these shared beliefs, values, and communicative patterns form the discourse(s) of our taken-for-granted ways of being. Such a view resonates with an ecological conception of mind (Bateson, 1972). Here, the mind is not limited to residing only within an individual but as emerging and manifesting as discourse; that is, a "pattern which connects" (Bateson, 1980, p. 9) you, me, and us simultaneously both a part and a whole of larger collectives (e.g., class, deaf education, community, society, and the world).

At its core, our work seeks to interrupt the status quo; that is, deaf education as an entrenched system, which despite best intentions, continues to manifest deaf education as a wicked problem (Weber & Skyer, 2022). The primary motivation compelling us is this: For the past, present, and foreseeable future, most, if not all, decisions concerning the education of deaf learners have been, are, and will be made by program coordinators, school administrators, boards of education, superintendents, and the medical profession without substantial input from those whom it concerns most—deaf children, deaf youth, and their parents. This chapter concerns four key issues that are often sites of abstractions and conflations commonly held by stakeholders in deaf education. As such, these sites lend to the proliferation and persistence of problems in deaf education. To consider the issues differently, we attend to the discourses which underlie and contribute to four stakeholder views: (a) deaf cultural critique (Mauldin 2016), (b) inclusive education, (c) deaf education, and (d) direct recipients of services.

Context

While deaf children share characteristics with the larger student population, including being educated within general education, they are remarkably diverse. Deaf children may vary according to factors such as placement in the educational settings (mainstream, congregated); language choices (ASL, spoken/print English); etiology, degree, and type of hearing loss; and usage of hearing technologies (FM systems, sound field systems). Moreover, they are subjected to the educational philosophies held by administrators, teachers, and parents or guardians, and are subject to the availability of programs and services (Kennon & Patterson, 2016). The recent influx of deaf students to the United States and Canada (Cannon & Luckner, 2016; Engelman & Izquierdo, 2025; Millett, 2024) from different countries and the growing presence of deaf children with additional needs adds to the complexity of teaching (Cannon et al., 2016; Millett, 2021; Silvestri & Harman, 2022), requiring teachers of the deaf and hard of hearing (TODHHs) to be culturally and linguistically responsive in their pedagogies (Cannon et al., 2016; Kurz et al., 2021).

Traditionally, deaf children received special services out of the concern that they were experiencing language delays due to hearing loss (Luft, 2017). The focus was on "catchup" upon reaching spoken language or sign language commensurate with hearing and deaf peers to ameliorate historically limited educational outcomes and achievement (Humphries et al., 2016, 2019, 2022; Ladd, 2003; Lane, 1984, 1992). More recently, however, discourses concerning language deprivation as an outcome of incomplete and inconsistent exposure to oral and/or sign language began to circulate mostly during the past 10 to 15 years (Cheng et al., 2019; Glickman & Hall, 2019; Hall et al., 2017; Mayberry, 2010; Mayberry et al., 2002, 2011; Mayberry & Kluender, 2018; Mayberry & Lock, 2003; Pénicaud et al., 2013). The lack of exposure to a language is considered to result in irreversible cognitive deficits (Glickman & Hall, 2019; Hall et al., 2017). Now, language deprivation is being identified as the primary cause for lifelong difficulties in learning and communication across the diverse spectrum of deaf people (Goodwin et al. 2022; Gulati, 2019; Hall et al., 2017; Hall et al., 2019; Hecht, 2020; Humphries et al., 2016, 2019, 2022).

The growth of the cochlear implant (CI) industry has profoundly changed the professional discourses about language acquisition (Mauldin, 2016). Deafness is no longer defined as sensory loss, but rather as a neurological processing problem where a CI serves as a tool for the brain to acquire language (Mauldin, 2016). Advocates for listening and speech skills argue that the neuroplasticity cannot accommodate both senses equally but favors one or the other (Mauldin, 2016). This leads to the assumption that sign language will interfere with the neurological development of hearing and speech in CI users and that the brain must be molded in an "explicitly nonvisual way" (Mauldin, 2016, p. 52).

Meanwhile, Jasinska and Pettito (2013) affirm that the brain does not differentiate between auditory and visual input, giving rise to the possibility for the development of both languages if exposure is sustained and consistent. Delcenserie et. al. (2024) affirm that sign language and spoken language provided during early childhood reduces the risk of language deprivation in young deaf children

Mapping the Territory of Language Deprivation in Deaf Education

While language deprivation topics appear to be first and foremost on everyone's minds, we are unaware of any efforts that consolidate the research findings and, in turn, suggest solutions to address this overwhelming crisis. What is holding us stakeholders—medical professionals, administrators, teachers, and researchers in deaf education—back? Clearly, there is both a need for and an opportunity to examine language deprivation research, particularly the issues it provokes in deaf education. To begin this work, we will examine four broad issues and their key problems as an attempt to map this territory of deaf education research. The issues concern support services for all communication modalities and language choices; structures for planning and providing resources to all deaf children in multiple education environments; provisions for professionals, paraprofessionals, general special education teachers, and school district administrators; and assessments and documentation of language acquisition and academic achievement.

Services for All Language and Communication Modalities

Biomedical interventions have resulted in multiple systems of aural/oral habilitation services comprising CI clinics, audiological services, speech and language pathology services, preschool programs, and the K–12 system. In some cases, a sign language educational interpreter is provided to work with those who cannot benefit fully from hearing technologies, within the context of spoken language learning environments (Caselli et al., 2021). Biomedical interventions, however, have a long outreach and impact the deaf person from birth through 18 years of age (Mauldin, 2016). As such, these services receive dedicated funding, primarily from ministries of health and education in Canada (Snoddon, 2021), for providing services to facilitate the development of listening and speaking in deaf children. Miller (2014) identifies the itinerant model as predominant; that is, teachers travel to different schools to individually support deaf learners. Thus, education in oral language environments as the default model brings forth the associated service delivery to all deaf children, regardless of their degree of hearing loss.

The bimodal-bilingual path (using ASL-English or Langue des Signes Québécoise [LSQ]-French in Canada as dual languages of instruction) or bimodal multilingualism (in which home languages are also included in daily life and at school) is often considered a "fallback" in case the child does not develop the requisite speech and listening skills to navigate inclusive education environments (Luft, 2017). Funding for those who must learn and access the curriculum through sign language is often precarious, and resources are limited at best (Snoddon, 2021; Snoddon & Weber, 2021). In contrast, the highly supported route to listening and speaking appears to be a well-oiled machine in comparison to its alternative, bimodal-bilingual programs which are often thrown together within inclusive education environments on a case-by-case basis as a last resort for the child who has not benefited from the speaking and listening route (Newfoundland and Labrador Human Rights Commission, 2022). Each province in Canada offers differing levels of services related to the use of bimodal bilingualism (CAEDHH, n.d.). Despite advances in neuroscience and language (Mayberry & Kluender, 2018; Petitto & Jasinska, 2014), bimodal-bilingual pedagogy (Czubek, 2021; Di Perri, 2021; Kuntze & Golos, 2021), curriculum (Ladd, 2022; Skyer, 2021), and assessments (McQuarrie & Enns, 2021), these programs remain underdeveloped in the context of inclusive education (Howerton-Fox & Falk, 2019).

Structures for Planning and Providing Resources to All Deaf Children in Multiple Education Environments

The inclusive education philosophy—simply put, placement with other children who communicate through hearing and speaking, has and continues to shape programs and services for deaf children (Luft, 2017). Itinerant TODHHs work in rural and urban settings with the aim of integrating deaf children in their home community (British Columbia Teachers' Federation, Research Department, 2018). Despite this model being well-established in practice but not well-substantiated by research (Luckner & Ayantoye, 2013), it persists as the dominant model for supporting deaf students. Often decisions made about educational placements must be made before the availability of assessments concerning the deaf child's language, learning preferences, and strengths (Luft, 2017). And, while there are provincial schools for the Deaf in some provinces in Canada, such schools are considered a last resort when efforts for aural/oral rehabilitation have failed in oral language education environments (Luft, 2017).

In this model, itinerant TODHHs provide services to many individual deaf children who are significantly language deprived and are falling further behind their same-age peers in all aspects of development (Newfoundland and Labrador Human Rights Commission, 2022). This case-by-case approach which focuses on the deaf child's language acquisition via spoken language and sign language remains one of the most highly problematic aspects of deaf education due to the inability to provide consistent, quality, and meaningful access to language.

Provisions for Professionals, Paraprofessionals, General Special Education Teachers, and School District Administrators

TODHHs

Currently, deaf education is facing dwindling numbers of TODHHs (Luft, 2017; Meyer, 2021). Kurz et al. (2021) signal the need for radical change in teacher preparation programs to ensure there are TODHHs who have the knowledge and expertise to support deaf children throughout their K–12 schooling. Recruitment of culturally and linguistically diverse teachers, support for multilingual pedagogies, as well as multimodality in teaching and learning are needed transformations within existing teacher preparation programs (Kurz et al., 2021).

There is already a costly and lengthy period of initial qualification for TODHH specialist professional preparation (British Columbia Teachers' Federation, Research Department, 2018). TODHHs must also earn credits for courses in audiology, oral language development, linguistics and language development, instructional methodology, management of hearing technologies, ASL language fluency, additional disabilities management, assessment, parent-infant development, and literacy development (Di Perri, 2021). The average time for a full-time graduate school training program in Canada is 2 years at the University of British Columbia, Vancouver, and 1 year at York University, Toronto, Ontario. TODHHs are expected to have this knowledge base to develop effective individual programs. Despite intensive training, there remains confusion about the roles and responsibilities of TODHHs (British Columbia Teachers' Federation, Research Department, 2018, p. 5). TODHHs are recognized as having a more specialized skill set than those of classroom teachers and special educational teachers (British Columbia Teachers' Federation, Research Department, 2018). This was a point of contention for all parties during the Newfoundland and Labrador Human Rights Commission hearing for the Churchills; that there was a lack of trained TODHHs (and assistants and education interpreters) fluent in ASL (Newfoundland and Labrador Human Rights Commission, 2022). Since 2016, the parents of Carter Churchill had advocated for their deaf son, placed within the Newfoundland English School District, to be educated in ASL by fluent ASL signers, interpreters, and teachers (Newfoundland and Labrador Human Rights Commission, 2022). The Human Rights Commission concluded that the school board did not provide these needed services throughout his early schooling.

Many TODHHs are expected to deliver effective instruction without formal training and be knowledgeable about available instructional approaches and resources. Moreover, many TODHHs are required to attend professional development pertaining to literacy development in hearing children with the expectation that they will then "adapt" these resources and strategies. This adds to an already excessive workload. Burnout and frustration are common in this profession, resulting in many early career TODHHs requesting a transfer to the general classroom (Di Perri, 2021; Kennon & Patterson, 2016). Itinerant TODHHs indicate that their service provision is compromised through high caseloads, the logistics of traveling to and from sites, and the general lack of awareness in schools about needed supports for deaf and hard of hearing (DHH) students (Antia & Rivera, 2016; Davison-Mowle et al., 2018; Luckner & Dorn, 2017; Pedersen & Anderson, 2019).

Educational Interpreters

Access to classroom conversations via sign language interpreters in the inclusive education setting is highly problematic (Caselli et al., 2020; Russell, 2021; Salehomoum, 2020). In Canada and the United States, there are no national standards established for education interpreters (Johnson et al., 2018). There is no provincial standardized supervision and accountability system in place. Some states in the United States have adopted the use of the Educational Interpreter Performance Assessment to rate sign language interpreting competencies. This assessment, however, does not assess or evaluate educational interpreter competencies required to enable access to "complex, layered and theoretical communication," even in much less subject-specific courses (Johnson et al., 2018, p. 5). Caselli et al. (2020) suggest that unskilled interpreters may well be contributing to the language deprivation in deaf students. We are not aware of any Canadian assessment equivalents for interpreting in educational settings to date. Compound these challenges with the study by Russell (2021) in which only six of 35 educational interpreters in various school settings in Canada were able to fully convey classroom conversations despite years of experience, training, and certification.

Generalist, Special Education, and Administration Personnel. Special education or general education teachers may not recognize the depth of language-learning issues arising from language deprivation. Miller (2014) notes that TODHHs often face the challenge of educating general administrators, and teachers about language learning issues. Miller (2014) reported on the trends impacting a public school program for DHH students, noting that administrators may question whether deaf students who have spoken language skills need the specialized services of a TODHH. At the same time, it would be quite common for a principal to accept the need for a TODHH if the student were a signing student. Moreover, because of the sheer diversity of deaf learners, services are complexified (Kennon & Patterson, 2016). Deaf students receive primary labels denoting additional disabilities that are not necessarily related to their hearing loss, and consequently, the provision of language services is often impacted accordingly (Borders et al., 2016).

Assessments and Documentation of Language Acquisition and Academic Achievement

Assessment and documentation of needed services and planning pose other challenges for providing services to deaf students, including issues regarding appropriate assessments, development of Individualized Education Plans (IEPs), program delivery, and research agendas. Often language and communication assessments are the responsibility of diagnosticians who do not have the sign language skills to assess deaf children. Therefore, standardized testing is rarely implemented (Luft, 2017). The lack of data is compounded by the absence of training and research concerning the assessment of language deprivation and its variable impacts upon academic achievement and social and emotional development (Glickman & Hall, 2018; Luft, 2017). Without documented language goals in IEPs and appropriate yearly assessments (Easterbrooks & Beal-Alvarez, 2013), there can be no systematic data collection which means identification of levels of needed programs and services for DHH children will be unlikely. For instance, Musyoka and Clark (2017) found that the predominant IEP goals for American preschool children were school reading, communication, and pre-academic skills. With this, goals for listening and spoken language skills tended to focus mostly on the production of speech as supported by speech and language pathologists. Another study revealed that school teams generally underestimated the learning needs when developing IEPs for DHH students (Millett, 2021). Research efforts are often confounded by the inability to acquire data about school-based cohorts of deaf children's language acquisition and academic achievement (Arnold, 2022; Hall, 2019). Millett (2021) reports on the lack of available Canadian statistical data on the population of DHH students, citing the growing trend to decrease the number of TODHHs "because of a misunderstanding of the research literature, that students with hearing loss today are doing so well that they no longer need services at all" (Millett, 2019, p. 3).

For this reason, the provision of services to support the development of academic language may not be as prevalent in later years in IEPs (Easterbrooks, 2016; Musyoka & Clark, 2017). Clark et al. (2019) promotes a "bioecological systems approach for early and continuous assessment of deaf infants and children" in lieu of the prevalent emphasis on social and individual models of health which allow unacceptable levels of language deprivation to persist (Clark et al., 2019, p. 443).

Putting "It" on the Table

Our review of the literature on language deprivation in deaf education reveals longstanding challenges and how best to respond to the proliferation of concerns regarding the four identified issues. This review prompts further examination into these educational issues surrounding language deprivation of deaf children and youth.

For the next part of the chapter, we explore the four issues by making them topical and "putting them (as *it*) on the table" to enable frank conversations. To do this, we constructed four dialogues indicative of common parlance in deaf education. As each conversation unfolds, one of the concerns is taken up and (re)presented through each of the four stakeholder discourses within deaf education: deaf cultural critique, inclusive education, deaf education, and direct recipient of services.

The conversations offer a shared context in which we, as authors and our readers, can grapple with the topics of concern, and in all seriousness, come to deeper and hopefully new understandings. These dialogues are neither trivial nor novel in performance but inherently political and pedagogical. As such, we see(k) frank conversation as an alternative response to challenging issues in deaf education; one which holds potential for enriching and complementing more familiar lines of logics, discourses, argumentation, and conclusions.

It is also important for readers to be mindful that the character(istic) discourses do not represent actual people or individual perspectives but grander narratives within deaf education. Each voice and conversation are a weaving together of beliefs, ideas, and meanings that cohere past, current, and recent literature from the field; views of a parent to a deaf child in Western Canada whom we interviewed; our experiences as a TODHH as well as a parent of a deaf child; and our sensibilities, motivations, and reflections as teacher educators and educational researchers. Thus, each character as discourse is a collectivity of perspectives and serves as a means with which we can engage the four issues.

Each conversation opens with a quotation that frames and identifies the specific topic. And while we have situated the conversations within the 2022 *Carter Churchill v. the Newfoundland and Labrador English School District* hearings, the voices and dialogues that ensue more than expose the topics as an inexhaustible maze of contradictory and seemingly irreconcilable interests within deaf education writ large.

Frank Conversation 1: About Accommodation Services

The concept of the duty to accommodate is used as a way for people to gain access to these systems without really addressing the underlying barriers that exist. Accommodations are necessary because these systems were built without consideration of the needs of people, in this case people with disabilities, in the first place. The system is the barrier, not the disability. (Carey Majid, executive director, Newfoundland and Labrador Human Rights Commission, *Carter Churchill v. the Newfoundland and Labrador English School District*, Aug. 29 opening statement; [Majid, 2022, p. 8])

Inclusive education: We need to focus on keeping every[-]one in the same classroom. We have a duty to accommodate, within reason of course.

Deaf cultural critique: Yes, but Article 24 in United Nations Convention on the Rights of Persons with Disabilities (United Nations, 2006) says that the best learning environment for the deaf child is one that provides full access to a language, that is, sign language.

Deaf education: We have to support all approaches and languages. We also have to respect the desires of parents who may only want their child to speak and listen and not use sign language.

Direct recipient of services: I want to create a network of resources that accommodate the different needs of my child and provide them with many options and options that are not yet known. It doesn't make sense to blindly follow one direction.

Frank Conversation 2: About Resources for All Deaf Children

Part of this question looks at whether Carter, in this case, was accommodated to the point of undue hardship. Questions such as: were alternative approaches or possibilities investigated; were creative solutions proposed; did the parties work together to find solutions, for example, are all part of this equation. (Carey Majid, executive director, Newfoundland and Labrador Human Rights Commission, *Carter Churchill v. the Newfoundland and Labrador English School District*, Aug. 29 opening statement; [Majid, 2022, p. 6])

Inclusive education: We work with the parents to develop an IEP, which helps us to identify the resources, services, and personnel needed to support the deaf child.

Deaf cultural critique: We need to build up resources and services for bimodal-bilingual education, support deaf communities, and ensure the vitality of sign languages.

Deaf education: We believe that special services for deaf children are in place and are according to research-based evidence, ministry guidelines, and state/province standards.

Direct recipient of services: I can't get any straight answers from anyone at the school. They say they are doing all they can for my child who is falling further and further behind. My child cannot have a conversation with anyone.

Frank Conversation 3: About Professionals, Paraprofessionals, Teachers, and Administrators

[A]dequate inclusive education therefore is not a dispensable luxury. It is a ramp that provides access to our commitment to education made to all children. Truly inclusive education must be designed with input from all stakeholders and must be properly supported and financed. (Justice Abella, in his commentary on the Moore case [*Moore v. British Columbia (Education)*]; quotation supplied by Carey Majid, executive director, Newfoundland and Labrador Human Rights Commission, *Carter Churchill v. the Newfoundland and Labrador English School District*, Aug. 29 opening statement; [Majid, 2022, p. 10]. For the reader, Moore was a student with severe dyslexia in Western Canada who was denied accommodation for his disability).

Inclusive education: We need all hands on deck. It takes a whole village to raise a child.

Deaf cultural critique: We need to train more deaf teachers who are native signers and who are immersed in deaf culture and their deaf communities.

Deaf education: We must train more teachers and personnel to address these complex problems. One size does not fit all.

Direct recipient of services: No one stays in the system for very long but are often switching to other positions, other schools, and other parts of the country! I find myself having to reeducate different people repeatedly.

Frank Conversation 4: About Assessment, Progress, Acquisition, and Achievement

[T]he purpose of the school system, as stated in this case from the BC School Act, is to enable all learners to develop their individual potential and to acquire the knowledge, skills and attitudes needed to contribute to a healthy, democratic and pluralistic society and a prosperous and sustainable economy. (Justice Abella, in his commentary on the Moore case; quotation supplied by Carey Majid, executive director, Newfoundland and Labrador Human Rights Commission, *Carter Churchill v. the Newfoundland and Labrador English School District*, Aug. 29 opening statement; [Majid, 2022, p. 9])

Inclusive education: Each of our students receives formal and informal literacy assessments and student achievement and language acquisition benchmarks.

Deaf cultural critique: Sign language assessments should be administered by persons who are native speakers of sign language on a yearly basis, and the results should be compared with the general population of deaf children (norm referenced).

Deaf education: Without this vital statistical data, we cannot plan programs, develop resources, and hire the personnel to provide all options.

Direct recipient of services: I am completely in the dark. I want to know if he is language deprived. How bad is it? And if so, what will they do to address it?

What?!

Taking the four conversations at face value, the idea of resolving the issues does not appear to be a simple matter of identifying and filling "gaps." This would presume the current system to be generally working well and that all there exists are minor deficiencies to be addressed; when on the contrary, there may be a substantial population of deaf children who are language deprived (Hall, 2019; Humphries et al., 2022) and the system in place does not work well for any of the deaf children. The conversations obviate how each identified difficulty, simply upon mention, triggers a never ending series of related challenges and dilemmas. A complex entanglement of inappropriate solutions, tenuous differences, and competing interests within the deaf education field at large.

The result closely resembles what Weber and Skyer (2022) characterize as "wicked problems." That is, "unresolved problems [which] exist despite considerable work by students, parents, educators, school administrators, curriculum developers, and lawmakers" (Weber & Skyer, 2022, p. 74). Problems such as these adversely affect policy, curriculum, and pedagogy, and they produce unwanted outcomes across agency, stakeholder, jurisdictional, and geopolitical boundaries (Sydelko et al., 2021).

Take, for example, the inclusive education dictum that we must support all parental desires regarding language choices. Such a viewpoint can wreak havoc on a child who cannot meet those expectations concerning the chosen language and bring about deep-seated frustrations on the part of the assigned personnel for the child. Moreover, these kinds of problems tend to persist over long periods of time despite implementation of solutions, strategies, provisions of needed resources, and services (Rittel & Webber, 1973). Indeed, this is especially true when there is a lack of yearly assessments and statistical data with which to plan for resource implementation and services in many jurisdictions. Further still, wicked problems seem to arise when stakeholder groups who hold different values, goals, levels of decision-making power, and bureaucratic positions implement processes and procedures (Skyer, 2021). Within the four conversations, language ideologies, identity choices, and cultural values range from spoken monolingualism—identification with the hearing majority or as a disabled person, or embracing the cultural values of the family—to the deaf cultural critique in which bimodal multilingualism seeks to dismantle language hierarchies and embrace multiple identities. The dizzying array of perspectives that contribute to wicked problems are only compounded by racial, ethnical, cultural, linguistic, and socioeconomic variables (Foster & Kinuthia, 2003: Kinuthia, 2021).

Why is it that regardless of the deaf child, varying stakeholder discourses, and everyone's best intentions, the reality is that all too often, significant rates of language deprivation continue for deaf children? That parents have difficulty locating needed resources and services? That academic achievement lags well behind hearing peers?

Why is it that even when we (i.e., all four voices) recognize the futility of efforts and the administrative, programmatic, and pedagogical dead ends associated with them, somehow there always seems to be a whole host of narratives that willingly emerge, take over our conversations, and proceed to deny, negate, and oversimplify the situation(s) at hand so that we end up back where we began, unsuccessfully searching for a few gaps in the deaf education system to fill and fix? Why are we okay with narratives that erase deaf children altogether from these conversations again and again? The obfuscation is unrelenting and unchanging, and disconcertingly, there appears to be no answer in sight here. So, what are these conversations about? Or more appropriately, what are we in deaf education really communicating? What is "it" that we might not be putting on the table? What is "it" that makes it possible for us to do so? And more pointedly, how does "it" enable us to see certain issues while not seeing others that are so urgently calling for our attention?

Next, we explore these questions as they relate to the four frank conversations and (re)examine them in ways that can occasion new insight and deeper understanding. Taking a similar approach to the four issues, we now take these questions and make them topics for further frank discussion. The questions as posed then, serve to open spaces in which to inquire and reveal at least some of the "it" which underlies and gives rise to such wicked problems.

Re-Searching for Authentic Conversation

Make no mistake, these questions regarding what is being communicated in deaf education are neither glib nor made in jest. In all seriousness, amidst all these questions is a question that calls for understanding the very discourses embodied and enacted within the deaf education field; the discursive ways we bring theoretical and practical meaning into being; why so often teachers, parents, and most of all, deaf learners are left out of the conversation; and how it is that we become completely ignorant of the realities (being put) in place—realities that deaf children and youth ultimately must live out.

In the absence of authentic conversation—"conversation [that is] guided by an interest in understanding more fully what is not said by going beyond what is said" (Aoki, 2004c, p. 227) and the undeniable presence of stakeholder voices which persist in only talking to themselves—this question calls attention to the ways in which seemingly disparate convictions surrounding the language deprivation of deaf children might somehow be connected. Instead of conceding to the conclusion that the stakeholder discourses are irreconcilable and therefore incapable of talking *with* each other, we seek a possible "pattern which connects" (Bateson, 1980, p. 9) and cohere them together for better understanding. We are particularly interested in discovering and examining the underlying forms of knowledge, actions, and identities that actually foment the disparities in the deaf education systems and at the same time, serve to sustain and bind those systems together. "Without this going beyond, the participants in conversation will not be able to [extend past] each other's unspoken taken-for-granted, that is, each other's ideology, which is the cultural crucible and context that make possible what is said by each in the conversational situation" (Aoki, 2004a, p. 227).

This examination then is inherently an *ecological* one, not in the sense of empirical ecology which involves biological, meteorological, and geographical studies of earth, how it is changing, and the effect of these changes on earth's natural systems. And not in terms of environmental ecology which focuses on the human impact on earth's systems. Our inquiry, rather, is situated in Bateson's ecology of mind (Bateson, 1972), which assumes that the mind does not reside solely within the individual but dynamically interrelates with and is inseparable from social, cultural, and natural (i.e., more-than-human) environments as an integrated whole. Akin to ecologies in nature, ecologies of mind are information-rich and brought forth into being through social "relationships, cultural norms, shared ideas, traditions, and language [such that] it becomes impossible to separate off components or 'individuals' from the systems of which they are a part" (Flinders, 2022, p. 2).

Our inquiry, as situated within this conception of mind, explores how a more expansive view of language can offer insight into the wickedness of problems associated with language deprivation and how we might talk differently and begin new conversations. To do this, we draw on both the decades-long, parallel, yet radically intersecting works of curriculum scholars Bowers and Aoki, and particularly their theorizing of language (see Thom, 2022 for more detailed discussion).

Language and Languaging

Much more than the spoken, written, or signed word, Bowers (e.g., 1997) and Aoki (e.g., 2004b) understand language to include physical (e.g., buildings), spatial (e.g., left-to-right order), temporal (e.g., past, present, future), spiritual (e.g., materialized as rivers, mountains, weather, stars), and symbolic patterns (e.g., text) of communication.

Language in this more expansive sense serves to relate and/or differentiate one social or cultural group with/from another, including how they recursively bring forth particular ways of knowing, doing, and being. For Aoki and Bowers, and akin to Bateson (1972), language as culture thought patterns serve as a "pattern which connects" (Bateson, 180, p. 9) members of a social or cultural group with one another, render them inseparable from the (im)material world, and enable them to carry on within institutionalized aspects of sociocultural life. Language conceived as such elucidates the impossibility of it ever being neutral or a "mere communication tool" (Aoki, 2004b, p. 324) with which to transfer information. Instead, "language as the very means by which [socio-]cultural norms are specified and materialize" (Thom, 2019, p. 513), implicates how "it" *is* through language "the very 'languaging' participates in creating [these] effects" (Aoki, 2004b, p. 324). In other words, "Language thinks us as we think with language" (Heidegger, 1962, as paraphrased by Bowers in Thom, 2019, p. 516). Consequently, it becomes imperative within deaf education for studies to examine and explicate the culture language thought patterns which are being conveyed, embedded, and enacted within the field.

We return to our flux of question(s): What are these conversations about? What are we in deaf education *really* conversing about? What is "it" that we might not be putting on the table? What is "it" that makes it possible for us to do so? And how does "it" enable us to see certain issues while not seeing others that are so urgently calling for our attention?

Continuing, we turn to the metaphorical nature of language and languaging. More so, how such an understanding of the two might offer insight into what we may or may not be seeing in deaf education and what " it" is that could be obscuring our vision.

Putting "It" Back on the Table

If language is really more than the simple exchange of ideas, purposive plans, descriptions, and viewpoints, and communication is different from the transmission of these (Aoki, 2004b; Bowers, 1997), then understanding the power of language lies in making sense of how these systems, as ecologies, (re)emerge, evolve, and are carried forth. These processes, what we call languaging (Aoki, 2004b; Bowers, 2005), concern the ways certain ideas, events, and meanings frame and specify how we as humans (including all of us in deaf education) come to know, act, and be in the world.

Metaphorical Nature of Language and Languaging

Postman (1995) reminds us that "we must keep in mind that language does much more than construct concepts about the events and things in the world; it *tells* us what sorts of concepts we *ought* to construct" (emphasis added, p. 181). To recognize "how culturally embedded our lives are to consider the cultural experiences, beliefs, and values that emerge from recurrent interactions of a group and metaphorically become what Bateson (1972) and Bowers (1997) refer to as a culture's *map*" (Thom, 2019, emphasis added, p. 26). Moreover,

> The term and concept [of a cultural map] borrowed from Korzybski (1931) means that a culture's map identifies what its members will and won't perceive as having significance by rooting these features within the culture's . . . language. Because these cultural distinctions permeate the group's languaging, . . . [when] these features become embedded in a culture's language, they are metaphorized [from the Greek word *metaphora*, "to carry over"] and taken for granted by the members (e.g., *linear* time and *objectified* knowledge). [Far beyond literary tools,] [m]etaphors then, as unseen aspects of a culture's language and features of the map, are deeply rooted in the collective mindset and mediate how the members perceive and subsequently experience the world. (Thom, 2019, p. 26)

Frankly, we wonder what metaphors might be rooted and entrenched within the language of the four conversations. Further, how, in deaf education, is such "language *thinking us* as we think with it[?]" (Heidegger, 1962, as paraphrased by Bowers in Thom, 2019, p. 516). For example, what are some of the discursive ways in which the collective mindset of deaf education is metaphorically defined by such culturally specific and deeply entrenched conceptions regarding the nature of deafness? How do such well-intentioned ideas and meanings, conscious or tacit, conflate and abstract deafness as a state of being within educational placements, such as when deaf students who have spoken language skills are deemed as needing minimal specialized services from a TODHH?

Metaphorical Patterns Which Connect

Returning to the frank conversations, we examine them together and ecologically as a diverse (not disparate) and integrated (not irreconcilable) whole. Here, we re-search within and across the conversations for possible metaphorical patterns which connect (Bateson, 1980) and cohere them together so that we might better understand them as well as gain insight and new understanding. In this way, we see(k) opportunities to open new spaces for authentic conversations wherein a generative reciprocity of perspectives (Aoki, 2004a) can arise.

At first glance, the four conversations present as if they concern each of their own separate topics in deaf education, each of their own set of unique issues within the field, and perspectives unto themselves. Looking deeper, however, what is revealed is not so much dissimilarity but a striking familiarity with each other. Not merely in the sense that the conversations resemble one another but how, in radical ways, they grow from the very metaphors rooted, embedded, and promoted within the larger field of education and more so, those discursively entrenched in dominant society such as universalism, scientism, mechanism, economism, individualism, progressivism, anthropocentrism, and colonialism. While the scope of this chapter does not allow us to explicate each of the metaphors and how they manifest within society, education, and the four conversations, we will attempt to put three of these root metaphors—universalism, mechanism, and progressivism—on the table as conversation starters.

Universalism

By definition, words such as *universe, universal,* and *universalism* imbue a sense of oneness or singularity. For example, "including or covering all or a whole collectively or distributively without limit or exception"; "available equitably to all members of a society"; "existent or operative everywhere or under all conditions"; "a predicable of traditional logic"; "adapted or adjustable to meet varied requirements"; and "a behavior pattern or institution (such as the family) existing in all cultures" (Universal, 2023). Metaphorically, these tacit meanings ubiquitously re(pro)duce and carry forth societal desires and intentions for *uni*formity and sameness. The need to involve every*one*. To find *one* solution which addresses *all* concerns. How a *universal* design process for creating environments, products, and communications applies to even the way homes are "built and remodeled to better meet the needs of *every*one at *every* life stage" (Mace, 2019).

This notion of universalism plays out ideologically in everyday life in how spoken and written English is the universal language of the United States and Canada (Canagarajah, 2013). As such, spoken English language educational environments are always "superior" to placement in a bimodal-multilingual classroom. In the first conversation, inclusive education supports the focus on keeping everyone in the *same* classroom, while deaf education tries to support parental wishes that their child speak *the dominant* language. The deaf cultural critique positions sign language *over* spoken language, emphasizing it is *the only* language that is *fully accessible*, therefore suggesting that access to sign language is a universal right (Murray et al., 2020). Universalism in the second conversation manifests as a teleological goal in which *everyone*'s needs will be *fully* met. Within IEPs, resources and services are presumed to be *adequate* and *fully* available upon request. If resources for sign language acquisition must be built up, resources must be built to "code" or to *normative* ways of learning, instead of supporting the vitality of communities that might provide those resources according to their own epistemologies. Inclusive education points to the "*whole* village" that will raise the child in the third conversation. The idiom obscures the practicalities of language acquisition acquired through interaction with a whole village. For instance, how many people in the village are conversant in sign language? Then in the fourth conversation, it is the experts in contrast to communities that can provide organic solutions to some problems, are armed with assessments based on universal *norms*, which, through instrumental means of measuring, quantifying, and *standardizing* approaches, will solve all problems. Regardless of the four discourses, each assumes and creates its own hubris when the goal of deaf education is to be universally all-inclusive by providing every(-)thing to every(-)one.

Mechanism

The word *mechanism*, as from the Greek word *mēkhanē*, means "machine, instrument, device" (Mechanism, 2023). In a metaphorical sense, mechanism assumes objectification of any and all phenomena. That such things are knowable, predictable, and can be broken down into smaller bits. As mechanistic objects then, they are, at most, the sum of their component parts. They can be (re)designed; (re)manufactured; taken apart; fixed or repaired; and (re)assembled. This also means they and any of their parts can be switched out and replaced without concern for losing or compromising the integrity of the machine. In the news, online, and all around us, we see this metaphor enacted as factory assembly lines, from the industrialization of farming and the manufacturing of food, to education as the production of programs, services, personnel, and resource packages guaranteed to meet the individual needs of every deaf child.

Within the first conversation, the root metaphor of mechanism is implied in the word *accommodations*. It is about repair, after all, of a system assumed to be working well for the most part. Accommodations as mechanisms are necessary because the present system is not meeting the needs of disabled persons. Therefore, the system needs redesign, repair, and reassembling. Mechanism as metaphor continues in the second conversation where emphasis is on the development of plans, personnel, resources, and services as modular pieces that can be plugged into the system when it is not functioning well. In the third conversation, inclusive education is described as a "ramp that provides access" and "all hands on deck," implying the boat is afloat but that much is required to keep it that way. The fourth conversation focuses on a normalized society and a prosperous and sustainable economy. To achieve these ends, knowledge, skills, and attitudes are measured and quantified through standardized assessments as the way to identify what is broken and what must be repaired, adjusted, or modified to integrate and normalize the deaf child into mainstream society. Even more telling is how the deaf child is conceived as a unit that will contribute to economic prosperity and sustainability. The emphasis on services, personnel, and resources to the deaf child indexes parts, pieces, and assessments that all contribute to a mechanistic view of the world. Mechanistically, many assessments attempt to drill down to the problem such as what the child is not doing correctly, where is the missing link, or what is not working. If the source of the problem can be identified, then appropriate interventions can enable the child to acquire language. Mechanism is all about troubleshooting, inputting, and making the correct, missing, or appropriate part operational so that the deaf child acquires language.

Progressivism

Progress as a term appears benign and innocuous. However, the culturally specific ways that *progressivism* becomes rooted and metaphorically specific, like universalism and mechanism (e.g.,

Bowers, 1997), is nothing less than stark and surprisingly revealing. Hence, there is no such thing as independent thoughts or ideas. Just as Postman (1995) contends, not only does language construct concepts for objects and events in the world, but also language gives rise to the very ideas each of us thinks we have come up with by ourselves. What we consider as "progress" takes on particular meanings as it is discursively informed by culture language thought patterns of (dominant) society. Just think about "it" for a moment. (Un)consciously, a common meaning for progress is to *move forward*. In contrast, lack of progress is to remain in the *same place* or to *fall behind*. Here, progress metaphorically conjures linearity. The belief and value that change and moving forward are necessary, inherently "good"' and conducive to progress, then embeds notions of stability and return as counterintuitive for "it." The advancement of knowledge, whether scientific, technological, economic, or otherwise, is framed, perceived, and experienced within these concepts and their meanings. As such, offshoots of these meanings eventuate universal and mechanistic-industrial-consumer views of progress. Moreover, ideas associated with change become ideas that emphasize replacing and discarding any and all things to maximize their rates and grades of performance and efficiency.

In the first conversation, gaining access to programs, services, and resources communicates progress as facilitating the acquisition of language in a deaf child or youth. The duty to accommodate is what prompts us to provide access, which mechanistically fuels and drives a forward-moving progression. In the second conversation, progress is about working together to troubleshoot and find solutions. Progress is equated with changed or alternative actions, which are often taken without question as radical, "all part of the equation," and creative answers. In the third conversation, progress is a matter of engineering and financing which suggests all resources are funneled through those who have decision-making power and who move forward with evidence-based practices and solutions. In the fourth conversation, the efficacy of these solutions is measured with statistical data used to plan programs, develop resources, and hire personnel. The deaf cultural critique advocates for yearly assessments to be performed by trained native users of sign language. Always and all too often, at all costs, the momentum is to move forward, plan, assess, and implement solutions based on benchmarks, indicators, and student assessments.

Reason to Pause

"It" is nothing trivial when all four frank conversations disclose, as entangled in the wickedness of deaf education problems, that "we are the language [and language is us]" (Aoki, 2004a, p. 264). Moreover, the deeply insightful conversations demonstrate how precious little is even possible to accomplish, except for dead ends and stalemates which prevent further conversation or dialogic cul-de-sacs that circuitously return to the starting point (e.g., raising the issue of concern), when unawareness persists regarding the metaphors tacitly rooted in the (un)consciousness of the collective. Importantly, such metaphors are bigger than deaf education and extend well beyond general education. Rather, they lie at the heart of mainstream society, giving rise to grand or master metanarratives which define and wholly cohere all three together. As dominant culture language thought-patterns, the metaphors which are embedded, entrenched, and metaphorically "carry over" are indeed our very ways of knowing, acting, and be(com)ing in the world. Language then, as inherently metaphorical (Aoki, 2004b; Bowers, 1997), is always and implicitly specifying what we (can) know, (can) do, and (can) be(come), including what ideas and approaches we can(not) see(k) for understanding and responding to problems within deaf education.

Where to Now?

As we pause to reflect on wicked problems in deaf education and wonder where the conversation might go next, the court decision of *Carter Churchill v. the Newfoundland and Labrador English School District* is announced. On March 1, 2023, the court ruled mostly in favor of Carter Churchill's parents. This landmark case will have repercussions across Canada for years to come (Newfoundland and Labrador Human Rights Commission, 2023).

The case proceedings held between August 29 and September 9, 2022, serve as a carefully laid out exposé of the conflations and abstractions held by key stakeholders embedded within the school district which contributed to the language deprivation of Carter Churchill (Newfoundland and Labrador Human Rights Commission, 2022). Compellingly, particular attention must be paid to the ways that the Churchills' lawyer Kyle Rees revealed the actual discourses re-represented by the four stakeholders featured in the frank conversations of this chapter. As such, the case points to huge fault lines and not mere gaps that can be resolved by simple tinkering within the deaf education system.

The chief adjudicator, C. Brodie Gallant, ruled that Carter Churchill experienced discrimination during his kindergarten to grade 3 years because he was not receiving meaningful access to his education. Furthermore, the adjudicator ruled that Carter received meaningful access in grade 4, upon being immersed in a special DHH classroom that offered him direct instruction in ASL and opportunities for interacting with deaf peers and adults. Finally, Gallant found issues with the school district's procedural implementation of the duty to accommodate, that is, their failure to consider the available information from TODHHs and the parents when developing IEPs for Carter (Newfoundland and Labrador Human Rights Commission, 2023). Carter's parents, Kimberley and Todd Churchill, despite their many efforts to point out problems with, inform, suggest, guide, and support the efforts of the school district, were effectively silenced and erased. Carter effectively became invisible to many of his teachers, administrators, and the higher levels of bureaucracy in the school district.

Carter Churchill v. the Newfoundland and Labrador English School District thus serves as a cautionary narrative of how language thinks us. How "it" limits responses to wicked problems when there is not an awareness of the metaphorical nature of language and the ways it discursively shapes thinking in deaf education. Perhaps for the first time in Canada, the parent voices on behalf of their deaf child, amplified, heard, and broadcasted across the country and reported in the media, have established an important precedent. The hope and promise of this case is that more parent voices will be heard, and more deaf children and youth will be seen.

This victory must be taken as bittersweet, given that the effects of language deprivation are known to be irreversible and are onerous at best to resolve. And while future litigation could raise awareness about language deprivation, issues concerning language that lie much deeper and at the root of wicked problems in deaf education would be missed. Real and lasting change calls for conversations that see(k) the vitality of a reciprocity of perspectives (Aoki, 2004a) to authentically (Aoki, 2004c) recognize what *is* "it" that we see and do not see when "[l]anguage thinks us as we think with language" (Heidegger, 1962, as paraphrased by Bowers in Thom, 2019, p. 516).

Invitation

We have chosen to conclude this chapter by continuing it. Now, turning to you as a reader interested in deaf education, we invite you to join us. The following serve as three provocations we see(k) as further prompts for continuing these frank conversations. As mentioned early on in this chapter, if the topic of language deprivation is first and foremost on everyone's minds, *why is there not a concerted effort to consolidate the research findings and implement solutions to address this overwhelming crisis?* What is holding deaf education back?

We know that "[w]ords matter. Appropriately used, they can build people up and acknowledge their worth, [and, t]he careless and insensitive use of words can have the opposite effect" (*Carter Churchill v. the Newfoundland and Labrador English School District,* 2023, p. 6). What are ways that deaf education can take up the work to (re)examine the linguistic metaphors that are at the root and give rise to activities, programs, plans, and research agendas? Here lies a possibility for returning to the live(d) experiences of parents, deaf children, and youth. In turn, doing so occasions opportunities with which to reveal and deepen understanding for their vulnerabilities and potentialities which are often hidden from view when deaf children and youth are perceived as individuals to be shaped, monitored, rehabilitated, and restored to the normalized world. If words really do *matter*; if "language is [more than a] mere communication tool [but instead is] the very 'languaging' [that] participates in creating effects" (Aoki, 2004b, p. 324)—and if we *are* the language and language *is* us (Aoki, 2004b; Bowers, 1997; Heidegger, 1962; Postman, 1995; Thom, 2019, 2022)—then what could this mean for deaf education? More urgently, what hope and promise could "it" and insights gained from "it" bring to deaf children and deaf youth? How might that which is wicked become that which is generative and flourishes?

References

Antia S. D., & Rivera M. C. (2016). Instruction and service time decisions: Itinerant services to deaf and hard-of-hearing students. *Journal of Deaf Studies and Deaf Education, 21*(3), 293–302. https://doi.org/10.1093/deafed/enw032.

Aoki, T. T. (2004a). In the midst of slippery theme-words: Living as designers of Japanese Canadian curriculum 1 (1992). In W. F. Pinar & R. L. Irwin (Eds.), *Curriculum in a new key: The collected works of Ted T. Aoki* (pp. 263–77). Routledge.

Aoki, T. T. (2004b). Language, culture, and curriculum . . . In W. F. Pinar & R. L. Irwin (Eds.), *Curriculum in a new key: The collected works of Ted T. Aoki* (pp. 321–29). Routledge.

Aoki, T. T. (2004c). Toward Understanding Curriculum: Talk Through Reciprocity of Perspectives 1. In W. F. Pinar & R. L. Irwin (Eds.), *Curriculum in a new key: The collected works of Ted T. Aoki* (pp. 219–28). Routledge.

Arnold, P. (2022). The Education of the deaf child: For integration or autonomy? *American Annals of the Deaf, 167*(4), 557–68. https://doi.org/10.1353/aad.2022.0052.

Bateson, G. (1980). *Mind and nature: A necessary unity.* Dutton.

Bateson, G. (1972). *Steps to an ecology of mind.* The University of Chicago Press.

Bateson M. C. (1996). Democracy, ecology, and participation. In Soder R. (Ed.), *Democracy, education, and the schools* (pp. 69–86). Jossey-Bass.

Borders, C. M., Bock, S. J., & Probst, K. M. (2016) A review of educational practices for deaf/hard of hearing students with comorbid autism. *Deafness and Education International, 18*(4), 189–205. https://doi.org/10.1080/14643154.2016.1255416.

Bowers, C. A. (1996). The cultural dimensions of ecological literacy. *Journal of Environmental Education, 27*(2), 5–10.

Bowers, C. A. (1997). *The culture of denial: Why the environmental movement needs a strategy for reforming universities and public schools.* SUNY.

Bowers, C. A. (2005). *The false promises of constructivist theories of learning: A global and ecological critique.* Peter Lang.

Bowers, C. A. (2016). *Reforming higher education in an era of ecological crisis and growing digital insecurity.* Process Century Press.

British Columbia Teachers' Federation, Research Department (May 11, 2018). *Research: Recruitment and Retention of Teachers of the Deaf and Hard of Hearing in BC Public Schools*, May 11, 2018. BS Teacher's Federation. https://www.bctf.ca/news-and-opportunities/news-details/2018/05/11/recruitment-and-retention-of-teachers-of-the-deaf-and-hard-of-hearing-in-bc-public-schools.

Canadian Association of Educators of the Deaf and Hard of Hearing (CAEDHH). (n.d.). Resources for TDHHs in Canada. https://www.caedhh.ca/tdhh-resources.

Canagarajah, S. (2013). *Translingual practice: Global Englishes and cosmopolitan relations.* Routledge.

Cannon, J. E., & Luckner, J. L. (2016). Increasing cultural and linguistic diversity in deaf education teacher preparation programs. *American Annals of the Deaf, 161*(1), 89–103. http://doi.org/10.1353/aad.2016.0014

Cannon, J. E., Guardino, C., & Gallimore, E. (2016). A new kind of heterogeneity: What we can learn from d/Deaf and hard of hearing multilingual learners. *American Annals of the Deaf, 161*(1), 8–16. http://doi.org/10.1353/aad.2016.0015

Cannon, J. E., & Luckner, J. L. (2016). Increasing cultural and linguistic diversity in deaf education teacher preparation programs. *American Annals of the Deaf, 161*(1), 89–103. http://doi.org/10.1353/aad.2016.0014

Carter Churchill v. the Newfoundland and Labrador English School District, 2023 CanLII 16071 (NL HRC). https://www.carterchurchill.ca/board-of-inquiry-decision-2023.html#/

Caselli, N. K., Hall, W. C., & Henner, J. (2020). American Sign Language interpreters in public schools: An illusion of inclusion that perpetuates language deprivation. *Maternal and Child Health Journal, 24*(11), 1323–1329. https://doi.org/10.1007/s10995-020-02975-7

Caselli, N. K., Pyers, J., & Lieberman, A. M. (2021). Deaf children of hearing parents have age-level vocabulary growth when exposed to American Sign Language by 6 months of age. *Journal of Pediatrics, 232*, 229–236. http://doi.org/10.1016/j.jpeds.2021.01.029

Cheng, Q., Roth, A., Halgren, E., & Mayberry, R. I. (2019). Effects of early language deprivation on brain connectivity: Language pathways in deaf native and late first-language learners of American Sign Language. *Frontiers in Human Neuroscience, 13*(Sept. 2019), Article 320. https://doi.org/10.3389/fnhum.2019.00320

Clark, M. D., Cue, K. R., Delgado, N. J., Greene-Woods, A. N., & Wolsey, J. A. (2020). Early intervention protocols: Proposing a default bimodal bilingual approach for deaf children. *Maternal and Child Health Journal, 24*(11), 1339–1344. https://doi.org/10.1007/s10995-020-03005-2

Czubek, T. (2021). Crossing the divide: The bilingual grammar curriculum. In C. Enns, J. Henner, & L. McQuarrie, (Eds.), *Discussing bilingualism in deaf children: Essays in honor of Robert Hoffmeister* (pp. 150–170). Routledge.

Davison-Mowle, J., Leigh, G., Duncan, J., & Arthur-Kelly, M. (2018). Description of the direct teaching activities of itinerant teachers of deaf and hard of hearing students. *Deafness and Education International, 20*(1), 23–40, https://doi.org/10.1080/14643154.2018.1442908

Delcenserie, A., Genesee, F., & Champoux, F. (2024). Exposure to sign language prior and after cochlear implantation increases language and cognitive skills in deaf children. *Developmental Science, 27*(4), e134811. https://doi.org/10.1111/desc.13481

Di Perri, K. (2021). The Bedrock Literacy curriculum. In C. Enns, J. Henner, & L. McQuarrie (Eds.), *Discussing bilingualism in deaf children: Essays in honor of Robert Hoffmeister* (pp.132–149). Routledge.

Disability Rights Coalition v. Nova Scotia (Attorney General), 2021 NSCA 70 (CanLII). ESCR-Net. https://www.escr-net.org/caselaw/2024/disability-rights-coalition-v-nova-scotia-attorney-general-2021-nsca-70-canlii/

Easterbrooks, S. R., Dostal, H. M., & Beal-Alvarez, J. S. (2013). *Literacy instruction for students who are deaf and hard of hearing.* Oxford University Press.

Easterbrooks, S. (2016, April 2). *What's really happening in literacy education? with Dr. Susan Easterbrooks transcript.* Minnesota Commission of the Deaf, DeafBlind & Hard of Hearing. https://mn.gov/deaf-commission/advocacy-issues/education/collaborative-experience/keynotes-and-presentations/whats-really-happening.jsp.

Engelman, A., & Izquierdo, A. (2025). Accessible services for deaf immigrants and refugees in the United States: Exploring the capacity of deaf-serving organizations. *Journal of Migration and Health, 11*, 100326. https://doi.org/10.1016/j.jmh.2025.100326

Flinders, D. J. (2022). An introduction to the curriculum and environmental scholarship of C. A. (Chet) Bowers. In A. Dentith, D. Flinders, J. Lupinacci, & J. S. Thom (Eds.), *Curriculum, environment, and the work of C. A. Bowers: Ecological and cultural perspectives* (pp. 1–12). Routledge.

Foster, S., & Kinuthia, W. (2003). Deaf persons of Asian American, Hispanic American, and African American backgrounds: A study of intraindividual diversity and identity. *Journal of Deaf Studies and Deaf Education, 8*(3), 271–290. https://doi.org/10.1093/deafed/eng015.

Glickman, N. S., & Hall, W. C. (2018). *Language deprivation and Deaf mental health*. Routledge.

Goodwin, C., Carrigan, E., & Walker, K., Coppola, M. (2022). Language not auditory experience is related to parent-reported executive functioning in preschool-aged deaf and hard-of-hearing children. *Child Development, 93*(1), 209–224. https://doi.org/10.1111/cdev.13677.

Gulati, S. (2019). Language deprivation syndrome. In N. S. Glickman & W. C. Hall (Eds.), *Language deprivation and deaf mental health* (pp. 24–53). Routledge/Taylor & Francis Group.

Hall, M. (2019). *What do you mean, "language deprivation"?* YouTube. https://youtu.be/arCySZ80VKs

Hall, M. L., Hall, W. C., & Caselli, N. K. (2019). Deaf children need language, not (just) speech. *First Language, 39*(4), 367–395. https://doi.org/10.1177/0142723719834102

Hall, W. C., Levin, L., & Anderson, M. L. (2017). Language deprivation syndrome: A possible neurodevelopmental disorder with sociocultural origins. *Social Psychiatry and Psychiatric Epidemiology, 52*, 761–776. http://doi.org/10.1007/s00127-017-1351-7

Hecht J. L. (2020). Responsibility in the current epidemic of language deprivation (1990–Present). *Maternal and Child Health Journal, 24*(11), 1319–1322. https://doi.org/10.1007/s10995-020-02989-1

Heidegger, M. (1962). *Being and time.* (J. Macquarrie & E. Robinson, translators). Harper.

Howe, A. (Jan. 18, 2023). *Deaf students lawsuit against school district draws support from justices on both the left and the right.* SCOTUSblog. https://www.scotusblog.com/2023/01/deaf-students-lawsuit-against-school-district-draws-support-from-justices-on-both-the-left-and-the-right/

Howerton-Fox, A., & Falk, J. L. (2019). Deaf children as "English learners": The psycholinguistic turn in deaf education. *Education Sciences, 9*(2), Article 133. https://doi.org/10.3390/educsci9020133

Humphries, T., Kushalnagar, P., Mathur, G., Napoli, D. J., Padden, C., Rathmann, C., & Smith, S. (2016). Avoiding linguistic neglect of deaf children. *Social Service Review, 90*(4), 589–619. http://doi.org/10.1086/689543

Humphries, T., Kushalnagar, P., Mathur, G., Napoli, D. J., Rathmann, C., & Smith, S. (2019). Support for parents of deaf children: Common questions and informed, evidence-based answers. *International Journal of Pediatric Otorhinolaryngology, 118*, 124–142, https://doi.org/10.1016/j.ijporl.2018.12.036

Humphries, T, Mather, G.., Napoli, D. J., Padden, C., & Rathmann, C. (2022). Deaf children need rich language input from the start: Support in advising parents. *Children, 9*(11), Article 1609. https://doi.org/10.3390/children9111609

Jasinska, K. K., & Petitto, L. A. (2013). How age of bilingual exposure can change the neural systems for language in the developing brain: a functional near infrared spectroscopy investigation of syntactic processing in monolingual and bilingual children. *Developmental Cognitive Neuroscience, 6*, 87–101. https://doi.org/10.1016/j.dcn.2013.06.005

Johnson, L. J., Taylor, M. M., Schick, B. S., Brown, S., & Bolster, L. (2018). *Complexities in educational interpreting: An investigation into patterns of practice.* Interpreting Consolidated.

Kennon, J. L., & Patterson, M. H. (2016) What I didn't know about teaching: Stressors and burnout among deaf education teachers. *Journal of Human Services: Training, Research, and Practice, 1*(2), Article 2. https://scholarworks.sfasu.edu/jhstrp/vol1/iss2/2

Kinuthia, Heather. (2021). *Teacher professionalism, education reform and 21st century skills in the United Arab Emirates* [Doctoral dissertation, University College London].

Korzybski, A. (1933). A non-Aristotelian system and its necessity for rigour in mathematics and physics. In A. Korzybski *Science and sanity: An introduction to non-Aristotelian systems and general semantics* (pp. 747–761). Institute of General Semantics. (Originally given as a conference presentation at the American Mathematical Society at the New Orleans, Louisiana, meeting of the American Association for the Advancement of Science, December 28, 1931).

Kuntze, M., & Golos, D. (2021). Revisiting rethinking literacy. In C. Enns, J. Henner, & L. McQuarrie (Eds.), *Discussing bilingualism in deaf children: Essays in honor of Robert Hoffmeister* (pp. 99–112). Routledge.

Kurz, C., Golos, D., Kuntze, M., Henner, J., & Scott, J. (2021). *Guidelines for multilingual deaf education teacher preparation programs.* Gallaudet University Press. https://gallaudetupress.manifoldapp.org/projects/guidelines-for-multilingual-deaf-education-teacher-preparation-programs

Ladd, P. (2003). *Understanding deaf culture: In search of deafhood.* Multilingual Matters.

Ladd, P. (2022). *Seeing through new eyes: Deaf culture and deaf pedagogies: The unrecognized curriculum.* DawnSignPress.

Lane, H. (1984). *When the mind hears: A history of the deaf.* Random House.

Lane, H. (1992). *The mask of benevolence: Disabling the deaf community.* Knopf.

Luckner, J. L., & Ayantoye, C. (2013). Itinerant teachers of students who are deaf or hard of hearing: Practices and preparation. *Journal of Deaf Studies and Deaf Education, 18*(3), 409–423. https://doi.org/10.1093/deafed/ent015

Luckner, J. L., & Dorn, B. (2017). Job satisfaction of teachers of students who are deaf or hard of hearing. *Journal of Deaf Studies and Deaf Education, 22*(3), 336–345. https://doi.org/10.1093/deafed/enx016

Luft, P. (2017). What is different about deaf education? The effects of child and family factors on educational services. *Journal of Special Education, 51*(1), 27–37. https://doi.org/10.1177/0022466916660546

Mace, R. L. (2019). *Accessible housing.* Universal Design Institute. https://www.udinstitute.org/accessible housing.

Majid, C. (2022). *Opening comments. Newfoundland and Labrador Human Rights Commission (2022). Carter Churchill v. NL English School District. Official Transcripts from the Human Rights Board of Inquiry, August 29–Sept. 9, 2022*, pp. 2–10. https://www.carterchurchill.ca/transcripts-human-rights-board-of-inquiry-2022.html

Martusewicz, R. A., Edmundson, J., & Lupinacci, J. (2021). *EcoJustice education: Toward diverse, democratic, and sustainable communities*, 3rd ed. Routledge.

Maturana, H., & Varela, F. J. (1992). *The tree of knowledge: The biological roots of human understanding* (Rev. ed.). Shambhala.

Mauldin, L. (2016). *Made to hear: Cochlear implants and deaf children.* University of Minnesota Press.

Mayberry, R. I. (2010). Early language acquisition and adult language ability: What sign language reveals about the critical period for language. In M. Marschark & P. E. Spencer, *The Oxford handbook of deaf studies, language, and education, vol. 2*, (pp. 281–291). Oxford.

Mayberry, R. I., Chen, J., Witcher, P., & Klein, D. (2011). Age of acquisition effects on the functional organization of language in the adult brain. *Brain and Language, 119*(1), 16–29. http://doi.org/10.1016/j.bandl.2011.05.007

Mayberry, R. I., & Kluender, R. (2018). Rethinking the critical period for language: New insights into an old question from American Sign Language. *Bilingualism: Language and Cognition, 21*(5), 938–944. https://doi.org/10.1017/S1366728918000585

Mayberry, R. I., Lock, E., & Kazmi, H. (2002). Linguistic ability and early language exposure. *Nature, 417*(6884), Article 38.

Mayberry, R. I., & Lock, E. (2003). Age constraints on first versus second language acquisition: Evidence for linguistic plasticity and epigenesis. *Brain and Language, 87*(3), 369–84. https://doi.org/10.1016/S0093-934X(03)00137-8.

McQuarrie, L. & Enns, C., (2021). Assessing ASL: Comprehension, narrative, and phonological awareness. In C. Enns, J. Henner, & L. McQuarrie (Eds.), *Discussing bilingualism in deaf children: Essays in honor of Robert Hoffmeister* (pp. 217–228). Routledge.

Mechanism. (2023). In *etymonline: Online etymological dictionary*. https://www.etymonline.com/search?q=mechanism

Mellett, E. (2024). Immigrant deaf students in the United States: Linguistics injustices brought to light. *Deafness & Education International, 27*(2), 144–164. https://doi.org/10.1080/14643154.2024.2389589

Meyer, K. (2021). *Massachusetts teachers of deaf and hard of hearing students: A mixed methods workforce study* [Doctoral diss., University of Massachusetts, Amherst]. https://doi.org/10.7275/20321731

Millett, P. (2021). Are students still "alone in the mainstream"? *Canadian Audiologist, 8*(2). https://canadianaudiologist.ca/issue/volume-8-issue-2-2021/column/in-the-classrooms/

Miller, K. J. (2014). Trends impacting one public school program for students who are deaf or hard-of-hearing. *Communication Disorders Quarterly, 36*(1), 35–43. http://doi.org/10.1177/1525740114533380

Moore v. British Columbia (Education), 2012 SCC 61 (CanLII), [2012] 3 SCR 360. https://decisions.scc-csc.ca/scc-csc/scc-csc/en/item/12680/index.do

Murray, J. J., Snoddon, K., De Meulder, M., & Underwood, K. (2020) Intersectional inclusion for deaf learners: Moving beyond general comment no. 4 on article 24 of the United Nations Convention on the Rights of Persons with Disabilities. *International Journal of Inclusive Education, 24*(7), 691–705. http://doi.org/10.1080/13603116.2018.1482013

Musyoka, M. M., & Clark, M. D. (2017). Teachers' perceptions of Individualized Education Program (IEP) goals and related services. *Journal of Developmental and Physical Disabilities, 29*(1), 5–23. https://doi.org/10.1007/s10882-015-9462-0

Newfoundland and Labrador Human Rights Commission. (2022). *Carter Churchill v. NL English School District. Official Transcripts from the Human Rights Board of Inquiry, August 29–Sept 9, 2022*. https://www.carterchurchill.ca/transcripts-human-rights-board-of-inquiry-2022.html

Newfoundland and Labrador Human Rights Commission. (March 1, 2023). *Kimberly Churchill and Todd Churchill, on behalf of Carter Churchill v. Newfoundland and Labrador English School District et. al.* (Complaint File # 10171). https://www.carterchurchill.ca/uploads/1/1/9/5/11951403/decision_-_churchill_v_nlesd__final_.pdf

Pederson, H. F., & Anderson, K. L. (2019). The changing role of the itinerant teacher of the deaf: A snapshot of current teacher perceptions. *Journal of the American Academy of Special Education Professionals*, 63–80. https://www.naset.org/publications/jaasep-research-based-journal-in-special-education/jaasep-fall-2019/the-changing-role-of-the-itinerant-teacher-of-the-deaf-a-snapshot-of-current-teacher-perceptions

Pénicaud, S., Klein, D., Zatorre, R., Chen, J., Witcher, P., Hyde, K., & Mayberry, R. (2013). Structural brain changes linked to delayed first language acquisition in congenitally deaf individuals. *NeuroImage, 66*, 42–49. http://doi.org/10.1016/j.neuroimage.2012.09.076

Postman, N. (1995). *The end of education: Redefining the value of school.* Vintage Books.

Pettito, L. A., & Jasinska, K. K. (2014). Development of neural systems for reading in the monolingual and bilingual brain: New insights from functional near infrared spectroscopy. *Developmental Neuropsychology, 39*(6), 421–439. http://doi.org/10.1080/87565641.2014.939180

Rittel, H., & Webber, M. (1973). Dilemmas in a general theory of planning. *Policy Sciences, 4*(2), 155–169. https://doi.org/10.1007/BF01405730

Russell, D. (2021). Critical perspectives on mediated education: Inclusion or the illusion of inclusion? In K. Snoddon & J. C. Weber (Eds.), *Critical perspectives on plurilingualism in deaf education* (pp. 217–239). Multilingual Matters.

Salehomoum, M. (2020). Inclusion of signing deaf or hard-of-hearing students: Factors that facilitate versus challenge access and participation. *Perspectives of the ASHAWIRE Special Interest Groups, 5*(4), 971–983. https://doi.org/10.1044/2020_PERSP-19-00124

Silvestri, J. A., & Hartman, M. C. (2022). Inclusion and deaf and hard of hearing students: Finding asylum in the LRE. *Education Sciences, 12*(11), Article 773. https://doi.org/10.3390/educsci12110773

Snoddon, K. (2021). "It seemed like if you chose sign language you were going to be punished": A narrative case study of participant experiences with supporting a deaf child in Ontario early childhood education and care. *Deafness & Education International, 23*(4), 276–294. https://doi.org/10.1080/14643154.2020.1840763

Snoddon, K., & Weber, J. (2021). *Critical perspectives on plurilingualism in deaf education.* Multilingual Matters.

Skyer, M. E. (2021). Pupil ⇄ Pedagogue: Grounded theories about biosocial interactions and axiology for deaf educators [Doctoral diss., University of Rochester]. ProQuest. https://www.proquest.com/docview/2572606741?pq-origsite=gscholar&fromopenview=true

Skyer, M. E. (2023). The deaf biosocial condition: Metaparadigmatic lessons from and beyond Vygotsky's deaf pedagogy research. *American Annals of the Deaf, 168*(1), 128–161.

Sydelko, P., Midgley, G., & Espinosa, A. (2021). Designing interagency responses to wicked problems: Creating a common, cross-agency understanding. *European Journal of Operational Research, 294*(1), 250–263. https://doi .org/10.1016/j.ejor.2020.11.045

Thom, J. S. (2019). Ecological revelations: Recovering the unseen. *Educational Studies, 55*(5), 510–530.

Thom, J. S. (2022). Co/inspiriting ecological conversations with Chet A. Bowers (1935–2017) and Ted T. Aoki (1919–2012). In A. Dentith, D. Flinders, J. Lupinacci, & J. Thom (Eds.), *Curriculum, environment, and the work of C. A. Bowers: Ecological and cultural perspectives* (pp. 22–43). Routledge.

United Nations. (2006). *Convention on the Rights of Persons with Disabilities, Article 24—Education.* https://www.un.org/development/desa/disabilities/convention-on-the-rights-of-persons-%20%20%20with-%20%20disabilities/article-24-education.html

Universal. (2023). *Merriam-Webster Dictionary.* https://www.merriam-webster.com/dictionary/universal

Weber, J., & Skyer, M. (2022). The aesthetics of OER, deaf pedagogy, and curriculum design contra the "wicked" policy of deaf education. *RIED: Revista Iberoamericana de Educación a Distancia,* 25 (2), 73–90. http://doi.org/10.5944/ried.25.2.33083

3

Psychological Assessment of Deaf and Hard of Hearing Individuals

Translating and Implementing the ASL Strengths and Difficulties Questionnaire

Justin Mulder and Cathy J. Chovaz

Construct

This chapter outlines challenges and complexities in the mental health assessment of Deaf and Hard of Hearing (DHH) individuals. Culturally and linguistically appropriate assessments ideally require assessors who understand the factors affecting mental health and deafness and who are fluent in the language of the DHH individual. Some challenges to think about before and during mental assessment include the governance of the clinician, the client's language and fluency, the use of mental health interpreters, the adaptation and translation of psychometric tests, and finally, language dysfluency or deprivation.

Head-to-Head and Heart-to-Heart

Mental health assessment of DHH individuals requires clinically crucial competencies as well as compassionate cultural knowledge. Translating tools from spoken to sign language relies on research that has been developed for both head-to-head and heart-to-heart work. In this chapter, head-to-head findings are shared from our work translating the Strengths and Difficulties Questionnaire (SDQ) into American Sign Language (ASL), the establishment of psychometric properties, and the results from an initial pilot study with DHH children. Heart-to-heart descriptions will be shared that highlight the context in which improper assessment can cause marked harm, and how appropriate assessment can facilitate adequate care.

Statements of Reflexivity

First Author: Justin Mulder

As a hearing researcher with primary knowledge in psychological measures, I am new to the culture of the DHH community. My aim is to combine my assessment skills with a respect for the community's unique and diverse experiences. Much of my knowledge comes from working collaboratively with Dr. Chovaz, and I recognize the importance of approaching this work with a beginner's mind. Being a hearing person, I am aware that I must consciously deconstruct the biases I have acquired through my life experiences as I write about psychological assessment. I am committed to learning from the DHH community and ensuring that my research is inclusive and respective of all perspectives.

Second Author: Cathy J. Chovaz

I acknowledge my view as deafened, white, female clinical psychologist. I was deafened as a young adult and grew up with spoken English as my first language and as such do not share the same early experiences of many of my patients. After becoming deaf, I learned ASL as a second language and culture. I identify with the tenets of hearing culture, as that was my first language and culture, yet also identify with and appreciate many of the tenets of a visual world and signed language. My reflection of the head-to-head information comes from decades of study in this area, and my appreciation of the heart-to-heart comes from intentional reflection of stories as they have been told to me by DHH patients and their families as well as my own life experience.

Recommendations

We conclude with recommendations for identifying and creating guidelines for the complex challenges inherent in the assessment of DHH individuals.

The clinical assessments of DHH individuals can be challenging for mental health professionals who may have little knowledge about the interactions between mental health presentations and linguistic and disability aspects of working with the diverse population of deaf people. Cultural and language discordance in addition to a fundamental lack of knowledge regarding mental health in this population is worrisome, potentially leading to erroneous diagnoses based on faulty assessments (Glickman, 2013).

Edna Levine (1960) addressed these issues within the context of the rehabilitation of DHH individuals in a foundational article which was then followed by other seminal work focused on psychometric delivery and analysis of data. For a more fulsome background, the interested reader is encouraged to read the work of Mindel and Vernon (1987), Brauer et al. (1998), Vernon (2005), and the prolific work of Pollard (1996, 1998, 2002) as well as Pollard and Berlinski (2017) and Pollard and Fox (2018.) In addition to these, Braden (1992, 2017) and Maller and Braden (2011) published important work on the core concepts involved in the intellectual assessment of deaf people. The purpose of this chapter is to build even further on past research and highlight the areas of assessment for clinicians which deserve intentional thought and consideration. For further discussion of the challenges of assessment, particularly with DHH children, the reader is encouraged to read Chapter 4.

Governance of the Clinician

Clinical governance refers to a system for improving the standards of clinical practice. It is essentially a shared responsibility among managers and clinicians to ensure that all patients/clients receive the best possible care. Starey (2001) describes the elements of clinical governance as including education, clinical audits, clinical effectiveness, risk management, research and development, and openness. The system of clinical governance integrates all these elements with the goal of promoting the quality of care.

The clinician's specific duties regarding clinical governance may differ by role and training (e.g., medical doctor, social worker, clinical psychologist, manager, administrator), yet each of their individual roles should be aligned with the systemic goal of effective clinical care. Each mental health care professional is bound by their respective profession's code of ethics and licensing requirement. This, however, is the bare minimum of best practices, given the numerous areas of specialty practice as well as types of clinicians. What does this mean then for clinicians working with DHH individuals?

The ethical principles for all mental health professionals in any kind of clinical relationship are based on professional values and moral decision-making. This is the minimum standard to ensure clinicians act in the best interest of the client. Yet, working with DHH individuals demands that the clinician also be mindful of the challenging ethical considerations related to competence to provide treatment, multiple relationships and boundary issues, confidentiality, assessment, diagnosis and evaluation, communication, and the use of interpreters (Boness, 2016). These are not trivial considerations, given the complexity of many DHH clients. For example, the clinician must not only adhere to their own specific health discipline code of best practices but also must be cognizant of the myriad of contributing factors such as Deaf culture, use of sign language, traditions and mores, language delay and deprivation, audism, appropriate assessment measures, discrimination, lived experiences, and risk factors regarding mental health (Maller & Braden, 2011; Pollard, 2002). As all mental health assessments, no matter the age of the client, should consider childhood influences, clinicians need to have the requisite knowledge of the typical development of a DHH child (which may qualitatively differ from that of a hearing child in terms of attachment, developmental milestones, and theory of mind). A good grasp of these issues can enhance clinical governance, while a lack of understanding will harm it. This is important because suboptimal practices could have profoundly negative impacts on the life trajectory of a DHH client.

The Client's Language and Fluency

It is essential in any assessment of a DHH individual to conduct testing in the preferred language of the client as well as evaluate their fluency using that language. This testing pertains to sign language and/or spoken language. As Chapter 1 of this volume explained, the language which a DHH individual uses, as well as their fluency in it, depends on many factors such as age of exposure, extent of exposure, quality of exposure, and the ability of the deaf child to access the exposure and modality of the language modeled around them. Other factors will include the individual's family of origin (deaf vs. hearing), the language used in their school experience as well as the degree of fluency of people using it, the type of school attended (Deaf school or mainstream school), and finally, the individual's own engagement with the language as their own. For example, Deaf individuals highly involved with the Deaf community may develop a far superior native fluency than a Deaf child who only sees ASL on the hands of an educational interpreter who may or may not be fluent. Pragmatically, choosing the language to assess a client in is not as straightforward as just determining if a client uses ASL or spoken English. The implications of the factors listed above may yield multiple language/communication modalities. The following are the combinations and/or variations of possible languages/communication modalities:

- sign language such as ASL
- spoken language such as English
- Manually Coded English—a signed system or visual code for spoken languages
- Signing Exact English (SEE)—a system of manual communication to exactly represent English vocabulary and grammar

- Signed English—a simpler form of SEE using 14 marker signs
- fingerspelling
- Total Communication—a philosophy which incorporates all means of communication such as formal signs, gestures, spoken language, lipreading, and body language
- Cued Speech—a visual mode of communication using handshapes in different locations near the mouth
- Pidgin Signed English—a communication system used to bridge the gap between ASL users and spoken language users
- gesture

It is unlikely that one clinician will have mastered or be fluent in all these modalities. In many cases, the client will present with either spoken language or sign language. In these instances, best practices indicate that it is optimal if the assessor can match the preferred language of the client (Du Feu & Chovaz, 2014). In situations where the clinician is not fluent in ASL and is working with a patient who considers ASL their first language, then a qualified interpreter with specialized training in mental health interpreting is recommended (Landsberger et al., 2013). In terms of communication strategies or systems rather than languages, it may be advantageous for the clinician to seek support from another professional familiar with that communicative strategy such as a Deaf interpreter (DI; Canadian equivalent of an American certified Deaf interpreter (Russell & Shaw, 2016).

Some Deaf patients will present with varying degrees of fluency in either their preferred language or communicative modality. The ideal strategy, although not always feasible, is to have a communication assessment completed (Williams & Crump, 2018). A communication assessment provides detailed information about language fluency and is especially helpful if the patient presents with any suspected impoverished or inconsistent language exposure during the critical language period (Lansberger et al. 2013). Such an assessment will reveal potential language mastery, dysfluency, or deprivation (Glickman & Hall, 2018), all of which are integral to well-being.

The Use of Mental Health Interpreters

A nonsigning clinician working with a Deaf client who uses ASL is strongly recommended to engage the services of a qualified ASL interpreter who has had training in mental health interpreting. The ASL interpreter, as a language and culture broker, can facilitate communication in very meaningful ways. Deaf clients with any degree of language dysfluency or deprivation, however, pose an even greater challenge to the assessment process. In these situations, the clinician should also engage the services of a DI. A DI is a skilled communication expert who is Deaf, and through lived experience, as well as specialized training, brings a unique critical skill set to the setting. The DI and the ASL/English interpreter work together to ensure maximal message equivalence across multilingual, multicultural, and multimodal approaches (Russell & Shaw, 2016).

Clinicians should be mindful that although the use of interpreters represents best practices, it also changes the therapeutic dyad into a triad or possibly even a quartet. This may qualitatively change the dynamics of the relationship between the clinician and Deaf patient, thereby necessitating dedicated thought as to how to respond to these possible challenges. In an earlier study, Chovaz (2013) presented a theory of intersectionality to better understand the complex interplay of factors inherent in these relationships utilizing interpreters. Intersectionality theory posits that we move beyond "we just work well together" (p. 9) by facilitating all involved professionals to operationalize, evaluate, and improve upon the process of their work as well as the outcomes (Chovaz, 2013).

The reader is encouraged to read Hlavac's (2017) succinct mental health interpreting guidelines on definitions, protocols, ethics, practices, self-care, and content knowledge for interpreters working in mental health settings with Deaf patients. This manifesto is specific to Australia but has universally useful suggestions. It has been my clinical experience (C. Chovaz) that constant evaluation and reevaluation of dynamics, message equivalency, therapeutic content, and the relationship itself is critical to the effective use of an interpreter in a role that is traditionally a clinician/patient dyad. Please see Chapters 7 and 10 in this volume for more detailed discussions of mental health interpreters in Canada.

The Adaptation and Translation of Psychometric Tests

Psychometric (coined from the Greek words *mental* and *measurement*) tests are used by psychologists to objectively and formally measure different domains of personality, behavior, cognitive ability, emotional status, educational achievement, skill sets, and psychological functioning. Psychometrics refers to the theory and technique of psychological measurement. Focusing on measurement theory, psychometrics is the construction and validation of psychological measures with the subsequent application in the assessment of individual differences (Balsamo et al., 2019). Psychologists who administer and interpret tests are interested in the validity of a test (Does it measure the construct it claims to?), the reliability of a test (Are test scores precise and free from measurement error?), in addition to standardization which is the process that ensures a test is administered following a specific standard. Valid, reliable, and standardized tests enable psychologists to answer difficult diagnostic questions through direct observation or clinical interview. In addition to diagnostic classification, psychometric testing is useful for planning treatment, monitoring progress, and evaluating outcomes.

The complexity for clinicians assessing DHH individuals typically arises from the fact that most tests used for assessment purposes are designed for individuals within mainstream culture or spoken language contexts and are thus not appropriate for individuals outside of this cultural and linguistic framework. Lane's (1999) pivotal book, *The Mask of Benevolence*, highlighted the inequities of assessment of Deaf people and coined the term *audist psychology of the deaf*. To illustrate this, the second author was asked to assess an elderly deaf woman who had been previously assessed at the age of 14 years and then sent to live in an institution for severely intellectually disabled individuals. The referral was to update an intellectual assessment when this woman was 80 years old which was done in a culturally and linguistically appropriate manner. Results indicated that her intelligence was within the average range. Likely, psychometric inequities in testing and inaccurate assumptions completed at a much earlier time sentenced her to 66 years of living in an institution for individuals with significant developmental disabilities despite her typical levels of intelligence. The interested reader will find further examples in Lane's book where he describes the erroneous use of psychological tests that have more often labeled Deaf people as emotionally disturbed than their hearing peers.

The compelling point is that psychometric practices are designed to ensure equitable and meaningful assessment. Some assessment measures will be useful with Deaf clients, and the astute clinician must carefully consider the psychometrics before choosing. For example, I (C. Chovaz) find the Comprehensive Test of Nonverbal Intelligence (Hammill et al., 2009) helpful for assessing skills in reasoning and problem-solving in Deaf individuals, Raven's Progressive Matrices Test (Raven et al., 2000) useful for yielding a nonverbal IQ score, and finally, the Test of Memory Malingering (TOMM; Tombaugh, 1996) both useful and appropriate (Chovaz et al., 2021) for the malingering of memory deficits. Pollard (Pollard & Fox, 2018) described many of the psychological tests he uses with Deaf clients specifically in terms of forensic evaluations.

There are, however, many other formal tests that I do not find useful with DHH clients. For example, English-based questionnaires that ask patients if they hear voices may be entirely misconstrued by a Deaf patient who has some residual hearing, may hear some degree of speech, and consequently may reply yes that they hear voices. Or, in other situations, the Deaf person may have no framework or lived experience for understanding the construct of voices and either avoids the question or randomly picks a response. Other examples include some tests of cognition. For example, the Montreal Cognitive Assessment (Nasreddine et al., 2005) is a widely used tool for detection of mild cognitive impairment but uses language and culture-bound items that do not translate effectively to sign language (Atkinson et al., 2015).

Some tests have been adapted for use with Deaf adults by translating them into sign language and evaluating their psychometric properties. For example, the following eight measures were all translated from English to ASL and validated for use with DHH adults (Guthmann et al., 2017):

- Alcohol Use Disorders Identification Test (AUDIT-C; Bush et al., 1998)
- Drug Abuse Screening Test (DAST-10; Skinner, 1982)
- Satisfaction with Life Scale (SWLS; Diener et al., 1985)
- Rosenberg Self-Esteem Scale (RSES; Rosenberg, 1979)
- The Beck Depression Inventory (BDI-II; Beck, et al., 1996)
- The Patient Health Questionnaire (PHQ-9; Kroenke & Spitzer, 2002)
- Generalized Anxiety Disorder (GAD-7; Spitzer et. al., 2006)
- Occupational Information Network (O*NET) Interest Profiler (IP; Rounds et al., 1999)
- Global Appraisal of Individual Needs—Short Screener (GAIN-SS; Dennis et al., 2013)

The process of effectively translating a psychometric test into sign language is both complex and challenging, including forward-and-back translations with multiple checks. We describe this process in more detail later in this chapter.

Fewer tests for DHH children have been translated into ASL which is problematic for clinicians working in this area. The SDQ (Goodman, 1997) is a brief emotional and behavioral screening questionnaire for children and young people. The SDQ has been translated into several sign languages, which the reader can find free for use on the Youth in Mind site (https://www.sdqinfo.org/a0.html). This includes the translation of the SDQ into ASL by the Chovaz research lab (Plimmer, 2018). We have also evaluated the psychometric qualities of the translated SDQ (Mulder & Chovaz, 2025), and this process is described in more detail later in this chapter.

Overall, clinicians assessing DHH individuals should consider the following in their selection of psychometric tests:

- Are tests *valid* and do they measure the intended construct? An example is the inappropriate use of verbal items on intelligence tests. These test items typically require reading, writing, and incidental knowledge or familiarity with concepts, such as idioms, strictly tied to a spoken language. Using these items in their intended way with a culturally Deaf person whose first language is sign language with limited proficiency or literacy in the majority spoken language may potentially violate the standard of validity. A relatively recent exploratory study (Ross, 2019) investigated, however, the diagnostic value of administering Verbal scale items and concluded that there may be some merit in using these items as predictors of potential for how successful the Deaf individual has been in developing verbal abilities in comparison with hypothesized potential (performance IQ). This approach does not use the Verbal items as intended but it realizes that some useful information may still be obtained when administered and interpreted by experienced clinicians.

- Is test administration *standardized*? Standard administration means that all participants take the same test item under the same conditions and are scored by the same criteria, thereby ensuring that results can be compared to each other. If test administration is altered even slightly, such as with the use of an interpreter, an assessor signing, or changing the concept to be more "deaf friendly," than the chance of error is introduced. Standardized administration typically yields normative data. When standardization is broken, norms become less reliable (Morere et al., 2019).
- Do test materials or items *discriminate* against Deaf people? This must be considered carefully when using tests with Deaf individuals that have been developed for hearing people. Dean et al. (2009) investigated the use of the Mini Mental State Exam (MMSE) in culturally Deaf adults, concluding that there was an increased rate of false positives, suggesting cognitive impairment when no impairment is actually present. This issue pertained to items such as "serial 7's" and instructions, such as "close your eyes," which have been shown to be problematic with Deaf adults. Conversely, Chovaz et al. (2021) found that the TOMM and cut-off scores were both appropriate for use with Deaf individuals.

The reader further interested in these constructs is encouraged to read Braden's (2017) work summarizing best practices in assessing those who are DHH.

Language Dysfluency or Deprivation

Children, hearing or deaf, are born with an innate ability to learn language. This typically happens naturally when the child is fully exposed to an accessible language. When DHH children do not have full access or sufficient exposure to any language (either spoken or signed) during their critical, language-learning years (typically birth to approximately 5 years of age), the term *language deprivation* is used to describe the negative effects that the child experiences often throughout their lifetime. Essentially, language deprivation is limited exposure to language during the brain's formative years that can potentially result in very serious cognitive delays and mental health difficulties across the lifespan. The reader is directed to Chapter 1 for a more extensive discussion of language acquisition and deprivation.

A Deaf child or adult with any degree of language deprivation poses considerable complexities for assessment. Language dysfluency or deprivation can be very challenging for the assessor, as language patterns are typically assessed to determine psychosis or thought disorders. In the case of a Deaf adult, however, their abnormal language discourse may not be due to mental illness and instead be due to late or inadequate exposure to ASL during critical developmental periods (Glickman, 2007). The knowledge deficits (a lack of concept and contextual knowledge), disordered thinking, moods, and behavior, which are also typically seen in Deaf individuals with language deprivation syndrome (Henner et al., 2018), may again not be due to or associated with mental illness such as we may expect to see in a hearing person with those same markers. The prudent clinician working with a Deaf patient, however, must remain diligent and aware that mental illness may indeed also be present in addition to language disorder. Untangling "what is what" becomes the task of the clinician such that appropriate diagnostic evaluations can be completed with commensurate treatment recommendations. It is our opinion that this untangling of constructs may or may not be related to mental illness, demanding a high degree of technical understanding of the measures used while remaining diligent regarding differential diagnosis.

Finally, consideration must be given when assessing Deaf individuals with any degree of diminished capacity. Appropriate tools used to establish capacity and/or competency must not unfairly penalize the Deaf adult regarding language differences, different worldviews, or differences in learning.

Heart-to-Heart

The heart-to-heart experiences showcasing the importance of carefully selecting and administering psychometric tests are described below with two descriptions followed by a review of the translation and psychometric evaluation process of the SDQ from written English to ASL.

#1 John

> John was a 12-year-old Deaf student attending a residential school for the Deaf. The language of instruction at the school was ASL. John was referred to a community psychologist for an assessment regarding his withdrawn behavior at home yet sustained interest in activities in his classroom and school residence. The psychologist Dr. Smith routinely used the Achenbach System of Empirically Based Assessment (ASEBA) in his practice and asked John's parents to complete the Child Behavior Checklist (CBCL6/18), his teacher to complete the Teacher's Report Form (TRF/6-18), and John to complete the Youth Self-Report (YSR/11-18).

John's parents completed and returned the form. John's teacher, who was culturally Deaf, completed the form but left a number of questions blank. John returned the form unanswered. Dr. Smith initially wrote notes back and forth with John but realized this was not effective. He then booked a community ASL interpreter to meet with John and go over the items on the YSR/11-18. After about a half hour, the interpreter came into Dr. Smith's office and told him she was not familiar with mental health inventories and was unsure how to interpret several of the items such as the following:

- Question #13: I feel confused or in a fog.
- Question #40: I hear sounds or voices that other people think aren't there.
- Question #68: I scream a lot.
- Question #79: I have a speech problem.
- Question #104: I am louder than other kids.

She shared with Dr. Smith that she was not comfortable interpreting the questionnaire, as she was not confident John was understanding her.

Based on the parents' scored responses, Dr. Smith felt that John was depressed. However, he was unable to confirm this from the two other informant questionnaires. When he met with the parents, they shared that they had never learned much ASL and could not communicate on any deep level with their son. They then told Dr. Smith that they guessed at many of their responses as "they just did not really know much about their son." Dr. Smith was perplexed and uncertain what to do, as he felt unable to rely on the psychometry.

#2 Rob

> Rob was a 35-year-old Deaf man who had graduated from a Deaf residential school. He had very little contact with his family, given that nobody in it knew how to sign, and he felt left out. Rob was fluent in ASL, very limited in English literacy, and had worked successfully since high school for the same warehouse, stacking products on shelves. Rob loved his work, as over the years many of his hearing coworkers had learned to sign conversationally with him, the salary was sufficient for him to live independently, and he felt useful. One year ago, Rob was suddenly laid off, as the pandemic had seriously threatened the financial stability of the company. Rob's savings were quickly depleted, and he had been evicted from his apartment and was living on the streets. Rob was not able to communicate with the workers he met in the homeless shelters, was threatened and physically attacked by others, and began stealing money for food. Rob's mental health deteriorated to the point where he felt hopeless and alone.

One evening, Rob was wandering the streets and was picked up by police for loitering. He was taken to the station where he became very frightened and physically began to struggle against the officers. He was handcuffed, which exacerbated his physical struggling, as Rob felt desperate without being able to use his hands to communicate. The officers escorted Rob to the local emergency room which made Rob even more anxious and physically reactive. Because of his physical struggling and striking out, the attending resident sedated Rob. Several hours later, the hospital staff removed his handcuffs, and the resident administered a suicide assessment checklist. The resident spoke the questions slowly and clearly to Rob. In his distress, mistrust, and inability to understand, Rob began nodding his head affirmatively to most of the questions he was asked. The resident tallied the score, concluding that Rob was a high risk of suicide and admitted him under their province's relevant form for authorizing the holding of a person for up to 72 hours at a psychiatric facility.

These case scenarios illustrate some of the challenges of using mental health questionnaires that have not passed psychometric scrutiny in addition to questionable clinical practices. For John, the psychologist attempted to use questionnaires that were not within the correct cultural or linguistic framework for a DHH child or for John's culturally Deaf teacher, and was not able to hire an interpreter adequately trained in mental health terminology. In Rob's story, the clinicians failed to evaluate his level of fluency in English and incorrectly administered the suicide assessment checklist which led to an invalid conclusion. The following section describes our process of translating a SDQ mental health screener, establishing psychometric properties, and administering it in a pilot sample of DHH children referred to a clinical agency.

Strengths and Difficulties Questionnaire (SDQ)

Until recently, there was a marked absence of signed measurement tools within North America specifically designed for DHH children and adolescents. Outside of North America, a popular clinical screening tool, the SDQ (Goodman, 1997), has been translated into British Sign Language (BSL; Roberts et al., 2015), Norwegian Sign Language (NSL; Aanondsen et al., 2019), and Australian Sign Language (Auslan; Cornes & Brown, 2012), although the Auslan translation was not accepted by the SDQ's copyright holder. These translations went through psychometric testing to ensure proper validity, reliability, and factor structure. Additionally, the BSL and NSL translations followed a standardized translation procedure to ensure congruence with other published SDQs.

Following the example of these past translations, Plimmer's (2018) thesis under the supervision of Dr. Chovaz produced a translation of the SDQ into ASL. Using the established forward/back-translation methodology, a panel of experts and an ASL interpreter organized the production of a self-report version of the SDQ for DHH children and adolescents. In this process, multiple forward translations were created by skilled bilingual translators from culturally different backgrounds who filmed their translations from printed English to ASL. Next, the team collectively evaluated each other's translations and came to a consensus about the most culturally sensitive and linguistically accurate translation of each question. The revised translation was recorded and subsequently sent to two separate back-translation teams who then independently translated the ASL-SDQ into printed English. The first back-translation team then compared their English translation to the original SDQ and formed a consensus about any adjustments required. The second back-translation team performed the same procedure as the first team. Both back-translation teams presented their translations to the supervising ASL interpreter who then requested the forward-translation team to incorporate the suggested changes. Finally, an expert panel compared the forward translation to the original English SDQ and the back translations. After reaching a consensus on all items, the panel requested the final translation of the ASL-SDQ to be filmed. The interested reader is encouraged to read Plimmer's (2018) work for an accessible, step-by-step, guided description of the translation methodology.

Initial findings indicated that with this translated questionnaire, DHH children and adolescents self-reported greater levels of mental health difficulties than their hearing parents who used a written English SDQ. Or, in other words, the DHH children were reporting a higher prevalence of mental health distress than was being identified by their hearing parents. It was postulated that these hearing parents may not be able to recognize the symptoms of mental health difficulties as experienced by their DHH children, given that many parents reported they did not share the same language as their child. This finding is like the literature indicating that the majority of hearing parents do not/cannot learn sign language beyond a very limited functional degree (Du Feu & Chovaz, 2014). However, the questionnaire's psychometric properties remained unevaluated, which constrained conclusions about the validity and reliability of its use in clinical screening contexts.

Therefore, we, the authors of this chapter, conducted a study to establish psychometric properties of the ASL-SDQ and confirm its comparability to written forms of the English SDQ (Mulder & Chovaz, 2025). For this study, information was gathered from a mental health program that conducts clinical work with DHH children and adolescents, as well as their support networks of parents and teachers. During intake, clinicians showed DHH children and adolescents a recording of the ASL-SDQ and endorsed their responses to the questions on the standard answer form. The intake clinician also distributed a demographics form and an English SDQ parent form and teacher form to be completed, respectively. If possible, after the child's clinical intervention was finished, children, parents, and teachers completed the SDQ for a second time. In total, 53 DHH children and adolescents completed the ASL-SDQ, along with 36 parents and 22 teachers who completed the written English-SDQ. From these questionnaires, the test-retest reliability, interrater reliability, internal consistency, and factor structure were analyzed.

Test-Retest Reliability

Due to clinical limitations that restricted on what day the ASL-SDQ was given a second time, test-retest reliability analyses were unable to be properly calculated. Past research by Stone et al. (2010) established that SDQ ratings tended to be less reliable over time, with time frames of approximately 6 months showing only moderate correlation. Therefore, research recommended time frames ranging from 2 to 15 weeks (Aanondsen et al., 2019; Roberts et al., 2015). This time frame was unable to be adhered to within the clinical setting, and an extended time frame of two months to over a year between tests contributed toward the insignificance of the reliability analysis. Additionally, as only nine children and adolescents completed the ASL-SDQ at two time points, the analysis was relatively underpowered and therefore would not be expected to produce a significant result. Future research is required to establish test-retest reliability.

Interrater Reliability

Interrater correlations were consistent with past research on DHH children and adolescents. Particularly, stronger correlations were observed between parents and children in this study than those reported by Roberts et al. (2015). Given that Roberts et al. (2015) focused on a BSL population rather than an ASL one, this finding could suggest a national difference in parental education and awareness of deafness. The strongest correlations were found in externalized behaviors that were more easily seen by parents, whereas the more language-based subscales yielded nonsignificant results. Researchers (Du Feu & Chovaz, 2014) have found that parents of DHH children or adolescents may have fundamentally different perceptions of their child's actions due to such language disconnects. Due to the absence of shared language, parents and children may view behavior in entirely different ways. If the family lacks proper communication supports, this language discordance could increase emotional and behavioral difficulties and contribute to a negative family dynamic. Additionally, DHH children and adolescents may struggle with relating their experiences to others due to language differences, including deprivation and delays, social isolation, and lack of peer models. As a result, DHH children and adolescents may not believe that their actions are socially problematic. Therefore, the interrater reliability analyses showed that DHH children and adolescents must be given adequate assessment so they can accurately report their context, as other adults may not understand their point of view.

Internal Consistency

Results for the ASL-SDQ's internal consistency were broadly like other signed SDQ versions. The subscale scores also approximately matched, established findings in Roberts et al. (2015) and several other studies (Du et al., 2008; Essau et al., 2012). These levels, however, markedly differ from seminal reports of the English self-report SDQ by Goodman (2001). As postulated by past authors (Roberts et al., 2015), individuals from languages and cultures other than Western cultures using spoken English may differ in their interpretation of items. Further, the unique translation challenges of signed questionnaires, such as contextual body language, facial expressions, and the need to rephrase statements as questions, can explain why items may load differently on subscales. As a result, the measures of internal consistency were within previously established ranges.

Factor Analysis

Following the methodology of Roberts et al. (2015), and Aanondsen et al. (2019), exploratory factor analysis and confirmatory factor analysis were conducted. However, the results were unclear, as items did not fully conform to the five-factor model. Firstly, the amount of variance accounted for broadly matched findings in Roberts et al. (2015), but the present study's exploratory factor analysis had a greater number of complex variables. This result corresponded with past studies where researchers have found inconsistencies with the SDQ's five-factor structure, using exploratory factor analysis in terms of its application in the DHH community (Niclasen & Dammeyer, 2016). Confirmatory factor analysis fit indices were also similar to those reported in the BSL-SDQ and the NSL-SDQ, as our sample only passed the normed chi-squared and Root Mean Square Error of Approximation (RMSEA) tests (Aanondsen et al., 2019; Roberts et al., 2015). These factor analyses may have also been impacted by our study's relatively small sample size, which, while similar to the size of Aanondsen et al.'s (2019) sample, would still have contributed to the lack of convergence. Additional difficulties interpreting these results arose from the fact that signed translations have historically not conformed to set standards, which has been postulated to indicate that there may be cultural differences which impact results. Therefore, greater analysis is required to solidify the fit of a five-factor model for the ASL-SDQ.

Overall Findings

Through conducting the pilot study, we gathered initial results regarding the validity and reliability of the ASL-SDQ and highlighted the importance of translating questionnaires into sign language following linguistically and culturally sensitive best practices. Additionally, our research demonstrated the complex interplay of variables which may be present within intervention and enumerated why potential language barriers between DHH children, adolescents, and hearing parents may impact the interpretation of questionnaire responses. Unequivocally, empowering DHH children and adolescents to self-report their own perspective plays a crucial role in providing accessible measures and effective intervention. Given that this was the first study within Canada to explore the psychometric properties of the ASL-SDQ, we hopefully look forward to additional research with more extensive community samples being conducted to establish this signed screening measure as a crucial component of clinical intervention.

Recommendations

- Clinicians should be mindful of their role in clinical governance and what that means when working with DHH clients.
- Clinicians should ensure language concordance through the assessment of their client's language fluency and optimal modality of communication into the clinical process. Understanding the client's ideal and preferred communication modality equips clinicians with the proper framework through which to engage in assessment and the therapeutic process. Appropriate assessment strategies ensure that appropriate and accessible clinical

interventions are developed which will avoid inequitable, or discriminatory outcomes, as well as ensuring that the client has the chance to fully participate in their assessment.

- Seeking specialized training to gain knowledge, insight, and a competent skill set for working with DHH people is invaluable. This can be achieved through formal education programs and by engaging in a mentoring or supervision process with experienced professionals in the field. A combination of academic and real-world experience ensures that clinicians are well-prepared to work with the diverse needs of DHH individuals.
- If the clinician is not fluent in the client's language, then sign language interpreters specifically qualified in mental health interpreting should be utilized. Given the complexities in mental health terminology, it is crucial for nonsigning clinicians to ensure that the sign language interpreters they are liaising with are trained in this specialized field. This component of training would empower interpreters to accurately convey pertinent healthcare information and facilitate the necessary therapeutic alliance which the clinician aims to form with the Deaf client. Furthermore, if the Deaf client has any degree of language dysfluency or deprivation, then clinicians should retain the services of a qualified DI.
- Clinicians should carefully select and administer assessments that have been validated for use with Deaf clients. The validity, reliability, and standardization of the assessment measure should be considered and empirically backed by research for use with a DHH population. If possible, relevant test norms should be used (Braden, 2017).
- Best practices essentially lead to more adaptive and effective lived experiences. Psychometrics should be a routine consideration for all clinicians conducting assessments with DHH individuals.

References

Aanondsen, C. M., Jozefiak, T., Heiling, K., & Rimehaug, T. (2019). Validation of the strengths and difficulties self-report in Norwegian Sign Language. *Journal of Deaf Studies and Deaf Education, 25*(9), 91–104. https://doi.org/10.1093/deafed/enz026

Atkinson, J., Denmark, T., Marshall, J., Mummery, C., & Woll, B. (2015). Detecting cognitive impairment and dementia in deaf people: The British Sign Language Cognitive Screening Test. *Archives of Clinical Neuropsychology: The Official Journal of the National Academy of Neuropsychologists, 30*(7), 694–711. https://doi.org/10.1093/arclin/acv042

Balsamo, M., Innamorati, M., & Lamis, D. A. (2019). Editorial: Clinical psychometrics: Old issues and new perspectives. *Frontiers in Psychology, 10*, Article 947. https://doi.org/10.3389/fpsyg.2019.00947

Beck, A. T., Brown, G. K., & Steer, R. A. (1996). *BDI-II: Beck depression inventory: Manual.* Psychological Corporation.

Boness, C. L. (2016). Treatment of deaf clients: Ethical considerations for professionals in psychology. *Ethics and Behavior, 26*(7), 562–585. https://doi.org/10.1080/10508422.2015.1084929

Braden, J. P. (1992). Intellectual assessment of deaf and hard-of-hearing people: A quantitative and qualitative research synthesis. *School Psychology Review, 21*(1), 82–94. https://doi.org/10.1080/02796015.1992.12085597

Braden, J. P. (2017). Best practices in assessing those who are deaf or hard-of-hearing. In R. S. McCallum (Ed.), *Handbook of nonverbal assessment* (pp. 47–58). Springer International Publishing/Springer Nature. https://doi.org/10.1007/978-3-319-50604-3_4

Brauer, B. A., Braden, J. P., Pollard, R. Q., & Hardy-Braz, S. T. (1998). Deaf and hard of hearing people. In J. H. Sandoval, C. L. Frisby, K. F. Geisinger, J. D. Scheuneman, & J. R. Grenier (Eds.), *Test interpretation and diversity: Achieving equity in assessment* (pp. 297–315). American Psychological Association. https://doi.org/10.1037/10279-011

Bush, K., Kivlahan, D. R., McDonell, M. B., Fihn, S. D., & Bradley, K. A., (1998). The AUDIT alcohol consumption questions (AUDIT-C): An effective brief screening test for problem drinking. *Archives of Internal Medicine, 158*, 1789–1795.

Chovaz, C. J. (2013). Intersectionality: Mental health interpreters and clinicians or finding the "sweet spot" in therapy. *International Journal on Mental Health and Deafness, 3*(1), 4–11.

Chovaz, C. J., Rennison, L. V., & Chorostecki, D. O., (2021) The validity of the test of memory malingering (TOMM) with deaf individuals. *The Clinical Neuropsychologist, 35*(3), 597–614. https://doi.org/10.1080/13854046.2019.1696408

Cornes, A. J., & Margaret Brown, P. (2012). Mental health of Australian deaf adolescents: An investigation using an Auslan version of the Strengths and Difficulties Questionnaire. *Deafness and Education International, 14*(3), 161–175. https://doi.org/10.1179/1557069X12Y.0000000009

Dean, P. M., Feldman, D. M., Morere, D., & Morton, D. (2009). Clinical evaluation of the mini-mental state exam with culturally deaf senior citizens. *Archives of Clinical Neuropsychology: The Official Journal of the National Academy of Neuropsychologists, 24*(8), 753–760. https://doi.org/10.1093/arclin/acp077

Dennis, M. L., Feeney, T., & Titus, J. C. (2013). *GAIN-SS—Global appraisal of individual needs—short screener: Administration and scoring manual, version 3*. Chestnut Health Systems.

Diener, E., Emmons, R. A., Larsen, R. J., & Griffin, S. (1985). The Satisfaction with Life Scale. *Journal of Personality Assessment, 49*, 71–75.

Du, Y., Kou, J., & Coghill, D. (2008). The validity, reliability and normative scores of the parent, teacher and self-report versions of the Strengths and Difficulties Questionnaire in China. *Child and Adolescent Psychiatry and Mental Health, 2*, 1–15. https://doi.org/10.1186/1753-2000-2-8

Du Feu, M., & Chovaz, C. (2014). *Mental health and deafness*. Oxford University Press.

Essau, C. A., Olaya, B., Anastassiou-Hadjicharalambous, X., Pauli, G., Gilvarry, C., Bray, D., O'Callaghan, J., & Ollendick, T. H. (2012). Psychometric properties of the Strength and Difficulties Questionnaire from five European countries. *International Journal of Methods in Psychiatric Research, 21*(3), 232–245. https://doi.org/10.1002/mpr.1364

Glickman N. (2007). Do you hear voices? Problems in assessment of mental status in deaf persons with severe language deprivation. *Journal of Deaf Studies and Deaf Education, 12*(2), 127–147. https://doi.org/10.1093/deafed/enm001

Glickman, N. S. (Ed.). (2013). *Deaf mental health care* (1st ed.). Routledge.

Glickman, N. S., & Hall, W. C. (Eds.). (2018). *Language deprivation and deaf mental health*. Routledge.

Goodman, R. (1997). The Strengths and Difficulties Questionnaire: A research note. *Journal of Child Psychology and Psychiatry, 38*(5), 581–586. https://doi.org/10.1111/j.1469-7610.1997.tb01545.x

Goodman, R. (2001). Psychometric properties of the Strengths and Difficulties Questionnaire. *Journal of the American Academy of Child and Adolescent Psychiatry, 40*(11), 1337–1345. https://doi.org/10.1097/00004583-200111000-00015

Guthmann, D., Titus, J., Embree, J., & Wilson, J. (2017). Translation and validation of an online suite of assessments in American Sign Language. *JADARA, 51*(1), 12–20. http://repository.wcsu.edu/jadara/vol51/iss1/5

Hammill D. D., Pearson N. A., Weiderholt J. L. (2009). *CTONI-2: Comprehensive test of nonverbal intelligence* (2nd ed.). PRO-ED. https://doi.org/10.1037/t73906-000

Henner, J., Novogrodsky, R., Reis, J., & Hoffmeister, R. (2018). Recent issues in the use of signed language assessments for diagnosis of language disorders in signing deaf and hard of hearing children. *Journal of Deaf Studies and Deaf Education, 23*(4), 307–316. https://doi.org/10.1093/deafed/eny014

Hlavac, J. (2017). *Mental health interpreting guidelines for interpreters*. https://static1.squarespace.com/static/571683f922482e219db7b3ae/t/5a86f0f64192028861457cda/1518792951958/Mental_Health_Interpreting_Guidelines_fo.pdf

Kroenke, K., & Spitzer, R. L. (2002). The PHQ-9: A new depression diagnostic and severity measure. *Psychiatric Annals, 32*(9), 509–515. https://doi.org/10.3928/0048-5713-20020901-06

Landsberger, S. A., Sajid, A., Schmelkin, L., Diaz, D. R. & Weiler, C. (2013). Assessment and treatment of deaf adults with psychiatric disorders: A review of the literature for practitioners. *Journal of Psychiatric Practice*, 19(2), 87–97. https://doi.org/10.1097/01.pra.0000428555.48588.f9

Lane, H. (1999). *The mask of benevolence: Disabling the deaf community*. DawnSignPress.

Levine, E. S. (1960). *The psychology of deafness: Techniques of appraisal for rehabilitation*. Columbia University Press.

Maller, S. J., & Braden, J. P. (2011). Intellectual assessment of deaf people: A critical review of core concepts and issues. In M. Marschark & P. E. Spencer (Eds.), *The Oxford handbook of deaf studies, language, and education* (2nd ed., pp. 473–485). Oxford University Press.

Mindel, E. D., & Vernon, M. (1987). *They grow in silence: Understanding deaf children and adults* (2nd ed.). College-Hill Press.

Morere, D. A., Dean, P. M., & Mompremoer, L. (2019). Mental health assessment of deaf clients: Issues with interpreters use and assessment of person with diminished capacity and psychiatric populations. *JADARA, 42*(4). https://repository.wcsu.edu/jadara/vol42/iss4/9.

Mulder, J. H., & Chovaz, C. J. (Manuscript in preparation). *Validation of the Strengths and Difficulties Questionnaire Youth Self-Report in American Sign Language*. Department of Psychology, King's University College at Western University.

Nasreddine, Z. S., Phillips, N. A., Bédirian, V., Charbonneau, S., Whitehead, V., Collin, I., Cummings, J. L., & Chertkow, H. (2005). The Montreal Cognitive Assessment, MoCA: A brief screening tool for mild cognitive impairment. *Journal of the American Geriatrics Society, 53*(4), 695–699. https://doi.org/10.1111/j.1532-5415.2005.53221.x

Niclasen, J., & Dammeyer, J. (2016). Psychometric properties of the Strengths and Difficulties Questionnaire and mental health problems among children with hearing loss. *Journal of Deaf Studies and Deaf Education, 21*(2), 129–140. https://doi.org/10.1093/deafed/env067

Plimmer, C. (2018). *Translating the Strengths and Difficulties Questionnaire into American Sign Language: A pilot study* [Undergraduate honors theses, King's University College]. https://hdl.handle.net/20.500.14721/26033.

Pollard, R. Q., Jr. (1996). Professional psychology and deaf people: The emergence of a discipline. *American Psychologist, 51*(4), 389–396. https://doi.org/10.1037/0003-066X.51.4.389

Pollard, R. Q., Jr. (1998). Psychopathology. In M. Marschark & M. D. Clark (Eds.), *Psychological perspectives on deafness* (vol. 2, pp. 171–197). Lawrence Erlbaum.

Pollard, R. Q., Jr. (2002). Ethical conduct in research involving deaf people. In V. Gutman (Ed.), *Ethics in mental health and deafness* (pp. 162–178). Gallaudet University Press.

Pollard, R. Q., Jr., & Berlinski, B. T. (2017). Forensic evaluation of deaf individuals: Challenges and strategies. *Journal of Social Work in Disability and Rehabilitation, 16*(3-4), 261–275. https://doi.org/10.1080/1536710X.2017.1372240

Pollard, R. Q., Jr., & Fox, M. L. (2018). Forensic evaluation of deaf adults with language deprivation. In Glickman, N. & Hall, W. C. (Eds.), *Language deprivation and deaf mental health* (pp. 101–135). Routledge.

Raven, J., Raven, J. C., & Court, J. H. (2000). *Manual for Raven's progressive matrices and vocabulary scales. Section 3: The standard progressive matrices*. Oxford Psychologists Press/The Psychological Corporation.

Roberts, S., Wright, B., Moore, K., Smith, J., Allgar, V., Tennant, A., Doherty, C., Hughes, E., Moore, D. C., Ogden, R., Phillips, H., Beese, L., & Rogers, K. (2015). Translation into British Sign Language and validation of the Strengths and Difficulties Questionnaire. *Health Services and Delivery Research, 3*(2), 1–96. https://www.ncbi.nlm.nih.gov/books/NBK274167/

Rosenberg, M. (1979). *Conceiving the self*. Basic Books.

Ross, D. R. (2019). A technique of verbal ability assessment of deaf adults. *JADARA, 3*(3). https://nsuworks.nova.edu/jadara/vol3/iss3/6

Rounds, J., Mazzeo, S. E., Smith, T. J., Hubert, L., Lewis, P., & Rivkin, D. (1999). *Development of the O*NET computerized interest profiler: Reliability, validity, and comparability.* National Center for O*NET Development. https://www.onetcenter.org/reports/CIP_RVC.html

Russell, D., & Shaw, R. (2016). Power and privilege: An exploration of decision-making of interpreters. *Journal of Interpretation, 25*(1), Article 7. https://digitalcommons.unf.edu/joi/vol25/iss1/7

Skinner, H. A. (1982). The drug abuse screening test. *Addictive Behavior, 7*(4), 363–371. https://doi.org/10.1016/0306-4603(82)90005-3

Spitzer, R. L., Kroenke, K., Williams, J. B., & Löwe, B. (2006). A brief measure for assessing generalized anxiety disorder: The GAD-7. *Archives of Internal Medicine, 166*(10), 1092C97. https://doi.org/10.1001/archinte.166.10.1092

Starey, N. (2001). *What is clinical governance?* [SCRIBD]. https://www.scribd.com/document/150705665/What-is-Clinical-Governance

Stone, L. L., Otten, R., Engels, R. C., Vermulst, A. A., & Janssens, J. M. (2010). Psychometric properties of the parent and teacher versions of the strengths and difficulties questionnaire for 4-to 12-year-olds: A review. *Clinical Child and Family Psychology Review, 13*, 254–274.

Tombaugh, T. N. (1996). *Test of Memory Malingering (TOMM).* Multi-Health Systems, Inc.

Vernon, M. (2005). Fifty years of research on the intelligence of deaf and hard-of-hearing children: A review of literature and discussion of implications. *Journal of Deaf Studies and Deaf Education, 10*(3), 225–231. https://doi.org/10.1093/deafed/eni024

Williams, R. C., & Crump, C. J. (2018). Communication skills assessment for individuals who are deaf in mental health settings. In S. Glickman, & W. Hall (Eds.), *Language deprivation and deaf mental health* (pp. 136–159). Routledge.

4

Mental Health of Deaf and Hard of Hearing Children and Youth

Cathy J. Chovaz

Construct

The prevalence rates of mental health disorders are higher in deaf and hard of hearing children (DHH) than hearing children. However, the risk factors as well as identification of mental health disorders are often not well understood. This chapter will review mental health disorders in DHH children and youth, including differences in clinical presentations.

Head-to-Head and Heart-to-Heart

Clearly, the experiences lived by DHH children need to be integrated into the research process as well as the translation of theoretical guidelines to practice. This is the art and science of clinical work and is highlighted here as head-to-heads and heart-to-hearts. Lack of evidence-based understandings of clinical presentations have the potential to lead to misidentifications or missed identifications. Both head-to heads and heart-to-hearts will be identified and described to highlight clinical differences in the symptom presentation of disorders.

Statement of Reflexivity

Author: Cathy J. Chovaz

I acknowledge my view as a deafened, white, female clinical psychologist. I was deafened as a young adult and grew up with spoken English as my first language and, as such, do not share the same early experiences of many of my patients. After becoming deaf, I learned American Sign Language (ASL) as a second language. I identify with the tenets of hearing culture, as that was my culture and English my first language, yet also identify with and appreciate many of the tenets of a visual world and signed language. My reflection of the head-to-heads information comes from decades of study in this area, and my appreciation of the heart-to-hearts comes from intentional reflection of stories as they have been told to me by DHH patients and their families as well as my own life experience.

Recommendations

It is critical that clinicians be well-informed about mental health disorders in DHH children. This chapter will conclude with strategies to recognize risk factors, accurately identify emotional and behavioral symptoms, as well as understand the importance of diagnostic evaluations of

DHH children. This will ultimately serve to better utilize research in clinical stories and minimize the gap between theory and practice.

This chapter is focused on mental health disorders and DHH children and youth. For brevity, they will be referred to as DHH children. The chapter starts with a discussion on prevalence rates followed by specific risk factors associated with deafness and mental health. This is followed by examples of clinical mental health presentations in DHH children, including case studies highlighting the lived experiences of DHH children. The chapter concludes with strategies to recognize risk factors, accurately identify emotional and behavioral symptoms, as well as understand the importance of diagnostic evaluations of DHH children.

Prevalence

Prevalence studies from all over the world have been consistent in finding higher levels of emotional and behavioral problems in DHH children than in hearing children and youth (Marschark et al., 2002; Wallis et al., 2004; Fellinger et al., 2012; Du Feu & Chovaz, 2014; Brown & Cornes, 2015; Niclasen & Dammeyer, 2016), with prevalence rates of mental and neurodevelopmental disorders ranging between 19% and 77% (Swanepoel et al., 2020). For example, in the United Kingdom, Hindley (2005) estimated that the prevalence of mental health problems in community samples of DHH children was approximately 40% and that they were estimated to be 1.5–2 times more vulnerable to mental health problems than hearing children. Data generated in the United States has suggested that DHH children exhibit higher levels of behavioral disorders and attention deficit hyperactivity disorder (ADHD) than the general population (Daza González, 2021), and Fellinger et al. (2008) reported that Austrian DHH children scored significantly higher on a mental health questionnaire, indicating more mental health distress completed by their parents and teachers than hearing children. They described marked differences on conduct issues, emotional problems, and peer problems and less of a difference on hyperactivity/inattention. Dammeyer (2010) reported that in their sample of Danish children, the prevalence of psychosocial difficulties was 3.7 times greater compared with a group of hearing children. In the group of Danish DHH children in their sample with additional disabilities, the prevalence was 3 times greater compared with DHH children without additional disabilities. Mulder & Chovaz (2025) report that, compared to a nationally representative sample, DHH Canadian children in a community agency sample demonstrated 2–3 times greater levels of mental health difficulties than normative scores. They further compared this to a sample of children within the Canadian welfare system, finding that DHH children were 67% more likely to display clinical levels of mental health issues. In contrast though and perhaps highlighting the heterogeneity of this population, Remine and Brown (2010) reported that the overall prevalence rate of mental health problems reported by parents and DHH children was comparable to that of the Australian hearing population.

The differences in prevalence rates within the literature is of interest to me both as a researcher and a clinician with an expertise in mental health and deafness. As a researcher, I appreciate that the validity of prevalence studies is a function of sampling, measurement, and analysis (Boyle, 1998). It is imperative that research accurately represents a defined target population which means that the target population needs to be defined very clearly and succinctly. However, from a clinical perspective, the target population of DHH children can be extremely diverse with different etiologies of deafness, different threshold hearing levels, different technological interventions, different language acquisitions and modalities, and vastly different lived experiences. As a researcher, I also value the importance of using valid and reliable measurement tools under standardized data collection processes. However, as a clinician, I am very aware of both the paucity of deaf-informed measurement tools as well as the tendency for uninformed clinicians to assume that tools developed for and standardized on hearing populations are always valid for DHH children. In some instances, as Pollard points out (Pollard & Fox, 20189), measures developed for use with hearing individuals may also be useful for the assessment of signing Deaf individuals, such as Raven's Progressive Matrices (Raven & Raven, 2000), but it takes an astute and informed clinician to establish the appropriateness of a tool prior to using it with Deaf individuals. Otherwise, one runs the high the risk of making erroneous interpretations/conclusions by using a tool that is not a valid measure. And finally, the analysis of evidence-based research reporting prevalence needs of mental health disorders in DHH children needs to consider sampling methods as well as the inclusion of confidence intervals. Research with DHH children is likely less randomized than purposeful, given the complexity of recruiting the sample, and as such may introduce design effects.

In sum, the prevalence rates, as reported in the literature, reflect possible methodological concerns as well as the epidemiology of diversity inherent in working with the DHH children population. This is well understood by those of us who are clinicians able to readily affirm that no two DHH children are alike. That presents its own clinical challenges yet also poses specific challenges for researchers.

Collectively, it appears that the rates of mental health disorders in DHH children are elevated compared to their hearing counterparts, yet we must remain vigilant (clinicians and researchers alike) in our understanding and use of measures, the formulation of our research questions, our methodological designs, and finally, the critical need for linguistically and culturally sensitive interpretations These inconsistencies have highlighted the importance of proper measurement methodologies, specific qualifications for interacting with, and gathering data from, DHH participants (Chovaz, 2013; Brown & Cornes, 2015; Wallis et al., 2004). The reader is encouraged to read chapter 3 for a more detailed discussion of the psychometrics involved in selecting appropriate measures for DHH children.

Risk Factors

DHH children experience uniquely negative circumstances surrounding mental health and deafness (Du Feu & Chovaz, 2014). These negative experiences may well be risk factors for mental health distress, yet it is important to recognize that deafness itself is not a causal factor. In other words, being deaf does not cause mental health disorders but does put a child at risk for, or contributes to, psychiatric problems (van Gent et al., 2007). Diagnostic overshadowing, or the assumption that deafness explains all problems in deaf children (Kitson & Thacker, 2000), is not only inaccurate but is a risk factor in and of itself, potentially perpetuating misdiagnoses and missed diagnoses. In general, DHH children are vulnerable to a number of factors that may add to the complexity of their mental health, including medical problems, adverse childhood experiences, language deprivation, peer relationships, theory of mind (ToM), and additional contributing factors.

Medical Problems

As a group, DHH children are more likely to experience additional disabilities than hearing children (Hindley, 2005). Children with syndromic and acquired hearing loss are at a greater risk for central nervous system disorders, other concomitant physical disorders (e.g., diabetes associated with congenital rubella; hypothyroidism associated with Pendred's Syndrome; cardiac abnormalities), and comorbid intellectual impairments (Hindley, 2005; van Gent et al., 2011), all of which greatly increase a child's risk of developing a mental health disorder (et al., 1971). Central nervous system (CNS) disorders are often specifically associated with etiologies of deafness, such as viral intrauterine infections like cytomegalovirus (CMV), or bacterial infections, such as meningitis, or viral infections, such as rubella in early infancy. Syndromes such as CHARGE syndrome or Goldenhaar's Syndrome, which cause deafness, may also cause CNS disorders (Hindley, 2005). Overall, studies suggest that about 25–30% of DHH children have additional disabilities (Knoors & Vervloed, 2003; Fellinger et al., 2012) such as learning disabilities, visual impairments, motor impairments, and intellectual disabilities, which increase the probability of experiencing mental health issues.

Adverse Childhood Experiences

Negative psychosocial experiences in the early years of any child's life can lead to poor health outcomes later in life such as chronic health problems, mental health issues, and substance misuse in adulthood (Øhre et al., 2015; Collishaw et al., 2007). Adverse childhood experiences (ACES) such as childhood maltreatment, neglect, trauma, and bullying occur more frequently in DHH children than in hearing children (Schenkel et al., 2014), increasing the risk for negative health outcomes. For example, Kvam (2004) found that DHH children were at 2–3 times greater risk of sexual abuse than hearing children. Other research corroborates this finding and details the general elevated prevalence of abuse (Sebald, 2008; Mertens, 1996; Sullivan et al., 1987) as well as maltreatment and trauma in DHH children (Schenkel et al., 2014). Outcomes data reported by DHH adults demonstrated that the lived experience of poorer direct child-caregiver communication and ongoing exclusion from incidental family communication were associated with increased risks for multiple chronic health outcomes (Kushalnagar et al., 2020; Kvam & Loeb, 2010). Given that the toxic stress from ACES can negatively affect children's brain development, immune systems, and stress-response systems, it is of concern that DHH children may be experience these life-altering events at even higher rates.

Language Deprivation

The development of language happens from birth to approximately 5 years of age. It is during these critical developmental years that a child's brain is most primed for learning language. After this age, the brain cells responsible for learning-language begin to gradually decrease and change, after which time it becomes much harder for children to ever develop a first language.

Children are not taught language but rather learn it through repeated and frequent exposure to and interaction with their parents, other adults, and children around them. Learning a language is so important that missing exposure to a natural language during this time-sensitive period may have very serious consequences. These range from a child being at risk for learning issues; difficulties with processing, memory, and understanding numbers; in addition to many serious mental health issues.

When DHH children do not have the chance to fully learn any language (either spoken or signed) during their critical language-learning years, the term *language deprivation* is used to describe the negative effects (Gulati, 2018). Language deprivation is very serious with irreversible effects and can potentially result in cognitive delays and mental health difficulties across the lifespan. As such, language deprivation is a very serious risk factor experienced by some DHH children with lifelong implications for mental health outcomes. The reader is encouraged to read chapter 1 for a more detailed discussion of language acquisition and deprivation.

Peer Relationships

Terlektsi and colleagues (2020) reported that DHH children experience more peer problems and lower levels of friendships than their hearing peers. These authors also found that adolescents with moderate hearing loss face the same or even greater challenges making new friends than adolescents with severe to profound hearing loss. Maintaining quality, peer-to peer-relationships can be difficult for DHH children due to language difficulties (Stevenson et al., 2010), fewer positive features of friendship such as companionship, a greater number of negative features such as conflict (Kouwenberg, 2013) and difficulties with emotional awareness and control (Rieffe et al., 2018).

Theory of Mind (ToM)

ToM is a cognitively complex mental state enabling children to understand the mental states of others with the realization that the thoughts, hopes, and feelings of others may be different from their own (Marschark et al., 2019; Garfield et al., 2001). ToM as a multifaceted set of skills develops as an intersectional construct between brain development and the social environment (e.g., parenting, friendships, education, social experiences) and involves memory, joint attention, complex perceptual recognition (i.e., face and gaze processing), language, executive functions, emotion-processing recognition, empathy, and imitation (Korkmaz, 2011).

ToM deficits have been reported in a number of childhood mental and neurodevelopmental disorders such as autism spectrum disorder (ASD), ADHD, developmental language disorders, obsessive-compulsive disorder, schizophrenia, oppositional defiant disorder, borderline personality disorder, posttraumatic stress disorder (PTSD), mood disorders, eating disorders, as well as acquired disorders of the right brain and traumatic brain injury (Sprung et al., 2022; Korkmaz, 2011, Szamburska-Lewandowska et al., 2021). The actual underlying mechanisms of the impairment of ToM in these mental disorders remains poorly understood, although progress is being made in treatment programs such as mentalization-based therapy or metacognitive training (Moritz et al., 2014; Malda-Castillo et al., 2019).

Studies have shown that DHH children from hearing families often have a delayed understanding of the false beliefs task which is a metric of ToM (Peterson, 2004; Peterson et al., 2005; Schick et al., 2007) and that these children also show lower degrees of empathy than their hearing peers (Peterson, 2016). Although this was initially attributed to communicative delays and disruptions in the early years, Marschark et al. (2019) reported that deaf participants scored significantly below hearing peers on ToM tasks, yet their performance on ToM tasks was unrelated to early access to social communication via either sign language (from Deaf parents) or spoken language (through cochlear implants), suggesting that deaf participants' performance was not solely a function of access to social communication in early childhood.

ToM skills are associated with social emotional maturity and social skills, and therefore, ToM deficits are conceptualized as negative predictors for social competence such as assertiveness and peer social skills (Vissers & Koolen, 2016). Fink et al., (2015) concluded that ToM was a predictor of mutual friendship and that chronic friendlessness in childhood predicts adverse mental health outcomes throughout life. Although research remains ongoing in terms of fully understanding the actual process of how ToM develops in DHH children, the delays in acquisition and/or ToM deficits raise concerns regarding mental health and well-being.

Additional Contributing Factors

Mental health disorders in any individual can be caused by a combination of biological, psychological, and environmental factors. Biological factors may include genetics (heredity), infections, brain injuries, prenatal damage or trauma, maternal substance abuse, poor nutrition, and exposure to toxins. Psychological factors may include severe childhood traumas, early loss (such as that of a parent), abuse, neglect, and isolation. Environmental factors may include stressors such as the death of an important person, dysfunctional family life, feelings of inadequacy, loneliness and low self-esteem, social cultural pressures such as discrimination, and substance abuse.

Clearly, DHH children are as vulnerable to these factors as hearing individuals, yet other factors may also be a concern. For example, inadequate teaching environments may contribute to isolation, discrimination/audism may cause internalization of negative self-labels (Admire & Ramirez, 2021), lack of incidental learning may contribute to dangerous or reckless decisions, language deprivation may place a child at risk for mental health issues, inaccessible family communication may contribute to a myriad of emotional sequalae, and finally, inaccessible health care may result in delayed or inaccurate diagnoses and treatment.

In summary, the risk factors described above may potentially intersect in many ways, culminating in greater vulnerability to mental health issues in DHH children.

Clinical Presentations

Most clinical psychologists and psychiatrists working in mainstream settings may never be asked to assess a DHH child. An estimated 1.2 million children and youth in Canada are affected by mental illness, with less than 20% accessing treatment. It is likely that a far smaller percentage of the DHH population is accessing care, given the lack of qualified clinicians, fewer evidence-based treatment interventions (Glickman & Pollard, 2013), language and communication barriers, very limited health literacy (Glickman, 2013), few mental health materials developed in ASL or translated from English to ASL (Mulder & Chovaz, 2025); McKee et al., 2011; Pollard et al., 2009), significantly flawed older research regarding DHH children, and a harsh history of mistreatment and discriminatory practices by mainstream hearing professionals (Myklebust, 1964; Pintner et al., 1941; Pollard, 1992). In fact, van Gent et al., (2007) suggests that less than 10% of the DHH children population in the Netherlands attempt to access mental health care. A significant number of DHH children are most certainly in need of mental health care.

For those DHH children who need mental health care, familiarization with this group is critical in terms of accurately recognizing symptoms of a mental health disorder. It is also incumbent upon those of us who work in this highly specialized area to share our knowledge. Missed diagnoses and misdiagnoses are problematic and potentially life-changing. Consider for example, the potential effects on the life of a DHH child given antipsychotic medication for social isolation or stimulant medication for a language disorder. This highlights the need to better understand the clinical presentations of some specific disorders that illustrate the clinical complexities inherent in working with these children and youth. The reader is also encouraged to review Chapter 5, Best Practices in Mental Health Assessment and Treatment of Deaf Children.

The next section describes clinical presentations that I, as a deaf clinician, have observed in my work with DHH children over the last three decades. The complexities of deafness in terms of mental health cannot be overstated. Clinicians need a thorough understanding of how these differences might present and how best to understand them within a clinical framework. It has become clear to me that the mind of a DHH child (regardless of their language modality) in some instances may be qualitatively different from that of a hearing child. This is not a binary statement that deaf and hearing children have a fundamental difference, as there likely is overlap between deaf and hearing children related to many mental functions. However, for those deaf children presenting with mental health issues, it has often been my experience that differences emerge. This refers to a difference in lived experiences which ultimately may effect neurophysiological changes. The mind of the DHH child is affected by risk factors, family dynamics, language, culture, and educational decisions, including various degrees of audism and acceptance. I am not convinced there is a "psychology of the Deaf," but I strongly believe that these fundamental differences between hearing and deaf minds demand educated, thoughtful, evidence-based, and intentionally driven clinical expertise.

DHH children are a very diverse group, and most of the following information pertains to DHH children who consider themselves part of Deaf culture and ASL is their first language. However, it is prudent to remember that any degree of hearing loss, degree of language acquisition or deprivation, and use or non-use of technical aids such as cochlear implants or hearing aids can potentially and significantly affect one's mental health.

The clinical presentations of mental health disorders in DHH children have three trajectories:

1. Clinical symptoms are accurately identified, for example, the DHH child is correctly diagnosed with ADHD.
2. Clinical symptoms are inaccurately identified e.g., the DHH child is diagnosed with ASD although the clinical symptoms are those of ADHD.
3. Clinical symptoms are attributed solely to the deafness (diagnostic overshadowing), for example, the DHH child has a mood disorder which is considered to be directly related to hearing loss.

The following section will present common symptoms/behaviors seen in ASD and ADHD, followed by a complex clinical presentation. Behaviors/symptoms will be identified within the context of lived experiences of DHH children with the disorders. These case studies come from my clinical practice. Please note that identifying features have been removed and some details have been added/omitted for teaching purposes.

Autism Spectrum Disorder (ASD)

ASD is a developmental neurological disorder characterized by core deficits in social communication and social interaction across multiple contexts and restricted, repetitive patterns of behavior, interests, or activities. Although children on the autism spectrum vary widely, the following symptoms are frequently observed:

- difficulties with language pragmatics
- difficulties with the social rules of conversation
- lack of or less eye contact
- difficulty with turn-taking in conversation
- difficulty responding appropriately to questions
- difficulty knowing how to insert oneself into a group setting
- perseverative behaviors

Table 1. highlights relevant clinical constructs with examples in a hearing child followed by examples of lived experiences in a DHH child with ASD, as well as a DHH child without ASD.

Table 1. Comparison of Constructs in Hearing Children with ASD, DHH Children with ASD, DHH Children with LD and a Typical DHH Child

Construct	**Hearing child with ASD**	**DHH Child with ASD**	**DHH Child with Language Deprivation (LD)**	**Typical DHH Child**
Language structure	Atypical language structure Pronoun reversal Echolalia Neologisms Repetitive Poor receptive language	Atypical language structure Hand (sign) reversals Echolalia Neologisms Repetitive Poor receptive language	Atypical language structure Limited vocabulary Repetitive Language dysfluency Knowledge gaps Difficulties with timelines Difficulties with receptive language	Typical sign language structure
Interests	Restricted Interests Repetitive behaviours	Restricted Interests Repetitive behaviours	Limited interests	Varied interests
Social Engagement	Poor social engagement Solitary play	Poor social engagement Solitary play	Awkward or limited social engagement	Social reciprocity May feel overwhelmed in settings with communicative barriers

(Continued)

Table 1. Continued

Construct	**Hearing child with ASD**	**DHH Child with ASD**	**DHH Child with Language Deprivation (LD)**	**Typical DHH Child**
Eye Contact	Avoids eye contact	Avoids eye contact May see eye contact for instrumental use	Variable eye contact	Good eye contact
Play	Unusual attachment to objects/toys Lack of imitative play Solitary play	Unusual attachment to objects/toys Lack of imitative play Solitary play	May engage in solitary play re: poor social skills Lack of incidental learning	Typical Play May see lack of incidental learning
Attention	Limited joint attention	Limited joint attention	Variable joint attention	Good attention
Sensory	Tactile over-responsiveness Sensory issues Response to specific triggers	Tactile over-responsiveness Sensory issues Response to specific triggers		
Gestures	Inappropriate use	Inappropriate use	Static use of gestures	Communicative use
Stimming	Present	Present		Not present
Executive functions	Deficits in EF	Deficits in EF	Variability in EF	Typical EF

Heart-to-Heart Experience

Betsy was a Deaf child of hearing parents. She had a bilateral sensorineural hearing loss of unknown etiology identified shortly after her birth. She attended a school for the Deaf since junior kindergarten where the philosophy was a bilingual approach with ASL and written English. Betsy was a quiet child who had always preferred to play by herself rather than with her peers. Her parents noticed at home that Betsy would spend long periods of time repeatedly lining up her younger brother's toy cars. When she was asked to stop, she would become very distressed. Her parents knew a little sign language but mostly tried to communicate with Betsy with gestures. They did feel she was different from her two hearing siblings (older, sister and younger, brother) but were convinced this was because she was deaf. Her mother felt that Betsy did not really care if she was there or not, whereas her two other children frequently came to her for comfort. Her mother also noticed that Betsy had an unusual way of spinning her index finger repeatedly and assumed this was somehow part of sign language. The couple met with their family doctor to share their observations and were relieved when the doctor confirmed that all children develop at different rates and likely Betsy's development was even more different given her deafness. He advised the couple to give it time.

In grade 2, Betsy's teacher met with her parents. The teacher felt that Betsy was not progressing in her language development, seemed to have few if any friends, became quite upset when her routine was changed, had odd facial expressions which caused her peers to mimic her, did not willingly participate in any classroom activities, instead spending inordinate amounts of time organizing colored pencils on her desk. Betsy's parents agreed for her to have a psychological evaluation with a Deaf clinical psychologist very familiar with Deaf children and mental health. The results of that assessment indicated that Betsy had persistent deficits in social communication and interaction as well as a pattern of restricted, repetitive behaviors yielding a diagnosis of ASD.

Head-to-Head Points to consider:

- Mainstream clinicians may not have the expertise to evaluate developmental progress in DHH children.
- Parents typically compare their children. This type of comparison can be problematic if parents' frame of reference does not include past experiences with DHH children.
- Symptoms such as preference for solitary play, unusual facial expressions, restricted interests, difficulties with transitions or terminating activities, and delayed or different language development are not seen in a typically developing DHH child with accessible language.
- Teachers with experience teaching DHH children will typically have excellent observations in terms of possible symptoms of mental health issues.
- It is essential that the psychologist or psychiatrist have experience diagnosing mental health disorders in DHH children to accurately identify symptoms.

Attention Deficit Hyperactivity Disorder (ADHD)

ADHD is a highly heritable, neurobiologically based disorder of attention and self-control presenting in childhood with serious implications for learning and success in life (Parasnis et al., 2003). ADHD is characterized by two distinct behavioral patterns of either inattentiveness or hyperactivity-impulsivity. Based on symptoms described in *Diagnostic and Statistical Manual of Mental Disorders—Fifth Edition* (*DSM-5*) (APA, 2022), there are three different presentations: predominantly inattentive, predominantly hyperactive/impulsive, or combined with symptom indicators of mild, moderate, or severe.

The following behaviors are frequently observed:

- difficulties with attention
- impulsive behaviors (may act without thinking about the result)
- hyperactivity
- difficulties with organization

ADHD can be caused by genetic, prenatal, and postnatal events, with the prevalence rate in the hearing population at approximately 3–7% (Barkley, 1997). Although there is no evidence that deafness causes ADHD, there is evidence that some of the recognized etiologies of ADHD (e.g., drug toxicity, anoxia) are also etiologies of deafness (Mauk & Mauk, 1992; Samar et al., 1998). Consequently, research studies have reported elevated rates of ADHD in the DHH population ranging from 3.55–38%, with the highest rates of ADHD identified in children with acquired deafness rather than hereditary deafness (Hindley & Kroll, 1998; Kelly et al., 1993).

Stevenson et al. (2010) specifically studied many of the behavior problems associated with ADHD (inattentiveness and impulsivity) in DHH children, reporting that hearing loss by itself is not a risk factor for behavior difficulties. Within the DHH group, increasing severity of hearing loss was not related to the level of behavior problems. Their conclusion was that hearing loss is related to an increased rate of behavior problems only because hearing loss is itself a risk factor for low language competence.

Table 2. Comparison of Constructs in Hearing Children with ADHD, DHH Children with ADHD, DHH Children with LD and a Typical DHH Child

Construct	**Hearing Children with ADHD**	**DHH Children with ADHD**	**DHH Children with Language Deprivation (LD)**	**Typical DHH Children**
Attention	Inattentive	Inattentive	Difficulties with attention	Attentive May look around the room frequently to monitor communication
Sustained Attention	Often easily distracted by extraneous stimuli	Often easily distracted by extraneous stimuli	Difficulties with sustained attention	Sustained attention May frequently scan environment for communication cues
Impulsivity	Difficulties regulating behaviour	Difficulties regulating behaviour May be reactive to not understanding and/or lack of accessible communication	May be impulsive	Regulates appropriately May be bored when excluded from communication
Activity	Hyperactive	Hyperactive	Difficulties regulating behaviour	Regulates appropriately May be hyperactive when excluded from communication

Table 2. Continued

Construct	**Hearing Children with ADHD**	**DHH Children with ADHD**	**DHH Children with Language Deprivation (LD)**	**Typical DHH Children**
Executive functions (EF)	Difficulties with self-awareness, inhibition, working memory, emotional self-regulation, self-motivation, planning, and problem-solving	Difficulties with self-awareness, inhibition, working memory, emotional self-regulation, self-motivation, planning, and problem-solving May be challenged in a visually inaccessible environment	Deficits in planning, organizing, problem solving, attention, and memory, sequencing, concepts of time, and spatial organization	Typical EF skills May be disruptive in a visually inaccessible environment
Intellect	Normal distribution Higher risk of learning disabilities	Normal distribution Higher risk of learning disabilities	Fund of knowledge deficits Risk of cognitive delays	

Given the higher prevalence rate reported with acquired deafness in addition to the higher rate of behavior problems related to language delay/deprivation, it is critical that clinicians understand the possible presentation of symptoms of ADHD (see Table 2).

Heart-to-Heart Experience

Michael was an 8-year-old deaf boy with hearing parents and one older hearing sibling. Michael was deafened after he had meningitis as a very young infant, was implanted at age 9 months, and his family was diligent about attending aural rehabilitation sessions. Michael was a student in a mainstreamed classroom where he was the only child with hearing loss.

His parents were told that Michael was a "cochlear implant success," noting that he communicated fairly well with his family and peers. The parents observed that Michael kept his room tidy, brought home all materials from school, and was interested in many different topics he found on his iPad such as dinosaurs and cars but did not always seem to understand the homework expectations. His parents also noticed that Michael became very hyperactive when there were family gatherings and typically ran around a lot, became disruptive, and did not sit calmly to visit with anybody.

Michael's teachers shared similar observations with the parents, including his tendency to frequently move around the classroom, not pay attention to the lesson, and struggle with mastery of the curriculum. When the parents visited the classroom, they noticed that all of Michael's belongings were well organized in his desk and cubicle and that the teacher's desk at the front of the room had a large window behind it.

The teacher suggested that the school psychologist assess Michael, and the parents agreed. Noting that Michael had an acquired deafness in addition to his hyperactivity and learning difficulties, the psychologist diagnosed Michael with ADHD—Combined Type. After sharing the psychological assessment with the family doctor, Michael was started on a stimulant medication. The parents, teacher, and Michael noticed no difference in behaviors, so Michael was switched to a different medication. Again, there were no benefits noted from the medication. Suspecting that perhaps Michael was also depressed, the family doctor added an antidepressant medication. Michael had also been aggressive toward his peers, especially during group discussions, so in addition to his stimulant (Ritalin) and antidepressant medication (Prozac), Michael was started on an antipsychotic medication (Risperidone) to address behavioral concerns.

By the time Michael was 12 years of age, there had still been no noticeable difference in his behavior or learning. The parents were referred to me as an expert in deafness and mental health. Following my assessment, I concluded that Michael did not have ADHD. The results of the assessment did not support that diagnosis; instead, I felt that when Michael became overwhelmed with communication demands, he responded behaviorally with increased movement, distractibility, and aggression. Working with the family doctor, Michael's medications were discontinued, and I carefully monitored his behavioral patterns. Clear patterns emerged showing that when communicative interactions became complex (group discussions), were not easily accessible (teacher at the front of the classroom with back turned, location of Michael's desk facing a window), or too exhausting (prolonged teaching time), Michael responded with negative behaviors. These behavior patterns were also clearly identified in the home setting. Over time, Michael's response to any communicative stress had become entrenched in his behavioral responses. I also completed a psychoeducational assessment which indicated that Michael was of average nonverbal intelligence with lower scores noted in verbal reasoning and comprehension. My recommendations to the school team and parents were largely around communication accessibility, and over time, Michael's behaviors improved. With one-to-one support reviewing academic instructions, Michael's grades slowly began to improve. With these improvements, it was noted that Michael seemed happier, more engaged, and more willing to try to communicate with his extended family members.

Head-to-Head Points to consider :

- Symptoms can be misunderstood/misidentified as clinical disorders in DHH children.
- Communicative abilities must be diligently and thoroughly assessed.
- The technological success of cochlear implants does not necessarily mean success in all communicative interactions.
- Strengths may be overlooked such as Michael's ability to keep his desk well organized and his responsibility in bringing home all school notices.
- Academic struggles may be rooted in accessibility to instruction rather than learning disabilities.
- Although medication can be very helpful, it is advantageous to thoroughly assess all contributing factors such as communication.
- It is well worth examining behavioral patterns as well as environmental configurations (lighting, seating, sightlines in front of windows).

Complex Presentation

The reality is that there are few clinicians who specialize in mental health and deafness. As a Deaf clinical psychologist, I am privileged to receive referrals for very complex clinical presentations of DHH children who typically have been seen by multiple clinicians prior to me and who have also usually received multiple clinical diagnoses. It is my job then to carefully review the history, better understand the clinical presentation, and often tease apart what I feel have been clinically astute decisions from those I consider having less veracity. The following is intended to illustrate for the reader one such case as well as my process of understanding the presentation of clinical symptoms. For the purposes of this case study, identifying features have been altered, some details have been omitted for brevity and only portions of the clinical presentations and assessment are described.

Heart-to-Heart Experience

I received a referral for Sofia who was a 14-year-old Deaf adolescent with an extensive history of repeated psychiatric hospitalizations and frequent interactions with the police for suicidal thoughts and disruptive behaviors. There was a significant concern of vulnerability to human trafficking.

Sofia's family immigrated from a South Asian country when she was 4 years old. Sofia had been identified as deaf at age 2 years with a bilateral, severe-to-profound sensorineural hearing loss of unknown etiology. The family communicated with her using only homemade gestures and spoken Hindi. Sofia had two older, hearing sisters and one younger, hearing sister. After arriving in Canada, the family moved several times to various provinces as the parents sought employment and a familiar community in which to live. Sofia received bilateral hearing aids at age 5 years and was enrolled in a mainstream school the following year. At age 8 years, due to ongoing difficulties following classroom rules and lack of academic progress, she was transferred to a Deaf school where she was exposed to ASL for the first time. The family history according to the parents (obtained through a Hindi interpreter and an ASL interpreter) was negative for mental health issues, disorders, or trauma.

Hospital clinicians repeatedly noted that communication was very difficult with Sofia even when using ASL interpreters. At times, clinicians elected to write notes back and forth with Sofia. Hospital reports outlined the following concerns:

- sad affect
- negative mood most days
- difficulties with communication even with ASL interpreters
- self-harm (cutting, scratching)
- suicidal thoughts/behaviors (ingestion of pills)
- physically aggressive/threatening statements and behaviors toward family
- unsubstantiated allegations of abuse by parents and teachers
- defiance
- vandalism of property
- irrational decisions
- incorrect assumptions about family and immigration decisions
- excessive and risky online behaviors
- school truancy

- academic failures
- few friends
- substance use (cannabis, crack, amphetamines)
- sleep issues
- inability to concentrate
- complaints of excessive fatigue
- little if any insight into consequences of actions
- frequent dramatic fabrication of events
- multiple expressions of frustration with home setting including lack of communication and resistance to rules

Head-to-head points to Consider:

The following diagnoses had been given by various clinicians:

1. ADHD
2. Learning Disorder
3. Intellectual Disability
4. Major Depressive Disorder
5. Disruptive Mood Regulation Disorder
6. PTSD
7. Conduct Disorder

It is noted that, although possible for one adolescent to have multiple diagnoses with comorbidities, the extensive nature of this list of diagnoses caused me to query the validity of some.

Although I am fluent in ASL, it is not my first language. I realized that although my fluency facilitates discourse within most parameters of assessment and treatment, communication expertise from the perspective of a first language fluency is critical. I therefore elected to meet with Sofia with a Deaf interpreter (DI) to ensure language discourse was as optimal as possible. I observed that she maintained moderately good eye contact (important for signed discourse) and was fairly oriented to time and place (was unsure of the day of the week as well as the province). She did not appear at any time to be distracted by or responding to internal stimuli.

The DI shared (and I agreed) that Sofia's discourse was receptively and expressively far less than age-appropriate and at times indicative of severe dysfluency. Sofia had impoverished vocabulary, often using signs incorrectly or repeatedly, tended to use unknown gestures/pantomine in addition to signs, had significant difficulties sequencing events in time, and did not follow typical grammar rules of ASL. Finally, we observed that there was often discord between her facial expression and sign execution.

It became apparent that Sofia had language deprivation (please see chapter 1 for an extensive description) underlying her clinical symptoms. The complicated history of a late identification of hearing loss (age 2 years); the family's communication modality of gestures, homemade signs, and spoken Hindi; her later age of acquiring hearing aids; switching of schools and language modalities; and the very late exposure to ASL (age 8 years) all contributed to Sofia missing out on language acquisition and first-language fluency. Therefore, many of the clinical symptoms observed were fundamentally rooted in the absence of a well-developed language.

Once the language deprivation was identified, it became more clear which clinical symptoms were indicative of language deprivation versus a mental health disorder. For example, Sofia's impulsive style of interacting and her inattentiveness was more related to language deprivation than ADHD. Her incorrect assumptions about her family as well as immigration decisions were again related to language deprivation (lack of incidental learning and deficits in abstract thought). Her inability to form relationships was more related to her lack of theory of mind, which is strongly tied to language acquisition and language development. Symptoms such as her low tolerance for frustration and her negative behaviors toward her family members were clearly rooted in her distress at not understanding the world around her, specifically her anger and frustration in not sharing a meaningful language with her family members.

Although language deprivation is not currently a *DSM-5* (APA, 2022) or *International Classification of Diseases—11th Revision* (*ICD-11*) (WHO, 2019/2021) diagnostic classification, the presence and identification of language deprivations informs a powerful story and developmental experience. Language deprivation clearly is a risk factor for mental health issues and can be comorbid with diagnosable mental health disorders. For example, Sofia's sad affect, self-harm, suicidal thought, inability to concentrate, and sleep issues met the criteria for Major Depressive Disorder. Lastly, appropriate psychometric testing did not support Intellectual Disability but confirmed Specific Learning Disorder.

The revised list of diagnostic classifications framed within the compelling implications of language deprivation included (a) Major Depressive Disorder, (b) Learning Disorder, (c) and Addiction of Substance Use Disorder.

Recommendations

Understanding clinical presentations in DHH children is complex. In many ways, this should be considered a specialized area of practice with clinicians knowledgeable about the typical development of DHH children, Deaf culture, language acquisition/deprivation, as well as presentations of mental health symptoms.

Recognizing that this level of expertise is often not easily available, clinicians should educate themselves as much as possible and establish allied partnerships with more specialized practitioners. It is ultimately the clinician's responsibility to determine if they have the requisite head-to-head knowledge, communication competence, and appreciation for and contextual understanding of the heart-to-hearts shared by the deaf community. The following recommendations are offered:

- Read credible resources and/or attend conferences and workshops to learn more about deafness and mental health in DHH children. Canadian resources include the Centre of Deaf Education and Accessibility Forum (CDEAF) at King's University, Ontario (https://cdeaf.kings.uwo.ca/) Canada, Deaf Centre Manitoba Inc. (https://deafcentremanitobainc.ca/page.php?pid=14&subpid=4), and the Canadian Hearing Services (https://www.chs.ca/about-canadian-hearing-services). American resources include the Deaf Wellness Center (https://www.urmc.rochester.edu/deaf-wellness-center.aspx), the National Deaf Center (https://nationaldeafcenter.org/resources/mental-health/), and The American Deafness and Rehabilitation Association (ADARA) (https://www.adara.org/). European resources include The European Society for Mental Health and Deaf people (ESMHD) (https://esmhd.org/). Lastly, the World Federation of the Deaf (https://wfdeaf.org/) post position papers as well as host the World Congress of the World Federation of the Deaf which typically includes topics related to mental health.
- Become familiar with the relevant risk factors in clinical histories.

- Be thoughtful about the selection and administration of psychometric tests, considering if tests are appropriate for use with DHH children.
- Seek support and supervision from individuals, organizations, and agencies who specialize in working with DHH children.
- Examine your own areas of competence, adding to it where necessary to work with this population.
- Learn sign language and/or develop your skill set for effectively working with a mental health interpreter.
- Be well-read in clinical theory and trust lived experiences.

References

Admire, A., & Ramirez, B. (2021). Violence and disability: Experiences and perceptions of victimization among deaf people. *Journal of Interpersonal Violence, 36*(1–2), NP1–NP25. https://doi.org/10.1177/0886260517730564

American Psychiatric Association. (2022). *Diagnostic and statistical manual of mental disorders* (5th ed., text rev.). https://doi.org/10.1176/appi.books.9780890425787

Barkley, R. A. (1997). Behavioral inhibition, sustained attention, and executive functions: Constructing a unifying theory of ADHD. *Psychological Bulletin, 121*(1), 65–94. https://doi.org/10.1037/0033-2909.121.1.65

Boyle, M. H. (1998). Guidelines for evaluating prevalence studies. *Evidence-Based Mental Health, 1*(2), 37–39. https://doi.org/10.1136/ebmh.1.2.37

Brown, P. M., & Cornes, A. (2015). Mental health of deaf and hard-of-hearing adolescents: what the students say. *Journal of Deaf Studies and Deaf Education, 20*(1), 75–81. https://doi.org/10.1093/deafed/enu031

Chovaz, C. J. (2013). Report of a deaf child with Tourette's disorder. *Journal of Deaf Studies and Deaf Education, 18*(3), 360–369. https://doi.org/10.1093/deafed/ent014

Collishaw, S., Pickles, A., Messer, J., Rutter, M., Shearer, C., & Maughan, B. (2007). Resilience to adult psychopathology following childhood maltreatment: Evidence from a community sample. *Child Abuse and Neglect, 31*(3), 211–229. https://doi.org/10.1016/j.chiabu.2007.02.004

Dammeyer, J. (2009). Congenitally deafblind children and cochlear implants: Effects on communication. *Journal of Deaf Studies and Deaf Education, 14*(2), 278–288. https://doi.org/10.1093/deafed/enn042

Dammeyer, J. (2010). Psychosocial development in a Danish population of children with cochlear implants and deaf and hard-of-hearing children. *Journal of Deaf Studies and Deaf Education, 15*(1), 50–58. https://doi.org/10.1093/deafed/enp024

Daza González, M. T., Phillips-Silver, J., López Liria, R., Gioiosa Maurno, N., Fernández García, L., & Ruiz-Castañeda, P. (2021). Inattention, impulsivity, and hyperactivity in deaf children are not due to deficits in inhibitory control but may reflect an adaptive strategy. *Frontiers in Psychology, 12*, Article 629032. https://doi.org/10.3389/fpsyg.2021.629032

Du Feu, M., & Chovaz, C. (2014). *Mental health and deafness*. Oxford University Press.

Fellinger, J., Holzinger, D., Sattel, H., & Laucht, M. (2008). Mental health and quality of life in deaf pupils. *European Child & Adolescent Psychiatry, 17*(7), 414–423. https://doi.org/10.1007/s00787-008-0683-y

Fellinger, J., Holzinger, D., & Pollard, R. (2012). Mental health of deaf people. *The Lancet, 379*(9820), 1037–1044. https://doi.org/10.1016/S0140-6736(11)61143-4

Fink, E., Begeer, S., Peterson, C. C., Slaughter, V., & de Rosnay, M. (2015). Friendlessness and theory of mind: A prospective longitudinal study. *The British Journal of Developmental Psychology, 33*(1), 1–17. https://doi.org/10.1111/bjdp.12060

Garfield, J. L., Peterson, C. C., & Perry, T. (2001). Social cognition, language acquisition and the development of the theory of mind. *Mind and Language, 16*(5), 494–541.

Glickman, N. S. (2013). Introduction: What is deaf mental health care? In N. S. Glickman (Ed.), *Deaf mental health care* (pp. 19–54). Routledge.

Glickman, N. S., & Pollard R. Q., Jr. (2013). Deaf mental health research: Where we've been and where we hope to go. In N. S. Glickman (Ed.), *Deaf mental health care* (pp. 358–387). Routledge.

Gulati, S., (2018). Language deprivation syndrome. In N. S. Glickman, and W. C. Hall (Eds.), *Language deprivation and deaf mental health* (pp. 24–46). Routledge/Taylor & Francis Group.

Hindley, P. A. (2005). Mental health problems in deaf children. *Current Paediatrics, 15*(2), 114–119. https://doi.org/10.1016/j.cupe.2004.12.008

Hindley, P., & Kroll, L. (1998). Theoretical and epidemiological aspects of attention deficit and overactivity in deaf children. *Journal of Deaf Studies and Deaf Education*, 3(1), 64–72. https://doi.org/10.1093/oxfordjournals.deafed.a014341

Kelly, D. P., Forney, J, Parker-Fisher, S., & Jones, M. (1993). Evaluating and managing Attention Deficit Disorder in children who are deaf or hard of hearing. *American Annals of the Deaf, 138*(4), 349–357.

Kitson, N. & Thacker, A. (2000) Adult psychiatry. In P. Hindley & N. Kitson (Eds.), *Mental health and deafness* (pp. 75–98). Whurr Publishers.

Knoors, H., & Vervloed, M. P. J. (2003). Educational programming for deaf children with multiple disabilities: Accommodating special needs. In M. Marschark & P. E. Spencer (Eds.), *Oxford handbook of deaf studies, language, and education* (vol. 2, pp. 82–94). Oxford University Press.

Korkmaz, B., (2011). Theory of mind and neurodevelopmental disorders of childhood. *Pediatric Research, 69*, 101–108. https://doi.org/10.1203/PDR.0b013e318212c177

Kouwenberg, M. (2013). *Social-emotional factors underlying internalizing problems and peer relations in deaf or hard of hearing youth* [Doctoral thesis, Leiden University]. https://scholarlypublications.universiteitleiden.nl/handle/1887/20757

Kushalnagar, P., Ryan, C., Paludneviciene, R., Spellun, A., & Gulati, S. (2020). Adverse childhood communication experiences associated with an increased risk of chronic diseases in adults who are deaf. *American Journal of Preventive Medicine, 59*(4), 548–554. https://doi.org/10.1016/j.amepre.2020.04.016

Kvam, M. H. (2004). Sexual abuse of deaf children. A retrospective analysis of the prevalence and characteristics of childhood sexual abuse among deaf adults in Norway. *Child Abuse and Neglect, 28*(3), 241–251. https://doi.org/10.1016/j.chiabu.2003.09.017

Kvam, M. H., & Loeb, M. (2010). The relation between adverse childhood experiences and later mental health among deaf adults. *Scandinavian Journal of Disability Research, 12*(4), 233–244.

Malda-Castillo, J., Browne, C., & Perez-Algorta, G. (2019). Mentalization-based treatment and its evidence-base status: A systematic literature review. *Psychology and Psychotherapy, 92*(4), 465–498. https://doi.org/10.1111/papt.12195

Marschark, M., Lang, H., & Albertini, J. A. (2002). *Educating deaf students: From research to practice*. Oxford University Press.

Marschark, M., Edwards, L., Peterson, C., Crowe, K., & Walton, D. (2019). Understanding theory of mind in deaf and hearing college students. *Journal of Deaf Studies and Deaf Education, 24*(2), 104–118. https://doi.org/10.1093/deafed/eny039

Mauk, G. W., & Mauk, P. P. (1992). Somewhere, out there: Preschool children with hearing impairment and learning disabilities. *Topics in Early Childhood Special Education, 12*(2), 174–195. https://doi.org/10.1177/027112149201200204

McKee, M. M., Barnett, S. L., Block, R. C., & Pearson, T. A. (2011). Impact of communication on preventive services among deaf American Sign Language users. *American Journal of Preventive Medicine, 41*(1), 75–79. https://doi.org/10.1016/j.amepre.2011.03.004

Mertens D. M. (1996). Breaking the silence about sexual abuse of deaf youth. *American Annals of the Deaf, 141*(5), 352–358. https://doi.org/10.1353/aad.2012.0257

Moritz, S., Andreou, C., Schneider, B. C., Wittekind, C. E., Menon, M., Balzan, R. P., & Woodward, T. S. (2014). Sowing the seeds of doubt: A narrative review on metacognitive training in schizophrenia. *Clinical Psychology Review*, *34*(4), 358–366. https://doi.org/10.1016/j.cpr.2014.04.004

Myklebust H. R. (1964). *The psychology of deafness*. Grune and Stratton.

Niclasen, J., & Dammeyer, J. (2016). Psychometric properties of the Strengths and Difficulties Questionnaire and mental health problems among children with hearing loss. *Journal of Deaf Studies and Deaf Education*, *21*(2), 129–140. https://doi.org/10.1093/deafed/env067

Øhre, B., Uthus, M. P., von Tetzchner, S., & Falkum, E. (2015). Traumatization in deaf and hard-of-hearing adult psychiatric outpatients. *Journal of Deaf Studies and Deaf Education*, *20*(3), 296–308. https://doi.org/10.1093/deafed/env013

Parasnis, I., Samar, V. J., & Berent, G. P. (2003). Deaf adults without Attention Deficit Hyperactivity Disorder display reduced perceptual sensitivity and elevated impulsivity on the Test of Variables of Attention (T.O.V.A.). *Journal of Speech, Language, and Hearing Research*, *46*(5), 1166–1183. https://link-gale-com.proxy1.lib.uwo.ca/apps/doc/A109265868/AONE?u=lond95336&sid=bookmark-AONE&xid=c5e0772f

Peterson C. C. (2004). Theory-of-mind development in oral deaf children with cochlear implants or conventional hearing aids. *Journal of Child Psychology and Psychiatry*, *45*(6), 1096–1106. https://doi.org/10.1111/j.1469-7610.2004.t01-1-00302.x

Peterson, C. C. (2016). Empathy and theory of mind in deaf and hearing children. *Journal of Deaf Studies and Deaf Education*, *21*(2), 141–147. https://doi.org/10.1093/deafed/env058

Peterson, C. C., Wellman, H. M., & Liu, D. (2005). Steps in theory-of-mind development for children with deafness or autism. *Child Development*, *76*(2), 502–517. https://doi.org/10.1111/j.1467-8624.2005.00859.x

Pintner, R., Eisenson, J., & Stanton, M. (1941). *The psychology of the physically handicapped.* Crofts.

Pollard, R. Q., Jr. (1992). Cross-cultural ethics in the conduct of deafness research. *Rehabilitation Psychology*, *37*(2), 87–101. https://doi.org/10.1037/h0079101

Pollard, R. Q., Jr., & ~~Meghan~~ Fox, M. (2018). Forensic evaluation of deaf adults with language deprivation. In N. S. Glickman & W. C. Hall (Eds.), *Language deprivation and deaf mental health* (pp. 101–135). Routledge

Pollard, R. Q., Jr., Dean, R. K., O'Hearn, A., & Haynes, S. L. (2009). Adapting health education material for deaf audiences. *Rehabilitation Psychology*, *54*(2), 232–238. https://doi.org/10.1037/a0015772

Raven, J., & Raven, J. (2003). Raven progressive matrices. In R. S. McCallum (Ed.), *Handbook of Nonverbal Assessment* (pp. 223–237). Kluwer Academic/Plenum Publishers. https://doi.org/10.1007/978-1-4615-0153-4_11

Remine, M. D., & Brown, P. M. (2010). Comparison of the prevalence of mental health problems in deaf and hearing children and adolescents in Australia. *Australian and New Zealand Journal of Psychiatry*, *44*(4), 351–357. https://doi.org/10.3109/00048670903489866

Rieffe, C., Broekhof, E., Eichengreen, A., Kouwenberg, M., Veiga, G., da Silva, B. M. S., van der Laan, A., & Frijns, J. H. M. (2018). Friendship and emotion control in pre-adolescents with or without hearing loss. *Journal of Deaf Studies and Deaf Education*, *23*(3), 209–218. https://doi.org/10.1093/deafed/eny012

Rutter, M. L., Graham, P., & Yule, W. (1971). A Neuropsychiatric Study in Childhood. *Archives of Disease in Childhood, 46*, 577.

Samar, V. J., Parasnis, I., & Berent, G. P. (1998). Learning disabilities, attention deficit disorders, and deafness. In M. Marschark & M. D. Clark (Eds.), *Psychological perspectives on deafness* (vol. 2, pp. 199–242). Lawrence Erlbaum.

Schenkel, L. S., Rothman-Marshall, G., Schlehofer, D. A., Towne, T. L., Burnash, D. L., & Priddy, B. M. (2014). Child maltreatment and trauma exposure among deaf and hard of hearing young adults. *Child Abuse and Neglect*, 38(10), 1581–1589.

Schick, B., de Villiers, P., de Villiers, J., & Hoffmeister, R. (2007). Language and theory of mind: A study of deaf children. *Child Development*, *78*(2), 376–396. https://doi.org/10.1111/j.1467-8624.2007.01004.x

Sebald, A. M. (2008). Child abuse and deafness: An overview. *American Annals of the Deaf, 153*(4), 376–383. https://doi.org/10.1353/aad.0.0059

Sprung, M., Burghardt, J., Mazza, M., & Riffer, F. (2022). Editorial: Misunderstanding others: Theory of mind in psychological disorders. *Frontiers in Psychology, 13*, Article 838853. https://doi.org/10.3389/fpsyg.2022.838853

Stevenson, J., McCann, D., Watkin, P., Worsfold, S., & Kennedy, C. (2010). The relationship between language development and behaviour problems in children with hearing loss. *Journal of Child Psychology and Psychiatry, 51*(1), 77–83. https://doi.org/10.1111/j.1469-7610.2009.02124.x

Sullivan, P. M., Vernon, M., & Scanlan, J. M. (1987). Sexual abuse of deaf youth. *American Annals of the Deaf, 132*(4), 256–262. https://doi.org/10.1353/aad.2012.0614

Swanepoel, B., Swartz, L., Gericke, R., & Mall, S. (2020). Prevalence and correlates of mental and neurodevelopmental symptoms and disorders among deaf children and adolescents: A systematic review protocol. *BMJ Open, 10*(10), Article e038431. https://doi.org/10.1136/bmjopen-2020-038431

Szamburska-Lewandowska, K., Konowałek, Ł., & Bryńska, A. (2021). Theory of mind deficits in childhood mental and neurodevelopmental disorders. *Psychiatria Polska, 55*(4), 801–813. https://doi.org/10.12740/PP/OnlineFirst/112708

Terlektsi, E., Kreppner, J., Mahon, M., Worsfold, S., & Kennedy, C. R. (2020). Peer relationship experiences of deaf and hard-of-hearing adolescents. *Journal of Deaf Studies and Deaf Education, 25*(2), 153–166. https://doi.org/10.1093/deafed/enz048

van Gent, T., Goedhart, A. W., Hindley, P. A., & Treffers, P. D. A. (2007). Prevalence and correlates of psychopathology in a sample of deaf adolescents. *Journal of Child Psychology and Psychiatry, 48*(9), 950–958. https://doi.org/10.1111/j.1469-7610.2007.01775.x

van Gent, T., Goedhart, A. W., & Treffers, P. D. (2011). Self-concept and psychopathology in deaf adolescents: preliminary support for moderating effects of deafness-related characteristics and peer problems. *Journal of Child Psychology and Psychiatry, 52*(6), 720–728. https://doi.org/10.1111/j.1469- 7610.2011.02392.x

Vissers, C., & Koolen, S. (2016). Theory of mind deficits and social emotional functioning in preschoolers with specific language impairment. *Frontiers in Psychology, 7*, Article 1734. https://doi.org/10.3389/fpsyg.2016.01734

Wallis, D., Musselman, C., & MacKay, S. (2004). Hearing mothers and their deaf children: The relationship between early, ongoing mode match and subsequent mental health functioning in adolescence. *Journal of Deaf Studies and Deaf Education, 9*(1), 2–14. https://doi.org/10.1093/deafed/enh014

World Health Organization (WHO). (2019/2021). *International Classification of Diseases—11th Revision* (ICD-11). https://icd.who.int/browse11

5

Best Practices in Mental Health Assessment and Treatment of Deaf Children

Patrick Boudreault and Lori A. Day

Construct

Appropriate mental health care for children necessitates accurate assessment and efficacious treatment, even more so for deaf children given the potential for misdiagnosis and the health disparities faced by deaf people (Fellinger et al., 2012). We present an overview of the challenges to providing effective mental health services for deaf children and the implications for potential misdiagnosis and ineffective intervention. We also address considerations of language and communication for assessment and intervention, and interpretation of assessment results based on different sociolinguistic factors, which is often more complex for deaf children as compared to adults.

Head-to-Head and Heart-to-Heart

The number of empirical studies addressing assessment and treatment for deaf children is limited. With the lack of sound empirical guidance about the provision of mental health services for deaf children, there is a wide range of quality in clinical practice. Common concerns encountered in everyday clinical practice with deaf children are discussed, and available guidelines regarding best practices, where available, are highlighted here as head-to-heads and heart-to-hearts. This includes discussions of best practices in selecting and/or adapting assessment tools, communication strategies, and evaluating and adapting available interventions, as well as vignettes to illustrate how various factors impact everyday practice.

Statements of Self-Reflexivity

First Author: Patrick Boudreault

Growing up as a Deaf child of grassroots Deaf parents, I was immersed in the Deaf community, where mental health issues are widespread and communication in sign language—the preferred language of the community—is often inaccessible. My personal experiences have deeply connected me to the challenges faced by my community. This study is shaped by the shared experiences of many Deaf individuals who, like me, encountered a lack of accessible and appropriate assessments in sign language during their childhoods. While my expertise in sign language underpins my work, I recognize that my perspective as a Deaf white male does not encompass the full diversity of our community. Effective intervention and diagnosis for a Deaf child must begin with an understanding of their lived experiences, combined with an inclusive approach that integrates sign language as a key component of holistic mental health assessment. I acknowledge that this is an ongoing effort, and there are multiple dimensions within our society that must be continually addressed.

Second Author: Lori A. Day

My experience has been shaped by my identity as a white, hearing woman raised in a hearing family with English as my first language, and by the privileges associated with these identities. My training as a licensed psychologist, including my doctoral education and now my work at Gallaudet University, has deeply informed my understanding of the intersectionality of identity, languages, and culture, particularly within the Deaf and Hard of Hearing (DHH) communities. I am grateful to the deaf children and families that have not only trusted me with their care, but also taught me how to show care. I am committed to leveraging my skills and position to work alongside my Deaf colleagues to improve the accessibility and quality of mental health services for those who our systems of care have not been traditionally designed to serve.

Recommendations

The chapter concludes with a series of recommendations for effective mental health clinical practice with deaf children, focusing on two areas: clinician competencies and clinical practices. We also discuss necessary next steps to address the serious gaps between research and practice to improve the provision of assessment and treatment for deaf children.

The provision of quality mental health services for children requires appropriate screening, assessment, diagnosis, and treatment. The mental health profession has a number of guidelines to support the provision of services that are sensitive to a client's unique background, including recommendations about appropriate training, the selection and use of psychological measures, and the application of interventions to diverse client needs (e.g., AERA et al., 2014; APA, 2017). However, adherence to these guidelines when serving marginalized communities, including deaf[1] individuals, becomes a challenge because of barriers to providing appropriate levels of high-quality mental health services. Barriers include limited training opportunities for clinicians, very few measures and interventions that have either been developed for and/or culturally and linguistically adapted to meet the needs of deaf children, and a limited number of qualified mental health professionals to conduct research and provide clinical services (Wilkins et al., 2022). These limitations are an urgent problem today, where children and adolescent mental health has quickly become a global health crisis (Benton et al., 2021; Weine et al., 2020). Further compounding this issue is findings that emotional, social, and behavioral issues are up to 2 to 4 times higher for deaf children as compared to hearing children (Dammeyer, 2010; Fellinger et al., 2012).

1. Throughout this chapter, we use the term "deaf" with a lowercase "d" to include a broad range of hearing status, including individuals who are hard of hearing.

Clinicians must have a grasp of not only the unique considerations for working with deaf individuals, but also of the heterogeneity within this group. In the United States, approximately 0.3% of school-aged children are deaf or hard of hearing (Gaffney et al., 2010). Deaf children using sign language represent a fraction of approximately half a million individuals who identify as members of the Deaf community and use American Sign Language (ASL). Within the broad deaf population, there is heterogeneity among cultural affiliation, language access, language use, levels of education, and additional disabilities (WHO, 2023). Furthermore, members may also identify with other marginalized groups, including Black and Indigenous People of Color (BIPOC), people from the lesbian, gay, bisexual, transgender, queer, intersex, asexual, and ally (LGBTQIA) community, people with additional disabilities, and immigrants (Anderson et al., 2023; Dunne, 2013). There are no universal guidelines that apply to all deaf people. Instead, practitioners need to think about understanding standards of practice within a complexity of other relevant factors. These professionals confront a wide array of clinical needs and must develop multilayered skills, even with scant resources at their disposal.

The Deaf Community's Perception of Mental Health Services

Access to mental health services has significant barriers for deaf people, stemming from the unavailability of qualified professionals, limited access to medical insurance, stigmas surrounding mental health, and mistrust of healthcare providers (Anderson et al., 2023; Fellinger et al., 2012). Given the historical context of the medicalization of people with disabilities, including the eugenics movement in the 19th century and early part of the 20th century, it is unsurprising that access barriers continue to exist for individuals with disabilities. The impact of the eugenics movement on the deaf community had a broader effect, given it was geared toward eradicating the deaf community's language and culture in favor of using auditory rehabilitation and integration with the general society (Baynton, 1996). Such acts were and continue to be based on ideological beliefs that speech is superior, namely systemic audism, where deaf people regularly experience communication barriers and are often misunderstood and misdiagnosed.

The prevalence of systemic audism in our society where the attitude of the audiocentric value oppresses the deaf community is an integral part of the collective memory and ongoing experience of the deaf community (Anderson et al., 2023; Bauman, 2004; Eckert & Rowley, 2013; Gertz, 2008; Lane, 1999). The phenomenon of audism is a significant form of trauma among the deaf community in multiple aspects of life, particularly those geared around communication (Johnson et al., 2018). Generational trauma can be passed down from one generation to the next, such as through exposure to family trauma narratives. It may also be passed among intergenerational members through oral stories (e.g., art, performances), historical events, resharing of similar experiences, and social media. The latter one is prevalent, given common ways of information sharing and learning in the deaf population (Holcomb, 2013). Awareness of the deaf community's generational trauma is one way to acknowledge and understand their experiences and may foster trust between clinicians and their clients. Perhaps not surprisingly, the deaf community has historically been resistant to seeking mental health services and continues to struggle to get appropriate services (Chovaz et al., 2022; Fellinger et al., 2012; Leigh & Pollard, 2012).

In addition, it is critical to recognize the multidimensional nature of trauma that can occur for people with additional marginalized identities, including deaf women, deaf BIPOC, deaf immigrants, and/or the deaf queer community (Anderson et al., 2023). Individuals with multiple marginalized identities are at greater risk of experiencing mental health concerns (Vargas et al., 2020). Yet individuals from marginalized groups face difficulties in accessing mental health services, including cost, cultural and linguistic discordance, transportation, and discrimination from providers (Barfield & Martinelli, 2021; DeSa et al., 2020; Rodgers et al., 2022).

Ethical Considerations and Guidelines

Clinicians generally adhere to their respective field's ethical principles and guidelines when providing mental health services. While the specific guidelines may differ across fields and/or countries, the overarching theme of providing services that benefit clients and do no harm is universal. For example, the American Psychological Association's *Ethical Principles of Psychologists and Code of Conduct* (APA, 2017) requires psychologists to base their opinions from assessment on information that is sufficient to support their findings (section 9.01). Tests should be used in a manner that is consistent with research or evidence available and appropriate to an individual's language preference (section 9.02). And furthermore, psychologists need to consider the characteristics of the client when interpreting assessment results and to report the limitations of their interpretations (section 9.06).

Additionally, the APA's 2022 *Guidelines for Assessment and Intervention with Persons with Disabilities* state that psychologists working with people with disabilities should be familiar with how disability and related factors influence their client's functioning, and that one's experience can be impacted by their experience of the community. There are few opportunities available, however, for psychologists to receive advanced training in disability issues (APA, 2022). These guidelines recognize the intersectional identities of people with disabilities and highlight the need for appropriate test access to support accurate diagnosis and treatment. Psychologists have a clear responsibility to ensure that assessment tools measure the intended construct and not disability-related factors (guideline 15).

The challenge that mental health clinicians encounter, regardless of specialization or country of practice, is that often, they are asked to provide services for which there are no appropriate resources available and/or evidence to support the effectiveness of tools or interventions, particularly with deaf children. Because the specialized field of mental health research with deaf children has not yet caught up with the broader community, clinicians often find themselves in situations where they need to make decisions and/or provide services even if there is no good evidence to support their practice. In these cases, clinicians must evaluate how to provide services in a way that provides maximal benefit to the client while minimizing potential harm.

Mental Health Tools and Interventions for Deaf Children

The mental health field is overflowing with measures and treatments to evaluate and support children. Yet, when it comes to specific populations that may have unique cultural and access needs from the majority population, such as deaf children, the resources available are often far fewer. There are a limited number of measures that have either been developed for this population or adapted and empirically studied with this population. There are even fewer resources when it comes to mental health interventions.

Tools Developed for Deaf Children

While several tools have been developed specifically for deaf children, they generally focus on the language domain and have primarily been developed for research purposes rather than for wide public dissemination (Hauser et al., 2016; Simms et al., 2013). This is an important start, but we also need accessible measures and tools that are developed to assess broad psychological domains in addition to language. Additionally, we need normative data on how diverse deaf children perform on these measures. Very few mental health measures include data from deaf individuals, and those with data are often limited in their sample size and/or clear descriptions of the sample of deaf children (e.g., language, education, etc.).

The current research landscape with deaf people is focused on identifying language development in order to identify potential language development issues. These measures are the cumulation of growing evidence-based research that helped to understand the social-emotional impacts of language deprivation while acknowledging how widespread this issue is for deaf individuals (Gulati, 2018; W. C. Hall et al., 2017). Indeed, it is beneficial for clinicians to identify atypical language development and to use that information to inform their selection and interpretation of psychological assessments (Henner et al., 2018). Table 1 includes selected examples of language-based measures that assess various aspects of children's language development.

Table 1. Examples of Language-Based Measures of Children's Language Development.

Measure	Description	References
ASL Assessment Instrument 4.0 (ASLAI)	A battery of assessment measuring vocabulary, morphology, syntax, and narrative comprehension for deaf children from 4 to 17 years old	Hoffmeister et al., 2015
ASL Communicative Development Inventory (ASL-CDI 2.0	A normed assessment adapted from MacArthur Bates Communicative Development Inventory in ASL. Measures receptive and expressive vocabulary, and a section on gestures and phrases from 9 to 73 months old	Caselli et al., 2020
ASL Comprehension Test (ASL-CT)	Measures ASL receptive skills for both children and adults	Hauser et al., 2016
ASL & Nonlinguistic Perspective Taking Test (ASL-PTCT)	Assesses the perspective in respect to comprehension of classifiers, looking at visual-spatial cognition for people from 7 to 20 years old	Quinto-Pozos et al., 2013
ASL Phonological Awareness Test (ASL-PAT)	Assesses the phonology of ASL (handshape, movement, and location) for children between 4 to 10 years old	McQuarrie & Abbott, 2012; 2013

(*Continued*)

Table 1. Continued

Measure	Description	References
DHH Language Exposure Assessment Tool (D-LEAT)	Developed to provide a quantitative estimate of DHH children's experience with different forms of language input from birth to age 3	Hall & De Anda, 2022
Language Access Profile Tool (LAPT)	Designed to estimate a child's language access between birth and age 3	Hall & De Anda, 2022
Receptive Skills Test (ASL-RST, AUSLAN-RST, BSL-RST, DGS-RST)	Assesses signed language grammar for children aged 3 to 13 years old (age range varies between measures); Adapted versions in several languages based on Herman, Holmes & Woll, 1999	ASL: Enns et al., 2013 AUSLAN: Herman et al., 2014 BSL: Herman et al., 1999 DGS: Haug, 2011
Visual Communication and Sign Language Checklist (VCSL)	Tracks and identifies children's sign language development milestones up to 5 years old using a checklist; also adapted into Flemish Sign Language	ASL: Simms et al., 2013 NSL: Wille et al., 2020
Web-based Vocabulary Test (ASL-VT, BSL-VT)	Assesses children's vocabulary from 4 to 15 years old for BSL and from 6 to 10 years old for ASL	ASL: Mann et al., 2016 BSL: Mann & Marshall, 2012

The growing list of measures outlined in Table 1 is promising, yet it also highlights the gaps. It is a significant improvement from previous practices where clinicians primarily used assessment tools only to evaluate children's performance-based and visually-based skills in their evaluations. Clinicians now have a number of resources to assess language-based skills, too. A gap remains, however, in measures that address other sociolinguistic factors. This highlights the importance of having an evaluator who shares the same background or identity as the client to understand potential omissions in our measurement tools when conducting language-based assessments. Further, there continues to be a serious gap in mental health measures originally designed for deaf children.

Tools Adapted for or Used in Research with Deaf Children

There are a growing number of self/informant-report mental health measures that have been translated and/or adapted for deaf adults (e.g., Substance Abuse Screener in ASL, Rosenberg Self-Esteem Scale, ASL-STAR [screeners, tests, assessments, and resources] portal of screening measures) (Crowe, 2002; Guthmann et al., 2017). However, self-report measures translated into ASL for signing deaf children and/or their caregivers are almost nonexistent aside from the Strengths and Difficulties Questionnaire, a screening tool to assess the mental health of children and adolescents

(Goodman, 1997; Plimmer, 2018; Roberts et al., 2015). Having accurate information from clients, caregivers, and related professionals is critical to accurate conceptualization and intervention.

A greater number of measures provide some level of accommodation for standard administration and/or comment on the appropriateness of administration with deaf children. Reesman et al. (2014) reviewed 13 commonly utilized intellectual assessment measures and provided an analysis of their applicability for use with deaf children. Each selected test was reviewed to determine if it provided information about (a) administration and accommodations guidance, (b) score interpretation guidance, (c) the described group of deaf children, (d) empirical reports of deaf children, and (e) an empirical assessment of possible bias. Table 2 includes the commonly utilized measures of intelligence for deaf children as reviewed by Reesman et al. (2014) that have been updated to fit current editions of each measure. As is clear from the table, only a few measures have empirical studies with samples of deaf children.

Table 2. Updated Test Review Scorecard for Children Who Are Deaf or Hard of Hearing.

Test	Administration Accommodation Guidance	Score Interpretation Guidance	Described Group in manual	Empirical Reports of D/HH in Literature	Empirical Assessment of Possible Bias
Bayley-IV	Yes	No	No	No	No
CTONI-2	Yes	No	No	Yes	Yes
DAS-II	Yes	Yes	Yes	Yes	Yes
KABC-II NU	Yes	Yes	Yes	No	No
Leiter-3	Yes	Yes	Yes	No	Yes
UNIT-2	Yes	Yes	Yes	No	No
RIAS-2	No	No	No	No	No
SB5	Yes	No	No	No	No
WISC-V	Yes	Yes	No	Yes	Yes
WJ-IV COG	Yes	No	No	No	No
WNV	Yes	Yes	Yes	Yes	Yes
WPPSI-IV	Yes	Yes	No	No	No

Note. Bayley-IV Bayley Scales of Infant and Toddler Development—Fourth Edition; SB5 Stanford-Binet Intelligence Scales, Fifth Edition; Leiter-3 Leiter International Performance Scale—Third Edition; WJ-IV COG Woodcock-Johnson, Fourth Edition, Tests of Cognitive Abilities; WPPSI–IV Wechsler Preschool and Primary Scale of Intelligence—Fourth Edition; DAS-II Differential Ability Scales–Second Edition; KABC-II NU Kaufman Assessment Battery for Children, Second Edition Normative Update; RIAS Reynolds Intellectual Assessment Scales, Second Edition; WNV Wechsler Nonverbal Scale of Ability; WISC–V Wechsler Intelligence Scale for Children—Fifth Edition; CTONI-2 Comprehensive Test of Nonverbal Intelligence, Second Edition; UNIT Universal Nonverbal Intelligence Test, Second Edition; D/HH deaf or hard of hearing.

Interventions Adapted for Deaf Children

Research regarding treatments that have been adapted for use with deaf children is scant. One evidence-based intervention, parent-child interaction therapy (PCIT), has been adapted for use with a wide range of deaf families, including those who communicate via ASL and spoken language (Costa et al., 2019; Day et al., 2018). PCIT is a parent-training program that supports parents/caregivers in building secure relationships with their children and effectively utilizing developmentally appropriate discipline (McNeil et al., 2010). Initial evidence suggests that it can be a helpful intervention for deaf children and their parents (Barrett, 2020; Costa et al., 2019; Previ, 2018); however, this data is preliminary because these studies are limited by small sample sizes.

There is promising work happening with several other child-focused psychotherapeutic interventions. At the Walden School in Framingham, Massachusetts (United States), clinicians have been implementing Sensory Motor Arousal Regular Treatment, (SMART; Warner et al., 2020) with their clients and are currently developing ASL-based materials and guidance for this intervention. Clinicians at Partners Advocating for Healing (PAH!) in Milton, Ontario (Canada), are adapting the Circle of Security intervention (Powell et al., 2013) and running the program with various parent/child dyads. The PAH! program has also recently developed a screener tool in ASL assessing theory of mind (ToM). Their premise is that if a DHH child is delayed in the acquisition of language, prework may be necessary prior to the onset of counseling to maximize effective outcomes. Clinicians at the Deaf and Hard of Hearing Child Resilience Center in Washington, DC, are currently adapting and implementing Trauma-Focused Cognitive Behavior Therapy (TF-CBT; Mannarino et al., 2014) with deaf youth. Published guidance for each of these interventions with deaf children is forthcoming. Each of these interventions has a growing body of evidence to support their effectiveness for a range of presenting problems, and they hold promise for supporting deaf children. However, significantly more work is needed in terms of dissemination of these interventions broadly to clinicians, collecting data on their effectiveness, and including a broader range of interventions.

The field of mental health and deaf children is slowly making gains in knowledge, research, and resources. Yet, this progress still lags behind the general population. When considering the historical mistreatment of deaf individuals, combined with the continued lack of research to support effective assessment and intervention with deaf children, it is easy to see why many deaf individuals struggle to obtain appropriate mental health services. This current lack serves to perpetuate the ongoing disparity of mental health support for deaf children.

Head-to-Heads and Heart-to Hearts

This section addresses practical head-to-head topics for clinicians who work with deaf children, including accessibility issues, practice-related considerations, and trends among practicing clinicians. Corresponding heart-to-heart experiences highlight ways that this may present in everyday settings for both clients and clinicians.

Accessibility for Deaf Clients

In the last two decades, accessibility services provided to clients in some countries have steadily improved with growing awareness and training among mental health professionals. For example, in the United States, the Americans with Disabilities Act (2008) requires that mental health clinicians provide reasonable accommodations. Indeed, provision of communication access for deaf clients through accommodations such as interpreting and captioning services has gradually increased. However, equitable access for deaf individuals goes far beyond merely providing interpreting and/or captions and includes the need for changes in beliefs and systems (Chovaz et al., 2022). Further, accessing accommodations often falls on the clients, who must advocate for their needs. In the case of deaf children, this responsibility falls mainly on their parents/caregivers as the primary people seeking support. While some parents may have the knowledge and skills required, this remains largely challenging. Additionally, parents may be unaware of their child's actual language issues to advocate efficiently. For those who work with interpreters, this might require learning about local agencies and understanding different types of interpreting services as well as the varied qualities of interpreters.

Securing interpreting services can be challenging for both parties—clinicians and clients—due to a myriad of interpreter factors, including availability, qualifications (e.g., certified, specialty in mental health), linguistic proficiency in working with children and young adults, and consistency in the use of regular providers. In some cases, the costs of the interpreting services may exceed the amount the clinician gets paid for rendering the service. All clinicians should have established budgets for interpreting services, but smaller agencies and practices may be more financially burdened by absorbing interpreting costs. The following vignette underscores the fact that meeting accessibility needs goes far beyond providing an interpreter:

> Kesha, a 15-year-old deaf teenager who communicates primarily via ASL, was referred for outpatient mental health services by her school counselor due to elevated symptoms of depression and active suicidal ideation. Her parents made an appointment with a psychologist at a local outpatient clinic. They requested interpreter services when making an appointment, and the clinic staff reported that they would secure a remote interpreter. During the initial appointment, Kesha met in person with the clinician, and a remote interpreter joined via an iPad placed in the room where Kesha could see it. This interpreter had some initial difficulty understanding Kesha's signing style, although over the course of the appointment, the interpreter became more comfortable. However, a new interpreter was assigned to the next session. This new interpreter did not have the context from the prior session, making it difficult to discuss issues raised in the last session without providing repetitive explanations. After several sessions of constantly changing interpreters, Kesha did not want to continue services, as it was too exhausting to continue to repeat and restate information and work with inconsistent remote interpreters.

Linguistic barriers can exacerbate existing mental health issues and prevent individuals from obtaining much needed services. Having a consistent, qualified interpreter for the same client or clinician is part of best practices (Vernon & Miller, 2001). Existent linguistic barriers highlight the need for deaf and hearing clinicians with the language and cultural skills necessary to serve deaf clients directly, without the use of third-party interpreting services.

Accessibility for Deaf Clinicians

There is an increasing number of deaf clinicians in the United States, but the number is still insufficient, given the higher risk of mental health issues among the deaf population (Brice et al., 2013;

Wilkins et al., 2022). There are barriers in the training pipeline for deaf individuals in the mental health workforce (Schooler et al., 2021). Systematic oppression creates barriers for many deaf individuals to participate in the advanced training required for mental health professionals (Brice et al., 2013; Dowtin & Day, 2019). For example, *access* was one of the major themes in a qualitative study of training experiences for clinicians who use play therapy with deaf clients (Dowtin & Day, 2019). Specifically, hearing therapists noted a disparity in access to peer supervision and consultation between deaf and hearing clinicians. A deaf clinician shared, "I used to be very upset watching hearing students that I helped train become credentialed in play therapy, while I could not find enough trainings or supervisors to become credentialed" (Dowtin & Day, 2019, p. 200).

A significant barrier experienced by deaf clinicians is the lack of essential, but often overlooked, professional growth experience of professional networking. In the mental health profession, knowledge is commonly shared both within and outside formal educational channels. Those informal incidental learning opportunities are important for one's professional growth and opportunities for collaboration. Professionals must maintain current awareness and knowledge of the latest assessment measures and interventions. Deaf clinicians do not have the same level of access to webinars, conferences, and local or national professional organizations as most hearing clinicians. Another vignette illustrates the obstacle encountered by deaf clinicians.

> Dr. Jenkins is a deaf psychologist seeking specialty training in an evidence-based therapy approach to build upon her skills in supporting clients who have experienced trauma. She found an upcoming 3-day training for which she registered. Upon registering, she requested ASL interpreters. The training organizers told her that they would look into hiring interpreters. Several days later, they replied that they could not find interpreters and that, unfortunately, this training did not focus on supporting deaf clients. They suggested that she obtain her training elsewhere. Dr. Jenkins decided that it wasn't worth her time to pursue training with people who were not interested in supporting her, so she cancelled her registration.

Stories like Dr. Jenkins's are common. In addition, even when there are mechanisms in place to access critical training needs, systemic barriers often burden deaf individuals by requiring them to identify and secure funding to support the accommodations and/or handle the everyday logistics of scheduling and coordinating with interpreter services. This additional burden has become what many consider a "disability tax" (Robinson & Henner, 2018). These added responsibilities add up and can easily become chronic stressors, given ongoing struggles for accessibility on both personal and professional levels.

Professional Considerations When Providing Mental Health Services for Deaf Children

The provision of mental health services for deaf children is complex and requires an understanding of both the unique factors relevant to providing clinical services for this population and an appreciation for the heterogeneity of deaf children regarding cultural affiliation, educational background, socioeconomic status, use of and fluency in various languages, levels of hearing loss, and the presence of additional disabilities. This reflects the need for head-to-head in addition to heart-to-heart understanding. Such knowledge and experience require specialized education and training, which ideally includes graduate study, supervised training, and continuing education (Braden, 2005). Deaf children may present with mental health concerns that are different from those of hearing children. Mental health professionals who are unfamiliar with unique issues risk providing inappropriate treatment or delaying appropriate care.

Professional Qualifications

It can be easy for clinicians without specialized training and experience in providing services to deaf children to overestimate their competence and overlook the unique considerations needed when working with this population. Unique considerations for working with deaf children include knowledge that communication and linguistic proficiency vary widely among children and the professionals who work with them. Ideally, communication and linguistic proficiency for professionals will include fluency in the child's primary language(s). Mental health professionals who do not know sign language may have limited knowledge about where to locate qualified interpreters or specialized assessment tools and how to use such resources, limiting their ability to provide appropriate care. For example, while a clinician may have the knowledge to provide direct access to communication, they may not be aware that best practices in providing language access include working with qualified interpreters, preparing interpreters prior to sessions, providing clear guidance on the role of the interpreter in the testing session (e.g., are they able to provide clarification or examples, or must that all be communicated directly by the clinician?), and debriefing with the interpreter after the assessment to obtain key cultural information that the clinician may have missed (Day et al., 2015; Wilkens, 2017). In the context of ongoing services, such as intervention, another best practice is having the same interpreters to reduce the cognitive load of the client to clarify terminology and context (Vernon & Miller, 2001). Those clinicians who may have foundational sign language skills may lack the necessary advanced skills in codeswitching to fit their client's specific communication abilities. For example, an adult learner of ASL may sign following English structure and have difficulty with ASL structure. This places increased demands on the deaf client's receptive language skills, and that increased cognitive load hinders the efficiency of the interaction dyad between the professional and the client. They are still subjected to other communicative variables that hinder a successful communication process.

In addition to assessing one's communication and linguistic competence, clinicians are responsible for assessing their own cultural knowledge and professional competence in working with deaf children. Specialization in providing services for deaf clients includes graduate study, supervised clinical practice, and ongoing familiarity with research on deaf populations (Braden, 2005; Brice et al., 2013). At Gallaudet University, there are graduate programs in school psychology, mental health counseling, social work, and clinical psychology that specialize in preparing mental health clinicians to work with deaf clients (Anderson et al., 2023; Dunne, 2013). Across the United States, there are several pre- and postdoctoral training programs where individuals can obtain supervised clinical training experience (Wilkins et al., 2022). Additionally, specialized professional networks are available for appropriate consultation (e.g., the American Psychological Association, the Division 22 Special Interest Group in Deafness, and the National Association of School Psychologists' Deaf and Hard of Hearing Interest Group). Another source of ongoing professional development is through relationships with colleagues who practice in this field and those with lived experience as a deaf person. Hearing clinicians who work in predominantly hearing settings are not likely to have colleagues who are deaf. These various aspects of specialized training and development highlight the need for clinicians to have enough knowledge to do an accurate self-assessment of their own professional qualifications and limitations. Another vignette demonstrates considerations for clinicians.

> A 9-year-old hard of hearing child was referred for a psychological evaluation due to academic delays. The child communicates via Simultaneous Communication (SimCom). The family lives in an area where there are few options for psychological services, and no options for services available directly in SimCom. They are assigned to a hearing clinician who has minimal training in and experience with testing deaf children. The psychologist is aware that they are underqualified to perform this evaluation and also recognizes the importance of this child being accurately evaluated to support their academic and treatment planning. The psychologist reaches out to a professional organization and is connected with another psychologist with expertise in evaluating DHH children using both signed and spoken language. Both psychologists discuss the case, and together they develop an evaluation plan, including gathering appropriate background information, developing a battery to address referral questions, and planning to ensure appropriate language access during the evaluation via qualified and well-prepared interpreters, suitable to this individual's communication needs.

In the above scenario, the clinician acknowledged their limitations in working with deaf children and sought appropriate consultation. This process requires conducting an accurate self-assessment and having a professional network available to locate a qualified consultant. Together, the clinician and the consultant were able to identify the information that needed to be gathered, identify appropriate measures, and set up communication for the evaluation. It is important to note that some clinicians may work routinely with deaf children, while others will work with them on infrequent occasions; their experiences and the level of their linguistic and cultural backgrounds will play an important role in determining the level of support needed.

Considerations of Deaf Child Development

Working with children requires an appreciation of the complexity of a child's language skills. The clinician must understand the child's linguistic background and language proficiency and incorporate communication strategies that are effective for the child. When providing clinical services for a deaf child, it is imperative to identify the best way to communicate based on the child's preferred communication and linguistic proficiency. Knowledge of a deaf child's preferred modality does not necessarily provide information about their level of proficiency in that language. The language development of a deaf child is not linear, and language acquisition milestones are varied compared to hearing counterparts *if* the child's language acquisition is delayed (Mayberry et al., 2002; Mayberry & Kluender, 2018; Newport, 1990). Collecting information about the communication environments at home, school, and other settings important to the child is critical. This includes an in-depth understanding of not only the hearing status and language use of others in the environment, but also how much access one has to language. For example, one might assume that a deaf child with deaf parents has had full language access from birth, but this may not always be the case, depending on the parents' language history and skills and the communication strategies used within the family.

The impact of language deprivation applies to every deaf child regardless of communication modality (e.g., gestures, home signs, sign language, speech-based, using assistive technology) and their hearing levels. The prevalence of this problem has only been more recently widely understood and discussed. The impact of this phenomenon goes much deeper than the quality and quantity of one's language acquisition. A child's global development—cognition, social-emotional skills, and physical health—is also proportionally impacted, which increases the complex nature of the assessment (M. L. Hall et al., 2017; Kushalnagar et al., 2020). Clinicians who work with a sign language interpreter are cautioned against asking the interpreter to evaluate the child's language proficiency, given that interpreter training is not centered on evaluating language proficiency. The same may be true for a deaf mental health clinician. Being deaf does not imply that one is qualified to assess language proficiency either. Instead, language assessments should be conducted by professionals who have expertise (e.g., language or communication specialists) (Glickman et al., 2020). This is indeed rare, and having a professional evaluate a child based on the child's background is important to obtaining critical information regarding everyday communication skills and identifying if communication delays or disorders are present. The following scenario exemplifies this.

> Casey is a 7-year-old deaf child with hearing parents who have taken several sign language classes and use some signs at home, although they rely mainly on spoken language. Casey has attended a deaf school and utilized ASL since he was 4 years old. Casey is presently showing language and academic delays and has been referred by his educational team for a psychoeducational evaluation. The school psychologist assigned to the case recognized the complexity of the child's language background, and prior to the evaluation, he conducted a classroom observation, interviewed the student's parents to further understand language access in the home, reviewed audiological records, and consulted with the student's teacher and speech and language therapist to gather information about the child's language needs for the evaluation. Based on the information collected prior to the evaluation, the psychologist decided that it was important to have a certified Deaf interpreter (CDI) available during the assessment to ensure that Casey had adequate language access.

Often, language profiles for deaf children are complex. Failure to understand potential issues that may be related to language deprivation can lead to misdiagnosis and ineffective treatment. Thoughtful reflection about one's areas of competence and development, coupled with sensitivity to issues that may uniquely impact deaf children promotes effective mental health services.

Considerations Using Sign Language Interpreters in Assessment

Hearing sign language interpreters are trained to work in various situations and settings. Most often, their training is geared toward deaf adults with a solid language foundation. Interpreting training programs and professional development opportunities for specializing in mental health settings and/or with children is rare. There is a specialized certification and training to work in medical settings and mental health provided by the St. Catherine University, CATIE Center in Minnesota (CATIE, n.d.) and the Mental Health Interpreter Training Project that is a partnership between the Alabama Department of Mental Health's Office of Deaf Services and the American Deafness and Rehabilitation Association (MHIT, 2023). Providing mental health services for children requires a unique set of skills, and training and mentoring in this area is limited due to the challenge of identifying training settings that include children.

Too often, deaf children experience widespread language deprivation or lack of accessible linguistic models in their early formative years. These children are linguistically impoverished where their language mastery or the range of sign vocabulary is less than their hearing peers of the same age. Their language skills and needs can be challenging to disentangle by non-native sign language users or those who do not have experience interacting with young deaf children. One often-overlooked but highly encouraged option is to include CDIs with mental health training in settings that serve deaf children. CDIs are deaf individuals and members of the deaf community trained to provide a wider range of communication and linguistic services. CDIs work in tandem with a hearing interpreter; having a CDI can reduce the potential for misinterpretation and increases the likelihood of better supporting a deaf child's language and communication needs (Boudreault, 2005; CASLI, 2022; RID, n.d.; WASLI, n.d.). The additional resources might be burdensome for many professionals, as discussed in the context of this chapter. However, their importance cannot be overstated, when working with individuals who are linguistically deprived or have "dysfluent language," particularly in cases related to medical, developmental, and psychiatric issues. The advantages of involving an expert far outweigh the potential drawbacks. An expert can prevent misdiagnoses, reduce the number of sessions or time required, and significantly enhance the bonding process between the professional and the client. This is especially true with the involvement of a qualified CDI (Glickman et al., 2020).

When interpreters are asked to interpret for psychological evaluations and/or administration of mental health assessments, they need to understand the purpose of the assessment, how the measures are to be administered, and how the interpretation of content may change the nature of the assessment (Bridgett, 2022; Vernon & Miller, 2001). In the context of treatment, interpreters should be prepared to know the goals of treatment, types of interventions being used, and background information relevant to the linguistic competence of the child. In these contexts, interpreters provide access for all parties but cannot administer psychological assessments or lead interventions without the support of a trained clinician. Additionally, interpreters should be prepared to manage their own personal reactions to exposure to mental health topics. They are not immune to experiencing vicarious trauma that may arise from discussing sensitive topics (Darroch & Dempsey, 2016).

Several linguistic factors may affect the integrity and equivalence of messages interpreted in sign language (Gutman, 2002; Vernon & Miller, 2001). For instance, paraphrasing or expanding the message to include additional examples can deviate from the standard administration of specific content. In the case of informant-report measures, the presence of a "live" person signing the questionnaire removes the value of textual neutrality, which can be very important for assessments. During the interpreting process, the use of schema is commonly integrated into the process. Interpreters are influenced by their personal experiences, cultural norms, or other factors. The transfer of a message from the source language to the target language can be biased by one's personal experience. Utilizing measures that have formal translations in ASL is the gold standard. However, there are very few tests that are available in sign language.

There is no research on how measures are affected by interpreting or translating from spoken to sign language. Using existing readability measures to determine the level of complexity of a written text is a common practice to determine if content will be understood at a specific age or grade level. There is no comparable method to evaluate the grammatical complexity of sign language that is suitable for a young deaf child. Additionally, content can be interpreted or translated literally from spoken language (e.g., using more literal messaging instead of spatial-visual grammar), or it may be interpreted incorporating the use of role shift or personification. The use of role shift and personification is often beneficial in conveying the message by using facial expressions, body language, and sign choices that mimic the characteristics of a particular entity, object, or concept. Other considerations include providing unintentional cues or answers to the client, such as by asking, "Show me how you brush your teeth." The act of mirroring the brushing event gives away the intended response, compared to the more neutral phrasing, "How do you clean your teeth?" which avoids specifying the method of cleaning. This is an example of how the lack of carefully adapted instruments can lead to inaccurate information, and potential misdiagnosis. It can be either helpful or harmful when used during an assessment. Take, for example, the case of Mariella.

> Mariella is referred for a psychological evaluation. The psychologist is fluent in sign language but recognizes she does not have the skills to communicate with the child. Fortunately, in their area, there are several CDIs available, but without specific training or certification in medical or mental health interpreting. The psychologist meets briefly with the CDI prior to the evaluation to explain the purpose. Once the evaluation gets underway, the CDI begins by providing additional examples that violate the standard administration procedures. Because the psychologist has sign skills, she is able to recognize that the additional examples and teaching provided by the CDI are not appropriate in this situation. She realizes that she did not adequately prepare the CDI for the assessment. She schedules a break and meets privately with the CDI to discuss standardization and the importance of allowing for expansion and examples to be directed by the psychologist.

Despite the best intention of the clinician and interpreter, the likelihood of this scenario happening is frequent. Administering psychological assessment has its own parameters that requires specialized trainings.

Current Practices in Assessment

Following the realization that the use of language-based measures to estimate the intellectual ability of many deaf individuals was not appropriate (Vernon, 2005), assessment practices shifted to utilizing nonverbal and/or language-reduced measures. This practice may provide more valid scores for performance-based skills such as spatial reasoning and pattern recognition, and it may reduce the confounds of language-based tests; however, it overlooks the child's language skills, which are crucial in supporting deaf children. Akamatsu et al. (2008) pointed out, "Nonverbal aptitude tests . . . may rule out global cognitive delays, but they tell us precious little about the strengths and weaknesses a particular student brings to the learning enterprise, nor about an individual's language capacity" (p. 144). This type of approach risks missing important areas of strength and/or weakness that cannot be identified via performance measures alone (Miller et al., 2015; Reesman et al., 2014).

In the context of limitations in tools and resources, Wilkins (2017) surveyed 30 licensed clinical psychologists and certified school psychologists who routinely provided psychological evaluations of deaf clients. Forty-three percent of the participants identified as deaf, hard of hearing, late-deafened, or as a sibling of a deaf adult. Most of the participants received some type of specialized training, such as supervised clinical experience, specialized degree programs, or specialized courses. Factors that participants most commonly identified to influence their test selection included recommendations from colleagues, comprehensiveness of the measure, and measures that have evidence of high reliability and validity with the deaf population and produce results that accurately reflect performance in real-life settings (Wilkens, 2017). The majority of the participants made adaptations or modifications to their administration for communication access. The main considerations for interpreting test results included the client's history and language access and ability. Approximately one-third of the participants utilized nonstandard assessments in their batteries, such as qualitative writing samples (Wilkens, 2017).

The principal challenges reported by the clinicians surveyed by Wilkens (2017) included finding appropriate measures/norms, test validity, knowledge of deafness by others in the field, and translation of measures into ASL. The clinicians used a variety of factors to determine the appropriate communication method for their assessments, including client preferences, the reason for referral, and the type of assessment being used. Other information influencing communication included audiological and speech and language evaluations/recommendations. There was a wide variety of use of interpreters, ranging from regularly using interpreters to support assessments to not using them at all. Interpreter types included hearing ASL interpreters, Deaf interpreters, Cued Speech transliterators, and oral interpreters. There was also a range of practices regarding a meeting with interpreters before and/or after the assessment (Wilkens, 2017). The next scenario illustrates the importance of carefully considering language needs and access for assessments.

Luis is a 17-year-old deaf student who immigrated to the United States 5 years ago from the Middle East. Luis was referred for a psychological reevaluation to support academic planning and upcoming transition services. Luis has been evaluated several times in the past, and each evaluation has utilized primarily nonverbal measures of intellectual functioning where his performance is below the average range compared to the normative sample. As Luis' educational team prepares to identify appropriate postgraduation supports for him, comprehensive information is needed regarding his visually-based and language-based reasoning skills and his adaptive functioning to identify settings that will be able to best support his daily living, vocational, and social needs. A deaf psychologist is hired to conduct the evaluation. This psychologist reviews his available academic and medical records and prepares a battery that will access the domains of visually-based reasoning, language skills, and adaptive functioning. The psychologist also hires a CDI to support communication during the evaluation, given the student's history of severe language deprivation.

Effects of Misdiagnoses

In the context of the complex linguistic backgrounds and skills of deaf children, and the limited assessment tools available to support evaluations, it is not surprising that misdiagnosis continues to be prevalent in the deaf youth community. While the field of mental health of deaf people has evolved to better appreciate the impacts of language access on development, the practices through which we identify and label issues such as language deprivation and/or disentangle issues that stem from lack of access to language from other developmental disorders continue to be severely lagging. The result of this can range from undetected diagnoses to inaccurate diagnoses; each of which can have far reaching impacts on one's life, as shown in the next vignette.

Eliza is a 12-year-old deaf student who attends public school and is placed in her district's DHH program. At school, she is instructed in ASL and written English. At home, her family communicates primarily via spoken English and gestures. Eliza was identified as deaf at age 2 and received early intervention services until she began public school in kindergarten when she was placed in their

> DHH program. Across the years, Eliza has struggled to complete grade-level curricula, has made only a few friends, and requires a lot of assistance to get through the school day. In years past, her educational team consistently attributed her academic, social, and daily living delays to her being deaf and passed her each year to the next grade. However, during her seventh grade year, her teacher pressed the education team to refer Eliza for a psychoeducational evaluation. The district's deaf psychologist completed this evaluation, and it was revealed that her nonverbal reasoning and adaptive functioning skills were below average. During the next Individualized Educational Planning (IEP) meeting, her team discussed adding additional diagnoses to her IEP and revising her annual goals.

Scenarios such as Eliza's are not uncommon for deaf individuals. The lifelong impacts of overlooking relevant diagnoses and/or educational needs, or providing incorrect diagnoses, cannot be overstated. The need for qualified mental health clinicians to support deaf children is apparent.

Recommendations

The following information provides specific recommendations for clinicians who provide mental health services to deaf children. The first subsection focuses on clinician-specific recommendations as they relate to knowledge and skills, and the second subsection addresses recommendations for clinical practice. This information is not an exhaustive list, nor is it intended to serve as a substitute for individualized planning and preparation for clients.

Clinician Training/Competence

Mental health assessment and treatment for deaf children are complex and require an understanding of both the unique factors relevant to providing clinical services for this population and an appreciation for the heterogeneity of deaf children regarding cultural affiliation, educational background, socioeconomic status, levels of hearing loss, use of and fluency in various languages, and the presence of additional disabilities. Such knowledge and experience require specialized education and training that focuses on deaf children, ideally including graduate study, supervised training, and continuing education (Braden, 2005; Brice et al., 2013; Wilkins et al., 2022). The following recommendations focus on clinician competence for working with deaf children, but do not address other intersectionalities with the deaf community. This further underscores the strong need for clinicians to recognize their areas of competence and limitations for any client, to request consultation and support where needed (Wilkins et al., 2022), and/or refer to outside providers if certain skills are beyond their competence level. In addition to formal training and education, the following additional recommendations are made regarding clinician competence:

- **Familiarize oneself with deaf people's lived experiences and the unique challenges faced by deaf children (Chovaz et al., 2022).** Understanding generational trauma among the deaf community is the first step toward dismantling systemic audism and gaining a deeper understanding of deaf people's place in society. This sort of understanding comes from ongoing interactions with deaf individuals, such as attending community events and social gatherings, being familiar with deaf stories, reading books, attending events, and even using social media platforms where lived experiences are shared. The importance of stories shared within the deaf community gives us a glimpse into deaf people's childhoods, which can be helpful in clinical settings and when interpreting assessment results.

- **Learn sign language and/or develop knowledge and skills for working with a qualified sign language interpreter.** Although learning sign language or working with an interpreter will likely not meet all linguistic needs, nor does it alleviate other necessary qualifications described earlier, it is an essential step in providing appropriate mental health services for deaf children. Further, it may help to develop a level of trust with the client. For clinicians not fluent in sign language, learning some basic conversational signs/phrases can be helpful in demonstrating respect for a client's language and building rapport. Clinicians will also need to know where and how to access qualified interpreters with appropriate credentials (e.g., mental health and working with children) and experiences, and how to utilize interpreters appropriately in their clinical work.
- **Familiarize oneself with the literature on deaf mental health.** Readers are referred to additional chapters in this textbook as a starting point as well as to the many scholarly references included herein. Other recommended texts include *Deaf Mental Health Care* edited by Glickman (2012), *Assessing Literacy in Deaf Individuals: Neurocognitive Measurement and Predictors* edited by Morere and Allen (2012), *Mental health and Deafness* by Du Feu and Chovaz (2014), *Psychological and Psychoeducational Assessment of Deaf and Hard of Hearing Children and Adolescents* edited by Miller and colleagues (2015), and *Language Deprivation and Deaf Mental Health* edited by Glickman and Hall (2018). Peer-reviewed journals that regularly publish scholarly work on Deaf mental health include the *Journal of Deaf Studies and Deaf Education*, *Rehabilitation Psychology*, and *Journal of the American Deafness and Rehabilitation Association.*
- **Seek resources and support from organizations specializing in working with deaf children.** Professionals should become aware of and seek possible involvement with national organizations that serve deaf children, such as the United Kingdom–based National Deaf Children's Society or the American Society for Deaf Children. They should also connect with professional networks within their respective field that include resources and/or colleagues who provide clinical services for deaf children, such as the American Psychological Association's Rehabilitation Psychology Special Interest Group on Deafness or the National Association for School Psychologists' Deaf and Hard of Hearing Interest Group. Such organizations can provide access to resources and training, as well as connections with colleagues with a wide range of experience and expertise.
- **Demonstrate skills in flexibility, adaptation, and clinical judgment (Wilkins, 2019).** Clinicians may need a dynamic approach to psychological testing that includes testing the limits, for example, where after attempting standardized administration of a measure, they try alternative approaches to evaluate if additional support is helpful. They may also need to unexpectedly revise their testing battery based on the client's performance. This requires that one have the knowledge and skills to administer tests that were unplanned. Further, the psychologists in Wilkens' (2019) study reported often taking on roles and responsibilities that were outside of their specific job requirements, like case management and attending IEP meetings. This might include creative ways of scheduling to include time for these additional support opportunities and/or budget planning to account for time that may not get reimbursed by third-parties.

Clinical Practice

The provision of mental health services includes a variety of activities, including assessment, intervention, and consultation. The recommendations that follow are intended to provide practical considerations for everyday work.

- Utilize a multimodal approach for assessment. The American Psychological Association recommends a multimodal approach to assessment for persons with disabilities, which includes clinical interviews, behavior observations, collateral interviews with family/caregivers/others in their daily life, and review of records (APA, 2022, Guideline 17). This is particularly true when working with deaf children. Given the limitations of many of the assessment tools that are available, obtaining information from multiple sources is crucial.
- Conduct a thorough clinical interview. Whether supporting assessment or treatment, conducting a thorough clinical interview that accounts for unique language and communication factors is crucial. Unique language and communication factors include the age of identification of being deaf, degree and etiology of hearing loss, age of onset, presence of additional neurological factors, parental hearing status, communication modalities used in the child's environment(s), communication modalities used by the child, parental/caregiver communication abilities, opportunities for accessible social interaction, language support services, and educational placements (Braden, 2005; M. L. Hall & De Anda, 2022; Hill-Briggs et al., 2007; Maller & Braden, 2010). The Language Access Profile Tool and the Deaf of Hard of Hearing Language Exposure Assessment Tool (Hall, 2020; Hall & De Anda, 2022) are two tools that may be useful in collecting robust language histories for children. Thorough knowledge of a child's language history will support the clinician's understanding of the quality and quantity of language input that the child is receiving in their everyday environment (Hall, 2020; Hall & De Anda, 2022) and can help support differential diagnosis.
- Design culturally and linguistically appropriate test batteries for assessment and determine necessary test accommodations or modifications. Interpreting a test into ASL does not necessarily mean it will be accessible to a deaf child or that it will be testing the construct that it was intended to measure. Instructions for many tasks, even those that are language-reduced, are often language-heavy. Even when appropriately translated, instructions may not be clear to the child (Day et al.,2015; Guthmann et al., 2017). Additionally, the practice of translating instructions or items from one language modality to another may impact the underlying skill being assessed. For example, digit span tasks can be interpreted from a spoken language to a sign language. However, research has shown that the average amount of information a person can recall in sign language is shorter than a person can recall in spoken language because of the modality of the stimulus (i.e., visual- rather than auditory-based information) and not because of a deficit in working memory skills (Boutla et al., 2004). Thus, comparison to normative data may underestimate working memory skills and normative data on sign spans is needed.
- Utilize the framework from Reesman and colleagues (2014) to evaluate the appropriateness of individual measures for the client. Following this framework, clinicians can evaluate whether the measure provides (a) administration and accommodations guidance, (b) score

interpretation guidance, (c) a well-described group of children who are deaf, (d) empirical reports of children who are deaf and/or empirical assessment of possible bias. Depending on the nature of the evaluation, meeting certain criteria may be more important than others and can help guide one's test selection. Additionally, Hillbriggs et al. (2007) provide examples of commonly used measures with deaf individuals based on the functional areas of assessment with limitations and precautions for their use.

- Conduct an assessment in the client's most effective language(s) and/or communication modality and interpret results in light of the client's history and accommodations/ modifications made (Wilkins et al., 2022). When testing deaf children, standardized administration of measures is generally altered to make communication accessible (Braden, 1994; Maller, 2003). Document the use of test modifications (e.g., restating instructions for clarification, providing additional teaching opportunities to ensure comprehension of instructions) and clearly state limitations of interpretations based on nonstandard administration procedures. If utilizing interpreters, ensure interpreters are hired with the requisite skills needed for the evaluation. Consider including CDIs on the interpreting team, if warranted by the client's language background and skill level. Meet with interpreters before and after the assessment/session to ensure they are adequately prepared to support the evaluation and that they have time to provide observations/ information that was not able to be conveyed during the evaluation. Consultation with teachers and parents is important but not a substitute for the appropriate use of a qualified interpreter (Arroyos et al., 2018).
- Provide intervention services in the client's preferred language. Clinicians are responsible to ensure that the client has language access during their treatment. Relying on family members to relay information or provide interpretation is not appropriate. For sessions where interpreters are utilized, work with interpreters with training and experience in mental health and working with children. Providing a consistent interpreting team throughout treatment services is strongly recommended. Interpreters should be adequately prepped prior to the start of sessions and provided with an opportunity to debrief with clinicians following the session. In addition to considerations about which language to use and whether interpreters are needed, clinicians need to be sensitive to environmental factors that may affect a client's language access (e.g., background noise, visibility of one's face) and the varied ways through which clients may best learn information (e.g., use of visuals to convey concepts).

Future Directions

In many ways, mental health assessment and treatments for deaf children have improved significantly, yet ample work remains. Ongoing systemic barriers to the well-being of all deaf individuals need to be dismantled, which includes greater access to qualified mental health providers and ongoing efforts within the community to rebuild trust in healthcare systems. The decline of Deaf schools has led to a decrease in specialized services. This, along with the linguistic and cultural diaspora of deaf children, exemplifies the challenges in assessing their mental health. Significant work remains to be done within the area of language deprivation. Research is needed to identify valid and reliable criteria for diagnosing language deprivation, and on the developmental impacts of language deprivation. Without these pieces, significant progress toward eliminating language deprivation will be difficult. Additionally, there is a need for guidelines about who is qualified to work with deaf clients so that clinicians can more accurately assess their competency in this area. These gaps highlight the need for clinicians and allied professionals to continue to work together to provide quality mental health services for deaf children.

References

Akamatsu, C. T., Mayer, C., & Hardy-Braz, S. (2008). Why considerations of verbal aptitude are important in educating deaf and hard-of-hearing students. In M. Marschark & P. C. Hauser (Eds.), *Deaf cognition: Foundations and outcomes* (p. 131–169). Oxford University Press. https://doi.org/10.1093/acprof:oso/9780195368673.003.0005

American Educational Research Association (AERA), American Psychological Association (APA), & National Council on Measurement in Education (NCME). (2014). *Standards for educational and psychological testing.* American Educational Research Association. https://www.aera.net/Publications/Books/Standards-for-Educational-Psychological-Testing-2014-Edition

Americans with Disabilities Act (ADA) Amendments Act of 2008, Pub. L. No. 110-325, 122 Stat. 3553 (2008). https://www.govinfo.gov/app/details/PLAW-110publ325

Anderson, M. L., Riker, T., & Wilkins, A. M. (2023). Application of the truth and reconciliation model to meaningfully engage deaf sign language users in the research process. *Cultural Diversity and Ethnic Minority Psychology, 29*(1), 15–23. https://doi.org/10.1037/cdp0000445

American Psychological Association (APA). (2017). *Ethical principles of psychologists and code of conduct.* https://www.apa.org/ethics/code

American Psychological Association (APA). (2022). *APA guidelines for assessment and intervention with persons with disabilities.* https://www.apa.org/about/policy/guidelines-assessment-intervention-disabilities.pdf

Arroyos, A., Diaz, D., & Torres, I. (2018). *Best practices in collaborating with interpreters: Lessons learned.* National Association of School Psychologists (NASP). https://www.nasponline.org/publications/periodicals/communique/issues/volume-46-issue-5/best-practices-in-collaborating-with-interpreters-lessons-learned

Barfield, K., & Martinelli, L. (2021). *School-based health centers and mental health access among minority and low-socioeconomic adolescents.* Poster presented at the Mercer University Atlanta Research Conference, April 10, 2021. Mercer University Libraries. https://galileo-mum.primo.exlibrisgroup.com/discovery/fulldisplay/alma991005673682805956/01GALI_MUM:MainLibrary

Barrett, G. E. (2020). *An exploration of questions as they apply to signing and oral deaf children participating in the baseline session of parent-child interaction therapy (PCIT)* [Doctoral diss., Gallaudet University]. Proquest. https://www.proquest.com/docview/2377677631?fromopenview=true&pq-origsite=gscholar

Bauman, H.-D. L. (2004). Audism: Exploring the metaphysics of oppression. *Journal of Deaf Studies and Deaf Education, 9*(2), 239–246. https://doi.org/10.1093/deafed/enh025

Baynton, D. C. (1996). *Forbidden signs: American culture and the campaign against sign language.* University of Chicago Press.

Benton, T. D., Boyd, R. C., & Njoroge, W. F. (2021). Addressing the global crisis of child and adolescent mental health. *JAMA Pediatrics, 175*(11), 1108–1110.

Boudreault, P. (2005). Deaf interpreters. In T. Janzen (Ed.), *Benjamins Translation Library* (vol. 63, pp. 323–355). John Benjamins. https://doi.org/10.1075/btl.63.17bou

Boutla, M., Supalla, T., Newport, E. L., & Bavelier, D. (2004). Short-term memory span: Insights from sign language. *Nature Neuroscience, 7*(9), 997–1002. https://doi.org/10.1038/nn1298

Braden, J. P. (1994). *Deafness, deprivation, and IQ.* Springer Science & Business Media.

Braden, J. P. (2005). Hard-of-hearing and deaf clients: Using the WISC-IV with clients who are hard-of-hearing or deaf. In A. Prifitera, L. G. Weiss, & D. H. Saklofske (Eds.), *WISC-IV clinical use and interpretation: A volume of practical resources for the metal health professional* (pp. 351–380). Academic Press.

Brice, P. J., Leigh, I. W., Sheridan, M., & Smith, K. (2013). Training of mental health professionals: Yesterday, today, and tomorrow. In N. S. Glickman (Ed.), *Deaf mental health care* (pp. 298–322). Routledge.

Bridgett, T. N. (2022). *American Sign Language translation of the VCI from WISC-V* [Doctoral diss., Gallaudet University]. ProQuest. https://www.proquest.com/openview/cc0c646d453e2880b5410 48055a6a040/1?pq-origsite=gscholar&cbl=18750&diss=y

Caselli, N. K., Lieberman, A. M., & Pyers, J. E. (2020). The ASL-CDI 2.0: An updated, normed adaptation of the MacArthur Bates Communicative Development Inventory for American Sign Language. *Behavior Research Methods*, *52*(5), 2071–2084. https://doi.org/10.3758/s13428-020-01376-6

Canadian Association of Sign Language Interpreters (CASLI). (2022). *CASLI - Deaf Interpreter Position Paper*. https://www.casli.ca/page-18143

CATIE Center, St. Catherine University. (n.d.). *Mental and behavioral health interpreting*. CATIE Center. https://www.stkate.edu/academics/shas/asl-interpreting-department/catie-center

Chovaz, C. J., Russell, D., & Daly, B. (2022). Lived experiences of deaf Canadians: What we want you to know! *Canadian Psychology / Psychologie Canadienne*, *63*(4), 651–666. https://doi.org/10.1037/cap0000313

Costa, E. A., Day, L., Caverly, C., Mellon, N., Ouellette, M., & Wilson Ottley, S. (2019). Parent–child interaction therapy as a behavior and spoken language intervention for young children with hearing loss. *Language, Speech, and Hearing Services in Schools*, *50*(1), 34–52. https://doi.org/10.1044/2018_LSHSS-18-0054

Crowe, T. V. (2002). Translation of the Rosenberg Self-Esteem Scale into American Sign Language: A principal components analysis. *Social Work Research*, *26*(1), 57–63.

Dammeyer, J. (2010). Psychosocial development in a Danish population of children with cochlear implants and deaf and hard-of-hearing children. *Journal of Deaf Studies and Deaf Education*, *15*(1), 50–58. https://doi.org/10.1093/deafed/enp024

Darroch, E., & Dempsey, R. (2016). Interpreters' experiences of transferential dynamics, vicarious traumatization, and their need for support and supervision: A systematic literature review. *The European Journal of Counselling Psychology*, *4*(2), 166–190.

Day, L. A., Costa, E. A., Previ, D., & Caverly, C. (2018). Adapting parent–child interaction therapy for deaf families that communicate via American Sign Language: A formal adaptation approach. *Cognitive and Behavioral Practice*, *25*(1), 7–21. https://doi.org/10.1016/j.cbpra.2017.01.008

Day, L. A., Adams Costa, E. B., Raiford, S. E. (2015). *Testing children who are deaf or hard of hearing* (Wechsler Intelligence Scale for Children, Fifth Edition, Technical Report No. 2). Pearson. https://www.pearsonassessments.com/content/dam/school/global/clinical/us/assets/wisc-v/wisc-v-technical-report-2.pdf?srsltid=AfmBOoorvaxebj6B16UnhMgN5N9kB65JBNvSjxGZcHbuTeiTHY3bXIU2

DeSa, S., Gebremeskel, A. T., O. Omonaiye, & Yaya, S. (2020). Barriers and facilitators to access mental health services among refugee women in high-income countries: Study systematic review. *Systematic Reviews*, *1*, Article 62. https://doi.org/10.1186/s13643-022-01936-1

Dowtin, L. L., & Day, L. A. (2019). Signs and barriers: Play therapy training experiences of deaf and hearing clinicians. *International Journal of Play Therapy*, *28*(4), 195–206. https://doi.org/10.1037/pla0000105

Du Feu, M., & Chovaz, C. (2014). *Mental health and deafness*. Oxford University Press.

Dunne, C. M. (2013). *Deaf/LGBTQ intersectional invisibility in schools: The lived experiences of deaf lesbian students of color at a school for the deaf* [Doctoral diss., University of Pennsylvania]. Proquest. https://www.proquest.com/openview/025fba0890d61c3016df3e613fb6ecbc/1?pq-origsite=gscholar&cbl=18750

Eckert, R. C., & Rowley, A. J. (2013). Audism: A theory and practice of audiocentric privilege. *Humanity and Society*, *37*(2), 101–130. https://doi.org/10.1177/0160597613481731

Enns, C. E., Zimmer, K., & Boudreault, P. (2013). *American Sign Language Receptive Skills Test*. Northern Signs Research, Inc. https://northernsignsresearch.com/american-sign-language-receptive-skills-test/

Fellinger, J., Holzinger, D., & Pollard, R. (2012). Mental health of deaf people. *The Lancet, 379*(9820), 1037–1044. https://doi.org/10.1016/S0140-6736(11)61143-4

Gaffney, M., Eichwald, J., Grosse, S. D., & Mason, C. A. (2010). *Identifying infants with hearing loss—United States, 1999—2007* (Morbidity and Mortality Weekly Report). Centers for Disease Control and Prevention. https://www.cdc.gov/mmwr/preview/mmwrhtml/mm5908a2.htm

Gertz, G. (2008). Dysconscious audism: A theoretical proposition. In H. D. L. Bauman (Ed.), *Open your eyes: Deaf studies talking* (pp. 219–234). University of Minnesota Press.

Glickman, N. S. (Ed.). (2012). *Deaf mental health care*. Routledge. https://doi.org/10.4324/9780203810545

Glickman, N. S., Crump, C., & Hamerdinger, S. (2020). language deprivation is a game changer for the clinical specialty of deaf mental health. *Journal of American Deafness and Rehabilitation Association, 54*(1), 54–89.

Glickman, N. S., & Hall, W. C. (Eds.), *Language deprivation and deaf mental health*. Routledge/Taylor & Francis Group.

Goodman, R. (1997). The Strengths and Difficulties Questionnaire: A research note. *Journal of Child Psychology and Psychiatry, 38*(5), 581–586.

Gulati, S. (2018). Language deprivation syndrome. In N. S. Glickman (Ed.), *Language Deprivation and Deaf Mental Health* (1st ed., pp. 24–46). Routledge. https://doi.org/10.4324/9781315166728

Guthmann, D., Titus, J., Embree, J., & Wilson, J. (2017). Translation and validation of an online suite of assessments in American Sign Language. *Journal of American Deafness and Rehabilitation Association, 51*(1), 12–20.

Gutman, V. (2002). *Ethics in mental health and deafness*. Gallaudet University Press.

Hall, M. L. (2020). the input matters: Assessing cumulative language access in deaf and hard of hearing individuals and populations. *Frontiers in Psychology, 11*, Article 1407. https://doi.org/10.3389/fpsyg.2020.01407

Hall, M. L., & De Anda, S. (2022). *Estimating early language input in deaf and hard of hearing children with the Language Access Profile Tool*. American Journal of Speech-Language Pathology, 31(5), 2132–2144.

Hall, M. L., Eigsti, I.-M., Bortfeld, H., & Lillo-Martin, D. (2017). Auditory deprivation does not impair executive function, but language deprivation might: Evidence from a parent-report measure in deaf native signing children. *Journal of Deaf Studies and Deaf Education, 22*(1), 9–21. https://doi.org/10.1093/deafed/enw054

Hall, W. C., Levin, L. L., & Anderson, M. L. (2017). Language deprivation syndrome: A possible neurodevelopmental disorder with sociocultural origins. *Social Psychiatry and Psychiatric Epidemiology, 52*(6), 761–776. https://doi.org/10.1007/s00127-017-1351-7

Haug, T. (2011). Approaching sign language test construction: Adaptation of the German Sign Language Receptive Skills Test. *Journal of Deaf Studies and Deaf Education, 16*(3), 343–361. https://doi.org/10.1093/deafed/enq062

Hauser, P. C., Paludneviciene, R., Riddle, W., Kurz, K. B., Emmorey, K., & Contreras, J. (2016). American Sign Language Comprehension Test: A tool for sign language researchers. *Journal of Deaf Studies and Deaf Education, 21*(1), 64–69. https://doi.org/10.1093/deafed/env051

Henner, J., Reis, J., & Hoffmeister, R. (2018). Using standardized, receptive ASL assessments in deaf mental health. In N. S. Glickman (Ed.), *Language deprivation and deaf mental health* (1st ed., pp. 160–176). Routledge. https://doi.org/10.4324/9781315166728

Herman, R., Holmes, S., Woll, B., Schembri, A., Hodge, G., & Rogers, I. (2014). *Assessing Auslan (Australian sign language) development: The Auslan Receptive Skills Test and Productive Skills Test [assessment tool]*. Victorian Deaf Education Institute.

Hill-Briggs, F., Dial, J., Morere, D., & Joyce, A. (2007). Neuropsychological assessment of persons with physical disability, visual impairment or blindness, and hearing impairment or deafness. *Archives of Clinical Neuropsychology, 22*(3), 389–404. https://doi.org/10.1016/j.acn.2007.01.013

Hoffmeister, R. J., Fish, S., Benedict, R., Henner, J., Novogrodsky, R., & Rosenburg, P. (2015). *American Sign Language Assessment Instrument (ASLAI): Unpublished instrument*. Boston University Center for the Study of Communication and the Deaf.

Holcomb, T. K. (2013). *Introduction to American deaf culture*. Oxford University Press.

Johnson, P., Cawthon, S., Fink, B., Wendel, E., & Schoffstall, S. (2018). Trauma and resilience among deaf individuals. *The Journal of Deaf Studies and Deaf Education, 23*(4), 317–330. https://doi.org/10.1093/deafed/eny024

Kushalnagar, P., Ryan, C., Paludneviciene, R., Spellun, A., & Gulati, S. (2020). Adverse childhood communication experiences associated with an increased risk of chronic diseases in adults who are deaf. *American Journal of Preventive Medicine, 59*(4), 548–554. https://doi.org/10.1016/j.amepre.2020.04.016

Lane, H. L. (1999). *The mask of benevolence: Disabling the deaf community.* DawnSignPress.

Leigh, I. W., & Pollard, R. Q. (2012). Mental health and deaf adults. In M. Marschark & P. E. Spencer (Eds.), *The Oxford handbook of deaf studies, language, and education, Volume 1, Second Edition* (2nd ed., pp. 214–226). Oxford University Press. https://doi.org/10.1093/oxfordhb/9780199750986.013.0016

Maller, S. J. (2003). Intellectual assessment of deaf people. In M. Marschark & P. E. Spencer (Eds.), *Oxford handbook of deaf studies, language, and education, Volume 1, Second Edition* (2nd ed., pp. 451–63). Oxford University Press.

Maller, S. J., & Braden, P. (2010). Intellectual assessment of deaf people: A critical review of core concepts. In In M. Marschark & P. E. Spencer (Eds.), *Oxford handbook of deaf studies, language, and education* (vol. 1, 2nd ed., pp. 473–485). Oxford University Press.

Mann, W., & Marshall, C. (2012). Investigating deaf children's vocabulary knowledge in British Sign Language: Vocabulary development in sign language. *Language Learning, 62*(4), 1024–1051. https://doi.org/10.1111/j.1467-9922.2011.00670.x

Mann, W., Roy, P., & Morgan, G. (2016). Adaptation of a vocabulary test from British Sign Language to American Sign Language. *Language Testing, 33*(1), 3–22. https://doi.org/10.1177/0265532215575627

Mannarino, A. P., Cohen, J. A., & Deblinger, E. (2014). Trauma-focused cognitive-behavioral therapy. In S. Timmer & A. Urquiza (Eds.), *Evidence-based approaches for the treatment of maltreated children: Considering core components and treatment effectiveness* (pp. 165–185). Springer.

Mayberry, R. I., & Kluender, R. (2018). Rethinking the critical period for language: New insights into an old question from American Sign Language. *Bilingualism: Language and Cognition, 21*(5), 886–905.

Mayberry, R. I., Lock, E., & Kazmi, H. (2002). Linguistic ability and early language exposure. *Nature, 417*(6884), Article 38. https://doi.org/10.1038/417038a

McNeil, C. B., Hembree-Kigin, T. L., & Anhalt, K. (2010). *Parent-child interaction therapy.* Springer.

McQuarrie, L., & Abbott, M. (2012). Bilingual deaf students' phonological awareness in ASL and reading skills in English. *Sign Language Studies, 14*(1), 80–100. https://doi.org/10.1353/sls.2013.0028

Mental Health Interpreter Training (MHIT). (n.d.) *Alabama's mental health interpreter training project: A partnership between the Alabama Department of Mental Health's Office of Deaf Services and ADARA.* http://www.mhit.org/.

Miller, M. S., Thomas-Presswood, T. N., Metz, K., & Lukomski, J. (2015). *Psychological and psychoeducational assessment of deaf and hard of hearing children and adolescents.* Gallaudet University Press.

Morere, D. A., & Allen, T. (Eds.). (2012). *Assessing literacy in deaf individuals: Neurocognitive measurement and predictors.* Springer Science + Business Media. https://doi.org/10.1007/978-1-4614-5269-0

Newport, E. L. (1990). Maturational constraints on language learning. Cognitive Science, *14*(1), 11–28.

Plimmer, C. (2018). *Translating the Strengths and Difficulties Questionnaire into American Sign Language: A pilot study* [Undergraduate honors theses, King's University College]. https://ir.lib.uwo.ca/psychK_uht/75

Powell, B., Cooper, G., Hoffman, K., & Marvin, B. (2013). *The circle of security intervention: Enhancing attachment in early parent-child relationships.* Guilford publications.

Previ, D. (2018). *Parent-Child Interaction Therapy Dyadic Parent-Child Interaction Coding System (DPICS): Interrater reliability with live versus video coding* [Doctoral diss., Gallaudet University].

Quinto-Pozos, D., Singleton, J. L., Hauser, P. C., Levine, S. C., Garberoglio, C. L., & Hou, L. (2013). Atypical signed language development: A case study of challenges with visual–spatial processing. *Cognitive Neuropsychology, 30*(5), 332–359. https://doi.org/10.1080/02643294.2013.863756

Reesman, J. H., Day, L. A., Szymanski, C. A., Hughes-Wheatland, R., Witkin, G. A., Kalback, S. R., & Brice, P. J. (2014). Review of intellectual assessment measures for children who are deaf or hard of hearing. *Rehabilitation Psychology, 59*(1), 99–106. https://doi.org/10.1037/a0035829

Registry of Interpreters for the Deaf (RID). (n.d.). *Use of a Certified Deaf Interpreter; Standard Practice Paper.* Google Docs. https://drive.google.com/file/d/0B3DKvZMflFLdbXFLVVFsbmRzTVU/view?resourcekey=0-DOFwojDu1kIDMlsVKhi29g&usp=embed_facebook

Roberts, S., Wright, B., Moore, K., Smith, J., Allgar, V., Tennant, A., Doherty, C., Hughes, E., Moore, D. C., Ogden, R., Phillips, H., Beese, L., & Rogers, K. (2015). Translation into British Sign Language and validation of the Strengths and Difficulties Questionnaire. *Health Services and Delivery Research, 3*(2), 1–96. https://doi.org/10.3310/hsdr03020

Robinson, O., & Henner, J. (2018). Authentic voices, authentic encounters: Cripping the university through American Sign Language. *Disability Studies Quarterly, 38*(4). https://doi.org/10.18061/dsq.v38i4.6111

Rodgers, C. R. R., Flores, M. W., Bassey, O., Augenblick, J. M., & Lê Cook, B. (2022). Racial/ethnic disparity trends in children's mental health care access and expenditures from 2010-2017: Disparities remain despite sweeping policy reform. *Journal of the American Academy of Child & Adolescent Psychiatry, 61*(7), 915–925.

Schooler, D., Day, L. A., Maynard, S., Rosier, R., Pabon, A., Miller, C. A., & Wagner, K. (2021). Becoming psychologists: Barriers and bridges encountered by deaf and hard of hearing students in education and training settings. *Journal of American Deafness and Rehabilitation Association, 54*(2), Article 4.

Simms, L., Baker, S., & Clark, M. D. (2013). The standardized visual communication and sign language checklist for signing children. *Sign Language Studies, 14*(1), 101–124. https://doi.org/10.1353/sls.2013.0029

Vargas, S. M., Huey, S. J., Jr., & Miranda, J. (2020). A critical review of current evidence on multiple types of discrimination and mental health. *American Journal of Orthopsychiatry, 90*(3), 374–390.

Vernon, M. (2005). Fifty years of research on the intelligence of deaf and hard-of-hearing children: A review of literature and discussion of implications. *Journal of Deaf Studies and Deaf Education, 10*(3), 225–231. https://doi.org/10.1093/deafed/eni024

Vernon, M., & Miller, K. (2001). Interpreting in mental health settings: Issues and concerns. *American Annals of the Deaf, 146*(5), 429–434. https://doi.org/10.1353/aad.2012.0200

Warner, E., Finn, H., Wescott, A., & Cook, A. (2020). *Transforming trauma in children and adolescents: An embodied approach to somatic regulation, trauma processing, and attachment-building.* North Atlantic Books.

Weine, S., Horvath Marques, A., Singh, M., & Pringle, B. (2020). Global child mental health research: Time for the children. *Journal of the American Academy of Child and Adolescent Psychiatry, 59*(11), 1208–1211.

World Association of Sign Language Interpreters (WASLI). (n.d.). *Deaf Interpreters.* https://wasli.org/special-interest/deaf-interpreters.

World Health Organization (WHO). (February 26, 2023). *Deafness and hearing loss.* https://www.who.int/en/news-room/fact-sheets/detail/deafness-and-hearing-loss#.

Wilkins, A. M. (2019). *Current practice of psychological assessment of deaf and hard of hearing clients: A focus group study* [Doctoral diss., Gallaudet University\. ProQuest. https://www.proquest.com/docview/2324921341?pq-origsite=summon

Wilkins, A. M., Morere, D. A., Pick, L. H., Day, L. A., & Anderson, M. L. (2022). Characteristics of psychologists assessing deaf and hard of hearing clients. *The Journal of Deaf Studies and Deaf Education, 27*(2), 115–124. https://doi.org/10.1093/deafed/enab039

Wilkins, E. (2017). *Current assessment practices: Common tests, adaptations, and approaches used in psychological assessment of deaf and hard-of-hearing clients* [Doctoral diss., Gallaudet University].

Wille, B., Allen, T., Van Lierde, K., & Van Herreweghe, M. (2020). Using the Adapted Flemish Sign Language Visual Communication and Sign Language Checklist. *Journal of Deaf Studies and Deaf Education, 25*(2), 188–198. https://doi.org/10.1093/deafed/enz039

6

Stories About Challenges Supporting the Mental Health of Deaf and Hard of Hearing Children and Hearing Children of Deaf Families

Veronica Bickle and Cathy J. Chovaz

Construct

When working with Deaf and Hard of Hearing (DHH) children and youth and sometimes hearing children from Deaf families (children of Deaf adults or Codas), it is often assumed that counseling with a Deaf, or signing, therapist will ensure effective outcomes. However, we have learned that although a shared language and intimate knowledge of cultural mores are very important, many other factors must be considered to support the mental health of these children. For example, it can be critical for successful outcomes to have culturally and linguistically psychological diagnostic assessments, the option of an accessible in-patient component, ongoing and significant family involvement, and appropriate counseling strategies specifically developed for deaf children. These factors are above and beyond having a therapist who shares the same language as the child. These factors are just a few that can make the counseling process with DHH children/youth and Codas very challenging.

The intent of this chapter is to share the stories we have experienced with DHH children/youth in our roles at a children's mental health program serving DHH children/youth and their families as well as Codas and their families. The confidentiality of each of our young clients has been protected with changes to their names, ethnicity, family composition, and gender. We have sought to preserve the essence of their stories as they were told to us. Following each story, the lead clinician at the PAH! Mental Health Program for Deaf and Hard of Hearing Children and Youth under the Bob Rumball Canadian Centre of Excellence for the Deaf in Ontario, Canada, and first author of this chapter, Veronica Bickle, has offered her reflections, identified challenges, and provided recommendations regarding what may have improved the process and outcome. It is our hope that this chapter will educate, inform, and further our understanding of the complexities and challenges involved in supporting the mental health of DHH children and youth.

Head-to-Head and Heart-to-Heart

Through our work with DHH children, Codas, and their families, we have become very aware of some key issues, including a critical need for head-to-head information that clearly identifies the challenges facing counselors working with DHH children/youth and Codas. This means having a comprehensive understanding of some of the linguistic, developmental, and mental health differences that may impact the counseling process. The reader is encouraged to read chapters 4 and 5 in this textbook for a more detailed summary of these differences as well as specific strategies that may be useful.

Some of these challenges will be highlighted throughout this chapter as the reader reads the stories. For example, counselors in mainstream agencies working with hearing children typically assume that the children/youth have a solid foundation in language acquisition and theory of mind (ToM). This allows counseling strategies to be implemented that utilize dialogue turn-taking and some degree of introspection. However, within our program, we have become very aware of the profound impact of language deprivation, or the lack of full access to language, which is very much associated with differences in the development of ToM. Additional challenges that we have observed, such as lack of incidental learning and the differences in attachment with parents of DHH children and Deaf parents, means that traditional counseling which maybe be effective with hearing children often fails the DHH child/youth, or the hearing child/youth from a Deaf family.

We also feel there is a critical need for heart-to-heart sharing from the perspectives of the DHH child or Coda, their family members, their teachers, and the counselor themselves. It has become evident to us that often the DHH child may not developmentally, linguistically, or intellectually be able to tell their stories in ways that make sense to their parents, teachers, or doctors, especially if there is not a shared language. As such, it is our hope that sharing our stories in this chapter may bridge that gap and raise awareness of some of the challenges facing the DHH child or Coda and their families.

Statements of Reflexivity

First Author: Veronica Bickle

I am a culturally Deaf white woman, born to a Deaf mother and hearing father in a family who first used signed English and then later switched to American Sign Language (ASL) when my hearing siblings and I were children. I grew up at a provincial school for the Deaf, took some courses in the mainstreamed high school environment, and then attended university in Canada, graduating with a bachelor of arts degree in law and a master's degree in social work. I worked for many years in the social work field with DHH adults and then transitioned a few years ago to work with DHH children and youth and hearing children of Deaf families. I also volunteered with various organizations within the heart of the Deaf community for many years. Based on my life experiences, when it comes to my head and my heart, I am "at home" when working with this group of people.

Second Author: Cathy J. Chovaz

I acknowledge my view as a deafened, white female clinical psychologist. I was deafened as a young adult and grew up with spoken English as my first language and, as such, do not share the same early experiences of many of my patients. After becoming deaf, I learned American Sign Language (ASL) as a second language and culture. I identify with the tenets of hearing culture, as that was my first language and culture, yet also identify with and appreciate many of the tenets of a visual world and signed language. My reflection of the head-to-head information comes from decades of study in this area, and my appreciation of the heart-to-heart comes from intentional reflection of stories as they have been told to me by DHH patients and their families as well as my own life experience.

Recommendations

We have included recommendations throughout the chapter related to each story told and close the chapter with recommendations that we feel are important to address the challenges clinicians may face when supporting the mental health of DHH children/youth, Codas, and their families.

When one considers the popular saying that "it takes a village to raise a child," one needs to consider what this "village" looks like for the DHH child/youth. Since language is the medium of how people in this "village" communicate with and raise their children and youth, this community will look very different for many DHH children and youth. When access to language in their environment is considerably limited, it potentially creates a deficiency of opportunities for skill-building that is needed to promote and maintain the healthy development of mental health, resilience, and overall emotional well-being. This developmental and linguistic scaffolding in a child's life is not something that counseling alone can resolve.

One may question how can counseling can even begin when the child/youth does not share a language, much less a conceptual framework for "what we are doing here?" Unfortunately, our mental health program is funded only for counseling, relying on the assumption that it alone can "fix" the DHH child/youth like it does in many mainstream counseling environments. For some DHH children and youth, and for most Codas, it may be enough. Unfortunately, there are many cases where counseling alone is literally impossible. Even so, our program still tries to provide support with the goal of improving the child's quality of life and to provide a safe space for them with a focus on developing ToM skills, emotional regulation skills, interpersonal skills, and psychoeducation through the use of stories told in ASL, role-playing, and play therapy in addition to yet often traditional counseling techniques derived from cognitive or dialectical behavioral therapy.

An academic search using the words "counseling (or counselling) deaf children" reveals surprisingly few entries specifically dedicated to DHH children. There appears to be a paucity of published journals, articles, and books directly focusing on the challenges involved in counseling DHH children, yet there are considerable references for counseling strategies with DHH adults. An online library search at Gallaudet University (considered a mecca of research) yields 31 books related to the topic, yet relatively few of those include specific challenges encountered or strategies utilized when counseling deaf children. A search in the APA PsycINFO database over the last 10 years yields 42 results, of which only six have any direct attention given to counseling strategies or challenges when working with DHH children/youth. The most notable of these include Day et al.'s (2018) article on adapting parent-child interaction therapy for deaf families that communicate via ASL, Tapia-Fuselier and Ray's (2019) article adapting child-centered play therapy for deaf children, Dowtin and Day's (2019) qualitative study exploring play therapy training experiences of DHH clinicians.

There is considerable research, however, describing the prevalence rates of mental health disorders (Fellinger e al., 2012; Swanepoel et al., 2020), quality of mental health in DHH children (Aanondsen et al., 2020; Fellinger et al.,2008), clinical presentations of disorders in Deaf children (Chovaz, 2013; Du Feu & Chovaz, 2014; Scott & Hansen, 2020; Wright et al., 2022), the critical necessity of language acquisition in early developmental stages (Glickman & Hall, 2018), challenges associated with DHH children with additional special needs (Turner Dougherty & Day, 2022), in addition to some articles outlining the adaptation of clinical tools for use with DHH children and adolescents (Wright et al., 2020; Cornes & Brown, 2012; Roberts et al., 2015). Of note is the recent development and evaluation of a Deaf-accessible trauma/substance use disorder toolkit (Anderson et al., 2021). It is hoped that more evidence-based strategies and techniques developed specifically for DHH children will follow.

Although all this work is indeed helpful for counselors working with DHH children and Codas, there still appears to be a gap in the literature describing the stories shared with and learned by counselors working with DHH children and adolescents.

Our Work at PAH!

PAH! is a children's mental health program in a province in Canada providing service to DHH children/youth and their families as well as Codas. The program strives to support any level of hearing loss and the use of any type of assistive device as well as respects any choice of communication. PAH! currently employs three registered, Deaf social workers who are fluent in ASL. Veronica Bickle (first author of this chapter) is the clinical lead of the program. PAH! is supported by an ASL interpreter as well as a deaf clinical psychologist, Dr. Cathy Chovaz (second author of this chapter).

Bob Rumball Canadian Centre of Excellence for the Deaf, who oversees the PAH! program, has a partnership with the leading local mainstream children mental health agency—Reach Out Centre for Kids (ROCK), based in the municipality of Halton in Ontario, Canada. Through this partnership, the PAH! program utilizes some of ROCK's resources, such as their database and intake and assessment tools. They have a central intake program that accepts, screens, and connects with all referrals to their program as well as partner agencies, then determines which agency or program would be the best match. The goal of this regional central intake system is to reduce duplication of services, multiple referrals, and length of wait time before receiving services as well as the likelihood of being bounced from one program or agency to another in the search for the right fit.

Before the COVID pandemic, PAH! was funded to provide services to a specific geographical area (the greater Toronto area). With the transformation and growing acceptance of counseling through virtual platforms during COVID, PAH! provided mental health services to DHH children and Codas regardless of where in the province of Ontario they resided, and this has continued after the end of the pandemic.

Intake Process

We have a preference at PAH! to conduct intake interviews internally within our program as compared with receiving completed intake data through the regional central intake system. The information we want to collect from these families differs in some ways from the information requested by mainstream agencies. However, the pathway for referral to PAH! through this central intake agency remains open, and occasionally, we will receive a referral with information already collected from the family from them. We have found that there are gaps in the information we receive, which has meant that we typically set up another intake interview to ensure that we have an accurate understanding of the child and their needs.

For example, we received a referral for an 11-year-old Deaf girl through this central intake program. When reviewing the information from the initial intake interview done by central intake, there were no details about family composition, what kind of communication was used at home, and what kind of school the child was attending. For mental health therapists working with DHH children and youth, that kind of information is crucial because it offers significant insights about how the child is living and functioning as a DHH individual as well as a better understanding of potential challenges and protective factors to assess the level of need.

A second intake appointment was scheduled with the purpose of filling in the gaps and to confirm the accuracy of the information that was received. I, Veronica Bickle, connected with the hearing mother of the Deaf child who was being referred for anxiety, as the child's father was currently in very poor health with the possibility of death, and the child had also recently lost a close grandparent.

In the initial intake referral notes received from central intake, it was stated that the child "developmentally communicates and understands at a 6 y/o level." During my interview with the child's mother, she said her daughter had a cochlear implant, uses ASL and "speaks like a 5/6-year-old."

I asked for clarification if she meant her daughter's cognitive development was at the 5/6-year-old level. The mother advised that she was just referring to her speech and that she estimated her daughter's cognitive development was at the level of a 9-year-old child. With this clarification, the clinical presentation of the child's cognitive and developmental abilities and what kind of counseling and support she might need shifted, necessitating further assessment.

When reviewing the information from the initial referral, the initial screener noted that the child "struggles to make and maintain friendships—no current relationships reported." When I learned that the child attended a provincial school for the Deaf, as opposed to being the only Deaf child in a mainstream environment, I felt the need to double-check this statement about the lack of any relationship with her peers. As a Deaf person and a Deaf mental health therapist, it has been my experience that Deaf children attending a Deaf school have fewer difficulties forming and maintaining friendships than in a mainstream program, given there are many other Deaf peers to make friends with, all using a shared sign language.

The mother clarified that her daughter struggled to connect with other hearing children and did not want to participate in activities when no other Deaf child was present. As an example, her daughter recently quit her dancing classes. The previous summer, the mother tried to encourage her daughter to go to camp but after the first hour, the girl left because she did not want to be the only Deaf child there.

When I asked about friends at the provincial school for the Deaf, her mom confirmed that she had friends there. She described her daughter as "assertive" and "feisty" and already starting to show preteen behavior and attitude. Her mother was frustrated that play dates with friends from school were hard to set up because her friends did not live locally—geographically, the closest friend lived a 1-hour car drive away.

I had a Deaf intern student observe the intake meeting with this mother, and when we debriefed afterwards, she commented that it appeared that "many 'outside' agencies do not really understand what it's like to be a deaf child or they try to assess them in the mold of a hearing child." After reviewing notes from the initial referral and receiving clarifying information from the mother, we were able to see that the central intake screener assessed the Deaf child from the perspective of the average hearing child, where speech equals communication and that no friends to play with at home might indicate difficulties with making and maintaining friendships.

This interview indicated how important it is to have the right questions to ask, what information to know, and what areas in the life of a DHH child may warrant further clarification. This may be especially true when receiving information from parents who may not always be clear or accurate with the information that they share with us. It also shows how crucial it is to have interviewers with the relevant and accessible clinical knowledge, frame of reference, and experience with the community whom we work with to appropriately screen the stories parents share with us. Basically, sometimes it is not enough to have the head-to-head practical knowledge about the challenges DHH children experience; one needs to also have the underlying heart-to-heart innate understanding of the intricacies of life as a Deaf child in a hearing world.

The following are heart-to-heart stories of supporting DHH children and youth at PAH!. It is our belief that close attention to these stories is critical for a deeper understanding of the complexities inherent in working with this population.

Aashi

Aashi was a 14-year-old Deaf female referred to PAH! with a request for support by her school social worker from the provincial school for the Deaf that Aashi attended. The goal of the school social worker was to ensure that Aashi continued to receive support throughout the summer months. When connecting with her for the first time through a video call, Aashi cited family and peer conflict and shared that she felt depressed.

Aashi was born deaf in Bangladesh, and her hearing loss was first identified when she was 1 year old. The family moved to Canada when Aashi was 3 years old. She is the youngest of three children: She has an older sister and brother and is the only Deaf member in the family.

Aashi's journey in acquiring language had been challenging. Upon arrival in Canada, Aashi first attended a school that used Langue des Signes Québécois and spoken French. Five years later, the family moved to a different province, and Aashi started to learn ASL and written English at a provincial school for the Deaf as a day student.

The family's first language spoken at home was Bengali. Aashi's parents' acquisition of English was rudimentary, and Aashi's older sister often assisted with facilitating communication with various service providers. The parents and siblings did not communicate with Aashi in ASL, which was the language Aashi understood best—they communicated with her through speaking in Bengali or English, homemade signs, gesturing, and writing.

To offset the isolation she experienced at home, Aashi turned to various social media apps and video-chat platforms to seek connection with others, leading to toxic and unhealthy interactions with various Deaf youth and adults. Her main goal was to find a romantic partner, and she had a series of various attachments to other Deaf youth online. She had a history of sharing pictures and videos of herself in various stages of undress through social media channels, and often, naked pictures of her would appear and circulate online. Aashi's family also received sexually explicit pictures and videos of Aashi from others online after Aashi shared personal information such as their home address and parents' email addresses.

During counseling sessions, Aashi was very motivated in sharing details about the online drama in which she participated. She was most engaged when sharing about the threats she made or received with various people online, or when witnessing conflict between others. For a time, she repeatedly shared a story that her online boyfriend had a gun, had killed police officers, and her family "better watch out" as he can come to Canada, kill them, and it would be "too bad for them." She emphasized many times that the parents she was currently living with were her "fake" parents and that her real mother was either dead or still in Bangladesh, and that she had a twin sister.

Aashi's increasing reliance on social media resulted in her staying up late, missing school, communicating with acquaintances on the phone during class which resulted in poor academic performance, and escalating conflicts with her parents who attempted to regulate her behavior by shutting down Wi-Fi access at bedtime. In turn, Aashi became physically aggressive and attempted to harm her parents and siblings and often alleged that she was a victim of physical abuse. These allegations resulted in investigations on several occasions by the local child protection agency. The protection service agency, utilizing the use of English-ASL and Deaf interpreters, concluded each time that there was no substance behind these allegations.

It was during this time that Aashi began sneaking out of her home at night in search of free Wi-Fi, walking the streets at night to find a 24-hour coffee shop without regard for her own safety. When reminded in our counseling sessions about the risk to her personal safety, Aashi commented that she could fight off anyone if they attempted to harm her, despite her small physical stature.

When frustrated with her family members, Aashi often shared that she wanted to kill herself and had thoughts about dying. There were also incidents of self-harming, starting with scratching and cutting herself and eventually escalating to using a lighter on her foot. There was an incident when challenged by another youth, she downed some pills while "live" on social media, and the incident was recorded and circulated. There was also another picture where she wrapped a rope several times around her neck, which was also circulated online. These pictures and videos were often reported to school staff by other students.

There were multiple visits to Aashi's home by the police and paramedics triggered by calls made by Aashi through video relay services. There were also numerous contacts by her online acquaintances to police with requests to check on Aashi's well-being following self-harming statements and behavior from Aashi, as well as the occasional fabrications from others about Aashi's plans to harm herself. Sometimes Aashi was taken to the hospital to be assessed and then usually discharged, and sometimes the police determined that there was no safety concern and left her at home. Reports of every visit were sent to Aashi's child protection worker. Aashi was fortunate to have a child protection worker who was genuinely concerned about her well-being and worked to find various local service agencies to help Aashi and her family, but he stated that his requests often were turned down because these agencies did not have the funds to cover the costs of interpreting services.

The frequency with which first responders went to Aashi's house became a concern—in a 6-month period, the local police were called to Aashi's home 39 times. Aashi's family was advised that Aashi was at risk of being charged by the police with mischief. Aashi was cautioned to take care with requesting the involvement of first responders, with a reminder that constant visits to her home may mean the police and paramedics may not be available for other local emergencies, but she was not able to appreciate the serious nature of their involvement.

I once accompanied Aashi to the hospital after she disclosed that she had suicidal thoughts and had a plan to harm herself. When questioned by medical staff, her responses were vague and benign and to the undiscerning doctor, the situation didn't seem serious enough to continue to keep her at the hospital despite evidence of self-harm and advocacy on my part. After being kept overnight and assessed by an emergency room doctor and a psychiatrist, she was released with a referral to an outpatient mental health program for adolescents. Aashi did not follow through with appointments after her initial visit there.

School was also difficult for Aashi, as she struggled to make friends and did not do well academically. Her guidance teacher shared that she had observed Aashi spending time alone, signing to herself in the presence of no one else, and staying apart from her other peers during their free time. She would make comments about self-harming or threatening to harm someone else, resulting in the police and paramedics dispatched to the school 13 times.

Aashi's desire to leave home and live with her online boyfriend escalated to conflicts where Aashi would demand that her family hand over her passport and pay for her ticket to fly to visit him, perceiving this as her inherent right and failing to understand that her parents had the parental right to decline her requests. Other times, she would state that her Deaf boyfriend from the United States would come and get her. At one point, she believed this to be true to the point that she had her suitcase packed and was sitting out in the garage for hours waiting for him to come.

Aashi's conflicts with her family at home became distressing for her, and she found cannabis use and sometimes alcohol beneficial to cope with the stress she was experiencing. Although she would obtain cannabis from peers at school, she would also seek opportunities by connecting with strangers when loitering at a nearby department store. This resulted in her experiencing sexual assault by a hearing acquaintance of the family when he offered free cannabis in exchange for sex. Aashi did not fully understand, realize, or appreciate the consequences of accepting the offer. Her fund of information was extremely limited.

At this point, Aashi's mental health deteriorated to the point that she was brought to the hospital. With advocacy from her child protection worker, the police, and two local mental health agencies (which had become involved at the request of the police), she was admitted to the child and youth inpatient unit at the local hospital, citing that she was at high risk for self-harm, human trafficking, and a possible flight risk. By then, Aashi had lost significant weight and was not eating and sleeping well.

When Aashi was admitted to the inpatient department at the hospital, Dr. Chovaz, our program clinical consultant with extensive experience working with DHH children and youth, was requested to complete a psychological assessment. The results of that assessment concluded that she met the criteria for language deprivation syndrome, adjustment disorder with mixed anxiety and depressed mood directly related to the language deprivation, and an attachment disorder with symptoms of both reactive attachment disorder and disinhibited social engagement disorder. A query diagnosis of attention deficit hyperactivity disorder (ADHD) was also included. This was the first time the mental health team working with Aashi felt able to better conceptualize her clinical presentations within these diagnostic criteria and to try to formulate treatment strategies.

While admitted in the hospital, Aashi attended therapy with the use of a virtual interpreting service and started medication to target depression and symptoms of ADHD. After a few weeks, there was a noticeable improvement in her mood, ability to focus, and the coherence of her expressive sign skills. Aashi also showed more willingness to attend to and accept other people's perspectives, even if they differed from hers. Following a 2-month admission in the hospital, Aashi transferred to the Drury Program under the Bob Rumball Canadian Centre of Excellence for the Deaf. This is a group home environment where all staff were able to communicate in ASL that was used as a step-down facility where Aashi was able to stay for 6 weeks before returning home. During this brief period at the Drury program, Aashi was receptive to cognitive behavioral therapy (CBT) therapy. Unfortunately, there was not enough community funding for a longer stay and upon her return home, Aashi's symptoms started to appear again and the opportunity for further treatment was lost.

Residing at home again, Aashi began seeking romantic partners by connecting online with older, local hearing men. She engaged in sexual activity with the goal of moving out of the family home with unrealistic expectations of living permanently with one of these men. There was also an incident in which she brought home an older man, resulting in further conflict and a phone call to the police by her family.

Further conflicts with her family about her sexual relationships with men much older than her, stealing money from her parents, and smoking and vaping in their house led to an incident in which Aashi became angry and attempted to set the living room on fire. As a result, 6 months after her discharge from the Drury program, Aashi was returned to the child and adolescent inpatient unit at the local hospital. Adjustments to her medication were made, and Aashi agreed to the installment of a birth control implant. She was released home after a 2-week admission.

Aashi is now 18 years old and has been a client with PAH! for 3 years with limited improvement. She recently graduated from the provincial Deaf high school program. The clinical community team of the PAH therapist, community social worker, hospital outpatient social worker, in addition to our PAH clinical consultant, met regularly to try to maintain her stability. There have been no further incidents of suicidal thoughts, self-harm, or emotional outbursts at school. There have been fewer incidents of Aashi signing to herself (or an imaginary person) in public. While taking her medication regularly, her communication skills and ability to focus improved considerably. Aashi's attempts to find a romantic partner are still ongoing, conflicts within the home are still happening, and she continues to engage in very high-risk, online, sexually motivated behavior. Unfortunately, motivation from Aashi's family members to continue to engage with service providers has significantly lessened, as they are exhausted from her behaviors. The progress of transferring her to adult mental health services has begun. An application to get support services from the province's developmental disability services had been declined, due to the agency not recognizing language deprivation as instrumental of limited functional ability to live independently.

Reflections on Aashi

During the early months of working with Aashi before she was transferred to the inpatient unit at the local hospital, it was not clear what the underlying mental health issues were, as there were no diagnoses or any previous assessment. At PAH!, we had queried the presence of a possible intellectual or developmental disability. We had also wondered if she was, at times, psychotic with hallucinations, given her tendency to sign to herself when there was no one else there and her strong belief in stories that appeared delusional. Formal diagnostic clarification was very helpful.

When gently trying to challenge the credibility of her claims such as the story that her boyfriend had killed police officers, Aashi resisted to admitting that it was not true. She fabricated reasons to defend her story, without comprehending that I, as the therapist, could see through the gaps and untruths in her story. After a few failed attempts to challenge her perspective about the stories she shared, it was apparent that this kind of intervention was nothing more than a cat-and-mouse chase between the two of us and that it was not therapeutically helpful or beneficial.

There were few opportunities for genuine therapeutic interventions during counseling sessions. Aashi consistently viewed these sessions as her time to vent about her online interactions and her frustration with her family, with little motivation for introspection and development of coping strategies. When attempts were made to focus on psychoeducation or development of skills, she refused to cooperate. She dominated the conversation and would become irritated if she felt she was being interrupted or when asked for clarification too often. Her thoughts were scattered, her signed expression was unclear and disorganized, jumping from one topic to another without appropriate transition. It was clear that she did not have a realistic and age-appropriate perspective of the world she lived in.

One of the most difficult issues when working with Aashi was to help her understand boundaries, such as the fact that her parents had authority to make decisions for her while she was a minor and she had to respect their decisions. The fact that her parents refused to comply with what she wanted them to do led to outbursts, physical assaults against family members, and repeated allegations of abuse, oppression, and discrimination against her as a Deaf person.

Given her limits of communication, lack of ToM, and mental health disorders, Aashi's parents were not able to manage their daughter's behavior from childhood, resulting in serious issues of trust and attachment. If information or advice was presented in a way that she did not understand or if she perceived that it may not benefit her, Aashi often disregarded it. If encouraged to think about what other people might feel about how her actions may have impacted them, she would often disregard this advice by bringing the issue back to her own thoughts and feelings or changing the subject, suggesting a very weak ToM in terms of perspective-taking. Trying to approach the subject from different aspects, rephrasing, elaborating, and providing examples, as well as returning to the same subject later, in hopes that she would be more receptive, met with little to no success.

This client had little appreciation of the potential consequences of her actions, or any risks to her own personal safety when warned ahead of time, especially if it got in the way of what she wanted. She was distrustful of advice given out to her by adults. However, it was noted following her 2-month hospital admission and initiation of medication that she refrained from suicidal behavior. This may have been due to an elevation in her mood as well as the realization that she had learned that staying in the hospital was a threat to her independence. When discussing strategies to reduce being involuntarily brought to the hospital, she was open to the feedback about using more appropriate vocabulary to express her anger and frustration other than making statements about wanting to kill herself or someone else, because it benefitted what she wanted.

Although Aashi experienced issues at school, she did show more respect to the authority of teachers at the Deaf school than that of nonsigning hearing adults, such as her family or out in the community. During the 6 weeks she stayed at the Drury Program following her discharge from the hospital, despite being defiant on occasion, Aashi cooperated well with staff who could use ASL. She was not happy there, but for most of the time, she was well-behaved and respected the rules, and perhaps even appreciated the structure these rules gave her.

It became clear to us that Aashi's family were not able to provide the needed structure and communication support, and thus Aashi acted out significantly at home. Aashi was mostly cooperative while at school and at the Drury Program when she was in an ASL-inclusive environment. Had she been placed in an accessible group home for youth, such as the Drury Program, on a long-term basis, it is likely that much of the pain and suffering that had been experienced by Aashi and her family may have been avoided. There had been many times when I thought that had her admission at the Drury Program been considerably extended, at that crucial point in time for intervention, the trajectory of Aashi's mental health journey could have shifted with more positive results.

We feel that if there had been funding for Aashi to access recreational programs and activities via ASL interpreters to keep her busy and away from toxic online interactions, many negative incidents may have been avoided. Similarly, accessible in-home supports, respite care, and access to different language interpreters (for both Aashi and her parents) without being concerned about the costs, would have likely helped her parents better manage Aashi's behavior. Tailored, one-on-one ASL tutoring for the family could also have been beneficial. The local child protection agency paid for the parents to take ASL classes online, but it proved difficult for the parents to follow, given their limited English literacy. The minimal efforts of local mental health agencies to invest in Aashi's mental health well-being led her family to be disconnected and distrustful and as a result, their lack of engagement with local agencies was also a negative factor regarding Aashi's overall mental health and safety.

Fatima

Fatima was a 16-year-old Deaf girl referred to the PAH program by her guidance teacher at the school for the Deaf. The referral was related to family conflict, specifically Fatima's frequent and intense anger with her family.

Fatima is the middle child of three siblings who lived with their single mother. Fatima's family originally moved to a western Canadian province from Syria when she was 3 years old. Fatima is the only Deaf member of the family, and the etiology of her deafness is unknown. It was also unclear when she was identified as deaf but likely when she was an infant. While in Syria, the family communicated with Fatima using spoken Arabic and gestures.

At age 5 years, following the move to Canada, Fatima attended a self-contained classroom for deaf children within a hearing school. This classroom had an ASL interpreter, which was Fatima's first exposure to sign language. Fatima had bilateral cochlear implants when she was 8 years old. Shortly after the family's immigration to Canada, Fatima's parents separated, with the mother citing that her ex-husband abused both her and Fatima. After the initial separation, Fatima's father remained in Canada, although Fatima later reported that he returned to live in Syria, as most of their extended family still lives there.

Fatima's parents and siblings had made very little effort to learn ASL despite encouragement from service providers to do so and continued to interact with her using spoken language (Arabic or English). Fatima described feeling very lonely, sad, and frustrated when trying to communicate with her family. She also indicated that her mother and siblings often treated her poorly, such as expecting her to do more than her fair share of household chores and refusing to turn on captions on when they were watching television at home.

The family was Muslim Canadian which created further conflict when Fatima refused to wear a hijab, angering her parents and causing considerable distress within the family. In addition, her mother became angry upon learning that Fatima was dating a boy from school. As a result, she became furious and hit Fatima on the leg with a cellphone charger cable wire. Fatima's leisure time with friends was limited, and her older sister would often enter Fatima's social media accounts and change passwords so Fatima would not be able to contact other people online easily.

During her first virtual counseling session with her Deaf counselor at PAH!, the counselor noticed that Fatima's mom and older sister were in the room, pressuring her to end the video call, and that they appeared to be threatening to hit Fatima. The counselor documented that he was concerned about physical abuse, because he noticed something was wrong through Fatima's body language, as she was flinching and attempting to shield herself as if expecting to be hit. A report was made to the local children's protective services, culminating in long-term involvement with the agency that continued until Fatima turned 18 years old.

The referral noted that Fatima first demonstrated suicidal behavior the year before becoming involved with PAH!. Fatima had a second suicide attempt the following year and was admitted to the local hospital. This began a cycle of frequent suicidal, self-harming behaviors demonstrated both at school and at home and repeated hospital admissions. She was prescribed an antidepressant medication, which she decided to stop taking after a few days due to side effects, despite noticing some elevation in her mood.

Fatima also demonstrated depressive symptoms. She was frequently irritable, often expressing her unhappiness and struggled to sleep at night. It had been noted by her counselor at PAH! and school staff that Fatima's stress and self-harming behavior often escalated near the end of the school week, particularly before long weekends or extended school breaks. Fatima often became agitated and demonstrated this by becoming upset and tearful, demanding immediate support from her guidance teacher. Then, she gradually became angry and shared thoughts about self-harming and suicide with friends online.

Fatima's multiple end-of-life statements to friends resulted in being brought to the hospital several times. She demonstrated curiosity about suicide by asking questions about various methods to kill oneself. She self-harmed and started self-cutting during one of her hospital admissions, and once started to punch her own nose and her ears until they started to bleed when feeling stressed.

When asked about her experience with accessibility at the local hospital she attended, Fatima replied that based on her 13 visits to the hospital, often an ASL interpreter was provided through video relay interpreting (VRI), although there were a few times when an interpreter attended in-person. She said that VRI interpreters often misunderstood her, leading her to feel frustrated when she had to repeat herself often to provide clarification for the interpreter.

Fatima also described how in her first few visits to the hospital, an interpreter was not provided. Typically, a nurse would come in and check on her by writing to ask if she was doing okay, if she was hungry, or if she was thinking about suicide. Fatima would ask the nurse if they could get an interpreter, but she reported that most of the time, she was told no and that they didn't have time for that. The staff would continue to write back and forth on paper, ignoring Fatima's request for an interpreter. During her fourth hospital admission, Fatima finally had an in-person interpreter provided. During her fourth and eighth hospital admission only, a Deaf interpreter was also provided, and Fatima reported that communication with hospital staff at that time was optimal.

When asked about communication through paper and pen, Fatima commented that as English was not her first language (she considered ASL to be her first language), it was not easy to understand what was being communicated. Often, she struggled and reported that she did not actually understand what the notes said. She commented that it was not a successful means of communication.

Fatima did not do well academically. A psychoeducational assessment had not been done by the school professional staff to better understand possible learning difficulties. Support staff at Fatima's school developed two different safety plans for Fatima to manage her behavior. One was a noncrisis plan, such as when Fatima persisted with her negative talk, and the second one was a crisis plan in case Fatima demonstrated suicidal behavior.

Upon her multiple discharges from the hospital, Fatima was offered local and mainstream community mental health resources. After initially trying these services, Fatima began to continuously refuse their services and increasingly demand ASL-friendly mental health services. However, the extent and range of her mental health needs was more than what our PAH program could offer her. What Fatima needed was mental health supports in an ASL-inclusive group home setting in conjunction to the supports she was already receiving from PAH!, such as the Drury Program (previously described with the first story of Aashi).

The hospital clinical team that worked with Fatima strongly felt that they were not able to effectively offer treatment, given the lack of ASL-fluent clinicians and appropriate peers. The psychiatrist working with Fatima wrote in favor of the Drury Program:

> An investment in her treatment there will save the health system money in the long term. Fatima has presented to the hospital 11 times which is approximately the equivalent of $107,787 dollars (not including costs of specific procedures, interpretation services, medication costs, etc.). Without deaf and hard of hearing residential treatment services, we anticipate she will continue to represent to the hospital in crisis, which will be costly to the system but also is not helpful for Fatima's recovery because the lack of deaf and hard of hearing supports in the hospital only serves to re-traumatize and entrench her beliefs that people do not meet her needs. . . . If this was a youth who was not deaf or hard of hearing, she would have been in one of our "hearing" mental health residential treatment settings many months ago.

At this point, there had not been any formal mental health diagnosis for Fatima. The psychiatrist at the local hospital that Fatima attended initially brought forward a possible diagnosis of major depressive disorder vs. adjustment disorder and parent-child relational disorder with symptoms of oppositional defiant disorder. Dr. Chovaz initially queried an unspecified anxiety disorder.

Another barrier was that the Drury Program did not have base funding. As it was a fee-for-service program, other service providers in the province would have to provide funding for DHH youths to stay there. Fatima's counselor, Dr. Chovaz, and the chief operating officer for Bob Rumball spent months advocating the government for funding. The main problem was that we had to prove that the community services available for Fatima "failed" to provide what she needed, something that was difficult to establish given that Fatima refused these services before even really trying them.

Eventually, funding was obtained for a 2-month stay at the Drury Program, which was less time than we had initially hoped. Also included in that funding was money for a psychological assessment.

During her brief stay at the Drury Program, Fatima was happy and content with an absence of mental health issues. She met with Dr. Chovaz for a psychological assessment and was diagnosed with parent-child relational disorder and generalized anxiety disorder. In addition, given Fatima's disclosures of abuse and a history of childhood adverse experiences, she also met the criteria for unspecified trauma and stressor-related disorder. In her psychological assessment, Dr. Chovaz mentioned that Fatima's ASL was fairly age-appropriate. However, her knowledge and understanding of the world was limited—Dr. Chovaz noted that, for a young woman of 18 years old, Fatima was unaware of very basic facts relative to where she lived, attended school, or the local news around her.

It was also mentioned in the psychological assessment, after the completion of the clinical questionnaires by her primary worker at the Drury Program, her teacher, and her guidance counselor, that Fatima had a significantly poor ability to control her emotional responses with a tendency to overreact or present with overblown emotional reactions to seemingly minor events. It also indicated that Fatima had poor inhibition and a lack of ability to self-monitor her own behavior, suggesting that she was not aware of the effect that her behavior has on others. This continued to be evident in the time after she left the Drury Program.

Following her departure from the Drury Program, her suicidal behavior and incidents of self-harming stopped completely, and there have been no further visits to the hospital. However, she still struggled with the regulation of her own behavior and emotions. If other students were negative or there was some gossip about her, Fatima would overreact by crying and becoming emotionally distraught. When at a sports tournament being held at the school gym, Fatima's counselor observed an incident in which Fatima suddenly appeared in the hallway leading to the gymnasium, crying and visually upset, impulsively pouring out her thoughts and emotions with a teacher without regard of the attention she was garnering there. The teacher gently reminded her that it was not the right place or time, directing her how to appropriately manage her emotions and behavior.

After graduating from high school at 18 years old, Fatima was to attend a Deaf upgrading program at a local college. At the time of discharge (due to aging out of the PAH program), Fatima became engaged in a conflict with her mother. This conflict arose after Fatima had been recently approved for a disability pension and her mother requested that she pay a higher amount toward room and board at home. Fatima refused and her mother became angry with her and physically harmed her, resulting in Fatima calling the police. The police placed Fatima in a shelter for abused women. At this time, Fatima had already been transferred to an adult mental health and general social support services agency, which provided support to DHH adults. There, Fatima had the professional support that she needed to navigate through this new change in her life, such finding a new place to live on her own.

Reflections on Fatima

There were some similarities between Aashi and Fatima—they both had a late exposure to language, and both sets of parents moved to Canada as immigrants with a limited ability to communicate in English. Fatima's parents spoke limited English. Neither set of parents were able to communicate in ASL with their Deaf child, which likely contributed to attachment issues between the youths and their parents.

Although somewhat delayed with her literacy and understanding of the world, Fatima demonstrated a better ability to express herself, compared to Aashi. Fatima was able to recall events and communicate details of events coherently. She also had an ability to advocate for herself appropriately by consistently refusing services because they were not accessible for her. There was no complete disregard of other people's emotions and perspectives, like with Aashi, but Fatima would need prompting to consider them.

However, Fatima had challenges with her ability to cope with emotional distress and be able to use strategies to self-soothe appropriate for her age. She was very dependent on others to provide reassurance, regulate her emotions for her, and find solutions to her problems, also demonstrating poor executive functioning skills especially when overwrought. When experiencing emotional outbursts, there was a lack of awareness about how other people may perceive her, yet she was sensitive when hearing gossip or speculation about her following her emotional episodes.

Fatima was not receptive to learning coping skills, to become more independent in managing her own emotions. During her stay at the Drury Program, Fatima was given the expectation of learning some emotional regulation strategies. Despite patient counselor support, Fatima barely tolerated the instruction, instead rushing through these lessons so to leave some time for her counselor to help her address her immediate issues and concerns. It was not an issue of her inability to learn these skills but a matter of priority for her, as she had limited time with her counselor, who was one of the very few caring adults available to unconditionally listen to what was happening to her, pay attention to her thoughts and feelings, and provide emotional support in a way her parents were not able. Her relationship with her counselor was important to her—she requested that he be there as one of her guests on her high school graduation day.

When she was staying at the Drury Program, there were very few episodes of emotional distress and no expression of suicidal behavior. After she left the program, she continued to experience emotional distress and a need for someone to help her manage her emotions, but these occurrences were at a lower level of intensity, and there were no further trips to the hospital for mental and emotional distress.

Respite care, accessible in-home supports, and access to ASL and Arabic interpreters for both Fatima and her mother would have been very helpful. In addition, access to recreational programs and activities via ASL interpreters would have lessened the time spent feeling isolated when at home. Instead, she and her family were left alone to cope, and identification of Fatima's mental health issues was unnecessarily prolonged. Fatima's needs were never completely met and addressed before aging out of the children's mental health system.

Olivia

Olivia was first referred to PAH! in the fall of 2017, when she was 6 years old, due to her mother's concerns about Olivia's increasingly aggressive behavior at home. The mother reported that Olivia had frequent outbursts of anger and impulsive behavior, especially when she was told no. The mother also added that the strategies she tried at home, such as discipline and setting of expectations, were not successful in changing Olivia's behavior. Olivia's mother was concerned about safety at home, as her daughter had exhibited aggressive behavior toward her and her siblings.

Olivia was the third of four children of hearing Caucasian parents. She had an older sister and two younger brothers, and she was the only Deaf member in the family. Olivia was born with bilateral profound sensorineural deafness of unknown etiology and did not qualify for a cochlear implant. There was no family history of hearing loss. It was also reported in the referral that Olivia experienced developmental delays—sitting up at 1 year, signing at 18 months, walking at 2 years, and toilet-trained at 4 years old.

At the time of the initial intake appointment, Olivia was starting Grade 1 at a provincial school for the Deaf. Previously, she was in a DHH preschool program at a mainstreamed school. Upon transfer to the nearest provincial school for the Deaf, her parents commented during the intake process that after attending this school for only two months, they had already observed a huge improvement in Olivia's language and behavior.

The family had a home-visiting teacher whose role included teaching ASL to the family, but this service stopped when Olivia started school, and the family had to pay out of pocket for a private ASL tutor. It was noted that Olivia's mother was the main communicator at home, while Olivia's father tried to learn but shared that he felt frustrated at times with trying to learn and communicate using ASL.

Olivia's mother shared that when Olivia got upset about something she did not do well, or when she was told no while already feeling frustrated, she would scratch herself, poke her own eyes, or attack her siblings. Olivia's mother also added that Olivia used to bite when upset, but that stopped after applying some behavioral strategies. She also shared that they had a hard time getting Olivia to listen "right away." It was also commented that Olivia was not gentle, and that her mother had a hard time explaining to her why things break. Basically, disciplining Olivia was a challenge because she did not seem to care if her toys or privileges were being revoked as a consequence of her behavior.

During her early days as a client at PAH!, Olivia participated in art therapy, with limited success, and her counselor at the time (who was not Deaf and no longer working at PAH!) also provided supportive counseling for her mother. Her counselor reported noticing that Olivia was having a hard time identifying a feeling unless prompted. Her mother mentioned noticing that Olivia was not able to express herself well, particularly when complex feelings were involved—she felt Olivia was only able to understand basic emotions such as happy, sad, or mad.

As a result, the counselor and Olivia worked on creating a visual book of different feelings, but soon after, the counselor reported struggling to keep Olivia's attention on-task, as she preferred to color the book and chat about what she was doing, rather than work on understanding feelings. The counselor also reported that Olivia attempted to inappropriately tickle her, and the counselor had to redirect Olivia while trying to maximize the teaching moment regarding appropriate boundaries.

A few months later, Olivia's mother reported that she had no further concerns about Olivia's behavior, and her file was closed.

Less than a year later, Olivia's mother contacted PAH! again for service, citing increased aggressive behavior at home and was again concerned about the physical safety of other family members. Olivia's file was reopened. Olivia's mother reported that she was still the sole family member able to communicate well with Olivia at home, adding that she wished her husband was more involved in trying to manage Olivia's behavior.

The parents noted that when Olivia became angry, she would severely harm her mother by kicking or biting her (sometimes leaving marks), as well as punching or kicking anyone in proximity, such as her sister or brother. Olivia's mother reported two occasions when Olivia pushed and held her older sister underwater in a pool: once at camp and once when supervised by their mother. She also added that Olivia threw a knife when she was angry with her father for not allowing her to cut some fruit herself. Olivia's mother reported being very concerned about safety, as Olivia did not seem to understand the consequences of her actions.

The mother also added that there had been a few incidents when Olivia's violent behavior resulted in the parents contacting the police. However, when the police arrived at their home without an ASL interpreter, it resulted in Olivia's mother having to facilitate communication between Olivia and the officer which further frustrated the parents.

The PAH counselor also made note of Olivia's mother's efforts to make the household accessible for Olivia, and to have Olivia feel included in family moments, such as meals, conversations, and parties. It was also noted that Olivia's mother tried to encourage the entire family to learn sign language to better communicate with Olivia, but the rest of the family did not master this as well as the mother wished.

Olivia's mother also observed that her daughter did not understand what people were telling her unless it was explained in very basic ASL. She reported seeing similarities between Olivia and her younger brothers in terms of comprehension, following directions, and maturity level. Olivia's mother also noted that Olivia's siblings did not really want to play with her anymore.

It was reported that Olivia was now presenting with significant behavior problems at school—difficulties with following instructions from her teacher and inability to be compliant while in the classroom. Olivia often did as she pleased and if her teacher tried to redirect her, she would have a temper tantrum in the classroom. With her behavior so unpredictable and volatile, the school administration felt that Olivia was not able to accompany her classmates on school trips.

It was also suggested, at the time of the second intake appointment, that a psychological assessment be sought. The family was successful in obtaining a psychological assessment for Olivia, and it was done with a community psychologist hired by the provincial school for the Deaf. The psychological report noted that a referral was made due to concerns "regarding reasoning, problem solving, expressive and receptive language, social skills, memory, attention, impulsivity, mood, and behavior." The assessment concluded that Olivia met the criteria for borderline intellectual functioning, which meant "challenges in abstract thinking and executive functioning, that evidences a more concrete approach to problems and solutions and displays conversation that is less mature than expected."

Olivia also underwent a speech and language assessment. The results of the assessment indicated a "significant receptive and expressive language disorder." Finally, Olivia had a psychiatric assessment yielding the following diagnoses: oppositional defiant disorder, intermittent explosive disorder, and childhood onset conduct disorder with onset being at 5 years old. The psychiatrist also noted that autism spectrum disorder was ruled out, as Olivia was "affectionate, craves attention and enjoys imaginary play." He also noted that endorsed questionnaire responses from home and school did not indicate clinical symptoms of ADHD, but he was not opposed to reviewing this again later. Medication was initiated to reduce impulsivity, inattention, and hyperactivity with some improvements noted in Olivia's behavior.

There was a pause in the provision of services to Olivia during the COVID pandemic and when Olivia returned to PAH! at the age of 10 years, she was placed with a different counselor who was Deaf. With assessments done by a psychiatrist and psychologist, the counselor had some background knowledge of Olivia's diagnoses.

During sessions, Olivia would often want to do things her way. Every time she showed up for her session, she tried to negotiate to have the lights turned off in the room, even though both she and the counselor were Deaf and would not be able to communicate with each other in the dark. She grabbed her counselor's phone without permission and asked for her password to access it. She crumbled up a paper she had been working on and threw it at her counselor instead of handing it over to her. When she was advised that these actions were not appropriate behavior, she would often sign in ASL, "just joking." The counselor would often ask Olivia how she would feel if the roles were reversed, and sometimes, she would respond that she would not like it while at other times, she would say she would like it. This made the counselor wonder if Olivia was understanding the intent of the question, given her borderline intelligence.

Several months later, when Olivia was 11 years old, there was an incident at school during recess where two other students told Olivia that they did not like her. When she asked them why, they did not respond and walked away from her. Olivia tried to chase after them and then grabbed a tree branch, using it to slash her throat and causing a superficial cut. When her mother talked with Olivia about the incident at school, Olivia told her that she wanted to die. Olivia's mother mentioned that it was the first time Olivia stated this. The mother shared that in the past, Olivia would make "you die" comments when angry, but never about herself. A few weeks later, following another conflict with a friend, Olivia tried to put both of her thumbs into her eyelids, resulting in red eyes.

The following summer, Olivia's behavior continued to escalate. Olivia's mother shared that her daughter had several incidents in which she became angry and violent, to the level where Olivia's mother felt she had to lock Olivia's younger brothers in the bathroom to keep them safe. There was one situation when Olivia wanted to jump off a deck, situated at a dangerous height from the ground, and would not listen to reason—her father went below to be ready in case she jumped. Her mother left the scene upset and frustrated with Olivia's inability to listen, and Olivia, seeing that her mother was upset, changed course and ran after her and sank her teeth in her mother's back. Olivia's mother reported feeling exhausted and nearly at the breaking point in trying to manage her daughter's behavior. She shared that she started to look for additional community resources for the family to be able to manage Olivia's behavior.

When school resumed in the fall, it was decided that Olivia would stay full-time in the student dormitories during the week and go home on the weekends. Previously, she had been a day student, going home every evening after school. After a successful short trial of staying in a student residence part-time, Olivia's parents decided to make it permanent.

Over the next few months, the frequency and intensity of Olivia's explosive incidents abated. She cooperated well during her counseling sessions at PAH!. She thrived in a structured ASL environment where everyone signed, and she had opportunities to learn how to manage personal boundaries supervised by adults who were native ASL users and who could advise and redirect her behavior when needed. When Olivia's residence counselors were asked how Olivia was doing, they reported no serious concerns, although they commented that Olivia continued to struggle to respect other students' boundaries. This was something the counselors continued to help Olivia understand. Olivia's weekends at home were less chaotic, and Olivia's mom returned to work after being a stay-at-home mom.

Work with Olivia on respecting personal boundaries and managing strong feelings continues a weekly basis. She is a highly motivated client, eagerly appearing for her weekly sessions, sitting inside the tent in the PAH playroom and doing work with the use of frequent role-play, drawing, and therapeutic discourse in ASL. Olivia has a strong rapport with her present counselor, and her care plan goals include creating a safe place to work on developing skills to navigate what is, for her, a complex world of human interactions, as she goes through puberty and becomes a young adult.

Reflections on Olivia

Prior to Olivia staying during the week at the school's dormitories at the provincial school for the Deaf, it was noticed that when discussing scenarios about what kind of behavior was right or wrong during counseling sessions, Olivia would answer appropriately. When discussing the feelings of herself or someone else, she would offer correct answers during the counseling session. However, this contravened with her behavior at home, in which her mother continued to report aggressive conduct and impulsive behavior with a lack of consciousness about possible consequences, disregard for what other people may be thinking about her, and a disregard of other people's feelings when she was angry or wanted something.

When discussing with Olivia about her inappropriate behavior or outbursts during counseling sessions, she often acknowledged what she did was not right. Sometimes with or without prompting, she would provide some reflection about her thoughts and feelings during these altercations. Coping strategies and alternative courses of action were discussed with her, but when she went home, nothing changed. She was able to provide appropriate responses during counseling sessions but could not apply the strategies she learned while at home.

When Olivia started taking medication and staying in the student dormitories at the provincial school for the Deaf during the week, the frequency and severity of her episodes at home and at school lessened. She had more learning opportunities to modify her behavior in an environment where everyone could sign. While living in the residence, Olivia had access to incidental learning. She had staff who modeled appropriate behavior and could intervene when Olivia showed early signs of stress and reason with her before she completely lost control of her emotions. The residence and school staff could easily communicate constant reminders of various coping strategies that Olivia could apply. This was clearly very beneficial for her.

Olivia's counselor was also in regular contact with dormitory counselors and Olivia's mom for updates on Olivia's behavior, and if there were any incidents, they were reviewed during sessions, and work was done on identifying the feelings of all parties involved and strategies to use for next time a similar incident happened. In Olivia's case, she learned best from behavioral learning in her daily activities, rather than learning a skill in theory first and then applying it in practice later, and her counselor emphasized or clarified the importance of using specific strategies in response to specific incidents. With the incident where she commented she wanted to die following the conflict with her friends, she confirmed she didn't really want to die, so her counselor worked with her on strategies to better manage her feelings next time, such as using appropriate vocabulary to express how she felt about this and how to seek support from a safe adult when in distress.

In the absence of any incidents of concern, as they became less frequent, psychoeducational work was done on personal boundaries using hypothetical situations, role-play, figurines representing people, and drawing. She often played with kinetic sand while talking with her counselor.

At home, her mother was the only member of the family who could communicate with Olivia fluently, but she could not be everywhere and everything for her all at once. Isolation at home and the "dinner table syndrome" is hard for the average Deaf child to manage, but for a child like Olivia, living with her mental health diagnoses, it was more stressful.

Counseling at PAH! was helpful, yet this counseling intervention was not enough to help Olivia without additional supports. Without the option of living in the student dormitory at the Deaf school, Olivia's behavior would probably have escalated to greater levels of severity. The family needed respite care, in-home supports, or for Olivia to live in a group home, but these community supports were not available to the degree of accessibility found in the school dormitories. Access to recreational programs and activities with ASL interpreting would have been beneficial to keep Olivia occupied when not in school. Specialized one-on-one ASL tutoring for Olivia's family would have been helpful, so the burden was not entirely on Olivia's mother regarding family communication. Clearly, the mother was experiencing her own degree of distress and was becoming incapable of taking care of her own child.

Mahmoud

Mahmoud and his younger sister, Jamila, were first referred to PAH! by their father, following the breakup of his marriage with the children's mother. They were Codas of both Egyptian and Muslim ethnicity. Mahmoud was 12 years old at the time of referral, and his younger sister was 5 years old. They were referred due to family conflict and emotional concerns. Both children were seen by a Deaf therapist with an ASL interpreter.

The children's father shared that Mahmoud was unhappy that his parents were no longer together. Furthermore, the father shared that Mahmoud was distressed about his mother's relationship with a new same-sex partner. The father commented that Jamila seemed anxious and often wanted to stay with him and was frequently missing school.

During separate individual intake sessions with the parents, we learned that the family conflict started when the mother reunited with a former girlfriend who was also Deaf. She had been compelled to break up with her following family disapproval, in which she was sent to Egypt, met and married the father of her children, and returned to Canada with him soon after. Following a marriage of 15 years, she then reconnected with the former girlfriend which escalated into a love triangle and culminated in family discord. The mother indicated that her ex-husband and her own family were influencing her children's perspective of her relationship with a woman, citing homophobia.

The narrative, as we later understood it, was that during an argument, the girlfriend slashed the mom on the face with a sharp weapon in front of Jamila. The father, upon learning of this shortly after, called the police to ensure his ex-wife's safety. However, the mother reported that it was the father who harmed her, and as a result, the father was taken into police custody and charged with assault. The charge against the father was eventually dropped with the conditional promise of good behavior for one year. The agency for protective services for children became involved and recommended that the children be referred for mental health counseling.

They was nearly a year on the waitlist before the siblings were able to receive service from PAH!. As Mahmoud's file was about to be opened, we received an urgent request from an agency providing mental health services to DHH adults. Mahmoud's Deaf aunt had shared with that agency that Mahmoud had suicidal thoughts about jumping off the roof of his apartment building, as the door to the roof was sometimes left unlocked. When connecting through Zoom video for the first time shortly after, Mahmoud reassured the PAH counselor that he had had suicidal thoughts previously but confirmed that he did not have any current thoughts or plans to harm himself.

Over the course of the next few counseling sessions, Mahmoud shared that the main source of his stress was his mother's new partner. He shared that he felt afraid and uncomfortable when she was around, and that the partner threatened him with having her brother do some "black magic," so he "better be careful with her." Mahmoud also shared that his mother's partner occasionally swore at him and signed rude things to him when his mother was not watching, and that her eyes often followed him when he was inside his home.

Early in the counseling relationship, I, Veronica Bickle, the Deaf counselor, was shown a text conversation that the mother's partner had with Mahmoud in which she told Mahmoud that his father was a pedophile. In a later session, Mahmoud also shared while riding in his father's car that he saw a text message from his mother's partner showing up on his father's phone, threatening his father with dismemberment of his private parts.

Mahmoud shared in counseling that he was also struggling with flashbacks from the time when he was 11 years old when he heard and witnessed constant fighting and yelling between his parents and his mother's partner, and witnessed his father being taken into police custody. He commented that he noticed that he felt upset when hearing sudden noises, triggering his anxiety.

Mahmoud also shared that sometimes he felt unable to stay at home alone because it triggered memories of when his mother often left him at home alone when he was younger, so she could go and meet her partner. He commented about his current dislike of chicken nuggets, since that was the only thing he knew how to cook for himself and his sister when his mom was absent. His mother ceased to leave Mahmoud at home alone for lengthy periods of time, but sometimes when she left their home briefly to pick up his younger sister from school, he felt anxious and tried to distract himself by watching television.

When asked, Mahmoud confirmed he had problems sleeping at night and experienced nightmares. Since the family conflict started, Mahmoud shared that he had been sleeping in the same bed as his mom and his sister, as he felt unable to sleep by himself in his own bedroom. Mahmoud articulated many worrisome thoughts. He was nervous about the possibility of the fire alarm going off or someone breaking into their apartment. He worried about being able to pass Grade 7 due to being unable to concentrate well in school. He worried about his mother's physical safety with her partner given their turbulent relationship, and he also worried about what kind of woman his sister will grow up to be after being exposed to the "toxic" behavior of his mother's partner and her children. Finally, Mahmoud worried that his father often seemed sad.

During counseling sessions, Mahmoud shared details of numerous incidents involving his mother's partner, and in the retelling of these stories, he appeared disconnected from the present. Mahmoud struggled with headaches and tension in his shoulders. His father commented that Mahmoud gained weight when the family was experiencing discord, although his weight gain has since stabilized.

Mahmoud shared that he had already told the local child protection service worker and the police that he did not want to live with his mother, was not comfortable with her partner, and felt that no one was listening to him. He also commented that he did not feel completely safe with his mother as she "will tell her [his mother's partner] everything I share with her," and because she will listen to whatever her partner tells her to do. He added that when telling his mother that he felt uncomfortable with her partner, his mother would suggest that he stay in his bedroom for the time being and "just ignore her."

After reviewing his file and meeting with Mahmoud, the clinical consultant, Dr. Chovaz, diagnosed him with post-traumatic stress disorder (PTSD), noting that his symptoms fell into the three clusters of this disorder: reliving the traumatic events through intrusive memories and dreams, emotional avoidance, and hyper-arousal.

Early in the counseling relationship, the parents were advised that as Mahmoud was over the age of 12 years, he had a limited right to make some decisions for himself. It was explained that if Mahmoud felt unsafe, he could leave home to stay with his maternal aunt and uncle, maternal grandparents, or father without needing permission from his mother. It was recommended that Mahmoud be given a "break" from his mother's partner for a period of time. The rationale was that less contact with the partner as Mahmoud learned coping strategies in counseling may improve his current state of well-being.

His mother eventually complied with the suggestion that Mahmoud should not have any contact or exposure to her partner. Over the next 8 months of counseling at PAH!, during which trauma-focused CBT techniques were taught to Mahmoud, and with no contact with his mother's partner, there was a gradual reduction of symptoms. Counseling sessions included psychoeducation regarding trauma symptoms, development of coping strategies, a better understanding of how thoughts can influence our feelings, and using the techniques of relaxation skills and mindfulness.

Mahmoud then indicated that he felt well enough to terminate counseling. By this time, Mahmoud was receiving better grades in school, and he expressed a preference for spending time with his friends instead of attending counseling sessions. However, he was still sleeping in the same bed with his mother and sister. When discussing this during counseling, he indicated he was ready to try sleeping apart from his mother, if his younger sister was still in the same room as him.

Mahmoud's mother, upon seeing the improvement in Mahmoud's mental health, decided that it was a good time to "reintroduce" her partner by allowing her to visit her home when Mahmoud was there. Previously, she would spend time with her partner when the children were in school and on the weekends when her ex-husband had the kids. The decision by the mother to invite the partner back to the family home had not been discussed with Mahmoud, nor was he forewarned about this. At first, Mahmoud tried to tolerate this change but shortly after, he had another conflict with his mother's partner. When the partner was visiting at his mother's home, Mahmoud became anxious and left the apartment to go downstairs to wait in the lobby for her to leave. Mahmoud's mother went down to talk with him, and her partner followed, resulting in further conflict when the partner lectured him about the lack of respect that he showed her. Mahmoud reported that during the incident, his mother stood by and did not say anything. In retrospect, Mahmoud shared that he felt hurt that his mother did not stand up for him or took his side.

Following this conflict with his mother's partner and during a counseling session in which his mother also joined, Mahmoud shared his feelings about her partner and emphasized he wanted no contact with her. He shared that he understood that his mother wanted to continue to see her "friend," but requested that it did not happen when he was at home.

His mother, at first, was reluctant to confirm that the "break" from her partner needed continue. However, I followed up with a video call during which the mother confirmed that she had reconsidered and would make sure that Mahmoud did not have any contact with her partner and that if she wants this to change in the future, she will have a discussion with him beforehand.

With Mahmoud slowly improving, the frequency of counseling decreased to once a month, with a focus on the goal of being able to sleep alone. After a few months, Mahmoud reported that he is now sleeping alone in his bedroom, commenting that he didn't realize how easy the transition would be. Once he was able to achieve this, he stopped coming in for counseling and eventually, his file was closed, with follow-up meetings with both parents to review strategies to continue to support Mahmoud's mental health.

Jamila

Mahmoud's younger sister, Jamila, was assigned to another Deaf counselor at PAH!, and her file was opened around a month after I started working with her older brother. Jamila, who was 6 years old, had also been impacted by the family conflict. Due to her young age, however, the effects of the family discord on her mental well-being were not as clear, nor was she was able to articulate it well to her therapist.

The PAH therapist was told by the parents that Jamila refused to go to school. However, in the year she was on the PAH wait list for services, she started to attend school more regularly. Jamila had frequent and significant problems falling and staying asleep through the night and was often tired. She was often irritable and had outbursts of temper. Her mother described her as bossy, sassy, and easily frustrated.

However, during counseling sessions, Jamila presented as a quiet, serious young girl, providing answers with a maturity beyond her years, although she was often visibly tired. It was noticed by her counselor and the ASL-English interpreter that Jamila spoke with a flat monotone with few facial expressions, demonstrating none of the usual mannerisms of a child her age, such as giggling or engaging in silly talk.

Unlike her brother, Jamila had ambivalent feelings about her mother's partner and once commented that she liked her "when she was nice." The main source of her stress was her mother—it had been noticed that Jamila showed signs of an insecure attachment and felt that her mother was always mad at her, believing that her mother loved her partner more than her. She felt that her mother would believe other people's accounts about her, rather than believe what she was trying to tell her. When asked if these concerns could be shared with her mom to try and solve these issues, she refused to give consent, worried that her mother would be mad at her. Jamila also refused to have these feelings shared with her father, as she felt her father would share it with her mother.

During counseling, Jamila indicated she believed she was ugly. When asked why she felt this way, Jamila shared that the children of her mother's partner, who were older than her, had told her on a few occasions that she was ugly. Jamila internalized this and believed it. Jamila shared that her mother had made negative comments to her friends in front of her, like that she behaved like a "teenager," and Jamila felt hurt by that. Jamila also shared that when peering over her mother's shoulder to read texts on her phone when her mother was talking with her partner, she saw that her partner complained to her mother that Jamila was rude and annoying.

At the beginning of the counseling sessions, Jamila described school as a positive and supportive place, although this changed over time to the point where she shared that it was not as happy for her. Jamila commented that she was bullied by an older boy on the playground at school and that she was not believed when she initially reported the incident. When she shared it with her mother, Jamila reported that her mother did not do anything. After a few more incidents, her older brother, Mahmoud, asked their father to address this concern with the school principal, which he did. Jamila also shared that, in general, she felt other kids at school did not believe her when she shared stories with them.

Counseling sessions focused on identifying safe adults with whom Jamila could share her concerns or fears. She did not list or volunteer her mother and instead she listed her brother, father, maternal aunt and uncle, and maternal grandparents. It was observed that Jamila looked to her older brother as her main source of support and security. Counseling sessions also addressed Jamila's ongoing fatigue. She indicated that she did not know why she always felt tired. She mentioned a tendency to stay up late watching television, drawing, painting, or listening to music. She once mentioned that the light from her mother's phone bothered her when she was trying to sleep and that she had bad dreams.

Over the months she had been attending counseling at PAH!, Jamila noticeably gained weight. When her father was asked about this, he confirmed that he had noticed this too but was not sure if it was "genetic or not." However, when Jamila was asked about her eating habits, she shared that she felt she was eating less. Her father also noticed the increased frequency of Jamila's irritability, or "bad attitude."

Early in the counseling relationship, Jamila was assessed for symptoms of trauma. When assessing her, she was willing to answer questions. She also became more visibly distressed by questions, particularly when she chose to disclose and describe traumatic events involving her mother and her partner, as well as events that had occurred with the children of her mother's partner. Jamila shared that she had trouble sleeping every night, was tired every day, tried to avoid people that reminded her of unhappy events, had difficulty feeling happy, and found it hard to concentrate in school.

Even though she was clearly experiencing symptoms of trauma, Dr. Chovaz concluded that at that point in time, there was not enough evidence to diagnose PTSD, as there was no evidence of intrusive symptoms, significant negative alterations in mood, or hypervigilance. Dr. Chovaz advised that given Jamila's young age, further information-gathering would be beneficial within the context of play therapeutic approaches, as young children will often express trauma through play re-enactment. An attempt at play therapy with Jamila during a counseling session, however, did not go well—Jamila indicated she did not want to play with dolls or toys and commented she would prefer to draw, so sessions were tailored to meet this.

After a few more months of regular counseling sessions, Dr. Chovaz assessed and diagnosed Jamila with a major depressive disorder related to adverse childhood events (psychosocial stressors). Treatment had been focused on alleviating her depressive symptoms with a focus on improving her sleep patterns and self-esteem.

Reflections on Mahmoud and Jamila

Following my initial conversation with Mahmoud, one of the first things I, Veronica Bickle, noticed as his therapist was how he presented as someone much older. He had just turned 13 years old when we first connected, yet he talked and behaved like a youth closer to adulthood than a child. He was serious and spoke with a gravity of someone older than his years, which made me think of parentification. This tends to occur when parents look to their children for practical and emotional support rather than providing it. Mahmoud experienced the trauma of family discord, had been left alone at home when feeling vulnerable, and was asked frequently to care for his younger sister. His mother commented that when his father was arrested, Mahmoud interpreted for him at the police station. As a result, it was hypothesized that Mahmoud may have felt compelled to grow up faster than a typical boy his age. However, over time, as his life became more stable and his symptoms gradually lessened, Mahmoud started to behave and communicate more like a youth closer to his actual chronological age. The counselor working with Jamila also observed that she was a serious young girl who spoke as if she was an older child. Jamila also had been caught in a family conflict that was likely difficult for a child of her age to understand. She had seen violence between her mother and her partner. She was exposed to upsetting events and had to work through conflicts on her own. Her mother had made some candid comments about Jamila to others in front of her, such as remarking that she already behaved like a teenager, which were comments that may have confused Jamila.

Fundamentally, the siblings had not been protected by their parents as they should have been. As therapists, we queried if the parents were aware or completely understood the impact of the trauma on their children, as they tended to minimize many of the issues their children were expressing or experiencing. When working with Mahmoud and his mother to resolve issues between them, his mother often suspected and accused Mahmoud of not telling the whole story and seemed to expect that he would communicate the problem at the same level of competency as an adult. When discussing this with her later, the mother was encouraged to remember that while Mahmoud was a bright, communicative youth who may seem older than he was at times, he was still a child who had not yet developed a maturity to explain problems in the same way as an adult. Codas are not as vulnerable in terms of delays with language acquisition and the development of ToM. They are usually responsive to traditional mental health interventions, but they can potentially be exposed to various gaps in parenting and access to suitable community supports. We have also observed generational trauma as their parents struggle with their own language and knowledge deprivation, the trauma of their own upbringings with isolation, and parents who could not communicate well with them, as well as the frequent challenges of feeling included in mainstream society.

For Codas like Mahmoud and Jamila, it made sense for them to receive services from an agency that also provided services for DHH children and youth. Communication between Deaf parents and counselors was accessible, as it is important for parents to be involved in their children's mental health journey. At PAH!, the children's counselor was readily available to communicate directly with the Deaf parents without waiting or arranging for an interpreter which sometimes resulted in delayed provision of support. With Mahmoud and Jamila's parents, considerable psychoeducation and support were provided to help them be better able to manage their children's mental and emotional needs.

Communication with the children using an ASL-English interpreter was continuously evaluated. The children were advised they could use either spoken English or ASL. Both children elected to use an interpreter most of the time. With Mahmoud, it was noticed when longer and more complex answers were required, he would use an interpreter, but for shorter responses, he would choose to answer using ASL. It is important to respect the child's wishes of preferred language as well as their communicative competency. Finally, when using an interpreter, the Deaf therapists debriefed following each session requesting the interpreter's input on linguistic characteristics, such as tone of voice, volume, and congruence with facial expression.

Sometimes, mainstream therapists, limited by their own frame of reference and life experiences, may not realize how much a Deaf parent might not know regarding parenting, and may not be able to discern what general information or knowledge the parents may be missing. However as Deaf therapists, we are aware that this can happen quite easily in any area in the life of a Deaf adult. Deaf parents may be more comfortable with Deaf counselors in terms of requesting support or clarification. This may be because Deaf therapists are less likely to be surprised with these knowledge gaps in what hearing therapists may assume to be common knowledge.

We are also very aware of accessibility challenges when Deaf parents may depend on their young children to interpret for them in adult situations. This is clearly not ideal and may be something a mainstream counselor is unaware of in terms of the effect on the child. Mainstream mental health counselors may not be as aware of the intricacies of life as a Coda, the language deprivation that Deaf parents may have experienced, and the impact of accessibility challenges experienced while growing up which may potentially increase the likelihood of parentification, negatively affect the attachment between parent and child, contribute to their own mental health issues, and ultimately create conflict between Deaf parents and their hearing children.

Closing Recommendations

DHH children experience mental health issues just like other children in mainstream society. However, it has been our experience that the complexities related to the myriad etiologies of deafness, effects of language deprivation/delay, deficits in fund of information, delays in the development of ToM, potential differences in attachment with parents, and the lack of accessible resources may all contribute to very complex clinical presentations. All these factors may negatively affect the children's ability to function, their emotional resiliency, and potential to benefit from counseling, such as learning to apply strategies for emotional regulation. This then leads to the exacerbation of mental health symptoms, requiring more intensive and lengthy intervention.

Sometimes, there is no preexisting mental health concern or adverse childhood experience, rather it is a lack of access to language or language deprivation that is at the root of the child's mental health concerns. This may further affect the family's ability to communicate with and develop a secure attachment with their DHH child. Mental health symptoms often become more noticeable when the DHH child becomes older, relying more on communication as a means of connection rather than child play.

PAH! is a mental health program that provides counseling for DHH children and youth but currently does not have the resources and funding to appropriately meet all the varied complex needs. Yet, these clients remain with us for extended periods of time because our low-intensity intervention program is the most accessible and safe environment for them. The length of time that a child remains in our program reflects the complexity of their issues, our lack of resources such as a fully accessible in-patient component, and affects our wait list times. The longer our wait list, the fewer DHH children and youth with varying levels of mental health need can access the supports they critically need.

When complex mental health symptoms escalate with the DHH child or youth, mainstream agencies often do not have the funding or resources to provide intensive mental health support and services. This includes the costs needed for admissions to inpatient mental health units or group homes, as well as the costs needed to ensure equitable communication with ASL interpreters if required. This inability of our community to appropriately respond to the level of their considerable needs often further isolates the DHH child and their family, and families then are left to navigate crises themselves with limited, and often ineffective, support from the mainstream children's mental health system.

Our heart-to-heart experiences suggest the following:

- The need for Deaf friendly strategies:
  It is essential that the mental health care system realize that a number of traditional counseling strategies and approaches simply are not accessible for use with the DHH child, especially when they have varying levels of language deprivation and gaps in ToM development. There needs to be more research and development of deaf-focused or accessible counseling strategies and solutions, information about how to support and respond to the unique mental health issues of DHH children, always considering the intersectionality between Deaf culture, language deprivation, and mental health.
- Language deprivation syndrome:
  We feel our clientele would benefit from formal recognition of language deprivation as a disorder, by adding it to the *DSM-5* (APA, 2022) and acknowledged by various mainstream social service agencies—such as service providers providing support for those with developmental disabilities. We are aware that this is controversial (see chapter 10 where, in fact, the author feels language deprivation syndrome may be a problematic diagnosis in a forensic setting); however, we also have realized that within a mental health setting, we are, at times, struggling to ensure hearing mainstream funders fully realize the lifelong implications of such a classification. In addition to formal recognition of language deprivation as a mental health disorder, strategies to prevent or mobilize early intervention need to be developed. Ideally, DHH children and youth would be screened for early detection of language delay and deprivation and corresponding supports be made available for parents and educators to alleviate its detrimental impacts, going beyond the acquisition of language itself, such as the development of ToM and interpersonal skills.

- Theory of Mind:
  These issues have become apparent in our own clinic, and we are striving to meet these needs which again requires funding and appropriate expertise. For example, we have recently developed a screener to assess ToM in our clients. The results of this screener have confirmed that many of the DHH children referred to PAH! have delays or differences in their development of ToM, perhaps related to their difficulties in language acquisition (Peters & Pisoni, 2023). We hypothesize that if a child cannot understand the perspective of others or accurately identify emotions, then traditional counseling strategies may not be effective.
  We now administer this ToM screener on all children/youth at intake. If a DHH child is identified as significantly lacking in ToM, we then provide a set of modules designed to teach ToM skills. The child will complete these modules prior to the onset of counseling in the hopes of maximizing treatment effectiveness. This is somewhat similar to the pre-work model proposed by Glickman (2012), Glickman and Hall (2018), and Glickman et al. (2020).
- The importance of a fully accessible, in-patient component for DHH children/youth:
  With recent strides in gaining a better understanding of the detrimental effects of language deprivation and lack of ToM with DHH children and youth, there needs to be a better awareness and acceptance that appropriate treatment requires more support and infrastructure than what Deaf-specialized, low-intensity counseling programs or mainstream high-intensity, in-patient programs alone can provide. A better commitment to specialized treatment for all DHH children with high and complex needs that will appropriately respond to the challenges they present may be costly to implement and maintain, but in the long run, these children and youth will become less of a financial burden on the system in terms of their mental health, general health, and overall autonomy as adults. An excellent example of a fully accessible, in-patient component for DHH children/youth is the Walden School at The Learning Center for the Deaf (https://www.tlcdeaf.org/walden-school/about-walden-school), which is a residential therapeutic and educational program in Massachusetts, USA. This program provides treatment to learning- and language-challenged deaf youth with an emphasis on culturally affirmative adaptations to treatment strategies (Bishop, 2013). The PAH program is not residential, and as described in our stories, we recognize that this type of support in Canada would be extremely beneficial.
- Unique needs of Codas:
  We also need to consider the mental health needs of Codas who may experience the generational effects of their parents' adverse childhood experiences, mental health issues, and effects of language deprivation. The childhood experiences of Codas are often qualitatively and significantly different from hearing or DHH children, and mainstream mental health agencies may not always be able to fully appreciate this. The likelihood that there will be inadequate support for these children is high, due to the lack of understanding of the lived experience of their Deaf parents, cultural understanding and sensitivity, as well as lack of funding to provide optimal access to services for the family, such as ASL interpreting. To provide effective mental health assessment and treatment for these children, Deaf parents need to be involved with the process and not be treated as outsiders. Deaf parents should feel included and safe which is likely easiest when working with professionals knowledgeable about these relevant constructs and able to connect with the family unit from a bilingual and bicultural perspective.

- More accessible resources and support for Deaf parents:
  PAH! was able to optimize the translation into ASL of an internationally recognized parenting course, "Circle of Security," which focuses on improving parent-child attachment for Deaf parents with young children. However, while it was a success with hearing parents of Deaf children, the translation of its video clips into ASL, paid for by the organization providing this course, was only suitable for Deaf parents with high-literacy competency, and the course's reliance on an important auditory analogy was a barrier for other Deaf parents with lower literacy skills to utilize. Requests have also been received for accessible parenting courses for those with older children, but PAH! has not been able to respond to this as of this writing. More evidence-based resources designed or appropriately modified for Deaf parents, in addition to specialized counseling support, would help support the gaps that some Deaf parents are currently experiencing.

In conclusion, much more awareness and understanding at the mainstream level regarding the unique mental health issues and experiences of DHH children and Codas is needed for equitable service provision. Although there has been some progress in this area in recent years, much more is needed to translate into effective clinical practices. We understand the logistics of this is challenging related to the small size of Deaf communities, the paucity of well-trained clinicians in this area, and the corresponding sparse funding allocated for specialized programs. Additionally, ongoing meaningful training is needed for those specialized clinics already offering services to this population.

Working with DHH children and Codas can be challenging, sometimes overwhelming, especially when there is so much that we still don't know yet in terms of what the best evidence-based approaches are when with working with DHH children and youth, especially those with language deprivation. Heart-to-heart, we do understand the struggles and frustration of Deaf children and youth and how isolation and exclusion can have such an impact on their mental health, because at least at some level, we also lived through those experiences ourselves. There is no question about the desire, motivation, and passion of the PAH team to try and address these challenges. However, head-to-head, we acknowledge that how we feel, despite the PAH! providing dedicated efforts, is not enough. More research and clinical knowledge regarding these issues DHH children and Codas face is needed beyond the energy and motivation of individual therapists to really make a change. We often struggle with determining if what we are doing is enough for our clients. Yet, the idea of not providing at least some kind of mental health support for this group of children and youth is inconceivable and is why we continue this work. Although difficult, it remains very gratifying work.

We hope that sharing these heart-to-heart stories of counseling DHH children and youth will raise awareness of these issues and work toward creating solutions to improve the quality of specialized mental health services and support for DHH children/youth, Codas, and their families.

References

Aanondsen, C. M., Jozefiak, T., Lydersen, S., Heiling, K., & Rimehaug, T. (2023). Deaf and hard-of-hearing children and adolescents' mental health, quality of life and communication. *BMC Psychiatry*, *23*(1), Article 297. https://doi.org/10.1186/s12888-023-04787-9

American Psychiatric Association. (2022). *Diagnostic and statistical manual of mental disorders* (5th ed., text rev.). https://doi.org/10.1176/appi.books.9780890425787

Anderson, M. L., Glickman, N. S., Wolf Craig, K. S., Sortwell Crane, A. K., Wilkins, A. M., & Najavits, L. M. (2021). Developing Signs of Safety: A Deaf-accessible counselling toolkit for trauma and addiction. *Clinical Psychology & Psychotherapy, 28*(6), 1562–1573. https://doi.org/10.1002/cpp.2596

Bishop, K. (2013). Culturally affirmative adaptations to trauma treatment with deaf children in a residential setting. In N. S. Glickman (Ed.), *Deaf mental health care* (1st ed., pp. 268–297). Routledge. https://doi.org/10.4324/9780203810545-8

Chovaz, C. J. (2013). Report of a deaf child with Tourette's disorder. *Journal of Deaf Studies and Deaf Education, 18*(3), 360–369. https://doi.org/10.1093/deafed/ent014

Cornes, A. J., & Margaret Brown, P. (2012). Mental health of Australian deaf adolescents: An investigation using an Auslan version of the Strengths and Difficulties Questionnaire. *Deafness and Education International, 14*(3), 161–175. https://doi.org/10.1179/1557069X12Y.0000000009

Day, L. A., Costa, E. A., Previ, D., & Caverly, C. (2018). Adapting parent–child interaction therapy for deaf families that communicate via American Sign Language: A formal adaptation approach. *Cognitive and Behavioral Practice, 25*(1), 7–21. https://doi.org/10.1016/j.cbpra.2017.01.008

Dowtin, L. L., & Day, L. A. (2019). Signs and barriers: Play therapy training experiences of deaf and hearing clinicians. *International Journal of Play Therapy*, 28(4), 195–206.

Du Feu, M., & Chovaz, C. J. (2014). *Mental health and deafness*. Oxford University Press.

Fellinger, J., Holzinger, D., Sattel, H., & Laucht, M. (2008). Mental health and quality of life in deaf pupils. *European Child and Adolescent Psychiatry, 17*(7), 414–423. https://doi.org/10.1007/s00787-008-0683-y

Fellinger, J., Holzinger, D., & Pollard, R. (2012). Mental health of deaf people. *The Lancet, 379*(9820), 1037–1044. https://doi.org/10.1016/S0140-6736(11)61143-4

Glickman, N. S. (Ed.). (2012). *Deaf mental health care*. Taylor & Francis Group.

Glickman, N. S., & Hall, W.C. (Eds.). (2018). Language deprivation and deaf mental health (1st ed.). Routledge.

Glickman, N. S., Crump, C., & Hamerdinger, S. (2020). Language deprivation is a game changer for the clinical specialty of deaf mental health *Journal of American Deafness and Rehabilitation Association, 54*(1), 54–89.

Peters, K., Pisoni, D.B. (2023). Theory of Mind in children who are deaf: The importance of early language and conversational access. In T. Lopez-Soto, A. Garcia-Lopez, & F. J. Salguero-Lamillar (Eds.), *The Theory of mind under scrutiny: Psychopathology, neuroscience, philosophy of mind and artificial intelligence* (pp. 243–279). Springer.

Roberts, S., Wright, B., Moore, K., Smith, J., Allgar, V., Tennant, A., Doherty, C., Hughes, E., Moore, D. C., Ogden, R., Phillips, H., Beese, L., & Rogers, K. (2015). Translation into British Sign Language and validation of the Strengths and Difficulties Questionnaire. *Health Services and Delivery Research, 3*(2), 1–96. https://doi.org/10.3310/hsdr03020

Scott, J. A., & Grace Hansen, S. (2020). Working with dual diagnoses: A survey of teachers serving deaf or hard of hearing children who have autism spectrum disorder. *Journal of Autism and Developmental Disorders, 50*(5), 1539–1552.

Swanepoel, B., Swartz, L., Gericke, R., & Mall, S. (2020). Prevalence and correlates of mental and neurodevelopmental symptoms and disorders among deaf children and adolescents: A systematic review protocol. *BMJ Open, 10*(10), 1–7. https://doi.org/10.1136/bmjopen-2020-038431

Tapia-Fuselier, J. L., & Ray, D. C. (2019). Culturally and linguistically responsive play therapy: Adapting child-centered play therapy for deaf children. *International Journal of Play Therapy, 28*(2), 79–87. https://doi.org/10.1037/pla0000091

Turner Dougherty, A. C., & Day, L. A. (2022). Deaf and hard of hearing plus: Preliminary estimates of child and parent functioning. *Rehabilitation Psychology*, 67(2), 189–204. https://doi.org/10.1037/rep0000437

Wright, B., Phillips, H., Allgar, V., Sweetman, J., Hodkinson, R., Hayward, E., Ralph-Lewis, A., Teige, C., Bland, M., & Le Couteur, A. (2022). Adapting and validating the Autism Diagnostic Interview—Revised for use with deaf children and young people. *Autism, 26*(2), 446–449. https://doi.org/10.1177/13623613211029116

Wright, B., Phillips, H., Le Couteur, A., Sweetman, J., Hodkinson, R., Ralph-Lewis, A., Hayward, E., Brennan, A., Mulloy, J., Day, N., Bland, M., & Allgar, V. (2020). Modifying and validating the social responsiveness scale edition 2 for use with deaf children and young people. *PloS One, 15*(12), Article e0243162. https://doi.org/10.1371/journal.pone.0243162

7

Mental Health of Deaf and Hard of Hearing Adults

Meghan L. Fox and Mary K. Matchett

Construct

This chapter outlines research on risk and protective factors associated with Deaf adult mental health. Risk factors reviewed include language deprivation, stigma and discrimination, substance misuse, trauma, limited access to mental health services, and criminal system injustices. We then describe protective factors from the individual, family, community, and Deaf community perspectives. The benefits of positive meaning-making are outlined.

Head-to-Head and Heart-to-Heart

Research on deaf adult mental health began with a special interest in the stories of deaf individuals, families, and communities. Stories beget questions, which lead to research hypotheses, and so on. Human hearts and heads have always been involved in the deaf adult niche in the mental health field. In this chapter, we honor the importance of how head-to-head connections have developed and expanded research in deaf adult mental health on the topics of risk and protective factors. The heart-to-heart stories in this chapter contextualize the research with emotion, meaning, and community. Together, the head-to-head and heart-to-heart in this chapter push forward the boundaries of research and clinical care with deaf adults.

Statements of Reflexivity

First Author: Meghan L. Fox

I am a hearing clinical psychologist and sibling of a Deaf adult with intellectual disabilities and severe and persistent mental illness. I am fluent in American Sign Language (ASL) and contributed to this project by assisting in conceptualizing research questions and interpreting interview data. I led the collection and integration of research utilized in this chapter. I recognize that my roles intersect in a way that leaves me on the fringes of deafness and the Deaf community and influences the value of family members' experiences in this chapter.

Second Author: Mary K. Matchett

I am a Deaf social worker and parent of two Deaf adults, one with mental illness. My family and I are survivors of a family member's suicide. I contributed to developing interview questions, and through my connections in the Deaf community, I led the interview portion of this work. I contributed to interpreting interview data and reviewing the writing of this chapter. I identify with the challenges and experiences of growing up as a Deaf person in a hearing culture, living with a Deaf adult with mental health challenges, and navigating through the system to get help for my Deaf family member.

Heart-to-Heart Experiences

Findings are shared from interviews with 15 people with various kinds of personal and professional experiences with mental illness and related systems. These stories came from the lives of Deaf persons with mental illness, Deaf and hearing mental health professionals, Deaf family members, and hearing, ASL-fluent family members of Deaf adults with mental illness. Quotes from their stories are utilized to augment and highlight research gaps.

Recommendations

We conclude with recommendations for systems, clinicians, researchers, the Deaf community, and family members that stem from lived experience.

Deaf individuals have increased rates of mental health problems, social difficulties, and lower levels of psychological well-being than typically hearing individuals (Chovaz et al., 2022; Chapman & Dammeyer, 2017; Fellinger et al., 2012; Gryglewicz et al., 2017; Mousley & Chaudoir, 2018). Several studies have suggested that anxiety and depression are common among the Deaf population (Fellinger et al., 2012; Kvam et al., 2007; Kushalnagar et al., 2019). Relatedly, Deaf individuals indicated mental health, including stress, anxiety, and depression, as the greatest health concern in a recent survey (James et al., 2021). The prevalence of disability in the Deaf population, including genetic and syndromic conditions, is between 35% and 50% (Mitchell & Karchmer, 2006; Tranebjoerg, 2008). Some perinatal infections (e.g., rubella) and syndromic causes of deafness are associated with other disabilities and poor mental health (Young & Ng, 2023).

Deaf adults with mental illness are understudied (Fellinger et al., 2012; Øhre et al., 2016). Challenges in Deaf mental health research are bidirectional. Deaf communities are difficult for hearing professionals to access because of a lack of linguistic and cultural concordance, inaccessible informed-consent processes and research procedures, inadequate recruitment and engagement strategies, and culturally unfitting research approaches (McKee et al., 2013). The Deaf population has less mental and medical health knowledge and may neither recognize nor report symptoms (Fellinger et al., 2012; Øhre et al., 2016; Pollard & Barnett, 2009). Deaf individuals' fear, mistrust, and frustration toward research, divergence in communication with hearing providers, and obstacles in accessing mental health services lead to underdiagnosis or misdiagnosis and additional gaps in Deaf adult mental health research (Fellinger et al., 2012).

Lived experiences describe a person's ongoing journey involving their perceptions of their personal experiences, choices, and opinions (Chovaz et al., 2022). Our experiences with ourselves and others shape how we understand the world, society, and what happens in our lives. This is a forever-evolving process that builds and deepens infinitely. Understanding lived experience within the context of hearts-to-heart as well as head-to-head can be helpful for oneself and others to benefit research and clinical work. Incorporating heart-to-heart or lived experience into literature helps provide detailed examinations of individuals' personal experiences, deepens the literature, and benefits the community (Chovaz et al., 2022). This equalizes the importance of head-to-head and heart-to-heart connections. Published research has only recently focused on the narratives of Deaf people, and it calls for more attention to Deaf individuals' lived experiences, especially within the context of mental health (Chovaz et al., 2022).

From the coauthors' relationship to identifying research constructs, the value of lived experience and heart-to-heart relationships has led the way for this chapter. We interviewed 15 people from various walks of life and intersections of deafness and mental illness. We connected with these people and their stories through the authors' involvement in the local and national Deaf communities, professional connections, friends, friends' connections, civic involvement, and family members. Our heads brought us together through intellectual curiosity. Our hearts brought us together by valuing each other's stories. To be more specific, we interviewed Deaf persons with mental illness, Deaf and hearing mental health professionals, Deaf family members, and hearing ASL-fluent family members of Deaf adults with mental illness. They had variable backgrounds, including experience as administrators and direct-care professionals in Deaf education, rehabilitation, and art. Their roles in life were unique, including being swim directors, researchers, advocates, licensed professionals, Deaf interpreters, engineers, and actresses, to name a few. They identified as Chicana, Asian, and White. Ages ranged from the 20s through the 60s. Some came from first, second, third, and fifth generations of Deaf families. We dedicate this chapter to those who shared their stories with us and their families. We paraphrase and quote their stories with gratitude and care to illustrate research and note what research has not captured. Childhood and adolescent experiences cannot be separated when understanding adult mental health. However, this chapter focuses on Deaf adult mental health. We will discuss research and heart-to-heart experiences on risk and protective factors related to mental illness for Deaf adults. Our recommendations for systems, clinicians, researchers, the Deaf community, and family members stem from lived experience.

Risk Factors Associated with Deaf Adult Mental Health

Being deaf itself does not create a risk factor for suboptimal life outcomes, including mental illness; instead, it is the interaction between Deaf people and disabling environments that put Deaf people at risk for less optimal well-being (Listman et al., 2011; Young et al., 2008). Here, we identify the disabling environments and risk factors affecting Deaf adult mental health, including language deprivation, stigma, substance misuse, trauma, limited access to mental health services, and criminal system injustices.

Language Deprivation

Language deprivation is an essential topic in Deaf mental health (the reader is referred to Chapter 1 for a more detailed discussion). Most Deaf children are born to hearing parents who often have no prior knowledge of deafness and are not well-informed about the Deaf community (Humphries et al., 2016; Mitchell & Karchmer, 2006). Consequently, most Deaf people experience limited access to language and communication, including the "dinner table syndrome" where their hearing families are conversing. Thus, they cannot participate freely in conversations (Hauser et al., 2010; Humphries et al., 2016). Those conversations severely limit incidental learning for Deaf persons on topics such as coping with stress, family health history, and social etiquette. Barriers to incidental learning are lifelong risks that Deaf adults experience in their homes, jobs, and communities.

Limited incidental learning contributes to low English literacy. To reflect this, Pollard (1998) coined the term "fund-of-information (FOI) deficit," a distinct limitation in one's factual knowledge base compared to the general population, despite average intelligence and educational attainment. FOI deficits impact how deaf adults share about their mental health experiences, process information, and navigate systems of care.

Clinicians often see language deprivation and language dysfluency as common "symptoms" in deaf individuals who seek treatment and are subsequently hospitalized (Black & Glickman, 2006). A "language deprivation syndrome" involving language dysfluency, FOI deficits, and disruptions in thinking, mood, and behavior with neurological educational and developmental consequences has been proposed (Glickman, 2008; Hall et al., 2017; Humphries et al., 2016). Some of the leading theorists in deaf adult mental health have head-to-head connections that have benefitted the advancement of research and recommendations in this area.

Language deprivation contributes to behavioral, emotional regulation, and psychosocial difficulties in Deaf children (Dammeyer, 2010; Gulati, 2018). Please see Chapter 1 for a more detailed discussion of language acquisition and deprivation. The extent to which language-related stressors impact health outcomes later in life with Deaf persons has been demonstrated empirically in several studies. Poorer direct child–caregiver communication and ongoing exclusion from incidental family communication are associated with increased risk for depression, anxiety disorders, and other chronic health conditions (Kushalnagar et al., 2020). Perceived inability to understand what their caregivers said was significantly associated with lower quality of life and increased depressive symptoms (Kushalnagar et al., 2011). Poorer direct child–caregiver communication was strongly associated with greater symptoms of depression (Kushalnagar et al., 2017). Lastly, Deaf and Hard of Hearing (D/HH) adults who reported being unable to understand what their primary caregiver said during their formative years had significantly higher odds of experiencing food insecurity than D/HH adults who understood some to all of what their caregivers said (Kushalnagar et al., 2019).

The stories we captured in our interviews provided a true-to-life perspective on how language deprivation complicates a mental health crisis:

> In-person, mental health–trained ASL and certified Deaf interpreters (CDIs) must be present during the entire process and patient stay. When a Deaf person is in a psychotic or severe mood episode, an ASL interpreter will probably not be able to capture and communicate everything alone. Interpreters not showing up for assignments, the limited number of allowed persons in the room, and overreliance on video remote interpreting during the COVID-19 pandemic created more layers of language deprivation that impacted my mental health and treatment. (Interviewee 14)

> My husband's lifelong experience of language deprivation is a big part of understanding his mental illness. Starting with his family and childhood, where he did not have access to communication, and then at his job as an adult, where he was discriminated against and denied interpreters and technology accommodations, he felt abandoned, unimportant, and rejected. Then, he sought mental health treatment and faced further language deprivation and discrimination. He waited for days during inpatient hospitalization for an interpreter to be provided, and another time, he waited months to get a 30-minute virtual appointment with a Deaf expert. (Interviewee 13)

Stigma and Discrimination

Deaf individuals are considered an invisible minority because their deafness is not readily apparent (Abney et al., 2017; Stapleton, 2016). Many Deaf individuals experience institutional and structural discrimination because they communicate in a language without written form and live within societies that favor hearing and speaking privileges (Abney et al., 2017; Mousley & Chaudoir, 2018). This phonocentric hegemony often results in Deaf people being underestimated, pitied, and excluded from participating in common daily activities (Listman & Kurz, 2020). The effects of stigma and discrimination that Deaf people face impact educational achievement, employment, poverty, healthcare services, role models, and health and mental health literacy (Abney et al., 2017; Boutin, 2010; Fellinger et al., 2012; McKee et al., 2015; Stapleton, 2016). Deaf individuals with multiple intersections of diversity may experience stigma and discrimination concerning other aspects of their identity (Leigh et al., 2020). The intersectionality of being Deaf with other aspects of diversity (e.g., race, ethnicity, religion, sexual identity/orientation, age, and disability) is typical and adds unique layers and dimensions to understanding the well-being, happiness, and mental health of Deaf adults (Leigh et al., 2020). Research has documented the effects of stigma on Deaf individuals' mental illness, well-being, depressive symptoms, anxiety, and quality of life (Chapman & Dammeyer, 2017; Mousley & Chaudoir, 2018; Rogers et al., 2003). Similarly, the psychosocial impacts of acculturative stress include anger, anxiety, depression, exhaustion, resentment, and trauma (Aldalur et al., 2021). The lifelong and widespread experiences of stigma have been described as traumatic by Deaf people (Johnson et al., 2018).

Most of our interviewees' narratives included an underlying or obvious current about the stigma they faced living in an audistic society. A more prominent layer that research has not studied is the stigma associated with mental illness and how it further complicates getting help.

A Deaf mother of a Deaf son who died by suicide passionately shared the following:

> My son was determined to keep his academic grades up amid his downward mental health spiral. He convinced others that he was fine, but underneath, he was terrified of ruining his reputation if someone found out he needed help. He feared that getting help would be considered weak. (Interviewee 2)

A Deaf mental health professional with mental illness was feeling vulnerable about how intersections between his professional and personal lives complicated his mental health:

> I have many concerns about my reputation and misconceptions in the Deaf community. Those worries influence my choices in getting help and jobs I might pursue. What if the patients I refer for care see me at the same mental health clinics and support groups? There is a peer specialist position that I am very interested in, but I struggle with how working in this position would expose my mental health, family, and patients' confidentiality to the community. There are limited options for Deaf adults to have both privacy and accessibility in their mental health care. (Interviewee 14)

Our heart-to-heart narratives underscored another way that stigma impacts Deaf adult mental health, specifically how young Deaf adults are ill-prepared for adulthood and how this impacts their trajectory:

> Young Deaf adults often transition into being legal adults from schools and families who shelter them from the world. They struggle to gain maturity and assertive communication skills and understand how things work. Then this impacts their employment, finances, social life, living arrangements, self-esteem, and mental health. (Interviewee 8)

> The transition from high school to the working world or postsecondary education is a crucial time that impacts the trajectory of Deaf adults' mental health. They experience intense isolation after high school graduation, including a loss of daily interactions with teachers and peers who serve as role models, friends, and a source of shared information. There is a lack of job training, accessible employers, and postsecondary academic programs. This contributes to low self-esteem and negatively influences their mental health. (Interviewee 7)

Substance Misuse

Substance misuse could be at least as prevalent, of greater severity, and occur at an earlier age in Deaf adults when compared to hearing adults (Lipton & Goldstein, 1997; Titus et al., 2008). A lack of substance abuse education and prevention efforts, accessible information about signs and symptoms, culturally affirmative substance misuse treatment, fears about stigma from within the Deaf community, and the ignorance of family and friends (Guthmann & Blozis, 2001; Guthmann & Sandberg, 2003) contribute to the risk of Deaf persons developing a substance misuse disorder. Academic problems, low education level, unemployment, major depressive episodes, impairment in activities of daily living, and experiencing trauma without healthy coping strategies are other risk factors for alcohol use in the Deaf population (Anderson et al., 2016; Guthmann & Graham, 2005; Park et al., 2021). The comorbidity of substance misuse disorders and mental illness increases the likelihood of suicide attempts for Deaf adults (Guthmann & Graham, 2005). The head-to-head connections in the field have a long way to go before treatment for the deaf hearts impacted by substance use problems is meeting the needs of the community.

Few of our interviewees talked about substance misuse. Perhaps this is a result of the stigma that Deaf adults face in understanding and talking about substance misuse. One person shared his professional experiences in working with dual-diagnosis patients:

> I am working with a client who has schizophrenia and a substance misuse disorder and is very good at masking himself. When he is placed in a detox facility, and they find out he has schizophrenia, they discharge him, stating that he needs to be in another setting. However, when placed at a mental health hospital, he faces billing and insurance coverage issues and limited treatment for his substance misuse because that is not their expertise. There are so few facilities that provide dual-diagnosis treatment. I see no partnership between the state offices of mental health and public health; one pays for mental health treatment but not substance misuse, and vice versa. (Interviewee 14)

Trauma

Deaf individuals are nearly twice as likely to experience trauma than individuals from the general population, including higher rates of child maltreatment, interpersonal trauma, later revictimization, and intimate partner violence (Anderson & Leigh, 2011; Anderson et al., 2016; Pollard et al., 2014; Schenkel et al., 2014). Having a mother or father using corporal punishment, being bullied, and being the victim of serious childhood sexual abuse were significantly correlated with mental health problems for Deaf adults (Kvam & Loeb, 2010). Compared to individuals from the general population, Deaf individuals are more likely to develop posttraumatic stress disorder (PTSD) and demonstrate higher rates of lifetime trauma and PTSD symptoms (Porter & Williams, 2011; Schenkel et al., 2014; Schild & Dalenberg, 2012).

Language deprivation and delays, strained parental relationships, social isolation, societal prejudice and marginalization, and sociocultural barriers can create psychological and emotional difficulties that constitute a distinct trauma that Deaf individuals may experience (Anderson et al., 2016). Information deprivation trauma (IDT) is a historically prevalent type of trauma specific to Deaf experiences that explains how lacking knowledge or information can intensify traumatic experiences (Johnson et al., 2018). For example, FOI deficits in important health information (e.g., proper healthcare practices, coping strategies, and safety behaviors) (Pollard, 1998; Pollard & Barnett, 2009) increase the chance of developing severely chronic maladaptive coping strategies or life-threatening conditions that could have been avoided with adequate access to information (Schenkel et al., 2014). Limited communication with the hearing world can inhibit environmental cues and warnings (e.g., alarms, sirens, and calls from others) make an already traumatic experience seem more sudden, unpredictable, and uncontrollable, and increase the possibility of subsequent trauma (Anderson et al., 2016; Glickman, 2013; Schenkel et al., 2014; Schild & Dalenberg, 2012). When access to communication is limited in relationships, the effects of trauma can be escalated, especially if the abuser is the same person that a survivor relies on for access to information, social support, and interaction with the world (Vernon & Andrews, 1990). The expanded theorization that IDT adds to the field of deaf mental health is a profound development stemming from marrying head-to-heart connections.

Our interviewees disclosed many heartbreaking stories of abuse, bullying, and revictimization. Their narratives highlighted how inaccessibility exacerbated trauma, delayed help, and resulted in losing a loved one to suicide. Family members' vicarious trauma is a concept not often discussed in the literature.

A Deaf mother who is a social worker and had a Deaf son with autism spectrum disorder (ASD) die by suicide shared the following:

> With my graduate education and 28 years of experience in social work, it was very difficult witnessing our Deaf son not have the same rights and access as his hearing peers in inpatient psychiatric care. It was emotionally and mentally draining for the whole family to be constantly checking on him, thinking ahead about accessibility, trying to understand him when he could not explain himself, working around our schedules to make sure someone was present for his appointments and transitions, researching information to enhance our understanding of his diagnoses and needs, and checking in on each other's well-being. Having a Deaf family member with mental illness puts family members at higher risk for mental health challenges. (Interviewee 12)

A Deaf sister of a Deaf brother with ASD who died by suicide vulnerably said the following:

> I experienced guilt from wanting a "normal" life with a sibling without mental illness. I am also grateful for what we had. I worried about how others would treat my brother. I protected him in case others were unkind to him, but I did not want to hide his true self either. It was traumatic seeing him struggle and hoping for his good days. (Interviewee 10)

Another Deaf woman with a hearing brother with mental illness recalled how their mother was never the same after finding out about her son's trauma:

> My mom admitted to me that she was sickened to find out years later about the sexual abuse and bullying that my brother endured. My brother was sexually abused by his counselor, someone the family trusted! By the time he shared it with my mother, he was an adult and so severely self-medicating that he was dying on the inside. My mother felt so helpless. (Interviewee 3)

A Deaf male social worker shared insights from his work with families:

> People with Deaf family members with mental illness experience another disadvantage because they experience a lack of accessible resources and help for their ill family members and themselves. Loved ones experience emotional, mental, and physical challenges from being along for the ride. Support services must be available for the whole family, not just individuals with mental illness. (Interviewee 4)

Our interviewees noted how helpless, isolating, and exhausting it could be to wear so many hats in their loved one's mental illness journey. They often leaned on their families and had a small support system of people who respected their privacy, understood their unavailability, and did not judge their circumstances.

Limited Access to Mental Health Services

Deaf people experience significant challenges in accessing behavioral health care, including distrust and fear in medical settings, limited exposure to or knowledge of mental health disorders and treatment, and a negative view of mental health care providers (Fellinger et al., 2012; Pollard & Barnett, 2009; Steinberg et al., 1998). The lack of ASL-fluent and culturally knowledgeable providers and providers' lack of training in providing interpreters and culturally and linguistically appropriate accommodations disproportionately impacts Deaf individuals (Anderson et al., 2016; Crowe, 2019; Johnson et al., 2018; Mousley & Chaudoir, 2018).

All of the heart-to-heart narratives we collected highlighted what head-to-head research has emphasized for decades—the lack of accessible mental health services for Deaf adults. Some shared stories of how the lack of accessible mental health services led to additional trauma.

> During an inpatient mental health hospitalization during COVID-19, our Deaf son's hearing social worker insensitively and ignorantly met with our son without an interpreter and kept his mask on. This took away his communication accessibility and escalated his stress and anxiety. Our son's communication accessibility was even more important when he was psychologically unstable. He did not have any energy left to advocate for himself. (Interviewee 12)

> Uninformed hearing providers acting unethically and unprofessionally has long-lasting and far-reaching consequences for Deaf patients. A hearing psychiatrist who was not fluent in ASL accused me of being a know-it-all about my son's mental health. He scolded me in front of my son, destroying our mother-son bond. After that, my son became confused and suspicious about whether I was truthful. Our relationship was never the same. (Interviewee 2).

A Deaf sister added perspective about how hearing individuals in Deaf families suffer from the inaccessibility of mental health support for Deaf persons:

> It was very lonely for my brother as the only hearing person in our family. He navigated two different cultures, sets of values, education systems, and languages without his parents being able to support him fully. His hearing mental health counselor communicated with him only, and his Deaf family members were not encouraged or allowed to join the sessions. Although my brother was hearing, he experienced increased risk from the lack of accessible services for mixed Deaf and hearing families. (Interviewee 3)

Language and cultural inaccessibility during inpatient hospitalization and discharge was a pronounced theme in lived experience narratives:

> When our son was hospitalized, none of the staff was sensitive to working with Deaf patients and families. The nurses figured there was no harm in pointing at the medication and showing a note with a smile without an interpreter. Our son could not ask and respond to questions about medication or other aspects of his care. The hearing social worker met with our son repeatedly without an interpreter and never collaborated with the Deaf social worker and outpatient mental health program in the same hospital! We are a Deaf family, and all of us would have benefitted from the inpatient staff having training and working with the Deaf mental health professionals that were in the same building. It might have helped de-escalate our son's symptoms, build rapport, reduce isolation, and improve communication. (Interviewee 12)

> Inpatient psychiatric care has an ongoing issue of discharging Deaf adults when they are unstable and without an appropriate assessment and an accessible and comprehensive discharge plan. Inpatient psychiatric teams need to include several mental health professionals who work with Deaf adults to ensure that the assessment is accurate [and] Deaf patients can access inpatient activities and prepare a comprehensive and accessible discharge plan. (Interviewee 6)

> So often, when Deaf adults are discharged from inpatient treatment, their ability to continue recovering is cut off. The referrals made for them to housing, medication, and counseling services are not made with accessibility (e.g., interpreters, finding culturally appropriate clinical providers, transportation, or technology) in mind. The inpatient treatment programs rarely engage a trusted adult to support the Deaf adult and their discharge plan. (Interviewee 5)

To minimize the risk of misdiagnosis and suboptimal treatment, psychological assessments and treatment of Deaf individuals require clinically skilled, culturally sensitive, sign language–fluent professionals who can communicate directly with Deaf patients (Fellinger et al., 2012). Hiring an interpreter is insufficient for clinicians to thoroughly assess for psychosis, substance use, mood symptoms, and suicide with Deaf patients. Appropriate psychiatric assessment and treatment require clinicians to know and be able to assess language modality and language fluency, deafness/audiological history, social norms, and cultural identification. The lack of accurate and accessible clinicians, psychological assessments, and therapeutic approaches for Deaf persons can lead to significant errors that result in unnecessary and prolonged hospitalizations, missteps in medication treatment, and a failure to develop appropriate treatment programs and services (Glickman, 2008).

A Deaf couple who found a way through the husband's mental illness faced years of struggling with misdiagnosis, inaccurate assessments, and missed opportunities for treatment:

> For years my husband and I told our family doctor that we suspected that he had bipolar disorder, and that depression was not capturing all his symptoms. The family doctor is hearing and relies on interpreter services. The family doctor decided that my husband did not meet the diagnosis. However, I witnessed my husband's behaviors and moods and asked an accomplished Deaf therapist for her opinion. She agreed that he showed many symptoms of bipolar disorder and suggested he seek inpatient treatment. Once he was admitted to the hospital and had interpreter services, he was diagnosed with bipolar disorder and put on a better medication plan. All those years, I knew he had been prescribed the wrong medication, and it turned out that the antidepressant medication was causing more manic symptoms. (Interviewee 13)

> Misdiagnosis is common because of the lack of interpreters and inappropriate interpretation by interpreters who are not trained to work with Deaf adults with mental illness. This leads to misunderstandings of Deaf adults' behaviors, judgment clouded by pity, mistakes in evaluations, misdiagnosis, and poor treatment. (Interviewee 14)

> When I was discharged from the hospital, I expressed an interest in the partial hospitalization program (PHP), an intensive psychiatric outpatient virtual program. I knew I needed that next level of care to help me continue treatment and stabilize. The staff said I could not attend the PHP because no interpreters were available. I let the hospital team know that PHP was not in my discharge plan, and their response was, "Sorry, there is nothing we can do because it is not our department." One staff said, "Once you are discharged, we are no longer responsible for your care, and that applies to everyone." Because of my mental illness and barely being stable, I was exhausted and did not have the energy to continue fighting, so I gave up. The lack of partnership efforts between the hospital social worker and the outpatient agencies in the community needs to be improved. (Interviewee 14)

Other interviewees noted additional systemic barriers in Deaf mental health care:

> There is a need for more diversity (e.g., Deaf male, nonbinary) in mental health professionals who work with Deaf adults. However, there are licensure challenges, such as accessing ASL-fluent supervisors within the state where the supervisee is pursuing licensure. There are also limited opportunities for professional development and consultation for Deaf mental health professionals. (Interviewee 6)

> Crisis hotlines are often inaccessible. Appropriate and safe peer support programs do not exist for Deaf persons. State laws regarding family involvement in involuntary hospitalization proceedings also create a disadvantage for cases involving Deaf adults because important information is missing about the way a Deaf person's mental health is manifested. Health insurance coverage for mental health services (e.g., restricting the number of units allowed for psychological assessment and disallowing couples psychotherapy), lower reimbursement rates for Medicare and Medicaid plans, and the lack of in-network ASL-fluent providers create other logistical barriers. (Interviewee 9)

The stories shared with us emphasized how systems in Deaf adult mental health failed to communicate with one another and how systems that ideally support young deaf adults are unprepared to deal with mental illness.

> My Deaf sister lives in a mental-health-supported housing program for Deaf adults, a privilege, I know. I have close working relationships with all of the staff involved in her care, and it still took over a year of multiple hospitalizations, emails pleading for collaboration, staff changes, and ultimately me blowing up to get her housing coordinator, case manager, therapist, and medication provider to attend a virtual meeting. (Interviewee 15).

> I asked about local off-campus mental health inpatient psychiatric care services for my son but was told none existed. I later learned that there was a Deaf psychiatric care unit at a hospital about an hour from campus. The college did not collaborate with the community [in which] it resided. The lack of connection between college campuses and the community or other agencies has far-reaching consequences, including my son's life. (Interviewee 2)

Technology is associated with accessibility, and within the past few years, an increased focus on creating virtual access to mental health services has been widespread in inpatient and outpatient systems. Data shows support for the benefits and effectiveness of telemental health services with Deaf persons (Crowe, 2017; Afrin & Critchfeld, 1997; Wilson & Schild, 2014; Gournaris & Leigh, 2019; Wilson & Wells, 2009). Deaf individuals report more frequent and longer sessions (Afrin & Critchfield, 1997), decreased travel costs, increased satisfaction, increased savings in time, and improved accessibility when using telehealth technology (Afrin & Critchfield, 1997; Wilson & Wells, 2009; Wilson & Schild, 2014). Research has begun to explore the factors and obstacles contributing to Deaf perspectives in using telemental health (providing services over a virtual medium (e.g., HIPAA-compliant video platform or phone), including the availability of in-person therapy, therapists' ASL fluency, familiarity and experience with therapy and telemental health, financial compensation, licensure boundary limitations, and addressing mental health emergencies (Crowe, 2017; Wilson & Schild, 2014). One silver lining to come out of the COVID-19 pandemic is that it moved the needle on the acceptance of telehealth by stakeholders and enforceable legislative actions of providers advocating for the use of telehealth. Telemental health services with culturally and linguistically competent providers can effectively reduce disparities in mental health care and increase accessibility for Deaf adults.

Criminal System Injustices

Inaccessibility and the increased rates of language, psychosocial, and behavioral problems associated with Deaf populations extend to antisocial and criminal actions that may bring them into the criminal justice system (O'Rouke et al., 2013). While limited, research indicates that Deaf individuals are overrepresented among forensic populations (Mitchell & Braham, 2011; Zidenberg, 2021). Two significant factors related to this overrepresentation are language deprivation and biases in the criminal justice system. The reader is referred to Chapter 10 for a more detailed discussion on DHH persons in the Canadian criminal justice system.

FOI deficits and language deprivation result in Deaf persons often lacking legal competency knowledge and skills. In addition to the lack of necessary competency knowledge, inaccessibility leaves Deaf persons, especially those with language deprivation, vulnerable and disempowered (Miller & Vernon, 2001; Bramley, 2007). They may mistakenly confess to offenses, make poor witnesses, and their behavior may be misunderstood as lacking remorse (McAlister, 1994; Miller & Vernon, 2001; Vernon et al., 1996; Miller, 2004; Chovaz et al., 2023). Severe language deprivation is frequently observed among deaf persons accused of crimes (Miller et al., 2005; Young et al., 2001). Case law also has recognized the presence and legal significance of language deprivation (*Wisconsin v. Hindsley*, 2000; *Shook v. Mississippi*, 2000; *Wilson v. North Carolina*, 1996). Due to the frequent comorbidity of language deprivation and mental illness among Deaf people in forensic settings, it is hard to discern whether the dysfluency stems from a mental disorder and/or language deprivation (Pollard & Fox, 2018).

The legal system is complex, and without appropriate access, Deaf people experience many injustices, including being routinely denied access to sign language interpreters and assistive technology (e.g., videophones), given inaccessible information (e.g., Miranda warnings, orders in spoken or written English), and put in physically unsafe situations (e.g., inaccessible alerts and being targeted by hearing inmates). The marginalization of Deaf people in the criminal justice system is compounded by the lack of qualified interpreters and advocates, limited education and training about Deaf culture in criminal justice settings, trauma experiences, and oppression (Martin et al., 2021; Zidenberg, 2021, Chovaz et al., 2023). Many Deaf individuals in the criminal justice system need mental health and substance abuse treatment, which can be even less accessible (O'Rouke et al., 2013). The reader is encouraged to read Chapter 10 for a detailed discussion of these constructs.

Researchers and clinicians have consistently called for specialist mental health services in forensic settings, including comprehensive communication, safety, and threat assessments; specialized strategies in evaluations; accessible treatment including linguistic development and after-release support; and educating professionals working in the criminal justice system (Martin et al., 2021; O'Rourke & Grewer, 2005; Pollard & Fox, 2018; Pollard & Berlinksi, 2017; Zidenberg, 2021). The forensic field would greatly benefit from listening with their hearts to the stories of rampant injustice in the Deaf community to guide the next steps in research and political action.

A Deaf couple whose Deaf son with ASD died by suicide reflected on their multiple encounters with law enforcement shortly before his death:

> When our son had psychotic breakdowns at our house, we requested the police multiple times to help with a mental hygiene arrest (MHA). We were denied mental health help, and interpreters were repeatedly "unavailable." The officers did offer to help us press charges and left, stating that he was not eligible for MHA. There was also some confusion about if one officer was a "Deaf liaison" or not. That officer could barely sign. Our son's symptoms escalated to the point where he broke everything with a reflection, like glasses, televisions, picture frames, and much more. We looked at the officer who had been at our home before and asked him, "Is he eligible for MHA now?!" Law enforcement systems need training to understand Deaf mental health and the importance of ASL and CDI interpreters. They also need to follow up with families and persons from marginalized communities. Law enforcement needs to walk the talk about their professional values and beliefs in serving the public. (Interviewees 11 and 12)

Another person shared her observations and feelings of helplessness:

> It is frustrating to witness the discrimination and irrevocable consequences that uninformed legal systems and legal professionals have on Deaf persons and their families in criminal, civil, administrative, and family court cases. I have watched Deaf individuals try to educate professionals in the legal system by sharing information about local ASL-fluent experts with their attorneys and bringing Deaf advocates to their hearings, only to be met with attorneys and judges' preference for the professionals whom they know and work with often, but are ignorant about Deaf culture, language, and mental health. (Interviewee 15)

Protective Factors and Resilience

Resilience is overcoming adversity using assets and external resources (Crowe, 2021; Eichengreen et al., 2022). Resilience involves a dynamic interplay between assets, strengths, and external resources in multiple systems that can modify or prevent negative effects from aversive life circumstances and support successful adaptation (Eichengreen et al., 2022; Johnson et al., 2018; Rogers et al., 2003). Resilience is associated with health, well-being, achievement, healthy relationships, and financial freedom (Johnson et al., 2018).

Deaf individuals have historically been classified as at-risk, and their resilience in the face of multiple systematic challenges with obtaining equitable education, employment, and quality of life has been overlooked (Cawthon & Garberoglio, 2017; Luckner & Muir, 2001). Research has examined resilience-related assets and protective processes of Deaf adults (Chovaz et al., 2022; Rogers et al., 2003), case histories (Charlson et al.,1999), and autobiographical essays (Steinberg, 2000). Other research describes intrapersonal, behavioral, and environmental assets in navigating the Deaf and hearing worlds (Rogers et al., 2003) and promotive and protective factors in resilience development specific to Deaf people who experience trauma (Johnson et al., 2018). Recent research has examined the concept of anticipated work-family conflict management self-efficacy, psychological well-being as a multidimensional resilience factor, archival data, proposed theoretical models for future research, and how Deaf adult professionals described risk and protective factors encountered throughout their childhoods (Listman & Kurz, 2020; Lukomski, 2011; Meyer & Kashubeck-West, 2011; Michael et al., 2011). Research has called for more attention to Deaf adults' lived experiences and perspectives on their resilience (Eichengreen et al., 2022; Listman & Kurz, 2020; Young et al., 2011). Despite research's attempt to logically make sense of the underpinnings of resilience, we are still often amazed at stories of resilience. The desire to live and create a life worth living in the face of adversity is only fully understood when our hearts are involved. To capture resilience using a lived experience lens, we examine individual, family, environmental, and community factors.

Individual Factors

Individual factors contributing to resilience for Deaf persons are intrapersonal, perseverance, social, and insight-oriented. Intrapersonal assets that are protective for Deaf persons include a good sense of humor, a responsible personality, and a commitment to worthy goals (Eichengreen et al., 2022; Johnson et al., 2018; Rogers et al., 2003). Perseverance-related factors include goal-directed behavior, persistent problem-solving, embracing challenges, motivation, autonomy, and a purpose in life (Eichengreen et al., 2022; Johnson et al., 2018; Rogers et al., 2003). Socially oriented individual characteristics that benefit resilience development in Deaf experiences include a caring personality, strong social bonds, emotional perceptiveness, empathy, flexibility, gratitude, and comfort with solitude (Johnson et al., 2018; Rogers et al., 2003). Other noteworthy insightful attributes that foster resilience for Deaf persons are awareness of strengths, self-authenticity, self-advocacy, self-reliance, self-awareness, self-efficacy, and self-esteem (Johnson et al., 2018; Rogers et al., 2003).

Resilience research with Deaf persons identified some deafness-related attributes that impact resilience. Eichengreen et al. (2022) report in their study that having spoken communication skills, minimizing the appearance and importance of hearing loss, and accepting hearing loss are individual-level factors contributing to resilience among young Deaf adults (Eichengreen et al.,

2022). The value of developing an identity, including navigating intersections of diversity, deafness, and disability, was noted as a critical deaf-specific protective factor (Johnson et al., 2018). Deaf literature has repeatedly endorsed the development of a healthy deaf identity and other protective cultural identities as important for developing and enacting resilience (Jambor & Elliot, 2005; Lytle et al., 2011; Moore & Mertens, 2015; Young et al., 2008).

The limited focus on individual characteristics in our lived-experience interviews speaks to the understanding that resilience exists in interpersonal relationships and the heart-to-heart connection (Chovaz et al., 2022). Narratives like the following echoed the research:

> My education, combined with my knowledge about mental health challenges, including my experiences from my childhood trauma, my own therapy, and learned resources for healing, were protective factors for my son and me. (Interviewee 2)

> Good self-esteem, advocacy skills, desire for information and resources, and good interpersonal skills are necessary. You cannot be afraid to ask questions or seek information, but you must also be diplomatic. (Interviewee 8)

> Having some residual hearing, spoken language abilities, and English literacy was beneficial when my Deaf family needed to research and understand patients' rights, medical bills, insurance statements, and medical language. I gained a lot of experience through my job in a hearing environment that I applied to help our son; I could grasp the scope of organizations, understand how they function and anticipate challenges. (Interviewee 11)

Language Development and Family

Early language acquisition (signed or spoken) protects against mental illness (Sessa & Sutherland, 2013). Access to in-depth interpersonal conversations, sophisticated language acquisition, and literacy development are critical protective factors for Deaf individuals (Cawthon et al., 2015; Chovaz et al., 2022; Lytle et al., 2011). Building knowledge and acquiring information in safe ways (e.g., practice, role play) earlier in life and at critical developmental stages (e.g., transitioning into postsecondary settings) are essential (Johnson et al., 2018). Necessary prerequisites for language access include quality and meaningful educational experiences, the value of a trusted adult, high-caliber communication, having a foundation of emotional vocabulary, and opportunities to process experiences using their natural language (Chovaz et al., 2022; Johnson et al., 2018). There are multiple nuances in how family and parental support contribute to resilience for Deaf persons. Parental and family involvement, acceptance, full linguistic inclusion, high parental expectations, and emotional support can contribute to resilience and positive self-esteem for Deaf persons (Ahlert & Greef, 2012; Cawthon et al., 2015; Chovaz et al., 2022; Eichengreen et al., 2022; Johnson et al., 2018; Listman & Kurz, 2020; Rogers et al., 2003).

The stories we captured consistently highlighted the value of supportive and linguistically accessible families in coping with mental illness and fostering positive mental health.

> As a Deaf family with shared knowledge about each other's deafness and abilities, we maintained our roles and responsibilities with respect, clear boundaries, and open communication. (Interviewee 12)

> My Dad and I were very close. We kept each other going during difficult family times. We were each other's only support system. (Interviewee 1)

> My mom and I are very close. We support each other by exchanging ideas about what we can do to support my brother. In some ways, stigma encouraged the family to be close because we did not want to reach out to people outside the family. (Interviewee 3)

Community

The immense value of stories and heart-to-heart connections rings true in the concept of community. Research on the protective community factors contributing to Deaf mental health touched on relationships with peers and mental health providers and access to technology. Peer-group membership and a sense of belonging are protective factors against developing mental disorders for Deaf persons (Fellinger et al., 2009; Øhre et al., 2016). Positive peer relationships and socializing and learning together through a shared language with close Deaf and hearing friends are especially protective and can promote resilience for Deaf persons (Crowe, 2019; Eichengreen et al., 2022; Johnson et al., 2018; Rogers et al., 2003). Mental health providers who practice with unconditional acceptance, cultural competence, assured confidentiality, and explicit affirmations of strengths have also been identified as a community-based protective factor for Deaf individuals (Johnson et al., 2018). Virtual access and communities are gaining attention in Deaf mental health research. Research (Anderson et al., 2016; Johnson et al., 2018) has briefly noted the importance of access to technological resources and social media and their ability to buffer against isolation and serve as protective factors for building resilience. Many people in the Deaf community are at the forefront of technology, meeting self-care and interpersonal needs with various electronic resources such as videophones, vlogging, and smartphone apps (Anderson et al., 2016).

The people that we interviewed glossed over how geographical and technological access impacted mental health and resilience. However, many shared how friends and therapists helped them through.

> I have several connections with Deaf and hearing friends nationwide and globally who have similar experiences and understanding about supporting family members with mental illness. Now they know my entire family, and my family knows them too. We have also gone to family therapy to get another perspective to help our loved one with mental illness. (Interviewee 12)

> I have one close friend who has really been there for me. She stepped up for me and my brother with mental illness during a serious crisis when 911 was involved. I have also been lucky to have a great therapist who has helped me make sense of my past and build skills to cope with life now. (Interviewee 1)

Deaf Community

Research has consistently identified the Deaf community as a protective factor against developing mental illness and for perseverance when faced with oppression, discrimination, and logistical barriers (Anderson et al., 2016; Chovaz et al., 2022; Crowe, 2019; Johnson et al., 2018; Listman & Kurz, 2020; Rogers et al., 2003). Deaf community cultural wealth (DCCW) consists of knowledge, wisdom, strategies, and shared experiences that can help Deaf adults during hardships and contribute to their resilience (Listman et al., 2011). The Deaf community's protective cultural practices (e.g., exchanging information, consciously protecting one another from the exacerbating effects of a traumatic event, connection with others who have experienced similar types of negative experiences, leveraging assets on the collective level, and fueling loved ones' persistence) are beneficial for individual and community resilience (Johnson et al., 2018). Connection and involvement with the Deaf community can reduce the effects of stigmatization and marginalization faced in daily attitudinal and communication barriers and contribute to healthy identity development, positive self-regard, happiness, well-being, and satisfying deep psychological needs for love and belonging (Chovaz et al., 2022, Crowe, 2019; Johnson et al., 2018; Listman & Kurz, 2020; Rogers et al., 2003).

The stories we captured did not often comment on how the Deaf community was a protective factor in their mental health journey. We suspect that stigma interfered with how the people we interviewed connected with and utilized DCCW in coping with mental illness.

> My family and I were very fortunate to have our network and connections with several Deaf mental health professionals nationwide. This helped me get an appointment with a well-respected Deaf psychiatrist and services directly in ASL. Our connections with the Deaf community also helped us get interpreters in a pinch sometimes when agencies seemed unable to. (Interviewee 14)

Positive Meaning-Making

The concept of resilience not only considers a person's ability to withstand hardship but also looks at a person's ability to recover from adversity. This recovery often involves reframing stressful experiences more positively, including a growth perspective (Park, 2010; Park & Ai, 2006). Positive meaning-making is a core determinant of adaptive psychological adjustment (Park, 2016; Ching et al., 2012). "Benefit-finding" in one's deaf identity might moderate the impact of stigma on the well-being of Deaf adults (Mousley & Chaudoir, 2018). Acculturative stress research on Deaf adults' experiences in deaf and hearing cultures found that most experienced personal and emotional growth, wisdom, and cultural understanding (Aldalur et al., 2021). Participants mentioned increasing self-acceptance, developing meaningful relationships, involvement with social activism, and experiencing psychological growth, including positive coping and self-advocacy skills (Aldalur et al., 2021).

The people we interviewed shared remarkable stories of making positive meaning from their struggles. This is an area of deaf mental health where incorporating lived experiences, stories, and our hearts into research and how we make sense of resilience could be expanded. They were amazed that they and their families had survived and even thrived and gained purpose through the trauma and hardships they faced.

> I am a Deaf woman, and I come from a family with Deaf parents and hearing brothers. I am the oldest, bilingual (English and ASL), and without mental illness. When I was young, a child psychologist was puzzled by my advanced vocabulary development, which somehow led me to receive several electroconvulsive therapy (ECT) treatments. I still remember the pain and fear I experienced during ECT. Eventually, my father stopped the ECT treatments because it was so painful and traumatic for me. We later discovered that the psychologist was abusing his adopted deaf child. These biases and lack of professional oversight in the field have had a long-lasting effect on my life and family. I often

wonder if these early ECT treatments are why I do not have a mental illness like many in my family (e.g., Deaf grandmother, Deaf mom, and my twin hearing brothers). (Interviewee 1)

I was the glue that kept my family together. I always monitored my mother's body language and facial expressions to determine her mood. If she seemed to be feeling low or irritable, I would try to de-escalate any stress for her. I was my Dad's confidante too. My social, behavioral, and emotional development and awareness have developed twice as fast as a typical child. (Interviewee 1)

My daughter's experience living with a Deaf brother with mental illness has been helpful in her educational and professional journeys in psychology and school counseling. My experience of having a Deaf son with mental illness has given me the gift of empathy at the workplace and in the community, which is a must in any service field. (Interviewee 12)

After experiencing all of my family's tragedies, my empathy and understanding of others with mental illness are strong. That is why I went into counseling and became more involved in the caregiver community. I still check on my daughter and hearing brother every week and even several times a week to ensure they are okay. It is a lifelong commitment for me as a family member to look after them. (Interviewee 1)

I never fully understood how or why I maintained such a laser-like focus on becoming a psychologist. I was strongly committed to the field starting [in] high school, which never wavered. When I was in the eighth year of my career, my family discovered that my Deaf sister had a severe and persistent mental illness. Only then did I realize how this drive had become a professional and personal purpose. (Interviewee 15)

Recommendations

We echo many of the recommendations previously provided in Deaf mental health literature cited in this chapter and beyond. However, we want to draw upon the heart-to-heart connections to provide unique recommendations. We offer recommendations that extend beyond research and inform multiple systems, professionals, researchers, the Deaf community, and family members.

For Human Service Systems

Human service systems (e.g., emergency medical services, legal systems, senior health care, etc.) must mandate annual Deaf-affirming and Deaf-led training for all direct and management-level positions utilizing an engaging and collective approach. A multiple-series format that breaks down different topics (e.g., working with interpreters, Deaf culture) would encourage progressive learning.

Human services would benefit from incorporating "Deaf" as an intersection of diversity in agency missions and diversity efforts, including hiring and contracting with Deaf and ASL-fluent professionals with diverse backgrounds (e.g., Black, Indigenous) and removing employment barriers (e.g., minimum degree requirements) for hiring Deaf persons, especially for positions in the mental health field. Deaf professionals need workarounds for state-guided and financial barriers to professional development, licensure, and opportunities to connect and consult locally, nationally, and internationally.

Programmatic priorities in human services include forming a centralized agency that is accessible to Deaf persons and their family members that provides wraparound services (e.g., case management, education, therapy, crisis support, and medication services), creating housing programs that serve the different levels of care for Deaf persons with mental illness and other needs (e.g., senior citizens) and developing Deaf peer-support specialist training and positions. Another priority is integrating Deaf persons into early intervention programs where hearing parents with Deaf children can develop relationships with Deaf adults. Staff in human service systems must drastically enhance communication and collaboration between state-level offices for Deaf persons with mental health, developmental disabilities, and substance misuse problems.

For Education Systems

The people we interviewed pointed to high schools as the right place to create positions and programs to assist students and their parents with transitioning to life after graduation. A conglomerate of school districts and community mental health providers could provide resources and support to Deaf students and their families. Education and community systems must develop ongoing support plans focused on mental health, understanding logistical barriers (e.g., insurance), and identifying resources.

Higher education institutions are expected to prioritize the mental health of Deaf adults. The people we interviewed noted a need for more degrees and training programs focusing on Deaf mental health. Colleges and universities would benefit from forming cross-department committees focusing on processes, action plans, and resources to support Deaf students' mental health. Staff can ethically engage a student's support system (e.g., parents, siblings) in developing action and safety plans and communication about plan changes, new resources, and incidents. Committees could partner with Deaf educational institutions to share resources and protocols and create opportunities for consultation. Secondary education institutions need to establish a coordinator position that connects with the local, state, and national communities to enhance access to mental health services for Deaf students and their families.

For Healthcare Systems

Healthcare systems have a lot of power to improve mental health services for Deaf adults. Staff need to educate healthcare administrators, staff at all levels, and insurance companies about the importance of linguistically and culturally accessible services for Deaf persons, including fairly compensating ASL-fluent clinicians, negotiating with insurance for changes in medical necessity requirements and exceptions for ASL-fluent, out-of-network providers, and modifying policies to reduce barriers to accessing mental health care for Deaf persons. Our interviewees commonly mentioned inpatient treatment policies and breakdowns in Deaf patient care. Inpatient treatment staff and processes must consider equality and inclusiveness for Deaf persons in policies and procedures (e.g., providing access to a video phone or their cell phone to call and develop a discharge timeline that includes requesting interpreter services for outpatient appointments) and the accessibility of interpreters 24/7 during inpatient treatment.

Healthcare systems can implement technological and staff-level steps to make a huge difference in Deaf adult mental health care. More specifically, electronic medical records must include an obvious notation function that highlights Deaf accessibility needs and mental health concerns, so they are not overlooked or blocked. Staff must prioritize assigning professionals who can communicate directly with the Deaf patient before assigning indirect service professionals using interpreters. Direct services are far more effective—fewer people in the room and less distracting for the distressed patient. Clinicians working with Deaf patients are considering, planning, and providing multiple layers in their patient care (e.g., psychoeducation) and need support for administrative duties (e.g., insurance billing issues). Their time is better spent on patient care services.

For Clinical Providers

Community, clinical, and systems can emphasize and apply resilience concepts in their direct work with Deaf individuals while sharing this data with research. Other insights from our interviewees, especially the mental health professionals, focused on using CDIs and visual aids with Deaf adults and children with language deprivation and severe mental illness. Visual guides should be used more often in treatment, including guides with pictures, names, English words, and signs to help patients understand medication, different professionals' roles, and their rights.

Our interviewees highlighted the need for continuity of care and collaboration in patient care, including following Deaf patients through their inpatient stay and discharge; collaborating with agencies involved in the patient's past, present, and future, especially at the discharge phase of any level of treatment; engaging social workers and checking in with a patient's support system at every step of a patient's treatment; and encouraging partnership and mentorship between hearing and Deaf professionals. The need for providers serving mixed hearing and Deaf families was emphasized. The people we interviewed indicated a need for a nationally accessible virtual hub for Deaf mental health professionals that holds regular meetings, training, and consultations.

For Researchers

Deaf mental health research must address the gaps between research, clinical practice, and Deaf community needs for Deaf adults. Researchers would benefit from community-based participatory research methods to engage the Deaf community and prioritize community and clinical needs. Suggested research topics from lived experience include exploring barriers and solutions to collaborative care in professional organizations involved in Deaf adult mental health systems and identifying gaps and solutions in policies and laws that impact treatment. Other research priorities include identifying the needs and best treatment approaches for Deaf adults with other disabilities (e.g., DeafBlind) and caregivers supporting Deaf adults with mental illness. Deaf adult mental health research needs to continue to understand how stigma about mental illness is specific to Deaf experiences and happens within the Deaf community. Clinical approaches and Deaf community programs must address stigma and take steps to counteract the barriers it creates.

For the Deaf Community and Family Members

Deaf mental health literature consistently focuses on providing recommendations narrowed to the academic community. We believe it is vital to direct recommendations to the Deaf community to empower them to organize, advocate, and act in various systems. Our interviewees suggested that the Deaf community reduce stigmatization around mental illness by creating supportive spaces that minimize gossip and provide ongoing support for Deaf adults and their family members. Collaborative learning workshops and panel discussions that include different perspectives (e.g., Deaf persons and family members of Deaf persons with mental illness) on mental health topics (e.g., stress management, grief, mood disorders, healthy relationships, recognizing red flags, legal and financial resources, and developing safety plans) are strongly recommended. We also encourage the Deaf community to focus on engaging in local, state, and national political action on issues specific to Deaf adult mental health (e.g., access during mental hygiene arrests). This might involve partnering and learning from local, state, and national organizations with agendas paralleling Deaf issues.

Research and lived experience consistently noted the importance of family support and involvement in developing and enacting resilience in Deaf experiences. However, research has not focused on understanding family members' experiences. Research, clinical, and community programs focused on Deaf adult mental health must focus on family members' experiences and needs. Support and education programs for families and peers coping with mental illness, such as the National Alliance on Mental Illness, are often not linguistically or culturally accessible to Deaf adults or their loved ones.

Keeping with the value of empowering individuals and families, our interviewees offered recommendations for family members of Deaf adults with mental illness. Hearing parents must seek out and be provided education about Deaf abilities and mental health early on and regularly from a strengths-based approach and consider Deaf mental health risks and resources with the Deaf family member(s) in family discussions and decisions.

It was suggested that family members be visible and accessible to the providers in their family member's care team by building relationships in multiple spaces (e.g., housing, community, healthcare, legal) and with as many professionals (e.g., from administrators to direct-care staff) as possible. Family members should get involved in local, state, and national government and organizations associated with deafness, and/or mental health. In the USA, this may include agencies like the National Coalition on Mental Health and Deaf Individuals and American Foundation for Suicide Prevention. The people we interviewed emphasized the importance of educating and providing Deaf persons with mental illness information about medical and financial processes in mental healthcare, their rights, and diplomatic advocacy skills to advocate for themselves. Additionally, caregivers of Deaf adults with mental illness are encouraged to seek ongoing education about mental health and mental illness and be proactive in their mental health with a vast support system and a willingness to ask for help for themselves and their family members with mental illness.

Conclusion

The heart-to-heart stories of Deaf adults are often overlooked, especially in mental health and mental illness. Our head-to head research and heart-to-heart experiences identified areas for future research, clinical work, and community mental health efforts. Future work needs to focus on bridging the gap between relevant Deaf adult mental health experiences and research to produce applicable prevention, immediate, and aftercare programs accessible within various systems (e.g., education, healthcare, community, and forensic). Training with broad human service professions that interface with mental health must include a Deaf-affirming educational lens. Research and clinical approaches must prioritize family members, resilience, and protective factors to improve the mental health and well-being of Deaf adults and their families.

References

Abney, A. K., White, A., Shanahan, K. J., & Locander, W. B. (2017). In their shoes: Co-creating value from deaf/hearing perspectives. *Journal of Services Marketing, 31*(45), 313–325. https://doi.org/10.1108/jsm-05-2016-0201

Afrin, J. N., & Critchfield, A. B. (1997). Low-cost telepsychiatry for the deaf in South Carolina [Conference presentation]. *Proceedings of the AMIA Annual Fall Symposium*, Columbia, South Carolina (p. 901). American Medical Informatics Association. https://www.ncbi.nlm.nih.gov/pmc/articles/PMC2233381/

Ahlert, I. A., & Greeff, A. P. (2012). Resilience factors associated with adaptation in families with deaf and hard of hearing children. *American Annals of the Deaf, 157*(4), 391–404. https://doi.org/10.1353/aad.2012.1629

Aldalur, A., Pick, L. H., & Schooler, D. (2021). Navigating deaf and hearing cultures: An exploration of deaf acculturative stress. *The Journal of Deaf Studies and Deaf Education, 26*(3), 299–313. https://doi.org/10.1093/deafed/enab014.

Anderson, M. L., Glickman, N. S., Mistler, L. A., & Gonzalez, M. (2016). Working therapeutically with deaf people recovering from trauma and addiction. *Psychiatric Rehabilitation Journal, 39*(1), 27–32. https://doi.org/10.1037/prj0000146

Anderson, M. L., & Leigh, I. W. (2011). Intimate partner violence against deaf female college students. *Violence Against Women, 17*(7), 822–834.

Black, P. A., & Glickman, N. S. (2006). Demographics, psychiatric diagnoses, and other characteristics of North American deaf and hard-of-hearing inpatients. *Journal of Deaf Studies and Deaf Education, 11*(3), 303–321.

Boutin, D. L. (2010). Occupational outcomes for vocational rehabilitation consumers with hearing impairments. *Journal of Rehabilitation, 76*(3), 40–46.

Bramley, S. (2007). Working with deaf people who have committed sexual offences against children: The need for an increased awareness. *Journal of Sexual Aggression, 13*(1), 59–69. https://doi.org/10.1080/13552600701365530

Cawthon, S. W., Garberoglio, C. L., Caemmerer, J. M., Bond, M., & Wendel, E. (2015). Effect of parent involvement and parent expectations on postsecondary outcomes for individuals who are d/Deaf or hard of hearing. *Exceptionality, 23*(2), 73–99.

Cawthon, S. W., & Garberoglio, C. L. (2017). *Research in deaf education: Contexts, challenges, and considerations.* Oxford University Press. https://doi.org/10.1093/oso/9780190455651.001.0001

Chapman, M., & Dammeyer, J. (2017). The significance of deaf identity for psychological well-being. *Journal of Deaf Studies and Deaf Education, 22*(2), 187–194. https://doi.org/10.1093/deafed/enw073

Charlson, E. S., Bird, R. L., & Strong, M. (1999). Resilience and success among deaf high school students: Three case studies. *American Annals of the Deaf, 144*(3), 226–235.

Ching, S. S. Y., Martinson, I. M., & Wong, T. K. S. (2012). Meaning making: Psychological adjustment to breast cancer by Chinese women. *Qualitative Health Research, 22*(2), 250–262.

Chovaz, C. J., Russell, D., & Boudreault, P. (2023). Deaf community experiences in the Canadian justice system. *Psychology, Public Policy, and Law, 29*(4), 512–524. https://doi.org/10.1037/law0000404

Chovaz, C. J., Russell, D., & Daly, B. (2022). Lived experiences of deaf Canadians: What we want you to know! *Canadian Psychology/Psychologie Canadienne, 63*(4), 651–666.

Crowe, T. V. (2017). Is telemental health services a viable alternative to traditional psychotherapy for deaf individuals? *Community Mental Health Journal, 53*(2), 154–162.

Crowe, T. V. (2019). Factors associated with well-being in a sample of deaf adults. *Journal of Developmental and Physical Disabilities, 31*(3), 285–298.

Crowe, T. V. (2021). Psychiatric functioning, resilience, and recovery among deaf consumers of public behavioral health services. *Community Mental Health Journal, 57*(6), 1164–1174.

Dammeyer, J. (2010). Psychosocial development in a Danish population of children with cochlear implants and deaf and hard-of-hearing children. *Journal of Deaf Studies and Deaf Education, 15*(1), 50–58.

Eichengreen, A., Zaidman-Zait, A., Most, T., & Golik, G. (2022). Resilience from childhood to young adulthood: Retrospective perspectives of deaf and hard of hearing people who studied in regular schools. *Psychology and Health, 37*(3), 331–349.

Fellinger, J., Holzinger, D., & Pollard, R. (2012). Mental health of deaf people. *The Lancet, 379*(9820), 1037–1044. https://doi.org/10.1016/s0140-6736(11)61143-4

Glickman, N. (2008). Do you hear voices? Problems in assessment of mental status in deaf persons with severe language deprivation. *Journal of Deaf Studies and Deaf Education,* 12(2), 127–147. https://doi.org/10.4324/9780203893371-8

Glickman, N. S. (2013). Introduction: What is deaf mental health care? In N. S. Glickman (Ed.), *Deaf mental health care* (pp. 1–36). Routledge.

Gournaris, M. J., & Leigh, I. W. (2019). Comparison of face-to-face and video-mediated communication with deaf individuals: Implications for telepsychotherapy. *Journal of American Deafness and Rehabilitation Association, 37*(2), Article 5. https://nsuworks.nova.edu/jadara/vol37/iss2/5

Gryglewicz, K., Bozzay, M., Arthur-Jordon, B., Romero, G. D., Witmeier, M., Chapple, R., & Karver, M. S. (2017). A silenced population: Uncovering correlates of suicidal-related behavior among deaf and hard-of-hearing youth. *Crisis: The Journal of Crisis Intervention and Suicide Prevention, 38*(6), 433–442.

Gulati, S. (2018). Language deprivation syndrome. In N. S. Glickman & W. C. Hall (Eds.), *Language deprivation and deaf mental health* (pp. 24–53). Routledge.

Guthmann, D., & Blozis, S. A. (2001). Unique issues faced by deaf individuals entering substance abuse treatment and following discharge. *American Annals of the Deaf,* 146(3), 294–304.

Guthmann, D., & Graham III, V. (2005). Substance abuse: A hidden problem within the D/deaf and hard of hearing communities. *Journal of Teaching in the Addictions, 3*(1), 49–64. https://doi.org/10.1300/j188v03n01_04

Guthmann, D., & Sandberg, K. A. (2003) Culturally affirmative substance abuse treatment for deaf people: Approaches, materials, and administrative considerations. In N. S. Glickman & S. Gulati (Eds.), *Mental health care of deaf people: A culturally affirmative approach,* (pp. 261–303). Routledge. https://doi.org/10.4324/9781410607577-13

Hall, W. C., Levin, L. L., & Anderson, M. L. (2017). Language deprivation syndrome: A possible neurodevelopmental disorder with sociocultural origins. *Social Psychiatry and Psychiatric Epidemiology, 52,* 761–776. https://doi.org/10.1007/s00127-017-1351-7

Hauser, P. C., O'Hearn, A., McKee, M., Steider, A., & Thew, D. (2010). Deaf epistemology: Deafhood and deafness. *American annals of the deaf, 154*(5), 486–492. https://doi.org/10.1353/aad.0.0120

Health Insurance Portability and Accountability Act (The) (HIPAA). (1996). Public Law 104-191 or 42 U.S.C.§1320detseq. https://aspe.hhs.gov/reports/health-insurance-portability-accountability-act-1996.

Humphries, T., Kushalnagar, P., Mathur, G., Napoli, D. J., Padden, C., Rathmann, C., & Smith, S. (2016). Avoiding linguistic neglect of deaf children. *Social Service Review, 90*(4), 589–619. https://doi.org/10.1086/689543

Jambor, E., & Elliott, M. (2005). Self-esteem and coping strategies among deaf students. *Journal of Deaf Studies and Deaf Education, 10*(1), 63–81.

James, T. G., McKee, M. M., Sullivan, M. K., Ashton, G., Hardy, S. J., Santiago, Y., Phillips, D. G., & Cheong, J. (2021). Community-engaged needs assessment of Deaf American Sign Language users in Florida, 2018. *Public Health Reports, 137*(4), 730–738. https://doi.org/10.1177/00333549211026782

Johnson, P., Cawthon, S., Fink, B., Wendel, E., & Schoffstall, S. (2018). Trauma and resilience among deaf individuals. *Journal of Deaf Studies and Deaf Education, 23*(4), 317–330.

Kushalnagar, P., Topolski, T. D., Schick, B., Edwards, T. C., Skalicky, A. M., & Patrick, D. L. (2011). Mode of communication, perceived level of understanding, and perceived quality of life in youth who are deaf or hard of hearing. *Journal of Deaf Studies and Deaf Education, 16*(4), 512–523. https://doi.org/10.1093/deafed/enr015

Kushalnagar, P., Bruce, S., Sutton, T., & Leigh, I. W. (2017). Retrospective basic parent-child communication difficulties and risk of depression in deaf adults. *Journal of developmental and physical disabilities, 29*(1), 25–34. https://doi.org/10.1007/s10882-016-9501-5

Kushalnagar, P., Reesman, J., Holcomb, T., & Ryan, C. (2019). Prevalence of anxiety or depression diagnosis in deaf adults. *Journal of Deaf Studies and Deaf Education, 24*(4), 378–385. https://doi.org/10.1093/deafed/enz017

Kushalnagar, P., Ryan, C., Paludneviciene, R., Spellun, A., & Gulati, S. (2020). Adverse childhood communication experiences associated with an increased risk of chronic diseases in adults who are deaf. *American Journal of Preventive Medicine, 59*(4), 548–554. https://doi.org/10.1016/J.Amepre.2020.04.016

Kvam, M. H., & Loeb, M. (2010). The relation between adverse childhood experiences and later mental health among deaf adults. *Scandinavian Journal of Disability Research, 12*(4), 233–244. https://doi.org/10.1080/15017410903479004

Kvam, M. H., Loeb, M., & Tambs, K. (2007). Mental health in deaf adults: Symptoms of anxiety and depression among hearing and deaf individuals. *The Journal of deaf studies and Deaf Education, 12*(1), 1–7. https://doi.org/10.1093/deafed/enl015

Leigh, I. W., Andrews, J. F., Harris, R. L., & Ávila, T. G. (2020). *Deaf culture: Exploring deaf communities in the United States*. Plural Publishing.

Lipton, D. S., & Goldstein, M. F. (1997). Measuring substance abuse among the deaf. *Journal of Drug Issues, 27*(4), 733–754. https://doi.org/10.1177/002204269702700404

Listman, J. D., & Kurz, K. B. (2020). Lived experience: Deaf professionals' stories of resilience and risks. *The Journal of Deaf Studies and Deaf Education, 25*(2), 239–249. https://doi.org/10.1093/deafed/enz045

Listman, J., Rogers, K. D., & Hauser, P. C. (2011). Community cultural wealth and deaf adolescents' resilience. In D. Zand & K. Pierce (Eds.), *Resilience in deaf children: Adaptation through emerging adulthood* (pp. 279–297). Springer. https://doi.org/10.1007/978-1-4419-7796-0_11

Luckner, J. L., & Muir, S. (2001). Successful students who are deaf in general education settings. *American Annals of the Deaf*, 146(5), 435–446. https://doi.org/10.1353/aad.2012.0202

Lukomski, J. (2011). Resiliency and the emerging deaf adult. In D. Zand & K. Pierce (Eds.), *Resilience in deaf children: Adaptation through emerging adulthood* (pp. 375–390). Springer. https://doi.org/10.1007/978-1-4419-7796-0_15

Lytle, L. R., Oliva, G. A., Ostrove, J. M., & Cassady, C. (2011). Building resilience in adolescence: The influences of individual, family, school, and community perspectives and practices. In D. Zand & K. Pierce (Eds.), *Resilience in deaf children: Adaptation through emerging adulthood* (251–277). Springer. https://doi.org/10.1007/978-1-4419-7796-0_10

Martin, G. A., Paris, D. G., Lomas, G. I., & Guthmann, D. (2021). *Deaf people in the criminal justice system: Selected topics on advocacy, incarceration, and social justice*. Gallaudet University Press. https://doi.org/10.2307/j.ctv2rcngmd.15

McAlister, J. (1994). Deaf and hard of hearing criminal defendants: How you gonna get justice if you can't talk to the judge? *Arizona State Law Journal, 26,* 162–200.

McKee, M. M., Paasche-Orlow, M. K., Winters, P. C., Fiscella, K., Zazove, P., Sen, A., & Pearson, T. (2015). Assessing health literacy in deaf American Sign Language users. *Journal of Health Communication, 20*(sup2), 92–100. https://doi.org/10.1080/10810730.2015.1066468

McKee, M., Schlehofer, D., & Thew, D. (2013). Ethical issues in conducting research with deaf populations. *American Journal of Public Health, 103*(12), 2174–2178. https://doi.org/10.2105/ajph.2013.301343

Meyer, J., & Kashubeck-West, S. (2011). Psychological well-being in emerging adults who are deaf. In D. Zand & K. Pierce (Eds.), *Resilience in deaf children: Adaptation through emerging adulthood* (pp. 359–374). Springer.

Michael, R., Most, T., & Cinamon, R. G. (2011). Self-efficacy in the management of anticipated work–family conflict as a resilience factor among young deaf adults. In D. Zand & K. Pierce (Eds.), *Resilience in deaf children: Adaptation through emerging adulthood* (pp. 341–357). Springer. https://doi.org/10.1007/978-1-4419-7796-0_13

Miller, K. R. (2004). Linguistic diversity in a deaf prison population: Implications for due process. *Journal of Deaf Studies and Deaf Education, 9*(1), 112–119. https://doi.org/10.1093/deafed/enh007

Miller, K. R., & Vernon, M. (2001). Linguistic diversity in deaf defendants and due process rights. *Journal of Deaf Studies and Deaf Education, 6*(3), 226–234.

Miller, K. R., Vernon, M., & Capella, M. E. (2005). Violent offenders in a deaf prison population. *Journal of Deaf Studies and Deaf Education, 10*(4), 417–425.

Mitchell, R. E., & Karchmer, M. A. (2006). Demographics of deaf education: More students in more places. *American Annals of the deaf, 151*(2), 95–104.

Mitchell, T. R., & Braham, L. G. (2011). The psychological treatment needs of deaf mental health patients in high-secure settings: A review of the literature. *The International Journal of Forensic Mental Health, 10*(2), 92–106. https://doi.org/10.1080/14999013.2011.577135

Moore, E. A., & Mertens, D. M. (2015). Deaf culture and youth resilience in diverse American communities. *Youth resilience and culture: Commonalities and complexities*, 143–155. https://doi.org/10.1007/978-94-017-9415-2_11

Mousley, V. L., & Chaudoir, S. R. (2018). Deaf stigma: Links between stigma and well-being among deaf emerging adults. *Journal of Deaf Studies and Deaf Education, 23*(4), 341–350. https://doi.org/10.1093/deafed/eny018

Øhre, B., Volden, M., Falkum, E., & von Tetzchner, S. (2016). Mental disorders in deaf and hard of hearing adult outpatients: A comparison of linguistic subgroups. *Journal of Deaf Studies and Deaf Education, 22*(1), 1–13. https://doi.org/10.1093/deafed/enw061

O'Rourke, S. U. E., Glickman, N. S., & Austen, S. (2013). Deaf people in the criminal justice system: Is a culturally affirmative response possible or desirable? In N. S. Glickman (Ed.), *Deaf mental health care* (pp. 323–357). Routledge.

O'Rourke, S., & Grewer, G. (2005). Assessment of deaf people in forensic mental health settings: A risky business! *Journal of Forensic Psychiatry and Psychology, 16*(4), 671–684. https://doi.org/10.1080/14789940500279877

Park, C. L. (2010). Making sense of the meaning literature: An integrative review of meaning making and its effects on adjustment to stressful life events. *Psychological Bulletin, 136*(2), 257–301. https://doi.org/10.1037/a0018301

Park, C. L. (2016). Meaning making in the context of disasters. *Journal of Clinical Psychology, 72*(12), 1234–1246. https://doi.org/10.1002/jclp.22270

Park, C. L., & Ai, A. L. (2006). Meaning making and growth: New directions for research on survivors of trauma. *Journal of Loss and Trauma, 11*(5), 389–407. https://doi.org/10.1080/15325020600685295

Park, D., Lee, O. E., Park, J., & Minnick, D. (2021). Substance use disorders among adults who are deaf or hard of hearing in the United States. *Drug and Alcohol Dependence, 228*, 109106. https://doi.org/10.1016/j.drugalcdep.2021.109106

Pollard, R. Q, Jr. (1998). Psychopathology. In M. Marschark & D. Clark (Eds.), *Psychological perspectives on deafness* (Vol. 2, pp. 171–197). Erlbaum.

Pollard, R. Q, Jr., & Barnett, S. (2009). Health-related vocabulary knowledge among deaf adults. *Rehabilitation Psychology, 54*(2), 182–185. https://doi.org/10.1037/a0015771

Pollard, R. Q, Jr., & Berlinski, B. T. (2017). Forensic evaluation of deaf individuals: Challenges and strategies. *Journal Of Social Work in Disability and Rehabilitation, 16*(3-4), 261–275. https://doi.org/10.1080/1536710x.2017.1372240

Pollard, R. Q, Jr., & Fox, M. L. (2018). Forensic evaluation of deaf adults with language deprivation. In N. S. Glickman & W. C. Wyatte (Eds.), *Language deprivation and deaf mental health* (pp. 101–135). Routledge. https://doi.org/10.4324/9781315166728-5

Pollard, R. Q, Jr., Sutter, E., & Cerulli, C. (2014). Intimate partner violence reported by two samples of deaf adults via a computerized American Sign Language survey. *Journal of Interpersonal Violence, 29*(5), 948–965. https://doi.org/10.1177/0886260513505703

Porter, J., & Williams, L. M. (2011). Intimate violence among underrepresented groups on a college campus. *Journal of Interpersonal Violence, 26*(16), 3210–3224. https://doi.org/10.1177/0886260510393011

Rogers, S., Muir, K., & Evenson, C. R. (2003). Signs of resilience: Assets that support deaf adults' success in bridging the deaf and hearing worlds. *American Annals of the Deaf, 148*(3), 222–232. https://doi.org/10.1353/aad.2003.0023

Schenkel, L. S., Rothman-Marshall, G., Schlehofer, D. A., Towne, T. L., Burnash, D. L., & Priddy, B. M. (2014). Child maltreatment and trauma exposure among deaf and hard of hearing young adults. *Child Abuse and Neglect, 38*(10), 1581–1589.

Schild, S., & Dalenberg, C. J. (2012). Trauma exposure and traumatic symptoms in deaf adults. *Psychological Trauma: Theory, Research, Practice, and Policy, 4*(1), 117–127. https://doi.org/10.1037/a0021578

Sessa, B., & Sutherland, H. (2013). Addressing mental health needs of deaf children and their families: The National Deaf Child and Adolescent Mental Health Service. *The Psychiatrist, 37*(5), 175–178. https://doi.org/10.1192/pb.bp.112.038604

Shook v. Mississippi. (1989). 552 So. 2d 841 (Miss. 1989).

Stapleton, L. D. (2016). Audism and racism: The hidden curriculum impacting Black d/Deaf college students in the classroom. *Negro Educational Review, 67*(1–4), 149–168. https://www.proquest.com/scholarly-journals/audism-racism-hidden-curriculum-impacting-black-d/docview/1926479445/se-2

Steinberg, A. (2000). Autobiographical narrative on growing up deaf. In P. E. Spencer, C. J. Erting, & M. Marschark (Eds.), *The deaf child in the family and at school: Essays in honor of Kathryn P. Meadow-Orlans* (pp. 93–108). Lawrence Erlbaum Associates. https://doi.org/10.4324/9781410604699-13

Steinberg, A. G., Sullivan, V. J., & Loew, R. C. (1998). Cultural and linguistic barriers to mental health service access: the deaf consumer's perspective. *American Journal of Psychiatry, 155*(7), 982–984. https://doi.org/10.1176/ajp.155.7.982

Titus, J. C., Schiller, J. A., & Guthmann, D. (2008). Characteristics of youths with hearing loss admitted to substance abuse treatment. *Journal of Deaf Studies and Deaf Education, 13*(3), 336–350.

Tranebjærg, L. (2008). Genetics of congenital hearing impairment: A clinical approach. *International journal of audiology, 47*(9), 535–545. https://doi.org/10.1080/14992020802249259

Vernon, M., & Andrews, J. F. (1990). *The psychology of deafness: Understanding deaf and hard-of-hearing people.* Addison-Wesley Longman.

Vernon, M., Raifman, L. J., & Greenberg, S. F. (1996). The Miranda warnings and the deaf suspect. *Behavioral Sciences and the Law, 14*(1), 121–135. https://doi.org/10.1002/(sici)1099-0798(199624)14:1<121::aid-bsl200>3.0.co;2-r

Wilson v. North Carolina. (1898). 169 U.S. 586.

Wisconsin v. Hindsley. (2000). No. 99-1374-CR, 99-1374-CR.

Wilson, J. A. B., & Schild, S. (2014). Provision of mental health care services to deaf individuals using telehealth. *Professional Psychology: Research and Practice, 45*(5), 324–331. https://doi.org/10.1037/a0036811

Wilson, J. A. B., & Wells, M. G. (2009). Telehealth and the deaf: A comparison study. *Journal of Deaf Studies and Deaf Education, 14*(3), 386–402. https://doi.org/10.1093/deafed/enp008

Young, A., Green, L., & Rogers, K. (2008). Resilience and deaf children: A literature review. *Deafness and Education International, 10*(1), 40–55. https://doi.org/10.1179/146431508790559850

Young, A., Howarth, P., Ridgeway, S., & Monteiro, B. (2001). Forensic referrals to the three specialist psychiatric units for deaf people in the UK. *The Journal of Forensic Psychiatry, 12*(1), 19–35. https://doi.org/10.1080/09585180122591

Young, A., Rogers, K. D., Green, L., & Daniels, S. (2011). Critical issues in the application of resilience frameworks to the experiences of deaf children and young people. In D. Zand & K. Pierce (Eds.), *Resilience in deaf children: Adaptation through emerging adulthood* (pp. 3–24). Springer.

Young, A., & Ng, M. (April 17, 2023). *Genetic Hearing Loss.* NIH: National Library of Medicine. https://www.ncbi.nlm.nih.gov/books/NBK580517/

Zidenberg, A. M. (2021). Avoiding the deaf penalty: A review of the experiences of d/Deaf individuals in the criminal justice system. *Disability and Society, 38*(5), 842–864. https://doi.org/10.1080/09687599.2021.1965546

8

Unlocking the Potential of Deaf Adults With Multiple Disabilities

Johannes Fellinger

Construct

This chapter gives an overview about prevalence, etiologies, and especially specific developmental and living conditions of individuals who are deaf or hard of hearing from birth or at an early age and have mostly intellectual disabilities. The term "deaf+" is introduced, not only with respect to the presence of other disabilities, but also to highlight the positive potential of these individuals, which needs to be unlocked. Research data shows that this vulnerable population of people with special needs is large (about 40% of children born deaf or hard of hearing have additional medical or developmental difficulties (Gallaudet Research Institute, 2011). A huge variety of etiologies cause combinations of special conditions, especially genetic syndromes, prematurity, and congenital infections. Many of today's adult deaf+ population have experienced severe communicative deprivation beginning in their early lives and show very heterogeneous developmental profiles due to the interaction between deafness, cognitive abilities, and the opportunities to communicate in an accessible way and the education and the warmth of the social climate in their respective families. Study data illustrate discrepancies between cognitive functioning and adaptive skills, especially in the social and communicative domain.

Furthermore, the issue of challenging behavior is addressed by research data, which show that maladaptive behaviors were occurring 2 to 3 times more frequently in the deaf+ population compared to general populations. The study showed that higher language and social communication skills are significantly correlated with less maladaptive behavior.

Head-to-Head and Heart-to-Heart

This section of stories and experiences begins with descriptions of personal encounters with Austrian mothers of deaf+ individuals and deaf+ patients from an outpatient clinic for deaf people that foreshadowed the need to create a living environment for deaf+ individuals, with fully accessible sign language necessary. This then led to the establishment of three therapeutic communities in Austria, based on the idea that an enhancement of social communication abilities leads to an increase in social engagement and supports the establishment of satisfying social relationships. Social connectedness is seen as a major contributor to quality of life and mental life. The program of Lebenswelt (therapeutic living communities for deaf+ individuals) is introduced and the heart-to-heart stories of some residents and participants are told. Of particular interest are the stories telling about children of the mothers who stimulated the creation of the whole program.

Statement of Reflexivity

Author: Johannes Fellinger

I acknowledge my view as a son of a deaf artist and as a clinician (neurologist, psychiatrist, and child neurologist), who dedicated his life energy to serve deaf people with respect to health care and helping to create optimized developmental opportunities and living conditions for deaf people. Since 1991, I have had the privilege to set up different deaf+ services mainly in Linz at the hospital St. John of God, which are organized in the Institut für Sinnes- und Sprachneurologie (https://www.barmherzige-brueder.at/portal/issn/home). Furthermore, I have had the chance to support the deaf+ field with translational research activities and results at the Clinical Research Institute for Developmental Medicine of the Johannes Kepler University (https://www.jku.at/klinisches-forschungsinstitut-fuer-entwicklungsmedizin/). My relationships with deaf people exhibiting different degrees of hearing loss and different functional abilities and disabilities resemble, in many cases, more long-lasting friendships than just doctor-patient relationships.

Recommendations

The right to live in a communicative, accessible social environment, as mentioned in the UN Convention on the Rights of Persons with Disabilities (CRPD) (United Nations, 2006) and endorsed by the World Federation of the Deaf (2023) must be realized for deaf+ adults. Furthermore, parents of deaf+ children must be supported in fully meeting their children's communicative needs and in developing perspectives regarding future social environments.

Introduction

Humans do not develop in isolation. This concept is based on a wide range of evidence-based theories of human development (Bronfenbrenner, 1992; Cohen & Wills, 1985). Individuals who are deaf and have multiple disabilities are at a significantly greater risk of facing social exclusion. In most cases, the presence of multiple disabilities prevents them from living independently with free mobility and keeps them in a caring social environment. However, usually, these social environments are their families or staff members in institutions who are communicating in spoken language and are not able to provide constant, accessible, visual communication, which would give deaf+ individuals opportunities to fully participate and develop in a broad social context. Unlike the wealth of cultural solidarity and creativity described in Deaf culture (Ladd, 2003), there is very little empirical literature on how adults who are deaf and have multiple disabilities spend their lives.

Head-to-Head Information

1. **We know that the deaf+ population is large.** Prevalence rates indicate that 40% of children who are deaf or hard of hearing have medical or developmental difficulties (Gallaudet Research Institute, 2011). Data from the Atlanta birth registry shows that in 23% of children born with hearing loss, disorders of intellectual functioning were found (Van Naarden Braun et al., 2015). Of this group, 10% were found to have cerebral palsy and 7% were diagnosed

with autism spectrum disorder. A similar rate of cognitive disabilities (22%) in children with hearing loss was reported by the Gallaudet Research Institute (2011). Blindness or vision impairment was reported in 5.5% (Nikolopoulos et al, 2006). There are no epidemiologically representative data from deaf or hard of hearing adult populations.

2. **We know that a wide spectrum of etiologies is causing a huge variety of different combinations of special conditions, which are frequently attributed as handicaps.** (It is not the purpose of this chapter to provide an elaborated discussion on terminology of concepts or etiologies, including genetic syndromes, prematurity, congenital infections, meningoencephalitis, etc.). It is evident that, for most parents, the medical challenges are predominant. It is important to report that even in these times of universal, newborn hearing screening, hearing loss is identified in children with complex medical needs more than 2 months later than in children with hearing loss only (Chapman et al., 2011). This common underestimation of the impact of hearing loss on language acquisition and its consequences on cognitive, emotional, and social development has been leading to severe deprivation syndromes in generations of deaf and deaf+ individuals (Hall et al., 2017; Kushalnagar et al., 2020; Gulati, 2018).

   The presence of intellectual disabilities (IDs), especially, has a tremendous overshadowing effect. Developmental delays in language acquisition are frequently attributed to the cognitive limitations only, without assessments of auditive functions or intensive attempts to provide alternative communication pathways.

3. **We know that underdetection of hearing loss is a major issue in adult populations of people with intellectual and multiple disabilities.** This is demonstrated in two quite recent studies. Meuwese-Jongejeugd et al.'s (2006) large epidemiological study in the Netherlands included 1,598 adults with IDs and assessed their hearing and vision. In 35.8% of the participants, (previously unknown in 47,6% of them) hearing loss was detected. There was no relationship between the level of ID and the co-occurrence of a hearing impairment (Meuwese-Jongejeugd et al., 2006). An Austrian study (Fellinger et al. 2009) was conducted that included all 253 residents of an institution called Hartheim offering living quarters, health care, and opportunities for work for individuals with profound, severe, and moderate IDs. It was found that 46% of the participants had a hearing impairment, which was undetected in 72.8% of them prior to the systematic assessments. These findings point out that it is highly relevant to consider how many adults with multiple disabilities and IDs have undetected hearing loss and could benefit from communicative support meeting their needs.

4. **We know that today's adult deaf+ population has mostly experienced severe communicative deprivation beginning in their early life.** Hearing loss used to be detected very late. Hearing amplification, if available, was hardly efficient, and sign language was not implemented in families. Therefore, these children could not participate in family conversations. They also sometimes experienced harsh reprimands due to their limited cognitive abilities, which made them slow to react in specific situations. These traumatic, early childhood experiences are followed by further traumatic life events like separations from their parents due to hospitalization and treatment with respect to their complex medical needs. For many, the separation from their family when they were enrolled in a special school for deaf children was extremely painful. Although this was their opportunity to be exposed to sign language, which was not officially taught but used by other children, the time at the boarding school was another milieu for traumatization. As those with weaknesses in cognition and mobility,

many became victims of being mocked, bullied, and abused. While deaf children underwent vocational training after their time in school and had social relationships by staying in touch with signing deaf friends, deaf+ teenagers were simply sent home to their families or were brought into general institutions for people with IDs and multiple disabilities. In most cases, nobody paid attention to their communicative needs; they were either withdrawn or showed patterns of challenging behavior which increased their social exclusion.

Many children with deaf+ characteristics, especially those with more severe levels of ID, were not enrolled in any educational program at all. Simple gestures were used in their home environment to regulate their lives. In rural areas, many deaf+ individuals fulfilled simple tasks on farms without frequently getting proper respect or any kind of reimbursement. These descriptions of growing up as a deaf+ individual are derived from a plentitude of personal histories I followed in my work at the Health Center for the Deaf, which I founded in 1991 and which became the corner stone of the Institute for Neurology of Senses and Language of the Hospital St. John of God in Linz (Institut für Sinnes- und Sprachneurologie). In contrast most Deaf community members approached this multidisciplinary clinic with a fully signing staff on their own; deaf+ individuals were brought to the center by their family members or caretakers, who were desperate mainly due to the challenging behaviors of the deaf+ person or were anxious about future options. Parents of deaf+ adults were very worried about what would happen to their child after their passing. Before I share more about this journey together with deaf+ individuals and their families, I would like to share results from research studies we conducted with a clear focus on deaf adults with intellectual and multiple disabilities.

5. **We know that developmental profiles of deaf+ individuals are very heterogeneous.** As already mentioned, the interaction between deafness, cognitive abilities, adequate response to the existing communication needs, education provided, and warmth of the family social climate contributes to a large heterogeneity of developmental profiles.

We assessed 29 adults with prelingual deafness and mild intellectual functioning deficits with standardized instruments, the Snijders-Oomen Non-Verbal Intelligence Scale (SON-R 6-40) (Tellegen et al., 2012) and the Vineland Adaptive Behavior Scales II (Sparrow et al., 2005), regarding their nonverbal intelligence and their profiles of adaptive functioning. The Vineland II Scales are based on an extensive interview with a proxy person with respect to adaptive skills and provides standard scores for the communication, social, and practical domains and includes a maladaptive behavior index. Furthermore, we administered an adapted, easy-to-understand sign language version of the EURO-HIS-QOL eight-item index to assess participants' self-rated quality of life (Fellinger et al., 2021a). The 29 participants had a mean age of 46.9 years ($SD = 16.4$, range 20–73 years), and of those, 20 were male, six had cerebral palsy, and four had epilepsy. Four participants were on the autism spectrum, and 11 had experienced a lifetime depressive episode. More than half of the participants had intellectual disabilities with challenging behavior diagnosed according to International Classification of Diseases, 10th Revision (ICD-10; World Health Organization, 2004). These individuals were all participating in the therapeutic community programs, which will be introduced later in this chapter. The main results of this study can be observed in Figure 1, which is included in the journal article "Intellectual Disability Profiles, Quality of Life and Maladaptive Behavior in Deaf Adults: An Exploratory Study" (Eisinger et. al., 2022).

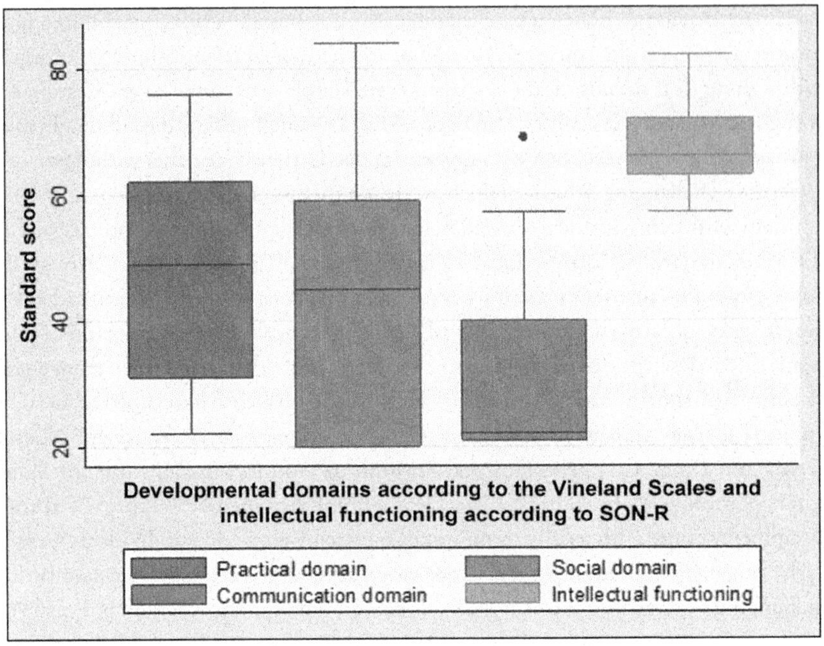

Figure 1. Intellectual Disability Profiles, Adaptive Skills assessed with Vineland scales, intellectual functioning measured by the SON 6-40 intelligence test.

The heterogeneity of the intellectual disability profiles in the sample is obvious. Whereas the levels of nonverbal intelligence were between borderline and mild intellectual functioning impairment (*mean IQ* = 67.3, *SD* = 6.5), the levels of adaptive functioning impairment were dramatically lower. For the practical domain, the mean standard score was 49 (*SD* = 17.4), with more than half of the sample having a deficit corresponding with moderate intellectual disability. The level of adaptive functioning for the social domain with a mean standard score of 41.5 (*SD* = 19.6) is equivalent to a moderate intellectual disability, according to the classification of the ICD-10. It should be noted that 12 individuals had scores indicating severe deficits. The communication domain of the Vineland II was assessed with a nonvalidated version adapted to the special situation of deaf people (items relating to comprehension or production of spoken language were replaced by equivalence for the visual modality and structured elements of Austrian sign language with similar complexity). The mean standard score for the communication domain was 31.4 (*SD* = 14.01.), which equals severe intellectual disability. Due to floor effects (a median score of 22), this domain could not be included for calculations.

To summarize, in this group of individuals with mild cognitive impairment, only 24% showed no discrepancy between intellectual and adaptive functioning. Nearly two-thirds of the sample had an intellectual disability domain discrepancy between the intellectual functioning level and the social domain (65.5%), and more than half had an intellectual disability domain discrepancy between their intellectual functioning and the practical domain (58.6%). A quarter had a discrepancy between the social and the practical domain, with the social domain being the weaker one. The most striking finding of this study (Eisinger et al, 2022) is that two-thirds of this intellectually quite-capable group had levels of adaptive skills in the communication domain similar to that of hearing people with severe intellectual disabilities.

These findings point out how language deprivation impacts independent living skills in a disastrous way. Language competence is the essential factor in acquiring practical or social skills, which exceed a basic level. Unfortunately, in so many cases, the social environment does not expect more and underestimates the human potential of these deaf+ individuals. This consequence of severe deprivation cannot be compensated for later in life. This was also shown in our participants, who at the time of the study, already had some access to a fully signing environment, which was designed to meet their needs.

Another finding of our study was that those individuals with a domain discrepancy between intellectual and social functioning were significantly more likely to have higher levels of internalizing maladaptive behavior (mainly symptoms of withdrawal and depression). This can be interpreted that it is painful to live a life where one cannot achieve one's potential. The higher levels of social functioning were significantly associated with better quality of life, a fact that underscores the importance of social connectedness for well-being.

6. **We know that challenging behavior is frequent in deaf+ adults and that communicative deficits are associated with maladaptive behavior**. In another study, (Fellinger et al, 2022), we investigated whether communicative deficits were associated with maladaptive behavior in a sample of 61 deaf+ individuals with different levels of intellectual functioning with a mean nonverbal developmental reference age of 6.5 years ($SD = 2.77$). All participants were part of three therapeutic communities, with a mean age of 54 years, and 64% were male. All were profoundly deaf and had no access to sign language before the age of 6 years. Around one quarter of the participants had epilepsy, and almost as many had cerebral palsy. Fifteen percent of the participants were diagnosed on the autism spectrum. Language and communication skills were assessed with different measures, which were combined to form a language competence score. Two standardized instruments were used to assess spoken language comprehension—the Reynell Developmental Language Scales III (Edwards et al., 1997) and the Comprehension Scale of the Child Development Inventory (Ireton, 1992)—which were adapted and validated for use with signing individuals by hearing and deaf linguists (Schreiber et al., 2020). Furthermore, the two eight-level scales of the Austrian sign language version of the Profile of Multiple Language Proficiencies (Goldstein & Bebko, 2003) were used by caregivers to estimate expressive and receptive language skills. Finally, a newly developed and validated social communication questionnaire in adults with IDs (QSC-ID; Weber et al., 2021) was used as a measure completed by caregivers that assessed the individuals' engagement in social communication, conversational skills, adaptation of communicative behavior to an interlocutor, prosocial communication, and the use of nonverbal communication.

Intellectual functioning was assessed with two versions of the SON-R 6-40 (Tellegen, 2012) and the SON-R 2 1/2-7 (Tellegen, 2007), which does not provide an IQ score but a reference age of intellectual functioning. Adaptive and maladaptive behavior was assessed with the Vineland II Scales (Sparrow et al. 2005).

The results of this study showed that, within this sample of deaf+ individuals, the prevalence rate of elevated maladaptive behavior was 41%, which is much higher than the general prevalence rate of 10–15% reported for people with IDs (Graves et al., 2020; Madduri et al., 2006). Although there might be differences in the definition of maladaptive behavior, our findings align with the work by Timehin and Timehin (2004), who found, in a large sample of residents in homes for people with learning disabilities, that problematic behavior was prevalent in 62% of individuals with hearing impairments.

Furthermore, the study (Fellinger et al. 2022) showed that the gap between a nonverbal developmental reference age of 6.5 years to the equivalent for the language measures for sign language competence of 3.5 years is huge and highlights the dimension of language deprivation and developmental disparity. In regression analyses, we showed that only language and social communication skills were significantly correlated with less maladaptive behavior, whereas the level of nonverbal cognitive functioning and other adaptive skills were not.

7. **We know that spirituality is important for deaf+ individuals and is associated with quality of life.** In another study with a mixed-methods approach (Fellinger et al, 2023), we explored quality of life and spirituality in 41 deaf+ individuals (*mean age* = 47, *SD* = 18) whose cognitive and signed communication skills were sufficient to respond to the above-mentioned EUROHIS-QOL eight-item index and to questions about their spirituality. The combination of qualitative and quantitative data indicated a fair picture of the importance of the spiritual dimension for this group of deaf+ individuals, who were enrolled in the above-mentioned therapeutic community programs. There was a high correlation especially between ratings of involvement in spiritual practice and self-reported quality of life.

   Proxy ratings by care staff show that this relationship is rather underestimated and stresses the importance of fully listening to what deaf+ individuals experience and have to share (Fellinger et al, 2020).

Heart-to-Heart Stories

The following section are heart-to-heart stories of individuals that highlight both the difficulties this population faces and their hidden potential. With respect to their names, pseudonyms are used.

Joseph

In 1991, when I started the outpatient clinic for the Deaf at the general hospital of St. John of God in Linz, a mother kept contacting me. Almost once a week, she came in crying and desperate. Her son, Joseph, 22 years of age, showed severe aggressive behavior. At this stage in his life, he was enrolled in a sheltered workshop, where he attacked other participants and staff. He was subsequently hospitalized in a closed psychiatric unit and then sent home again, where his sister was also a target of his attacks. His mother felt that she was the only person who could at least tolerate him and was desperate to get options regarding future places for him to live.

Joseph was the fifth of seven siblings. In the third trimester of the pregnancy, his mother was infected with rubella. After birth, a surgery on his left eye was necessary. Hearing loss was not detected until the age of 3. His motor development was delayed compared to his siblings. Joseph and his mother, who paid a lot of attention to him, communicated with simple gestures. The mother also reported problems with Joseph's father who sometimes became very angry with him. At the age of 7 years, Joseph was enrolled in a special boarding school for the Deaf, where he felt very uncomfortable, as he was bed-wetting. He was regarded as a difficult child with temper tantrums who ran away. Joseph had to leave school at the age of 15 due to problems with aggression.

After that time, he worked at the family farm and became very envious of his siblings, who were able to go out and earn their own money. He was very suspicious when others spoke about him. After a short time living at home and working in a nearby forest, he was admitted to a group home with seven hearing people with disabilities, where he was again discharged after only 3 months due to aggressive behavior. In direct contact, Joseph could make himself understood with simple sign language and was able to write a few words.

Frank

Frank's mother was another woman who constantly approached me in the outpatient clinic for the deaf with her worries for her son's future. She came from a privileged background and had so far dedicated her life to raising her son. Frank was a child born after she had lost three children before. His birth was complicated, and it took a long time until he could walk due to his cerebral palsy. He was about 2 when his hearing loss was diagnosed. She went to experts of her time, who recommended avoiding sign language and training him as much as possible in spoken language. He was enrolled in a general school for children with disabilities, without any specific expertise in educating deaf children. Numerous therapists were engaged to teach him to speak and read. He learned to write simple sentences and use a limited vocabulary. He was trained in polite behavior, for instance, standing up when greeting a person, wearing a tie, and raising a glass to toast with a glass of wine. After school, he stayed in his parents' house. I first met Frank as a 34-year-old deaf man, when he was hospitalized due to a hypoglycemic crisis. He was communicating only orally with a very limited level of language comprehension by lipreading and writing. He lived with his parents and attended as the only deaf person a sheltered workshop for people with handicaps. His family reported that he suffered from problems with depressive symptoms and aggressive behavior, which had already caused psychiatric admissions. As the relationship with his father was tense, his mother felt she was the only person able to really get along with Frank and was deeply concerned about his future.

Hank

The tremendous need of Hank's mother, who had been fighting for her son since birth, confronted me in 1991 with the challenges of deaf-blindness and patterns of autistic behavior. Hank and his mother have become great teachers for my whole professional life. When we first met, Hank was 14 years old and attended a school for children with disabilities for a few hours each week. His mother taught him on a one-to-one basis to speak, write, and understand situations by drawing social stories adapted to his visual abilities, and she structured the rest of his day. He had severe hearing and vision loss and had used hearing aids since he was 18 months old. He showed several patterns of challenging behavior, like stealing windshield wipers from cars and collecting them secretly or just running away when something stressed him, especially when he did not know what to do. His mother was busy structuring his day as well as she could but was very exhausted. As she had high expectations and was not satisfied with the support of the educational system, she sought help in the Netherlands especially from professor Jan van Dijk, the world expert on deaf-blindness at that time. It was she who brought us together in 1997, which was the beginning of a wonderful personal friendship that exceeded even the great impact of Jan van Dijk's mentorship on our professional development and the development of Lebenswelt, which was in preparation at that time and will be described later in this chapter.

Paul

Not only mothers stimulated the development of a specific service for deaf+ individuals. As a medical doctor working in an outpatient clinic for the deaf, I was contacted by the staff of a large institution for people with intellectual disabilities and special needs, concerning questions around contraception for two deaf residents with mild intellectual disabilities who were accommodated in different group homes, but had started to meet each other.

It turned out that Paul was the only deaf person in his group home. He reported being very bored while sitting around while the others were chatting. There were a lot of misunderstandings with staff and colleagues of the gardening project that he was involved in. He had attended the boarding school for deaf children and was placed in that institution for people with multiple disabilities immediately after school was finished at age 18. He fell in love with Carmen in 1992, who had also been placed in the same institution 15 years before. Carmen was involved in weaving in a sheltered workshop. Observing how much they benefitted from having met each other, as well as how much they benefitted from meeting other deaf people in the outpatient clinic for the deaf in Linz, was another important stimulus to consider the creation of a living environment, a community that fully met the communication and social needs of Deaf+ individuals in a culturally affirmative way.

Lebenswelt

The individuals mentioned above, together with others who had similar stories and worries, were the impetus to establish a living environment with fully accessible communication in sign language (see Figure 2). After intensive consultations with relatives, deaf community leaders and the government I planned and established a therapeutic living environment called Lebenswelt in the center of a village called Schenkenfelden in Austria. It was evident that only a high proportion of qualified deaf staff members could guarantee a constant signing environment. So parallel with the building process of the house, a three-year qualification and training program for Deaf people was prepared for future professional staff. In 1999, the unit was opened, and in 2011 and 2014, two other units were established, one in Pinsdorf (Upper Austria) and one in Wallsee (Lower Austria). Currently, 70 Deaf+ adults attend the working facilities, and 49 of them are living in group homes in these three units. Almost all have had profound hearing loss since birth. The participants have different levels of intellectual disabilities, ranging from mild to profound. Around one-quarter of them have epilepsy and cerebral palsy, and more than 50% have an ICD-10 diagnosis of IDs with challenging behavior. About 15% of the residents are on the autistic spectrum.

The mission of Lebenswelt is to offer a therapeutic environment where deaf+ individuals with histories of severe deprivation can develop socially, emotionally, mentally, spiritually, and in all other dimensions of human existence to the maximum of their potential. It is based on the idea that an enhancement of social communication can lead to an increase in social engagement and the establishment of satisfying social relationships. This increase in participation and social connectedness is seen as a major contributor to a person's quality of life and mental health, as illustrated in figure 2. Together, with other elements like meaningful work and healthy living conditions, this approach includes sufficient possibilities to establish social relationships in a big-enough network of people who constantly communicate in sign language or other modes of accessible communication, including deaf+ peers and trained deaf and hearing staff. A network

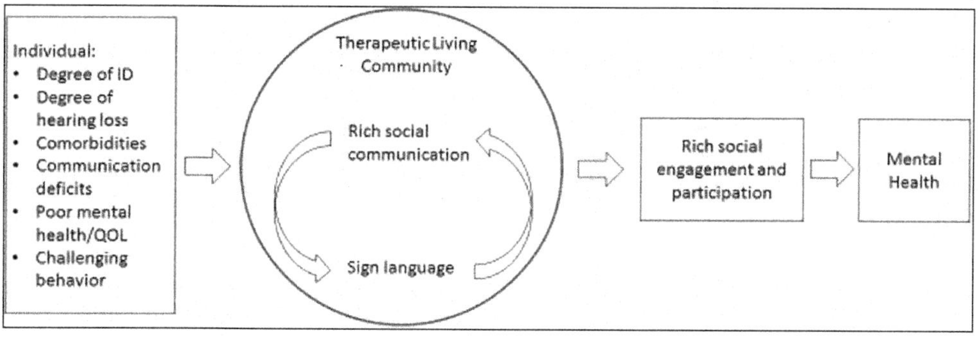

Figure 2. Mission of Lebenswelt, a conceptual model on the development of deaf+ adults in a therapeutic living community.

size of a therapeutic community includes 12 to 24 residents and the respective staff, altogether between 30 and 50 people. Lebenswelt exhibits the following characteristics:

1. Especially with respect to the traumatic experiences of many deaf+ individuals, an atmosphere of unconditional acceptance and forgiveness is seen as a precondition for personal development at all Lebenswelt sites. This personal development is the constant focus of all community activities. Increases in communication skills, self-determination, and establishment of social relationships are seen as the main outcome criteria.
2. Staff members are constantly trained to never give up and to try to fully understand what the residents want to express. This responsiveness training is very important to encourage deaf+ individuals who have experienced not being listened to or being overruled to express themselves, even in rudimentary signs.
3. The therapeutic communities are in the very center of the respective villages, where the residents are welcomed as citizens and where many inhabitants are trained to use sign language as much as possible and to give the Lebenswelt residents opportunities to participate in the infrastructure of the village, like using shops and the bank or participating in events. Furthermore, strong links to the deaf community are nurtured.
4. Regular morning meetings are offered, where the daily program is carefully explained, visitors are introduced, and issues in the community are discussed (e.g., illness and conflicts), giving the participants an opportunity to share what they want to tell. Stories from the gospel of Jesus are told by real-time, step-by-step paintings on flipcharts and through gestures, signs, and role-play. The impact of the stories on everyday life is discussed. At the beginning and the end of the meeting, songs in sign language let all join in, and the meeting is closed by residents who sign blessings.
5. The staff is intensively trained in how to enhance communication abilities and solve conflicts. There is a special emphasis on collecting "golden moments" of each participant. Golden moments are positive interactions with other residents, for instance, when initiation of communication or social behavior can be observed.

More about the program can be read in the articles "Development of Deaf Adults with Intellectual Disability in a Therapeutic Living Community" (Fellinger et al., 2020) and "Therapeutic

Living Communities for Adults Who Are Deaf and Have Intellectual Disabilities: A Conceptual Model Linking Social Communication and Mental Health" (Fellinger et al., 2021b).

The intensive involvement in setting up and developing these therapeutic communities formed the basis for close relationships with the individuals involved and is a source of ongoing lived experience and the stories told in the following subsections.

Joseph at Lebenswelt

When the Lebenswelt was built and the staff was trained, Joseph had a very hard time. In addition to his intellectual disability in the mild/moderate range and severe language deprivation, he developed symptoms of psychosis. He spent years in psychiatric hospitals. Neuroleptic medication could not make the hallucinations stop, but it did make him calmer. When he was again placed in a group home with hearing people, he attempted suicide by jumping out of a window. He incurred several broken bones but survived and was sent back to the psychiatric hospital. It was a challenge for us to get him out and accommodate him in this newly established setting. We were quite astonished how quickly he adapted to his new room and how he started to participate in the community activities. Even though he still hallucinates and has symptoms of anxiety, he participates in the morning meetings and experiences great relief when all the staff members make it frequently clear to him during the day that he is a beloved person. He takes the stories about Jesus very seriously and gets great comfort from Jesus being the one who loves him. Although he experienced some psychotic episodes, he never had to be readmitted to the psychiatric hospital.

Frank at Lebenswelt

When Frank was enrolled in the therapeutic community at Lebenswelt Schenkenfelden, he was exposed to sign language for the first time in his life. It was obvious how he acquired more and more abilities to understand signs and even express himself with a mixture of spoken and signed language. However, sometimes he made statements like "Speaking is better," which he was taught as a child. These statements and his orientation to staff alienated him somewhat from the other residents. Nevertheless, he is very interested in group activities and enjoys working together with others in the ceramic workshop, where he developed a very specific style of decorating pottery.

I want to share one very personal experience that I had with Frank, which shows that he could combine a lot from what was shared in the morning meetings about the Jesus stories. When my deaf father died in 2002, I invited the residents of Lebenswelt to participate at the funeral, as they knew him from several visits. My deaf father was quite a famous artist, and many prominent people like the governor attended the funeral and expressed their condolences. However, almost at the end of a long row of individuals who expressed their sympathy, Frank approached me in his hemi-spastic gait and expressed in his idiosyncratic mixture of signed and spoken language: "Do not be afraid, Jesus is alive!" His words touched me directly and have given me an unforgettable comfort.

Hank at Lebenswelt

The original plan to accommodate Hank as a resident had to be changed to participation in the day program only, where Hank became a very productive potter. As he was not willing to leave his parents' house where he had his aquariums, he traveled every day (almost 4 hours each day) with public transport, which he was taught carefully how to use.

In 2011, when the next Lebenswelt facility was opened in Pinsdorf, the town where he lived, he started to work there. He discovered running as an activity where he could use his energy also in preparation for inclusive competitions. He still lived at home, but his elderly parents were getting significant support by the therapeutic community staff at Pinsdorf, who helped planning provision for Hank's supported living needs. He just recently made a great step by moving into an apartment, where he lives on his own now.

Paul and Carmen at Lebenswelt

When Lebenswelt Schenkenfelden was opened, Paul and Carmen decided to leave the residential facility where they had been living for so many years and move to Lebenswelt. Initially, they lived in two separate rooms in the group home. They socialized with the other residents and developed a strong work identity. Paul has become a potter with a primary focus on decorating flowerpots and vases with ornaments that he developed himself. Carmen has been a very busy weaver. Paul increased his social network, not only within Lebenswelt but also with the citizens of the village. He enjoys going to the local inn and established a friendship with the owner of the inn, who has acquired some sign language. He has become a beloved citizen of the village; the village children often follow him when he rides his tricycle through the main square. Carmen developed more and more the ability to make decisions on her own, which she had not been able to do for so many years. Paul and Carmen continued their relationship and started to consider marriage. They both had legal custodians due to their intellectual disabilities, and so a very careful process was started to follow their wishes. We had to make clear that they knew what it meant to be married. During one of the marriage-preparation sessions, Paul said, "Marriage, to me, means that I will cook tea when Carmen is sick." It was very evident, by the end of the process, that the two of them were very dedicated to taking on the responsibility for each other and also understood the concept of being married. It was a touching experience for the whole village to join the two of them, not only at the ceremony but also afterwards, when they sat in a horse carriage like royal highnesses and were accompanied and cheered for by many citizens. They are still living together and are active participants in the therapeutic community and the village of Schenkenfelden.

Jim at Lebenswelt

It is important to share, that Lebenswelt took and is still taking in deaf+ individuals regardless of their level of intellectual functioning, their history of developmental trauma, and the severity of their behavior problems.

For instance, Jim was profoundly deaf and had a mild intellectual disability when he was enrolled at age 17, but he also had a terrible childhood. His mother suffered from a severe psychiatric disorder, which was the reason that he was transferred to institutional care early in life. He could hardly handle frustrations and showed highly aggressive behavior. Even in Lebenswelt, he broke the bones of staff members. It took a long time to reduce his outbursts by giving him opportunities for developing attachment to very stable staff members. Fortunately, the government funded this one-on-one treatment approach.

Ann at Lebenswelt

In contrast to Jim, Ann, who has a genetic syndrome (Cornelia-De-Lange syndrome) with various typical characteristics like having a small stature and moderate intellectual disability, grew up in a loving and signing family environment. In her active, very curious, and socially interested way of interacting with everybody, she is a welcoming and shining star for community participants and for people from outside.

These heart-to-heart stories are but a few examples of deaf+ individuals who represent the many Lebenswelt inhabitants with heterogeneous biographies and developmental profiles who experienced a new life in this signing therapeutic community environment. Almost all of them increased their sign language vocabulary and could at least understand what was going on around them, which was a great relief. In addition, with more encouragement to make decisions for themselves, it was observed that conflict between residents became more frequent. We welcomed these conflicts as indicators of positive human development, especially as in many cases, it was important to support participants to reconcile and develop more healthy social relationships. It seems contradictory, but the coexistence of happiness and the development of self-identity and social relationships with outbursts of challenging behavior in conflicts is a challenging, yet positive, everyday reality. I want to conclude this personal experience with a statement made by an experienced neuropediatrician upon visiting Lebenswelt: "Your participants are behaving like prisoners who have become free."

Recommendations From Our Heart-to Heart Experiences and Head-to-Head Information at Lebenswelt

- Have high respect for any deaf+ adults and their unlocked potential. This means identifying deaf+ adults wherever they are placed and considering how they could become part of a communicative and linguistically accessible social network, whose members are constantly using visual and signed communication. If there are no places known, be bold and start one. Don't think it is too late in life.
- The deaf community has a major responsibility for the care and support of deaf+ individuals, who live mostly at the fringes of Deaf society. The Position Paper on the Social Inclusion of Deaf People with Intellectual Disabilities was a strong message in that direction (WFD, 2023). In Austria, the Deaf association was supportive in setting up these therapeutic communities by helping to convince politicians to realize that every deaf person has the right to communication access.
- Support the parents of children with deaf+ characteristics as soon as possible, by putting the focus on communication and creating a signing social environment and supporting them in blending into adulthood. Support perspectives of self-determination and social participation in a communicative accessible environment and full realization of a deaf+ child's potential.
- Involve deaf+ individuals in policymaking, program implementation, and research.

These practical suggestions cannot be considered as "nice to have" but are essential expressions of how to realize the human right for communication. As stated in Article 19 of the UN Convention of Human Rights: "Everyone has the right to freedom of opinion and expression; this right includes freedom to hold opinions without interference and to seek, receive and impart information and ideas through any media and regardless of frontiers" (United Nations, 1948). Article 19 of the United Nations Convention on the Rights of Persons with Disabilities (United Nations, 2006) states that effective and appropriate measures must be taken to facilitate full enjoyment by persons with disabilities of the right to full inclusion and participation in the community, which is also true for deaf+ adults. This inclusion can also happen by including a community of deaf+ individuals and their signing social environment within mainstream society, whereas the inclusion of a single deaf+ individual without any accessible communication is, in fact, an act of isolation. Isolation is not the environment where humans can develop.

References

Brähler, E., Mühlan, H., Albani, C., & Schmidt, S. (2007). Teststatistische Prüfung und Normierung der deutschen Versionen des EUROHISQOL Lebensqualität-Index und des WHO-5Wohlbefindens-Index. *Diagnostica*, 53, 83–96.

Bronfenbrenner, U. (1992). Ecological systems theory. In R. Vasta (Ed.), *Six theories of child development: Revised formulations and current issues* (pp. 187–249). Jessica Kingsley Publishers.

Chapman, D. A., Stampfel, C. C., Bodurtha, J. N., Dodson, K. M., Pandya, A., Lynch, K. B., & Kirby, R. S. (2011). Impact of co-occurring birth defects on the timing of newborn hearing screening and diagnosis. *American Journal of Audiology*, *20*(2), 132–139. https://doi.org/10.1044/1059-0889(2011/10-0049)

Cohen, S., & Wills, T.A. (1985). Stress, social support, and the buffering hypothesis. *Psychological Bulletin*, *98*(2), 310–357.

Edwards S, Fletcher P, Garman M, Hughes A, Letts C, $ Sinka I. (1997). *Reynell Developmental Language Scales III.* Nfer-Nelson.

Eisinger, J., Dall, M., Fogler, J., Holzinger, D., & Fellinger, J. (2022). Intellectual disability profiles, quality of life and maladaptive behavior in deaf adults: An exploratory study. *International Journal of Environmental Research and Public Health*, *19*(16), Article 9919. https://doi.org/10.3390/ijerph19169919

Fellinger, J., Dall, M., Gerich, J., Fellinger, M., Schossleitner, K., Barbaresi, W. J., & Holzinger, D. (2021a). Is it feasible to assess self-reported quality of life in individuals who are deaf and have intellectual disabilities? *Social Psychiatry and Psychiatric Epidemiology*, *56*(10), 1881–1890. https://doi.org/10.1007/s00127-020-01957-y

Fellinger, J., Dall, M., & Holzinger, D. (2021b). Therapeutic living communities for adults who are deaf and have intellectual disabilities: A conceptual model linking social communication and mental health. *International Journal of Developmental Disabilities*, *67*(5), 391–396. https://doi.org/10.1080/20473869.2021.1953938

Fellinger, J., Dall, M., Weber, C. & Holzinger, D. (2022). Communicative deficits associated with maladaptive behavior in individuals with deafness and special needs. *Frontiers in Psychiatry 13*, 944719.

Fellinger, J., Holzinger, D., Dirmhirn, A., Van Dijk, J., & Goldberg, D. (2009). Failure to detect deaf-blindness in a population of people with intellectual disability. *Journal of Intellectual Disability Research*, *53*(10), 874–881. https://doi.org/10.1111/j.1365-2788.2009.01205.x

Fellinger, J., Linzner, D., Holzinger, D., Dall, M., Fellinger, M., & Fogler, J. (2020). Development of deaf adults with intellectual disability in a therapeutic living community. *Journal of Deaf Studies and Deaf Education*, *25*(3), 261–269. https://doi.org/10.1093/deafed/enz056

Fellinger, M, Holzinger, D, Fogler, J, & Fellinger, J. (2023). Exploring spirituality and quality of life in individuals who are deaf and have intellectual disabilities. *Social Psychiatry and Psychiatric Epidemiology*, *58*(11), 1709–1718. https://doi.org/10.1007/s00127-023-02451-x

Gallaudet Research Institute (2011). *Regional and national summary report of data from the 2009–2010 annual survey of deaf and hard of hearing children and youth*. Gallaudet University.

Goldstein, G., & Bebko, J. M. (2003). The profile of multiple language proficiencies: A measure for evaluating language samples of deaf children. *Journal of Deaf Studies and Deaf Education*, *8*, 452–463. https://doi.org/10.1093/deafed/eng027

Graves, R. J., Zlomke, K. R., Graff, J. C., & Hall, H. R. (2020). Adaptive behavior of adults with Down syndrome and their health-related quality of life. *Advances in Neurodevelopmental Disorders*, *4*, 27–35. https://doi.org/10.1007/s41252-019-00133-x

Gulati, S. (2018). Language deprivation syndrome. In N. S. Glickman & W. C. Hall (Eds.), *Language deprivation and deaf mental health* (pp. 24–53). Routledge. https://doi.org/10.4324/9781315166728

Hall, W. C., Levin, L. L., & Anderson, M. L. (2017). Language deprivation syndrome: A possible neurodevelopmental disorder with sociocultural origins. *Social Psychiatry and Psychiatric Epidemiology, 52*(6), 761–776. https://doi.org/10.1007/s00127-017-1351-7

Ireton, H. (1992). *Child Development Inventory.* Behavior Science Systems. https://doi.org/10.1037/t05317-000

Kushalnagar, P., Ryan, C., Paludneviciene, R., Spellun, A., & Gulati, S. (2020). Adverse childhood communication experiences associated with an increased risk of chronic diseases in adults who are deaf. *American Journal of Preventive Medicine, 59*(4), 548–554. https://doi.org/10.1016/j.amepre.2020.04.016

Ladd, P. (2003). *Understanding deaf culture: In search of deafhood.* Multilingual Matters. https://doi.org/10.21832/9781853595479

Madduri, N., Peters, S. U., Voigt, R. G., Llorente, A. M., Lupski, J. R., & Potocki, L. (2006). Cognitive and adaptive behavior profiles in Smith-Magenis syndrome. *Journal of Developmental and Behavioral Pediatrics, 27*(3), 188–192. https://doi.org/10.1097/00004703-200606000-00002

Meuwese-Jongejeugd, A., Vink, M., van Zanten, B., Verschuure, H., Eichhorn, E., Koopman, D., Bernsen, R., & Evenhuis, H. (2006) Prevalence of hearing loss in 1,589 adults with an intellectual disability: Cross-sectional population based study. *International Journal of Audiology, 45*(11), 660–669. https://doi.org/10.1080/14992020600920812

Nikolopoulos, T. P., Lioumi, D., Stamataki, S., O'Donoghue, G. M., Guest, M., & Hall, A.-M. (2006). Evidence-based overview of ophthalmic disorders in deaf children: a literature update. *Otology and Neurotology*, 27(2 Suppl 1), S1–S24. https://doi.org/10.1097/01.mao.0000185150.69704.18

Schreiber K, Dobner C, Stalzer C, & Holzinger D. (2020). Entwicklung praktikabler und zuverlässiger Verfahren zur Ermittlung des Sprachverstehens in der Österreichischen Gebärdensprache im Vorschulalter - eine Pilotstudie. *Hörgeschädigtenpädagogik,* 147–156.

Sparrow S, Cicchetti D, & Balla D. (2005). *Vineland-II: Vineland Adaptive Behavior Scales.* AGS Publishing. https://doi.org/10.1037/t15164-000

Tellegen, P., Laros, J., & Peterman, F. (2007). *SON-R 2 1/2 - 7.* Hogrefe.

Tellegen, P. J., Laros, J. A., & Petermann F. (2012). *SON-R 6-40 manual.* Hogrefe. https://www.hogrefe.com/uk/shop/manual-part-2-instructions.html

Timehin, C., & Timehin, E. (2004). Prevalence of hearing impairment in a community population of adults with learning disability: Access to audiology and impact on behaviour. *British Journal of Learning Disabilities, 32*(3), 128–132. https://doi.org/10.1111/j.1468-3156.2004.00289.x

United Nations (UN). (2006). *Convention on the Rights of Persons with Disabilities (CRPD).* https://social.desa.un.org/issues/disability/crpd/convention-on-the-rights-of-persons-with-disabilities-crpd

Van Naarden Braun, K., Christensen, D., Doernberg, N., Schieve, L., Rice, C., Wiggins, L., Schendel, D., & Yeargin-Allsopp, M. (2015). Trends in the prevalence of autism spectrum disorder, cerebral palsy, hearing loss, intellectual disability, and vision impairment, metropolitan Atlanta, 1991–2010. *PloS One, 10*(4), Article e0124120. https://doi.org/10.1371/journal.pone.0124120

Weber, C., Weber, C., Fellinger, J., & Holzinger, D. (2021). Development of a social communication questionnaire (QSC-ID) for people with intellectual disability in a deaf sample: a pilot and feasibility study. *Frontiers in Psychiatry 12,* 755993. https://doi.org/10.3389/fpsyt.2021.755993

World Federation of the Deaf (WFD). (2023). *Position paper on the social inclusion of deaf people with intellectual disabilities.* https://wfdeafnew.wpenginepowered.com/wp-content/uploads/2023/05/Position-paper-on-the-social-inclusion-of-deaf-people-with-intellectual-disabilities.pdf

World Health Organization (WHO). (2004). ICD-10: *International statistical classification of diseases and related health problems* (10th rev., 2d ed.). https://iris.who.int/handle/10665/42980

World Health Organization (WHO). (2004). *The World Health Organization quality of life (WHOQOL)—BREF, 2012 revision.* iris: Institutional Repository for Information Sharing. https://apps.who.int/iris/handle/10665/77773

World Health Organization (WHO). (1993). *The ICD-10 classification of mental and behavioural disorders: Clinical descriptions and diagnostic guidelines.* https://www.who.int/publications/i/item/9241544228

9

Mental Health Interpreting in Canada

A Call to Action

Debra Russell and Catriona J. Revell

Construct

This chapter discusses sign language interpreting services as one part of the important delivery of mental health and addiction support in Canada. We begin with an examination of the Canadian policies and practices that have shaped interpreting services in mental health contexts and then contrast these with international approaches. We also examine the Canadian landscape and the myriad approaches to mental health services for Deaf children, youth, and adults, which do not consistently serve Deaf people and clinicians in effective ways. The reasons why qualified mental health interpreters are needed are reviewed along with examples of inequities in the mental health programs in which interpreters work, particularly when interpreting for Deaf people living in correctional or congregate care facilities, rural or remote locations, and/or those attempting to access addiction treatment programs. We close with recommendations for improving the Canadian context of mental health interpreting.

Head-to-Head and Heart-to-Heart

The perspectives and lived experiences of Deaf and Hard of Hearing (DHH) children and adults are often shared with clinicians through the services of a sign language interpreter. The work of the sign language interpreter can involve head-to-heads, as clinicians may brief the interpreter on an individual's diagnosis, clinical presentation, or session goals, and the interpreter may, in turn, share feedback or insights about the interpreting and communication process. Heart-to-hearts emerge as interpreters become the vehicle through which emotions and personal stories are relayed to clinicians. The interpreter's ability to understand both the head-to-head interactions and the heart-to-heart stories and experiences of DHH people is key to ensuring proper diagnosis, effective treatment, and counseling approaches are taken with the DHH person. Given the critical role of sign language interpreters in mental health settings, we have chosen to seek out their insights and experiences in shaping this chapter.

Statements of Reflexivity

First Author: Debra Russell

I acknowledge that my views have been shaped by my experiences working within the Deaf community and as an interpreter with 4 decades of service. Much of my interpreting career has focused on community interpreting with a great deal of mental health and legal interpreting. I learned American Sign Language (ASL) as a young adult and did not grow up with Deaf family members. My commitment to the Deaf community and my drive to constantly improve my ability to serve the community well is inspired by the lived experiences and narratives of Deaf people that we are privileged to see and be trusted with through the nature of the interpreting assignments we accept.

Second Author: Catriona J. Revell

My perspective has been shaped by my experiences working and learning within the Deaf and interpreting communities. I began learning ASL as a young adult and was fortunate to meet, work with, and be taught by incredible Deaf educators during my undergraduate and graduate studies. I have also been inspired by interpreting mentors who have modeled the values of collaboration, respect for the Deaf community and their language, and the recognition that the interpreting profession is one of continuous learning and improvement. Through mental health interpreting, I have been humbled by the trust placed in me by Deaf individuals and the incredible responsibility and privilege of being privy to some of their most personal moments.

Research Shaping This Chapter

Findings are shared from a survey with over 107 Canadian interpreters. In addition to the survey, we conducted two targeted interviews to capture the perspectives of the francophone community and a counselor who has created a training program for Canadian interpreters working in mental health settings. The results reveal the pressing need for a pathway of training for interpreters wishing to work in mental health contexts. At present, this training is fragmented across the country, resulting in inequitable access when relying on interpreting services. There is also an urgent need for changes in the funding systems to cover the costs of interpreting services, as well as training for clinicians, so that they might better serve DHH clients from both a head-to-head and heart-to-heart perspective. While this chapter does not share stories in the ways that the other authors have done in this text, it exposes the lived experiences of the interpreter participants as they navigate the challenges of providing accessible mental health services for deaf people.

Recommendations

It is critical that interpreters have a solid foundation in understanding the clinical aspects that inform mental health with Deaf people. We conclude with a call to action and recommendations for government funders, service providers, and those training interpreters for this specialized domain of practice. By enhancing the training for interpreters working with Deaf people accessing mental health services, Deaf people and clinicians will be better served.

Healthcare interpreting is one of the more frequent settings in which sign language interpreters tend to work, as well as one of the most demanding; there has been considerable attention paid at the global level to healthcare interpreting, both in spoken and sign language literature (Russell, 2019). There are few studies, however, that explore the practices of interpreters working in mental health settings, and there have been no studies of the experiences of Canadian sign language interpreters to date. The lack of evidence-based studies upon which to plan for the delivery of effective mental health interpreting services is problematic.

There is legislation in place that protects people from discrimination based on disability, such as Section 14 of the Canadian Charter of Rights and Freedom. This section compels accessibility to an interpreter for any individual who does not understand or speak the language in which the legal proceedings are conducted or who is deaf (Canadian Charter of Rights and Freedoms, 1982). Section 15 of this same charter specifically mandates accessibility equality for Deaf[1] people using either American Sign Language (ASL) and/or Langue des Signes Québécoise (LSQ) (Canadian Charter of Rights and Freedoms, 1982). This jurisprudence is critical and fundamental to Deaf people's right to full access to interpreting in the courtroom; however, the provincial human rights codes have not traditionally ensured that Deaf people have access to healthcare and mental health interpreting. A landmark Supreme Court of Canada decision in 1997, *Eldridge v. British Columbia,* focused on access to interpreters to secure equal medical treatment for persons who are Deaf. This case changed the landscape for Deaf Canadians (Russell, 2019) and led to the development of medical interpreting services in each province. However, as health care is a provincial and territorial responsibility rather than a federal one, services are delivered differently across Canada. Canada is a bilingual country with English and French as official languages. Some Canadian Deaf communities use ASL while others use LSQ, and in recent years, more attention has been paid to Inuktitut Sign Language and other forms of indigenous sign languages (Oneida Sign Language, Plains Sign Language, etc.). In 2019, Canada passed the Accessible Canada Act (ACA), which further strengthens the legal requirement of access to interpreters for federal services. However, even with the *Eldridge v. British Columbia* decision and the passing of the ACA, the protection of Deaf people's rights to mental health services either directly from a clinician fluent in ASL or LSQ, or via mediated access with sign language interpreters, continues to fall short.

As Chovaz et al. (2023) stated, the experience of being Deaf goes above and beyond the presence of interpreters. The authors identify a number of challenges, including the lived experiences of marginalized Deaf people (Chovaz et al., 2022; Leigh et al., 2022a; Ziedenberg et al., 2021), the impact of audism (Bauman, 2004; Bauman & Murray, 2010; Humphries, 1975), the lack of access to education (Du Feu & Chovaz, 2014), unemployment and underemployment (Garberoglio et al., 2019), the prevalence of mental health issues (Du Feu & Chovaz, 2014; Fellinger, et al., 2012), matters stemming from language delay or deprivation (Gulati, 2018; Hall et al., 2017) and access to interpreters qualified to do the work (Russell, 2005, 2012).

We believe that these multiple challenges affecting access to the legal system are also true when accessing services in the healthcare and mental health systems. This study is one step in addressing the significant gap in the current literature informing Canadian policies and practices surrounding mental health support for Deaf people.

---

1. Throughout this chapter, the convention of capitalizing *Deaf* to distinguish members of a cultural and linguistic group has been used. The word *deaf* is used to indicate a larger group of people who may or may not be members of the Deaf community, their language or culture not made explicit (e.g., deaf students, deaf consumers, or interpreting services (Russell, 2002).

Positionality

As authors, we wish to acknowledge our positionality and how that influences our work. We are both Canadian interpreters. Our backgrounds bring together signed language interpreting in ASL, education, psychology, and mental health. The first author is an interpreter educator and researcher with a primary focus on legal and mental health settings. The second author is an interpreter with a practice that specializes in mental health interpreting. As a research team, we were prepared to approach the research process and any of the results with openness and a lens of curiosity. We are part of the Deaf and interpreter communities, and this study has allowed us to privilege our positions to highlight the experiences of Canadian ASL and LSQ interpreters and their interactions with the mental health system. Given the lack of empirical evidence that has included the perspectives of this subset of interpreters, our central research question was this: What do Canadian interpreters report as their lived experiences in providing interpreting services within the mental health system in Canada?

Review of the Literature

The Canadian Landscape

When examining the provision of mental health services for Deaf people, there has been considerable focus in the literature on the mental health experiences and diagnoses of Deaf individuals. Despite the recognition of resiliency (Chovaz et al., 2022; Zand, 2011), Deaf individuals are broadly considered to have higher rates of mental health disorders (Bone, 2019; Du Feu & Chovaz, 2014) and have less access to health care than people who can hear (Fellinger et al., 2012). Fellinger et al. (2012) also noted increased rates of mental health issues among Deaf people in both community and correctional settings, although Deaf correctional and forensic populations have been studied far less in the literature (Bone, 2019; Kelly, 2018; Wattman, 2018). Further, Fellinger et al. (2012) estimated that the incidence of Deaf inmates who are mentally ill surpasses that of their hearing prison peers. Finally, Zidenberg et al. (2021) stated that d/Deaf individuals with mental health issues appear to be overrepresented in prison settings, particularly for individuals with a history of violent sexual offending.

In the first Canadian study of Deaf people interacting with the legal system, Deaf individuals, whether victims or perpetrators of a crime, struggled to have their communication access rights recognized and met (Chovaz et al., 2023; Russell et al., 2018). Deaf inmates were incarcerated longer than nondeaf inmates based on a lack of access to treatment programs such as anger management, counseling groups, and/or individual therapy (Russell et al., 2018). This lack of access was most often linked to either an absence of interpreting services or a refusal to pay for and provide interpreting services on the part of the institution. While improvements have been made at some individual institutions since the study was published, there is no consistent policy guiding federal or provincial correctional facilities on the provision of mental health support and services for Deaf inmates.

As early as 2007, Woodcock and Pole studied community mental health services and reported that access for Deaf people disproportionately consisted of case management rather than clinical services. More recently, Chovaz et al. (2022) and Bone (2019) identified similar issues in current delivery services, suggesting that there has been little change over the ensuing 15 years. However, one interesting change in the Canadian approach has taken place in British Columbia, where the

Provincial Health Services Authority (PHSA) provides mental health interpreters for requests falling under the Medical Services Plan (MSP) and Hospital Insurance Act (HIA). For requests outside the scope of the MSP and HIA, a community-based agency, Vancouver Coastal Health's Deaf, Hard of Hearing, and Deaf-Blind Well-Being Program (https://deafwellbeing.vch.ca/), provides interpreters for mental health appointments. In addition, British Columbia ambulances now have access to video remote interpreting (VRI), enabling usage for emergency mental health calls in ASL (Vancouver Coastal Health, 2023). This service was initiated in 2022 and is provided by an American interpreting agency; however, the exact number of paramedic/first responder calls for Deaf individuals requiring mental health support is unknown (S. Jeffery, personal communication, January 15, 2023). PHSA maintains that for healthcare communication, particularly mental health, in-person interpreting is more effective than VRI, and encourages healthcare providers to access in-person services whenever possible.

Training Mental Health Interpreters in Canada

Across Canada, there are five Interpreter Education Programs (IEPs) that serve to educate most of the sign language interpreters in Canada. Some interpreters have entered the field through their own experience within the community, having learned ASL or LSQ through their families or community members. Canadian IEPs are generalist programs, however, working to simultaneously teach ASL or LSQ to learners and teaching those same learners how to interpret between two languages, leaving little time or opportunity for specialization (McDermid, 2009). No program offers a dedicated mental health interpreting course as part of its curriculum, but some may include discussion about mental health interpreting in the context of healthcare interpreting in general (A.M. Parisot, personal communication, September 13, 2022). The consensus across Canadian IEPs is that mental health interpreting is an advanced area of specialization that would not be appropriate for newly graduated interpreters. The general expectation is that graduates will pursue further training after having learned to interpret effectively in less high-stakes environments (R. Reynolds, personal communication, September 13, 2022). Instead, IEPs focus on teaching foundational interpreting skills and simply do not have the space in their curriculum for specialized training in areas such as mental health or legal interpreting.

Given this lack of specialized training, interpreters are left to their own devices in terms of seeking out additional training to work in several settings, including mental health appointments. There is no standard practice to follow nor a roadmap guiding interpreters through their entry into this field. Nationally and provincially, there is no required certification, screening, or test to become a mental health interpreter. Rather, interpreters seem to enter this specialty of their own volition, and at their own discretion, with essentially no oversight or gatekeeper determining qualifications for this work. Some interpreters seek mentorship from experienced interpreters, while others opt for additional training through an internship program or attend workshops or other professional development focused on mental health interpreting. Many interpreters may instead pursue no specialized training at all, yet are nonetheless able to take on mental health work. What is not known is how this fragmented landscape of interpreters working in mental health may be negatively impacting both Deaf Canadians seeking mental health support and clinicians who are unfamiliar with how to serve Deaf clients.

Training opportunities are both sparse and fragmented across the country; there is no unified approach to mental health training and no national standard in this area. Should an interpreter wish to pursue training in mental health interpreting, their options are limited and location-dependent.

In Ontario, the Ontario Interpreting Services (OIS) offers the Interpreter Internship Program (IIP), run by Canadian Hearing Services and funded by the Ministry of Health, which provides 9 months of intensive training for newer interpreters, with an "emphasis on specialized areas such as medical and mental health settings" (Canadian Hearing Services, n.d.). In its more than 20 years of operation, the OIS program has provided a baseline of exposure to various topics in mental health and offered situated role-plays that involved counselors. However, the program is weighted more toward medical and social interpreting, with only periodic 1-day workshops focused on mental health (T. Tamlin, personal communication, January 5, 2023).

Also in Ontario, King's University College at the University of Western Ontario hosts the Centre of Deaf Education & Accessibility Forum (CDEAF), which is "dedicated to the advancement and dissemination of knowledge related to mental health and deafness" (CDEAF, 2023). CDEAF is not focused exclusively on interpreter training but has offered several 2-day workshops on mental health interpreting in recent years. Outside of Ontario, mental health interpreter training exists primarily via individual workshops, presentations, or conferences that interpreters may or may not have the opportunity and the means to attend.

In past years, Douglas College in British Columbia offered a postdiploma, 1-week summer institute training for interpreters working in medical settings, which included some information on mental health interpreting and a specific ASL lexicon. This training served as the foundation for the screening tool used by British Columbia's Medical Interpreting Services, which included a performance assessment with a mental health scenario. Unfortunately, neither this post-diploma program nor the screening continues to be offered.

In 2020, Susi Bolender, a registered clinical counselor and certified ASL-English interpreter, attempted to address the training void in Canada by creating an online program for interpreters. Her program is entitled Mental Health Interpreter Training Essentials and is a self-guided online program with optional one-on-one support, aimed at providing interpreters with the equivalent of a three-day training (Bolender, 2025). The program is an entry point for interpreters interested in working in mental health. It places the onus on interpreters to learn how to talk about mental health work, diagnoses, therapeutic techniques, and the fundamentals of counselor training (S. Bolender, personal communication, December 8, 2022). This online program stands out as the only continuously offered mental health training for interpreters in the country (S. Bolender, personal communication, December 8, 2022). Unfortunately, with such a paucity of training options in Canada, many interpreters may be unable to pursue this type of specialized education or may be forced to seek their training outside of Canada.

Training Mental Health Interpreters in the United States

The Canadian picture stands in sharp contrast to the training that is available in the United States. Dean and Pollard (2009, 2011; Pollard, 1998) pioneered the development of mental health interpreter training and continue to refine an evidenced-based curriculum that specifically addresses this specialized area of interpreting. They have written extensively on the application of the demand-control schema in the training and supervision of interpreters working in mental health settings. The scholarship of Dean and Pollard has had a global influence, and their training model is thorough, leading to its implementation in several countries.

As well as the programs offered through Dean and Pollard, there are two primary centers offering training. The CATIE Center at St. Catherine University in Minnesota received federal funding for the Behavioral Health Interpreting (BHI) Project, which offered online training modules and self-directed workshops on various mental health topics, such as psychopharmacology, addiction recovery, domestic and sexual violence, and mental health and suicide.[2] The BHI Project also supports interpreters in both attending the Mental Health Interpreter Training (MHIT) program in Alabama (http://www.mhit.org/) and obtaining practicum experiences and credentialing after program completion. The CATIE Center offerings were designed to support the acquisition of skills and knowledge highlighted per the Healthcare Career Lattice (Swabey et al., 2016). This then provides a clear pathway to acquire the foundational experience required for healthcare interpreting in the United States. While the funding for the BHI project has concluded, archived resources and materials can still be found online. The CATIE Center has secured another 5-year grant (2021–2026) and is now offering Project Level Up, which has as its aim to "increase interpreters' knowledge, skills, and competencies; thereby, reducing the equity gaps in healthcare communication for Deaf, Hard of Hearing and DeafBlind individuals in healthcare settings" (https://healthcareinterpreting.org/level-up/). Participants can join either the self-directed or cohort track—the latter of which will accept 35 certified U.S. interpreters every year for 5 years and provide online instruction, discussion, group work with expert facilitators, interpreting role-plays with feedback, and observation hours.

There is also a well-established training program for mental health interpreters offered in Alabama, the Mental Health Interpreter Training (MHIT). Developed and codified in 2003 by Steve Hamerdinger, Charlene Crump, and various stakeholder groups, section 580-3-24 of the Administrative Code of Alabama: Certification of Mental Health Interpreters for Persons Who Are Deaf outlined the minimum competencies required for mental health interpreters (Alabama Department of Mental Health, 2022). Crump (2012) described these minimum competencies that form the basis for both the MHIT curriculum and the certification standards, including professional, cultural, and conduct competencies and knowledge. Given that this annual intensive week-long training is geared toward experienced ASL interpreters wanting to specialize in mental health interpreting, its focus has always been on developing knowledge, rather than on enhancing signing skills. To become certified as a Qualified Mental Health Interpreter, the training must be followed by a 40-hour practicum taking place in specific U.S. locations, a 6- to 8-hour formal written examination, and yearly maintenance of credentials (Alabama Department of Mental Health, 2022).

What is evident across the U.S. interpreter training field is the need for highly skilled interpreters who understand how to work with Deaf consumers, including those who may present with language deprivation syndrome and/or language dysfluency. Language deprivation syndrome results from a lack of consistent and full language exposure during the critical period for language acquisition and has been recognized to result in a range of social, emotional, and intellectual effects, in addition to communication issues and lack of fluency (Gulati, 2018). Mental health interpreters must have knowledge of therapeutic treatment processes and techniques, possess the specialized terminology across a range of presenting concerns (addiction, childhood trauma, attachment issues, suicidal ideation, etc.), and have both the tools and the ethical maturity to make effective professional decisions in the complicated landscape of mental health interpreting. The dynamics of interpreting in mental health settings can include working between individual

---

2. For further information, see the CATIE Center: https://healthcareinterpreting.org/

clinicians and clients, interpreting for families where not all parties use sign language, and working with Deaf mental health professionals. Hauser et al. (2015) suggests that because each of these scenarios can present unique challenges, interpreters must be adequately trained before accepting work in this specialized area.

The Consequences of a Lack of Trained Mental Health Interpreters

The lack of Canadian required training and certification not only presents challenges for interpreters but also makes the task of hiring qualified interpreters both confusing and difficult. With no way to know which interpreters are qualified for mental health assignments, interpreter referral services are left trying to figure this out for themselves. Service providers who are not Deaf themselves (counselors, hospitals, treatment centers) may have little to no knowledge about either Deaf people or the complexity of navigating issues such as language deprivation syndrome (Glickman & Hall, 2018; Hall, 2017) or language dysfluency (see Chapter 1 for greater discussion), let alone sign language interpreting, leaving them with no ability to screen the interpreters they hire. The consequence is that these providers may hire unqualified interpreters. Whether interpreters intend to deceive providers about their qualifications, or whether they simply do not have the ability to critically evaluate their own skills for the work, the result is the same: An unqualified interpreter is likely to impede communication access and may even affect treatment outcomes (Bontempo & Napier, 2007; Kruger & Dunning, 1999; Olson & Swabey, 2017).

Models of Mental Health Services in Canada

For Deaf consumers who use a signed language such as ASL or LSQ, direct mental health service requires a clinician (counselor, psychologist, therapist) fluent in the appropriate signed language. Ideally, this clinician would also be Deaf, allowing for a shared cultural understanding between counselor and client and avoiding the challenge of dealing with mental health professionals lacking knowledge of Deaf culture and language, as described by Bone (2019). Availability of this type of service is limited, however, and there appear to be only three organizations in Canada providing any form of direct service. In British Columbia, the Well-Being program offers bilingual and bicultural services for DHH and Deafblind children, adults, and seniors, such as individual and family counseling, group therapy, and peer support workers (Vancouver Coastal Health, 2023). In Ontario, the PAH! Program provides free mental health services for DHH children, youth, families, and hearing children of Deaf adults, while respecting communication choices (Bob Rumball Organizations, 2023). All three PAH! therapists are Deaf and able to provide direct service in ASL and work with interpreters and a consulting psychologist on a regular basis. Prior to the COVID-19 pandemic, PAH! covered a more limited catchment area, but is now providing virtual counseling services across the province, albeit with a months-long waitlist (V. Bickle, personal communication, February 16, 2023). Canadian Hearing Services (https://www.chs.ca/), also in Ontario, offers mainly mediated (interpreted) counseling through its Connect Counselling program, but in 2023 reports 30–35% of its counseling staff identify as Deaf or hard of hearing (M. Dawthorne, personal communication, January 10, 2023). These three organizations aside, there are private practitioners who provide direct service; we estimate no more than five practitioners each in British Columbia and Ontario, with a handful of Deaf and/or ASL- or LSQ-fluent practitioners throughout the country.

As a result of this gap, many Deaf individuals are forced to seek mental health care mediated via sign language interpreters. This care could occur through an organization such as Canadian Hearing Services, where clinicians are more familiar with both the Deaf community and how to work with interpreters. More often, the care likely occurs in local clinics, hospitals, and private practice settings where clinicians may have no such experience. Some of the limitations and challenges, in terms of clinician training to work with DHH people, are described below.

Clinician Training in Canada

Historically, the psychological research and mental health service for Deaf people that did exist were provided by hearing clinicians who were neither fluent signers nor generally well-versed in Deaf culture and whose practices were not informed by research (Glickman et al., 2020). Beginning in the 1970s, a culturally affirmative model of practice began to take hold, recognizing the importance of clinicians understanding both the language and culture of their Deaf clients; however, this approach still fell short of recognizing the unique communication needs of many Deaf people, particularly those dealing with language deprivation syndrome (Glickman et al., 2020).[3] The presence of language deprivation syndrome, then, necessitates both awareness on the part of the clinician as to its potential impact on counseling interactions and knowledge as to how to modify or adapt counseling techniques and communication approaches to ensure successful therapeutic outcomes.

As Deaf mental health has become a recognized clinical specialty, clinicians providing counseling services for Deaf individuals must be appropriately trained to do so. A hearing clinician may believe that arranging for an ASL-English interpreter will make their service accessible, but this is not always the case when Deaf clients are dealing with issues such as language dysfluency or language deprivation.

> The naïve hearing clinician who lacks any knowledge of the lived experiences of Deaf people, or language deprivation, but conscientiously arranges for an interpreter, will have little idea of the depth of the cognitive chasm that likely still separates them from the person they hope to serve. (Glickman, et al., 2020, p. 65)

Without appropriate training, clinicians may have no understanding of the interpreting process or of how the interpreter's presence may impact the therapeutic interaction. They may not, for instance, realize that an interpretation is not necessarily word-for-word and that the interpreter is making their own choices about the English words and phrases that they believe best represent what the Deaf person is saying. Clinicians must learn how to effectively screen the interpreters with whom they work, ensuring that interpreters have appropriate skills, training, and qualifications to work in mental health, and that they are available to consistently work with a particular Deaf consumer for any ongoing appointments (Hamerdinger & Crump, 2022). Clinicians must recognize interpreters as members of the treatment team, allowing for time to meet with them both before and after appointments for ongoing discussion of the work (Hamerdinger & Crump,

---

3 For further discussion of language deprivation, see Chapter 1 in this volume.

2022). One possible collaborative model for this work is described by Chovaz (2013) and uses intersectionality to describe the interaction between clinician and interpreter.

One example of potential best practices regarding mental health training for Canadian clinicians working with Deaf individuals could be found in the approaches taken by Canadian Hearing Services. Canadian Hearing Services aims to provide "culturally and linguistically sensitive counselling" and requires staff to take ASL classes and complete onboarding which "covers key concepts such as working with interpreters and Deaf residential schools," as well as providing newer staff with resources regarding language dysfluency and language deprivation (M. Dawthorne, personal communication, January 10, 2023)

Direct Healthcare Information Versus Mediated Information

Napier et al. (2014) conducted a study in Australia to examine the experiences of Deaf Australian Sign Language (Auslan) users in accessing health information. Their findings point to a consistent challenge noted by other researchers—that the literacy levels of many Deaf consumers are insufficient to reliably access information about specific health issues (Alexander et al., 2012; Pollard & Barnett, 2009). The authors cited earlier research by Harmer (1999) that showed that providing an interpreter is not sufficient to address the literacy challenges of Deaf consumers and can lead to Deaf consumers unable to play an active role in their own healthcare management. This barrier to accessing health information can, for example, lead to delays in self-diagnosis and treatment at home, or a visit to the doctor when medically necessary.

Two of the key recommendations that emerged from the Napier et al. (2014) study were that Deaf Australians require more Deaf-specific (direct) services as well as more access to sources of information in their preferred language, Auslan, through translated materials. They also found that Deaf Auslan users' experiences of accessing electronic information about their health were generally problematic, in that they felt as though the information was either insufficient, difficult to obtain, or simply incomprehensible. While this study was not specific to accessing mental health services or care, it would appear reasonable to extrapolate the findings to suggest that these same issues apply when accessing services and information in the domain of mental health.

In December 2022, the World Federation of the Deaf (WFD) published their position paper on Access to National Sign Languages as a Health Need, citing the United Nations Convention on the Rights of Persons with Disabilities (UNCRPD; United Nations, 2006) Articles 25 and 26 as obligations for all signatories (WFD, 2022). Canada is a signatory to the UNCRPD, and Article 25 of the convention states that governments shall provide health services as needed to persons with disabilities, including identification and intervention as appropriate, and services designed to minimize and prevent further disabilities. The WFD cites the important work of Kushalnagar et al. (2020), which found that adverse childhood communication experiences such as language deprivation and communication neglect can lead to an increased risk of chronic diseases as adults. Further, the work of Wilkenson and Morford (2020) identified the negative impacts on Deaf individuals of viewing spoken conversations between family members or others and not understanding what was being said. The ongoing exclusion from indirect family communication results in significant gaps in incidental learning about work knowledge, social and academic skills, and health literacy, along with additional psychological stress. The WFD initiated its global Health Resources Initiative, a 2010 survey that used data gathered from 44 countries (WFD, 2014). The most common health problems cited were mental health concerns and depression. While this global survey is somewhat dated, it appears that many countries, including Canada, are still not gathering sufficient data about Deaf people and their access to health care. One of the recommendations in the WFD survey was the need for Deaf people to gain access to healthcare information in their national sign languages, enroll in studies of health and mental health care, and participate in health education seminars targeted to the Deaf community provided directly in sign languages by Deaf healthcare specialists. A recent study by Jacob et al. (2022) stressed that the health care disparities faced by Deaf people are exacerbated by healthcare professionals' lack of knowledge of Deaf culture and health-related challenges. When Deaf people have lower literacy levels and prior negative experiences communicating with healthcare professionals, this can result in Deaf consumers opting to avoid accessing the healthcare system. As Jacob et al. (2022) stated:

> The interpretation process between sign language interpreters, Health Care Providers (HCPs), and Deaf signers is a dynamic one, and one which is compounded by the lack of in-depth medical training received by most interpreters. This makes a clear case for the need for HCPs themselves to be trained in cultural competency, which is currently lacking in health care education. Active learning approaches would seem suitable to ensure that future HCPs understand the challenges faced by Deaf signers and are trained on how to best care for this subset of patients. (p. 338)

The need is clear for healthcare professionals, including mental health specialists, to have additional training to effectively serve Deaf community members. One practice that has seen a steady increase is the pairs of Deaf and nondeaf interpreters working as a team to address the cultural competency required in complex settings. In the next section, we explore the role of Deaf interpreters in mental health work.

The Role of Deaf Interpreters in Mental Health

Morgan and Adam (2012) raised the importance of interpreters who are Deaf in mental health settings, stressing the need for the development of Deaf interpreter training programs. They suggested that it is also crucial to educate hearing professionals who may need to work with these highly skilled individuals in medical and mental health settings. Adam et al. (2011) found that Deaf people were more comfortable with a Deaf person performing translation or interpreting tasks, given their shared culture and background. Morgan and Adam (2012) noted that Deaf people were more comfortable asking for assistance and were either less or not embarrassed about their English literacy skills when working with Deaf interpreters. The importance of Deaf interpreters across the entire spectrum of community interpreting is becoming more of a norm, especially after the COVID-19 pandemic highlighted the important role of Deaf interpreters in media contexts relaying health information (Russell et al., 2022; Stone & Russell, 2022). Further, the complexity of mental health or child protection settings increases the risk of errors that may be made by nondeaf interpreters, who most often have learned ASL in a classroom and have ASL as a second language. A Deaf interpreter, by contrast, may be much more adept at recognizing atypical language use or adapting language for children, while simultaneously creating comfort for the Deaf consumer, given the common background of language and culture.

This literature review does not purport to be exhaustive but rather has canvassed some of the critical aspects of quality access to mental health services for Deaf citizens, with specific attention to Canadian issues. Given the dearth of evidence-based research that includes the perspectives of Canadian sign language interpreters with mental health interpreting experience, the current study could be considered a first step in addressing this gap.

Method

This study spanned 6 months and included an online survey (see appendix) of Canadian ASL-English interpreters, supplemented by targeted interviews with an interpreter representative of the French-LSQ community and a Canadian mental health therapist who currently delivers mental health training for sign language interpreters. An online survey was chosen, as Canada is a geographically large country, and we were interested in gathering as many experiences as possible to best reflect its regional diversity. The survey included questions that elicited quantitative and qualitative responses and was distributed in English, and we sought to include the French-LSQ community experiences with a targeted interview with a practitioner based in Quebec. Finally, given the limited interpreter training currently available in Canada, we chose to conduct a targeted interview with the one therapist who designed and offered a program for Canadian interpreters. In this chapter, we report on the analysis of the survey and interviews to offer a current picture of the Canadian landscape on interpreting in mental health settings.

Procedures

Qualitative and quantitative data were collected via an online survey, including both multiple-response questions ("check all that apply") and open-ended questions, and two individual interviews which utilized a semistructured approach and guiding questions. The interview protocol and prompts throughout were designed to allow for open-ended responses and elicit thick descriptions of participant experience (Lincoln & Guba, 1985). Thick descriptions provide rich and detailed accounts of contexts and attempt to uncover the nuances and complexities of social phenomena. Specific questions guided both survey and interview participants to describe experiences working in mental health settings. Data collected via interviews were in the preferred language of the participants (one in spoken English and one in ASL).

The data were analyzed using a constant comparison technique within content analysis (Corbin & Strauss, 2015). The constant comparison allowed for findings to emerge while the data were being collected and analyzed (Charmaz, 2005). Thematic analysis (Braun & Clarke, 2006) was used to identify, organize, and understand common participant experiences and was chosen for its flexibility. Open and axial coding, as well as a constant comparative method, were used to analyze the data, following Braun and Clarke's (2006, 2012) six-phase approach to thematic analysis: (a) familiarization with the data, (b) generating initial codes, (c) searching for themes, (d) reviewing themes, (e) defining and naming themes, and (f) writing up. According to Strauss and Corbin (1990), open coding refers to "the process of breaking down, examining, comparing, conceptualizing, and categorizing data" (p. 61), and axial coding refers to "a set of procedures whereby data are put back together in new ways after open coding by making connections between categories" (p. 96). The constant comparative approach involved continual attempts to pull information from the surveys and transcripts to provide insight into the categories being explored (Glaser & Strauss, 2017), allowing the findings to emerge (Charmaz, 2005)

Participants

Participants were recruited through email and video messages distributed by interpreter associations representing ASL-English interpreters in Canada, based on their experiences as interpreters who provided mental health interpreting services or were considering doing so in the future. Each participant was provided with information about the study and gave their consent to participate prior to data collection. Data were collected through initial quantitative and qualitative online survey questions. The digitally recorded qualitative data collected from the individual interview participants provided a depth of response that would have been difficult to achieve in a survey-only format. Two targeted interviews were conducted, one with a Deaf interpreter from Quebec whose working languages included English, French, ASL, and LSQ, and one former ASL-English interpreter who now works as a mental health therapist and has developed a specific training program for interpreters who wish to acquire the skills and knowledge needed for interpreting in mental health settings. All participants gave informed consent prior to completing a survey or participating in an interview.

Demographics

A total of 107 interpreters participated in the survey. All participants were above the age of 18, and 89% had completed an interpreter education program. Those who had not completed a formal interpreter program came to the profession through a combination of experience and professional development. In addition to those who had completed IEPs, 74 of 107 participants (69%) held additional educational qualifications, including bachelor's- and master's-level studies. Areas of study included ASL/Deaf studies, ASL-English interpretation, linguistics, community and rehabilitation studies, history, adult education, and psychology. Years of experience ranged from fewer than 5 years to more than 25 years, as shown in Table 1.

Of the 107 survey participants, 84 (79%) currently provide services in mental health settings, and a further eight (7.5%) are interested in working in this specialized area in the future. Fifteen participants, or 14%, indicated that they do not wish to work in this area.

The top four mental health settings interpreters reported working in included the following:

- Individual counseling: 78 participants (93%)
- Psychological assessments: 59 participants (70%)
- Hospital emergencies (psychological and psychiatric): 57 participants (68%)
- Treatment programs (including drug and alcohol, eating disorders, sexual disorders, etc.): 55 participants (66%)

Table 1. Interpreter Years of Experience (N = 107)

1-5 years	16 (15%)
6-10 years	13 (12%)
11-15 years	16 (15%)
16-20 years	17 (16%)
21-25 years	20 (19%)
25 plus	25 (23%)

Table 2. Training Completed (N = 84)

Type of Training	N/Percentage
Experience on the job	76 (91%)
Short-term professional development	61 (73%)
Basic orientation provided through IEP	20 (24%)
Mentorship from other interpreters	47 (56%)
Certificate program from Alabama	5 (6%)
Courses from the CATIE Centre	8 (10%)

When asked to describe the training that had supported respondents' interpreting in mental health settings, the following top six categories were offered, as shown in Table 2.

Other examples of training cited in individual responses included reading articles, completing an alcohol and drug counseling training program, completing a master's degree in counseling, in-house training offered by video relay service providers, and the lived experience of dealing with family members who were neurodivergent and/or had mental health issues.

Results and Discussion

Our findings provide insight into the perspectives of Canadian interpreters and have practical implications for the training of both interpreters and mental health clinicians. The analysis yielded four major themes: (a) lack of training and resources for interpreters working in mental health settings, (b) a perceived lack of awareness on the part of mental health professionals about how to effectively support Deaf patients, (c) systemic barriers such as a lack of funding for interpreting services and/or specialized, direct services, and (d) Deaf communities' limited understanding of mental health services, medications, and resources. Several subthemes within these four primary themes were identified, as described below.

Theme 1: Lack of Training and Resources for Interpreters Working in Mental Health Settings

Participants were asked to identify the top barriers that affect the delivery of interpreting services in mental health. Common barriers across all respondents included the following:

- lack of mental health training for interpreters, including observation and mentorship opportunities due to the highly sensitive nature of appointments
- interpreters' and counselors' lack of awareness about each other's roles and how to work as a team for effective service delivery
- a lack of skills among generalist-trained interpreters to perform well in mental health settings

These barriers are consistent with prior studies that emphasized the importance of training for interpreters working in mental health settings and education for mental health clinicians about the role of interpreters (Chovaz, 2013; Dean & Pollard, 2009; Morgan & Adam, 2012). Of note is that the study participants offered the idea of the interpreter as a *barrier* to the provision of effective service. One respondent said

> The fact that a third party is involved, period. I feel my presence in the room is a barrier. The other barriers are not necessarily knowing what exactly the therapist is looking for when they ask certain questions (i.e. treatment goal) and many therapists' lack of understanding about Deaf culture and issues Deaf individuals may experience. (Participant D)

Another interesting point arising from the data was that 56% of participants indicated their training for mental health work came via mentorship, yet the lack of mentorship was also frequently cited as a barrier. This call for greater mentorship reflects a desire for more formal or structured opportunities, in contrast to the informal mentorship that appears to have supported more than half of the participants in this study.

Theme 2: Lack of Awareness on the Part of Mental Health Professionals About How to Effectively Support Deaf Patients

Participants suggested that the lack of awareness and cultural sensitivity among mental health professionals about how to effectively serve Deaf clients leads to the potential for misdiagnosis and/or ineffective treatment plans. Therapists often misunderstand the nature of interpreting services, which can lead to unqualified interpreters being retained, a lack of interpreter consistency across regular appointments, and a lack of understanding about how and when to use a Deaf interpreter and the value they can add to the process. There also appears to be reluctance on the part of therapists to both prepare in advance and debrief with interpreters, despite these tasks being associated with better interpreting outcomes (Dean & Pollard, 2009; Bontempo & Malcolm, 2012). In addition, participants cited the following barriers:

- Standardized testing can be a barrier for many Deaf patients, and many therapists do not recognize the challenges experienced by interpreters in seeking ways to offer ASL-equivalent translations.
- Many standardized measures rely on English literacy skills and are normed based on populations who can hear and therefore are not valid for Deaf people.
- Therapist often have misconceptions about the language abilities of Deaf clients and the impact of language deprivation in the early years of life.

One respondent described these types of barriers as follows:

> Atypical use of language that requires a Deaf interpreter and one is not provided . . . leaves me to deal with question structure, deciding to include extralingual information or not, and acquiring prep information. (Participant K)

As with the work of Morgan and Adam (2012), these findings suggest that Deaf interpreters are critical to address the literacy challenges associated with standardized tests and the impact of language deprivation.

Another concern stated by one Deaf participant is that only when communication breaks down do the services hire Deaf interpreters, stating:

> The counsellor *thought* they were a fluent signer and based on miscommunication brought in a Deaf interpreter—and I [the Deaf interpreter] could barely understand the counselor . . . . [H]ow often had they counselled Deaf people before and not brought us in . . . . [T]his is a huge barrier to effective service! (Participant E)

Theme 3: Systemic Lack of Funding for Interpreting Services and/or Specialized, Direct Services

Across both survey and interview data, there was a strong theme centered on systemic barriers, including government policies claiming to support access to services for all citizens but which, in reality, are not accessible to the Deaf community (e.g., government-funded services refusing to budget for sign language interpreting and therapeutic services requiring Deaf people to access supports via lipreading or written interactions rather than ASL or LSQ). For example, participants identified the lack of accessibility for Deaf people entering women's shelters and/or homeless shelters, yet both of these settings often serve people with increased mental health needs, needs exacerbated by virtue of escaping intimate partner violence and/or living on the street. In addition, respondents also cited the following:

- systemic barriers such as institutional regulations, little or no government support for specialized services, and a lack of financial support for accessibility services
- a lack of awareness about the essential role of a Deaf interpreter, paired with the argument that paying for two interpreters is cost-prohibitive
- Service provision models such as lack of consistency in interpreters sent to ongoing appointments; clinicians booking interpreters who are not qualified
- lack of training for and/or availability of Deaf interpreters for mental health contexts

There are limited services that provide direct mental health support for Deaf people (with Deaf therapists or counselors who are fluent in ASL), with such specialized adult services available only in Ontario and British Columbia. In addition, Ontario appears to be the only province with specialized services for Deaf children. For the French-LSQ community, an interviewee in this study suggested that there is an even greater need in Quebec, which has a long history of not providing any suitable treatment and mental health support to the LSQ community either through direct services or with interpreters. Other provinces in Canada do not have access to specialized, direct services with counselors who are fluent in ASL or LSQ and/or have cultural and linguistic training to inform their practices. Participants stated the following:

> I believe the pursuit of rendering interpreting services is less favourable than pursuing access to Deaf professionals for Deaf clients/patients. (Participant C)

> We had a terrible situation where a young Deaf person required mental health programs, was denied access to a rehab center (because the government wouldn't pay for interpreters for residential treatment), and ultimately, they died because of the lack of treatment. (Participant E)

The situation in Quebec may also be more challenging, given both the lack of interpreters and the diverse community. Quebec is often the first destination for immigrants and serves people from Nunavut, resulting in a linguistic complexity that goes beyond English, French, ASL, and LSQ. A participant expressed frustration as follows:

> The medical profession has the power—they decide when and if to bring in an interpreter. And most often they don't, and if they do, the Deaf person has no say about whether they prefer that interpreter or even understand them! But the doctors diagnose people based on writing, or worse they call on the intercom for "signing staff" . . . like a janitor! This is not equitable mental health service for Deaf people! Professionals need to have specific training to work with Deaf people. (Participant B)

Currently, it appears that there are fewer than 10 qualified Deaf professionals to work with Canadian DHH patients. This is in sharp contrast to other linguistic communities that can access mental health support in their first language with therapists who speak the same language.

Theme 4: Deaf Communities' Understanding of Mental Health Services, Medications, and Resources

Survey respondents and interviewees suggested that there is an overall lack of awareness among Deaf communities about the role of mental health therapists, treatment programs, support in hospitals and community services, and the role of medications in treatment plans. This lack of awareness based on misinformation and/or negative stigmas about mental health concerns can result in a reluctance among members of the Deaf community to seek counseling and other mental health programs.

In the words of an ASL-LSQ interpreter:

> In Quebec there is a lack of awareness among the Deaf community about services because of the historical fact that the services were simply not provided. As well, Deaf interpreters are new to the LSQ community so there can be a reluctance to work with Deaf interpreters even though they should. (Participant F)

Another challenge is the potential of Deaf people not taking their medication as directed, especially if there is a limited appreciation about the role of medication in an overall approach to mental health treatment. There was also an identified need for resources in ASL and LSQ. For example, nondeaf individuals can locate mental health information on a variety of websites; however, at the time of writing this chapter, there appear to be no Canadian mental health websites with ASL and LSQ translations. These findings are consistent with the work of Napier et al. (2014) that addressed the need for accessible resources in sign language. Given that the UNCRPD recognizes the human rights of Deaf people to access publicly available government information in sign language and the need for professional interpreters in accessing health care and education, these Canadian findings suggest that the recommended practices identified in the convention are not being implemented in Canada. Similarly, this participant stated the following:

> Deaf people need training about their human and health rights, and they need to know how to complain about bad services, including bad interpreting! It would help if interpreters had to be members

> of the professional associations and be licensed for working in this area. And there should be guidelines and guidebooks for psychologists and doctors about interpreting. . . . [T]here is just so much needed . . . (Participant G)

Finally, this overall lack of awareness about mental health services and resources can also lead to an absence of support among community members for their Deaf friend or family member experiencing mental health issues.

In addition to the major themes identified above, the respondents offered advice for interpreters who are considering working in mental health settings, as described in the next section.

Advice for Interpreters

The survey included a question seeking respondents' advice for interpreters who might consider working in mental health settings in the future. The following are the key themes that arose in response.

Mental Health Discourse Is Everywhere: Tread Carefully

One recurrent piece of advice across respondents was that interpreters need to understand that mental health issues can arise in any setting. Interpreters must recognize that these types of topics may be embedded in any discourse. This, in turn, means that any interpreter choosing to take on mental health assignments has an obligation to ensure a suitable foundation of training and/or experience to support effective practice. In the words of these participants,

> . . . [S]tart slowly and tread lightly. Commit to therapy sessions for any given Deaf person only if you feel you can represent that client well, as constant interruption due to not understanding their signing can have a negative impact on therapy. (Participant F)

> . . . [E]very assignment is a mental health assignment, human interactions can change at any moment; predict and then be ready for the unexpected. Think, for example, about the impact on mental health at a [doctor's] appointment (such as where one receives a difficult diagnosis) or [when a person is] denied [a] loan application at a bank. (Participant L)

Further, interpreters recommended that prospective interpreters check in with interpreters who already work in mental health settings and seek their opinions on suitability. In the words of this interpreter,

> Consider this feedback as well as feedback from Deaf community members who have seen your work and assess your ethics and attitude in approaching the work. (Participant H)

While all respondents agreed that specific mental health training was important, there is currently very limited training available in Canada. What does exist is a patchwork of professional development presentations and workshops, as well as one online program offered by a mental health therapist who is a former mental health interpreter. One participant said the following:

> Seek out any and all educational opportunities and find an experienced interpreter to mentor you.... Never internalise and always remain calm no matter what happens or is witnessed... (Participant M)

Another strong theme suggested that interpreters should regularly work with Deaf interpreters to address the potential of linguistic and cultural barriers, and that interpreters should also have Deaf mentors to support their development.

Mentorship

All participants not yet working in mental health settings expressed a desire for mentorship opportunities through the pairing of experienced interpreters with those wishing to begin working in this specific field. This was also echoed by the following LSQ-ASL interpreter as a significant need in Quebec:

> If more experienced interpreters would talk more about their experiences in mental health settings, it would give me more of an idea of what the work entails. As of right now, I just hear "mental health" and picture a therapy session. I imagine that there is a lot more than that, but it feels secretive, and I haven't gotten a real sense of the nature of the work. It would help me if interpreters would share strategies and things they've learned. (Participant O)

Additionally, one participant stated the following:

> I would find casual mentorship beneficial—discussing the intricacies of the setting and tips or a guideline of sorts to know if one is suitable for the settings. Also, resources/vocabulary are always helpful even if I already have a solid schema... (Participant B)

The participants desired observation opportunities, but recognized that this is not ethically possible, so they suggested mock scenarios that are filmed and made available to interpreters, supported by guided conversations about each scenario. The participants also expressed a desire for regular postassignment debriefing conversations focused on strategies and specialized language demands and suggested that it is the duty of the Canadian Association of Sign Language Interpreters (CASLI; https://www.casli.ca/), the national professional body, to offer mentorship programs and professional development. The participants also stressed the need for CASLI to create a resource section on the organization's website, where specific mental health materials could be housed and accessible. This quote encapsulates the sentiments of many of the participants:

> Use membership dues to bring in higher-quality workshop opportunities that are a variety of interpreting skill-based, theory-based, as well as learning about mental health systems and practices. (Participant N)

Some participants also identified that professional development or training via courses offered at an accredited institution would be most useful in obtaining credentials to support effective practice. While this does not currently exist in Canada, it is an opportunity to be explored.

Participants also stressed that hiring agencies could support the transition to working in mental health settings by providing additional contextual information when sending out interpreter assignment opportunities. As a participant stated,

> If interpreter agencies were to provide a bit more information when sending out assignments, I may be more inclined to respond. At this point, a lot of assignments say "mental health" and I don't know if it's something I would be suited for . . . (Participant O)

This suggestion, if embraced by interpreter agencies, could contribute to greater numbers of interpreters developing the capacity to serve in this area.

Working as a Team

Another frequent suggestion was that interpreters need to develop a good working relationship with the therapist or service provider to obtain the information they need to interpret effectively. If interpreters and clinicians understand that they should prepare for appointments together, this allows for the discussion of therapeutic approaches, assessments, and goals for the session. This relationship, however, must be tempered with a healthy view of what information the therapist needs. This interpreter who was trained as a therapist stated the following:

> Be aware of how the interpreter impacts every situation they become involved with. . . . [F]rom my experience they spend so much time explaining the interpreting process and why some questions are not effective, versus what I need from the interpreter in this setting . . . (Participant G)

Once again, these results echo the work of Chovaz (2013) and Hamerdinger and Crump (2022), stressing the need for interpreters and clinicians to collaborate to deliver effective mental health support to Deaf clients. Part of effective collaboration and communication between the therapist and the interpreter(s) involves being mindful that for a recurring appointment, the same team of interpreters should be used if that is what best suits the Deaf consumer. By the same token, it also means knowing when it is appropriate for a different interpreter to step in. For example, if the therapist and interpreter(s) recognize that the therapeutic process is being impeded by an issue of transference between the client and interpreter, then a change of interpreter(s) is warranted.

Self-Care and Vicarious Trauma

All respondents identified self-care as a critical means of both staying healthy and being able to provide effective service. Suggestions for self-care included an emphasis on postassignment debriefings with mentors, as well as learning about vicarious trauma and the ways in which it can impact interpreters. Vicarious trauma was initially cited in the literature by Dr. Michael Harvey (2003a), which has spurred others to address this key area (Andert & Trites, 2014; Bontempo & Malcolm, 2012; Dean & Pollard, 2009; Knodel, 2018). An interpreter can have powerful emotional responses—both to clients and the topics discussed in a therapeutic session. If the interpreter is not prepared for this and/or does not have professional support to process that type of reaction, it can result in further trauma for the interpreter and may impact the therapeutic process. The following quote exemplifies the critical importance of training and self-care:

> Go to the Alabama MHIT, the work is much more in your self-management and ability to communicate the needs of the situation with other professionals involved than vocab or interpreting skills. Although a high level of ASL fluency and interpreting skill is important[, you] should be aware of the effects and impact of language deprivation and dysfluency. You should probably not do this work without being in therapy yourself and having done some solid trauma work if you have a trauma history to avoid secondary trauma. (Participant L)

Another participant stated,

> Make sure you have a good plan for your mental health—I suggest a counsellor to deal with vicarious trauma. Also, evaluate whether you are truly interested in this specialty and not just viewing it as just another job. I started working in mental health simply because there were no other interpreters in the community, and it is hard to say no when there is a need. It is important to remember that we aren't responsible for the dearth of interpreters. The more years I interpret, the more I self-reflect, and I have stepped back from Mental Health interpreting because it is not a good fit for me. This means there is a hole left in the community but that is not on me to fix. I suggest interpreters reflect on where their skills and capacities are before blindly accepting work. I felt I had the skill (could have used more as always) but not the passion which I feel is necessary to avoid burnout. (Participant N)

Fluency in ASL

Respondents stressed the need for interpreters to ensure that they are linguistically and ethically competent for the work. As a respondent said,

> Make sure your fluency in ASL is at a level where you won't struggle to understand the Deaf clients. It's difficult enough to voice psychosis without struggling to have a basic understanding of ASL. (Participant C)

Additionally, interpreters emphasized the importance of understanding affect and emotional overlays in ASL. In the words of this respondent,

> A lot of time the way things are conveyed have more meanings than the words or signs themselves. . . . [A]ffect is so important in these settings. (Participant I)

These responses also lend support to the idea that nondeaf interpreters should work with Deaf interpreters as frequently as possible in this complex area (Morgan & Adam, 2012). We also note that working with Deaf interpreters is an ethical obligation cited in the CASLI Code of Ethics and Guidelines for Professional Conduct, Tenet 3.3 (CASLI, 2000).

Implications and Recommendations

Based on the data gathered and the review of the literature, we conclude that the lack of training available for interpreters has a deleterious effect on mental health service delivery for the Canadian Deaf community. While this study has captured the perspectives and experiences of primarily ASL-English interpreters, other contributions in this volume have identified the perspectives of DHH people, citing the lack of equitable mental health access as exacerbating the risk of misdiagnosis and delayed treatment options.

Interpreters working in mental health require specific training, whether through a postsecondary institution and/or the professional bodies representing interpreters. There is also a significant need for both mentorship and regular supervision opportunities. This finding is consistent with the practices found in the Alabama-based MHIT program and in the scholarship of Dean and Pollard (2009), both of which stress the need for supervision of interpreters working in mental health contexts. There is also a role for hiring agencies to collaborate with professional bodies and/or training institutions to offer opportunities for teamed assignments, structured mentorship, and observation opportunities (even if these are mock appointments), and to provide structured debriefing opportunities for interpreters working in mental health settings. When creating offers of work, agencies need to offer greater detail to help interpreters determine whether they are appropriate for the assignment.

The four themes reflected in this study demonstrate the need for strategic planning on the part of professional associations and hiring agencies. However, there is also a need for government funding mechanisms to ensure a sufficient budget to cover the access needs of DHH people, enabling them to participate in the same programs and services available to all other citizens. There are also opportunities for experienced interpreters to immediately engage with colleagues wanting to develop the skills and knowledge required for this specialized area of practice. Thoughtful conversations among colleagues can start to build the confidence of interpreters who have not yet experienced mental health interpreting and expand their knowledge of strategies that can help them to begin accepting mental health assignments. Finally, the data points to additional training being required by clinicians to deliver linguistically and culturally sensitive services, as well as a need for greater awareness among Deaf community members about the nature of mental health support and the importance of accessing resources when needed.

From a practical standpoint, interpreters may feel as though they have no incentive to pursue additional training in a specialized area such as mental health. There is currently no requirement to do so, and for most interpreters, any such training would be self-funded. As most interpreters are self-employed, sometimes precariously, this financial barrier to training may be both real and insurmountable. In practical terms, participating in workshops, professional development, or other training opportunities does not afford interpreters the ability to charge more for their work, thus there is no "payoff," and therefore no financial incentive to seek out additional training. Given the precarious nature of freelance interpreting, interpreters may also feel incentivized to do work for which they are not explicitly qualified, since they may feel the financial pressure to do so. As many interpreters enter the profession because of their own connections to the Deaf community, unqualified interpreters may nonetheless feel the burden of responsibility to ensure that interpreters are present for counseling or treatment sessions and may take on the work themselves in a misguided attempt to ensure access. Based on the data, the following "calls to action" and recommendations are offered.

Government Funding for Mental Health Service

The data in this study point to funding as a major barrier preventing DHH people from accessing mental health programs within the community, be it treatment programs, individual counseling, or support groups. When organizations do not have the budget to cover interpreting costs, the burden of negotiating for interpreting services often falls on the shoulders of the Deaf consumer at a time when they are least likely to advocate for the same. In addition to funding for interpreting services, there are opportunities for government agencies to address funding gaps in services that can be linguistically and culturally appropriate. DHH citizens deserve options in the same way as other citizens, and this includes accessing therapeutic support provided by Deaf clinicians or clinicians fluent in ASL.

Funding to Develop Interpreting Capacity

There is a need to develop increased capacity within the interpreting community to ensure that the number of interpreters who are skilled and properly trained in mental health interpreting is sufficient to meet the needs of the Deaf community. This study confirmed that it can be challenging for interpreters to cover the costs associated with this type of specialized training. Institutional support from provincial governments and hiring agencies is needed to recruit a critical mass of Deaf and hearing interpreters to complete formal training such as the MHIT program in Alabama (Alabama Department of Mental Health, 2022) and/or an online program such as Mental Health Interpreter Training Essentials (Bolender, 2025), in similar ways to the CATIE Center's approach to developing capacity (https://healthcareinterpreting.org/level-up/).

Training and Mentorship for Interpreters

CASLI and/or its professional affiliates should develop partnership strategies with the goal of creating a rigorous professional development program. This program should be both thorough and structured, establishing a clear pathway to acquiring the skills and knowledge necessary for interpreting in mental health settings. Such a pathway could include combinations of online courses and face-to-face learning opportunities in collaboration with a postsecondary institution that can offer credit and professional recognition for this specialization. A cohort model would further support the development of a community of learners. Using a collaborative approach, CASLI and/or regional affiliate organizations and hiring agencies could create structured mentorship and supervision pathways to be required for interpreters working in mental health contexts.

Training for Clinicians

Given that the vast majority of clinicians have no professional training in or orientation to working with DHH individuals, it would be useful for the university programs preparing these professionals to include specific modules taught by Deaf clinicians. This type of exposure would develop awareness of the complexity of serving DHH individuals, as well as strategies for working with interpreters in clinical settings.

Information Access and Training for the Deaf Community

Organizations that host online mental health resources, especially if federally funded, have an obligation to collaborate with Deaf organizations to provide effective ASL and LSQ translation services and ensure that the resources are culturally and linguistically accessible for Deaf people. Such resources could offer the Deaf community both broad and specific information about the importance of mental health treatment and treatment options.

International Standards Organization (ISO) standards on mental health interpreting: While there are international standards published by the ISO for other specialized areas of interpreting practice—(ISO 18841:2018: Interpreting services—General requirements and recommendations; www.iso.org/standard/63544.html), such as community (ISO 13611:2044: Interpreting services—Community interpreting—Requirements and recommendations; www.iso.org/standard/82387.html), conference (ISO 23115:2022: Interpreting services—Conference interpreting—Requirements and recommendations: www.iso.org/standard/74749.html), and healthcare interpreting (ISO 21998:2020: Interpreting services—Healthcare interpreting—Requirements and recommendations: www.iso.org/standard/72344.html)—there is no published international standard on mental health interpreting. CASLI could lobby the Standards Council of Canada (SCC) for the development of such a standard for both spoken and signed language interpreters.

Limitations

This pilot study has captured the experiences of Canadian ASL-English interpreters, and future research could replicate the survey with French-LSQ interpreters. While this study was informed by one in-depth interview with a Deaf LSQ-ASL interpreter and an interpreter trainer with considerable experience, a broader segment of the francophone community would strengthen the findings. Future research should also examine the experiences of mental health clinicians along with the perspectives of Deaf people who have accessed mental health supports.

Conclusion

This chapter described the current state of the Canadian landscape as it pertains to mental health services for Deaf people. The data highlighted perspectives of Canadian ASL-English interpreters and demonstrated that the lack of specialized mental health training of ASL-English interpreters in Canada, in turn, impacts the delivery of services to the Deaf community. It also revealed additional systemic barriers affecting Deaf Canadians, including the lack of funding for interpreting services and the need for direct services provided by Deaf or ASL-fluent mental health clinicians. The findings support a call to action for collaboration among postsecondary institutions and professional organizations to develop a specialized foundational mental health training program for interpreters. Further, there are opportunities to collaborate with postsecondary institutions that train counselors in orienting professionals to the unique needs of the Deaf community in seeking mental health support. Finally, there are several ways in which professional organizations and interpreter agencies could increase the capacity of the pool of available interpreters, via structured mentorship and continued education. The current picture of mental health interpreting in Canada is disturbing, but this is not immutable. With the right training, funding, and support in place, mental health interpreters and clinicians alike will be able to provide more effective, accessible mental health services to Deaf Canadians.

References

Accessible Canada Act (ACA). (2019). (S. C. 2019, c. 10). https://laws-lois.justice.gc.ca/eng/acts/a-0.6/

Adam, R., Carty, B., & Stone, C. (2011). Ghostwriting: Deaf translators within the deaf community. *Babel, 57*(4), 375–393.

Alabama Department of Mental Health (2022). *Alabama's mental health interpreter training project.* http://www.mhit.org/practicum.html

Alexander, D., Gaillard, J. C., & Wisner, B. (2012). Disability and disaster. In B. Wisner, J. C. Gallaird, & I. Kelman (Eds.), *The Routledge handbook of hazards and disaster risk reduction* (pp. 413–423). Routledge.

Andert, O. L., & Trites, A. P. (2014). Vicarious trauma among sign language interpreters: A pilot study. *Journal of Undergraduate Interpreter Studies*, 1–36.

Bauman, H. D. L. (2004). Audism: Exploring the metaphysics of oppression. *Journal of Deaf Studies and Deaf Education, 9*(2), 239–246.

Bauman, H. D. L., & Murray, J. J. (2010). 14 Deaf studies in the 21st century: "Deaf-gain" and the future of human diversity. In M. Marschark & P. E. Spencer (Eds.), *The Oxford handbook of deaf studies, language, and education* (vol. 2, pp. 210–225). Oxford University Press.

Bob Rumball Organizations. (2023). *PAH! Children and youth mental health.* Bob Rumball Canadian Centre of Excellence for the Deaf. https://www.bobrumball.org/youth-family-services/pah-children-and-youth-mental-health/

Bolender, S. (2025). *Mental health interpreter training essentials.* https://mental-health-interpreter-training.teachable.com/p/mental-health-interpreting

Bone, T. A. (2019). No one is listening: Members of the deaf community share their depression narratives. *Social Work in Mental Health, 17*(1), 1–22.

Bontempo, K., & Malcolm, K. (2012). An ounce of prevention is worth a pound of cure: Educating interpreters about the risk of vicarious trauma in healthcare settings. In L. Swabey & K. Malcolm (Eds.), *In our hands: Educating healthcare interpreters* (pp. 105–130). Gallaudet University Press.

Bontempo, K., & Napier, J. (2007). Mind the gap: A skills analysis of sign language interpreters. *The Sign Language Translator and Interpreter, 1*(2), 275–299.

Braun, V., & Clarke, V. (2006). Using thematic analysis in psychology. *Qualitative Research in Psychology, 3*(2), 77–101.

Braun, V., & Clarke, V. (2012). *Thematic analysis.* In H. Cooper, P. M. Camic, D. L. Long, A. T. Panter, D. Rindskopf, & K. J. Sher (Eds.), *APA handbook of research methods in psychology, vol. 2. Research designs: Quantitative, qualitative, neuropsychological, and biological* (pp. 57–71). American Psychological Association.

Canadian Association of Sign Language Interpreters (CASLI). (2000, July). *Code of ethics and guidelines for professional conduct.* https://www.casli.ca/Code-of-Ethics.

Canadian Charter of Rights and Freedoms, s 14 and s 15. Part 1 of the *Constitution Act, 1982*, being Schedule B to the *Canada Act 1982* (UK), 1982, c 11 a.

Canadian Hearing Society (n. d.). *Expanding the vision: OIS interpreter internship program (IIP).* https://www.chs.ca/sites/default/files/iip_faq.pdf

Centre of Deaf Education and Accessibility Forum (CDEAF). (2023). *CDEAF: Mental health research and education.* https://cdeaf.kings.uwo.ca/

Charmaz, K. (2005). Grounded theory in the 21st century: Applications for advancing social justice research. In N. K. Denzin & Y. S. Lincoln (Eds.), *The Sage handbook of qualitative research* (pp. 507–535). Sage.

Chovaz, C. J. (2013). Intersectionality: Mental health interpreters and clinicians or finding the "sweet spot" in therapy. *International Journal on Mental Health and Deafness, 3*(1), 4–11.

Chovaz, C. J., Russell, D., & Daly, B. (2022). Lived experiences of deaf Canadians: What wewant you to know! *Canadian Psychology / Psychologie canadienne, 63*(4), 651–666.

Chovaz, C. J., Russell, D., & Boudreault, P. (2023). Deaf community experiences in the Canadian justice system. *Psychology, Public Policy, and Law*, *29*(4), 512–524. https://doi.org/10.1037/law0000404

Corbin, J., & Strauss, A. (2015) *Basics of qualitative research: Techniques and procedures for developing grounded theory* (4th ed.). Sage.

Crump, C. (2012). Mental health interpreting: Training, standards and certification. In L. A. Swabey, & K. Malcolm (Eds.), *In our hands: Educating healthcare interpreters* (pp. 54–76). Gallaudet University Press.

Du Feu, M., & Chovaz, C. J. (2014). *Mental health and deafness.* Oxford University Press.

Dean, R. K., & Pollard, R. Q, Jr. (2009). Effectiveness of observation-supervision training incommunity mental health interpreting settings. *REDIT E-journal on the Didactics of Translation and Interpreting*, *3*, 1–17.

Dean, R. K., & Pollard, R. Q., Jr. (2011). Context-based ethical reasoning in interpreting: A demand control schema perspective. *The Interpreter and Translator Trainer*, *5*(1), 155–182.

Eldridge v. British Columbia. (1997). 3 SCR 624, #24896. https://scc-csc.lexum.com/scc-csc/scc-csc/en/item/1552/index.do.

Fellinger, J., Holzinger, D., & Pollard, R. (2012). Mental health of deaf people. *The Lancet*, *379*(9820), 1037–1044. https://doi.org/10.1016/S0140-6736(11)61143-4

Garberoglio, C. L., Palmer, J. L., & Cawthon, S. W. (2019). *Undergraduate enrollment of deaf students in the United States.* National Deaf Center on Postsecondary Outcomes. https://nationaldeafcenter.org/wp-content/uploads/2021/03/Undergraduate-Enrollment-of-Deaf-Students-in-the-United-States.pdf

Glaser, B. G., & Strauss, A. L. (2017). *The discovery of grounded theory: Strategies for qualitative research.* Routledge.

Glickman, N. S., Crump, C., & Hamerdinger, S. (2020). Language deprivation is a game changer for the clinical specialty of Deaf mental health. *Journal of the American Deafness and Rehabilitation Association*, *54*(1), 54–89.

Glickman, N. S., & Hall, W. C. (2018). *Language deprivation and deaf mental health*. Routledge.

Gulati, S. (2018). Language deprivation syndrome. In N. S. Glickman & W. C. Hall (Eds.), *Language deprivation and deaf mental health* (pp. 24–53). Routledge.

Hall, M. L., Eigsti, I. M., Bortfeld, H., & Lillo-Martin, D. (2017). Auditory deprivation does not impair executive function, but language deprivation might: Evidence from a parent-report measure in deaf native signing children. *Journal of Deaf Studies and Deaf Education*, *22*(1), 9–21.

Hall, W. C. (2017). What you don't know can hurt you: The risk of language deprivation by impairing sign language development in deaf children. *Maternal and Child Health Journal*, *21*(5), 961–965. http://doi.org/10.1007/s10995-017-2287-y

Hamerdinger, S. H., & Crump, C. J. (2022). Collaboration: Sign language interpreters and clinicians working together in mental health settings. In C. Stone, R. Adam, R. Müller de Quadros, & C. Rathmann (Eds.), *The Routledge handbook of sign language translation and interpreting* (pp. 341–358). Routledge.

Harmer, L. (1999). Health care delivery and deaf people: Practice, problems, and recommendations for change. *Journal of Deaf Studies and Deaf Education*, *4*(2), 73–110.

Harvey, M. A. (2001) Vicarious emotional trauma of interpreters: A clinical psychologist's perspective. *Journal of Interpretation*, 7(2) 85–98.

Harvey, M. A. (2003a) Shielding yourself from the perils of empathy. *Journal of Deaf Studies and Deaf Education*, 8(2), 207–213.

Harvey, M. A. (2003b). *Psychotherapy with deaf and hard of hearing persons: A systemic model.* Routledge.

Hauser, P. C., Finch, K. L., & Hauser, A. B. (Eds.). (2015). *Deaf professionals and designated interpreters: A new paradigm*. Gallaudet University Press.

Humphries, T. (1975). *Audism: The making of a word* [Unpublished doctoral diss.], Union Graduate School, Cincinnati. https://docs.google.com/document/d/16D6h6JxZy8z84y4XczSfcce6IBf33BJ41ErvdxWASZA/preview?tab=t.0#bookmark=id.es4yxcrwabhb

Jacob, S. A., Palanisamy, U. D., Napier, J., Verstegen, D., Dhanoa, A., & Chong, E. Y.-C. (2022). Health care needs of deaf signers: The case for culturally competent health care providers. *Academic Medicine, 97*(3), 335–340.

Kelly, L. M. (2018). Sounding out d/Deafness: The experiences of d/Deaf prisoners. *Journal of Criminal Psychology, 8*(1), 20–32.

Knodel, R. K. (2018). Coping with vicarious trauma in mental health interpreting. *Journal of Interpretation, 26*(1), Article 2.

Kruger, J., & Dunning, D. (1999). Unskilled and unaware of it: How difficulties in recognizing one's own incompetence lead to inflated self-assessments. *Journal of Personality and Social Psychology, 77*(6), 1121–1134.

Kushalnagar, P., Ryan, C., Paludneviciene, R., Spellun, A., & Gulati, S. (2020). Adverse childhood communication experiences associated with an increased risk of chronic diseases in adults who are deaf. *American Journal of Preventive Medicine, 59*(4), 548–554.

Leigh, I. W., Andrews, J. F., Miller, C. A., & Wolsey, J.-L. A. (2022a). *Deaf people and society: Psychological, sociological, and educational perspectives* (3rd ed.). Routledge. https://doi.org/10.4324/9781003183686

Leigh I. W., Andrews, J. F, & Harris, R. L., & Gonzales Avila, T. (2022b). Deaf culture: Exploring deaf communities in the United States. Plural Publishing.

Lincoln, Y. S., & Guba, E. G. (1985). *Naturalistic inquiry*. Sage.

McDermid, C. (2009). The ontological beliefs and curriculum design of Canadian interpreter and ASL educators. *International Journal of Interpreter Education, 1*(1), 7–32.

Morgan, P., & Adam, R. (2012). Deaf interpreters in mental health settings: Some reflections on and thoughts about deaf interpreter education. In L. Swabey & K. Malcolm (Eds.), *In our hands: Educating healthcare interpreters* (pp. 190–208). Gallaudet University Press.

Napier, J., Sabolcec, J., Hodgetts, J., Linder, S., Mundy, G., Turcinov, M., & Warby, L. (2014). Direct, interpreter-mediated or translated? A qualitative study of access to preventive and ongoing healthcare information for Australian deaf people. In B. Nicodemus & M. Metzger (Eds.), *Investigations in healthcare interpreting* (pp. 233–276). Gallaudet University Press. https://doi.org/10.2307/j.ctv2rh2bq2.11

(2014). Direct, interpreter-mediated or translated? A qualitative study of access to preventive and ongoing healthcare information for Australian deaf people. In B. Nicodemus & M. Metzer (Eds.), *Investigations in healthcare interpreting* (pp. 233–276). Gallaudet University Press.

Olson, A. M., & Swabey, L. (2017). Communication access for deaf people in healthcare settings: Understanding the work of American Sign Language interpreters. *The Journal for Healthcare Quality, 39*(4), 191–199.

Pollard, R. (1998). *Mental health interpreting: A mentored curriculum*. Rochester Institute of Technology. https://www.urmc.rochester.edu/deaf-wellness-center/scholarship-research/mental-health-interpreting.

Pollard, R. Q, Jr., & Barnett, S. (2009). Health-related vocabulary knowledge among deaf adults. *Rehabilitation Psychology, 54*(2), 182–185.

Russell, D. (2005). Consecutive and simultaneous interpreting. In T. Janzen (Ed.), *Topics in signed language interpreting: Theory and practice* (pp. 135–164). John Benjamins.

Russell, D. (2012). Court/legal interpreting. In Y. Gambier & L. van Doorslaer (Eds)., *Handbook of translation studies*, (vol. 3, pp. 17–20). John Benjamins.

Russell, D. (2019). International perspectives and practices in healthcare interpreting with sign language interpreters: How does Canada compare? In M. Ji, M. Taibi, I. & H. M. Creeze (Eds.), *Multicultural health translation, interpreting and communication*, 37–66.

Russell, D., Chovaz, C., & Boudreault, P. (2018). *Administration of justice: The experiences of Deaf, Deaf-Blind, and Deaf people with additional disabilities in accessing the justice system*. Canadian Association of the Deaf. https://cad.ca/wp-content/uploads/2019/07/CAD-Report-Final-April-26-2018.pdf

Russell, D., Howard, N., & Nicholson, J. (2022). Canadian media interpreting: Public discourse and public discord. *Proceedings of the 2nd International Scientific Conference Space of Sign Languages Across Cultures: Interpretation, Communication, Research* (pp. 12–30). Atlantis Press.

Strauss, A., & Corbin, J. (1990). *Basics of qualitative research: Techniques and procedures for developing grounded theory*. Sage.

CATIE Center, St. Catherine University. (2023). *Mental health interpreter training*. Interpreting in Healthcare Settings. https://www.stkate.edu/academics/shas/asl-interpreting-department/catie-center

Stone, C., & Russell, C. (2022) *Media and emergency interpreting*. In C. Stone, R. Adam, R. Muller de Quadros, & C. Rathmann (Eds.), *The Routledge handbook of sign language translation and interpreting* (pp. 146–161). Routledge.

Swabey, L., Laurion, R., Patrie, C., & Ramirez, R. (2016). Using a career lattice to chart a path to competency in healthcare interpreting. In M. Rankin, R. Shaw, & M. Thumann (Eds.), *Out of the gate: Towards the triple crown* (pp. 1–16). Conference of Interpreter Trainers.

United Nations (UN). (2006). *Convention on the Rights of Persons with Disabilities (CRPD)*. https://social.desa.un.org/issues/disability/crpd/convention-on-the-rights-of-persons-with-disabilities-crpd

Vancouver Coastal Health. (2023). *What is the VCH Deaf, hard of hearing, and deaf-blind well-being program*. https://deafwellbeing.vch.ca/about-us/the-program/

Wattman, J. (2018). Interpreting for deaf people with dysfluent language in forensic settings: Application of the integrated model of interpreting. In N. Glickman & W. Hall, (Eds.), *Language deprivation and deaf mental health* (pp. 210–234). Routledge.

Wilkinson, E., & Morford, J. P. (2020). How bilingualism contributes to healthy development in deaf children: A public health perspective. *Maternal and Child Health Journal*, *24*, 1330–1338. https://doi.org/10.1007/s10995-020-02976-6

Woodcock, K., & Pole, J. D. (2007). Health profile of deaf Canadians: Analysis of the Canada Community Health Survey. *Canadian Family Physician*, *53*(12), 2140–2141.

World Federation of the Deaf (WFD). (March 25, 2014). *World Federation of the Deaf (WFD) Health resources initiative*. https://wfdeaf.org/world-federation-of-the-deaf-wfd-health-resources-initiative/.

World Federation of the Deaf (WFD). (2022). *Position paper on access to national sign languages as a health need*. https://wfdeaf.org/position-paper-on-access-to-national-sign-languages-as-a-health-need/

Zand, D. H., & Pierce, K. J. (2011). *Resilience in deaf children: Adaptation through emerging adulthood*. Springer.

Zidenberg, A. M., Rine, S. A. & Oliver, M. (2021 Zand, 2011;): Correctional and forensic contexts of d/Deaf persons: Implications for assessment and treatment. *Journal of Offender Rehabilitation*, *60*(6), 375–394. http://www.doi.org/10.1080/10509674.2021.1948945

Appendix

Interpreting in Mental Health Settings

Your responses to the following questions are being collected anonymously and will be used to help inform a chapter about mental health interpreting. The goal of this work is to provide a Canadian overview of ASL-English interpreting in mental health settings: legislation and policies affecting this work, training available (or not available), and recommendations for improvement. Should you be interested in reading the published work, please enter your name and email address on the final page of this survey.

Your participation in this survey is entirely voluntary, and your answers will not be saved until you click the "submit" button on the final page.

* Indicates required question

1. What best describes your background/training? *
   (select only one)
   — Completed an Interpreter Education Program (IEP)
   — Did not attend an IEP and have a combination of experience and professional development

2. If applicable, please indicate which IEP you completed.

3. Please list any/all additional education below, including subject area studied: (BA/MA/PhD/Post-Diploma)

4. How many years of interpreting experience do you have? *
   (select only one)
   — 1–5
   — 6–10
   — 11–15
   — 16–20
   — 21–25
   — > 25

5. Do you work in mental health related appointments and/or settings? *
   (select only one)
   — Yes (continue to question 6)
   — Not yet but I am interested (skip to question 10)
   — I do not want to work in this area (skip to question 15)

Working in Mental Health Settings

6. Please check all mental health settings in which you have interpreting experience: *
   (Please check all that apply)
   — Counselling (Individual, Couples, Group, Family, Children & Youth)

— Psychological Assessments
— Hospital Emergencies - psychological/psychiatric
— Treatment Centres (drug & alcohol, eating disorders, sexual disorders, other)
— Other:

7. Which of the following best describes your training for mental health interpreting? *
   (Please check all that apply)
   — Experience
   — Short-term professional development (workshops, presentations, etc.)
   — Basic orientation to the area through my IEP
   — Mentorship from other interpreters
   — Certificate program in Alabama
   — Courses offered by the Catie Center
   — Other:

8. What are the top three barriers that you believe affect the delivery of interpreting services in mental health appointments?

9. What advice would you offer interpreters who are considering accepting mental health appointments?

   Skip to end

Interpreters not yet working in Mental Health Settings

10. What could more experienced interpreters do/provide to enable you to begin working in this area?

11. What could professional interpreter associations such as CASLI do/provide to enable you to begin working in this area?

12. What could interpreter agencies do/provide to enable you to begin working in this area?

13. Can you think of any other support or training that you would need in order to begin to work in mental health settings?

14. Are there any other comments you would like to make?

    Skip to end

Interpreters who do not wish to work in mental health settings

15. Would you be interested in working in mental health settings if you had access to additional training in this area? *
    — Yes
    — No
    — Maybe

16. If you answered "yes" or "maybe" to the previous question, what type of training or support would you need to begin working in mental health settings?

Survey Completed!

Thank you for taking the time to participate in this survey. If you would like a copy of the written submission to Gallaudet University Press, please leave your name and email address below. Otherwise, leave the space blank and click "submit." Thank you for your time!

10

Deaf and Hard of Hearing Persons in the Canadian Criminal Justice System

A Time for Action

James C. MacDougall

Construct

This chapter is focused on barriers and issues related to equitable access to justice for Deaf and Hard of Hearing (DHH) persons. There is a particular concentration on mental health issues which impact various aspects of the justice system. The issue of fitness, or competence to stand trial, will be discussed in detail and legal cases involving deaf persons will be referenced. Explanation of these special cases demonstrates long-standing misunderstandings about the way deafness intersects with the justice system. Specifically, this chapter explains the complexities of determining fitness to stand trial for Deaf individuals in Canada who do not have a standard sign language, and who do not have a mental disorder.

Head-to-Head and Heart-to-Heart

The determination of fitness to stand trial is clearly challenging in the case of DHH persons who come from diverse linguistic and cultural backgrounds, and who for a variety of reasons, do not use a standard sign language. Part of the challenge is trying to understand the linguistic, cultural, and educational context experienced by these individuals, as well as the complex neurolinguistic and cognitive functioning of DHH persons who are accused of serious criminal behaviors. As far as the metaphor heart-to-heart is concerned, there is no lack of deeply felt emotion on all fronts; feelings of empathy for the victims of murder, sexual assault and other serious crimes are inevitable, however, at times these feelings need to be supressed rather than amplified during criminal justice proceedings. On the other hand, watching an accused deaf person who is unable to follow court proceedings, or who cannot adequately communicate with their lawyer, is equally unsettling. As far as head-to-head is concerned, trying to sort out the findings of empirical research and literature concerning the complex development of language and sign language—in light of the critical period language hypothesis—is equally challenging, particularly when a deaf person is languishing in jail awaiting a fair trial.

The complex interface of emotion, empirical evidence, and rational/logical thinking is heightened in small cultural contexts where the entire community may be affected by criminal proceedings. As well, there is often significant controversy and conflict within the community surrounding the determination of fitness to stand trail in serious cases involving murder or sexual assault. Head-to-head and heart-to-heart are amplified in these circumstances and take on a special meaning for all parties involved.

Reflection

My involvement with DHH people in the justice system has involved navigating between my professional training as a psychologist (head-to-head) and my own lived experiences as a child of deaf adults (Coda; heart-to-heart). The unforgiving complexities of the criminal justice system contrast sharply with the vulnerability of deaf persons and their families who often struggle to survive in unfavorable, and at times hostile, communication environments.

From the frozen tundra of Canada's Arctic to a small fishing village in a remote area of Nova Scotia, to the dank and dark corridors of the notorious Toronto Jail (built in 1860), I have been somewhat reluctantly thrust into issues with DHH persons in the justice system. I have had no formal training in forensics, and I found that progress in achieving any semblance of justice could only be realized by straddling many traditional professional barriers; a nerve-racking enterprise for any professional psychologist operating in a carefully regulated environment. I took only cases where the system was "stuck." I badly needed guidance for the forensic psychology aspect, and fortunately my mentor and good friend, the late pioneering psychologist, McCay Vernon, provided support and guidance every step of the way. Without Mac I would never have accepted to become involved in these forensic cases.

One of the most high-profile cases I participated in (which received significant media coverage) involved my wife Michele, a former social worker, who played an essential role facilitating communication cases which involved diverse cultural communities. My daughter Dr. Paige MacDougall, a sociocultural anthropologist, also provided essential guidance for navigating the diverse realities of deafness within Indigenous communities. When working in small Indigenous communities—where many people are related and where everyone knows and cares about everyone else—interactions become extremely personal. For me, the challenge was to be able to weave the personal with the professional without infringing on the rights of the accused/victim while at the same time upholding the highest professional standards This was not an easy task, and sadly there are very few solid guidelines in place for circumstances such as these.

I was extremely fortunate to have a long list of Crown, defense, and prominent judges who put extra effort into learning about the realities of deafness, and who provided careful guidance and counsel to a justice-novice such as myself. And of course, I relied on my own Deaf friends and trusted psychology colleagues for their wisdom and knowledge. I also made every effort to keep track of the empirical research which was quickly developing in this long-neglected area.

This unique journey involved acquiring a lot of new knowledge about the legal system, as well as venturing into as yet unexplored areas of language development in the context of mental fitness. What could be more serious than determining whether a person is fit or competent to stand trial? Standing trial is a cornerstone of democracy and human rights so it's essential that all persons—including diverse DHH persons—be afforded a fair trial, whether they be the accused or the victim.

The work I did in the forensic area involved a high degree of risk-taking on all fronts, moving swiftly and sometimes abruptly between head-to-head and heart-to-heart experiences. Fortunately, I received a lot of good advice and guidance from many different quarters, and particularly from a variety of deaf persons from diverse cultural and Indigenous communities. However, when I ultimately stood in the witness box in court, I was very much on my own and I alone take responsibility for the opinions expressed in this chapter.

Recommendations

The chapter I wrote provides some concrete recommendations for addressing the issues surrounding deafness that were raised during court proceedings, including changes to the Canadian Criminal Code (fitness section) as well as suggestions for restructuring the justice system overall. My suggestions refer to policing policies, interactions with defense and prosecution lawyers, court processes, and to the correction system itself (including support for community reintegration after a prison term has been served). I conclude by emphasizing a team-centered approach wherein legal and mental health professionals, as well as institutions, work together with professionals familiar with the issues faced by diverse DHH individuals in order to adequately understand their lived experiences.

Introduction

This chapter focuses on issues with access to criminal justice in the context of the ever-growing gaps between research, practice, and lived experience.[1] The specific focus will be on the issues of fitness to stand trial in the Canadian Justice system for deaf persons[2] who do not have a "standard" sign language and who do not have a mental disorder.[3]

For the past 30 years, I have been called to assist with issues determining the fitness of deaf persons to participate in court in a variety of criminal cases involving serious crimes such as murder, sexual interference and sexual assault, drug charges, sexual luring over the internet, and child pornography. Although each case was unique, they all presented challenges for the justice system to proceed with a fair trial, mainly due to the issue of fitness in the context of assessing communication and mental status.

I want to make clear that in focusing on this rather small and special population of diverse deaf people (i.e., those without a standard sign language), I am not in any way minimizing the wide range of other barriers and issues that are faced by deaf people in the justice system (Glickman & Hall, 2019; Guthmann et al., 2021; Russell et al., 2018).[4] In fact, there is a significant intersection

---

1. Note that the cases presented here are focused primarily on deaf people who use sign language rather than hard of hearing persons who primarily use speech and hearing to communicate.

2. Terminology note: "Deaf" with a capital "D" and "deaf" as a generic term will be used in different contexts as appropriate.

For additional information on terminology see: https://nationaldeafcenter.org/defining-deaf/

"The National Deaf Center is using the term *deaf* in an all-inclusive manner, to include people who may identify as deaf, deafblind, deafdisabled, hard of hearing, late-deafened, and hearing impaired. NDC recognizes that for many individuals, identity is fluid and can change over time or with setting. NDC has chosen to use one term, deaf, with the goal of recognizing experiences that are shared by all members of our diverse communities while also honoring all of our differences."

3. https://www.canada.ca/en/department-national-defence/corporate/policies-standards/legal-policies-directives/fitness-to-stand-trial-and-presence-of-a-mental-disorder-in-the-summary-trial-process.html

4. https://cad.ca/projects/access-to-justice/

between these more commonly discussed issues, such as general awareness of the realities of deafness, Deaf culture, and the need for appropriate interpretation and assessment at all stages of the criminal justice system—from initial interaction with the police, the defense counsel, the Crown, and the Judges in the courtroom as well as with corrections and community reintegration.

The *Roy* Case (1994): Can a Man Who Can't Hear, Speak, Sign, Read, or Write Get a Fair Trial in Canada?

My initial involvement with the issue of a deaf person being denied participation in a fair trial was when the associate chief justice of the Canadian Province of Nova Scotia (the Honorable Joseph P. Kennedy) asked if I would assist in the case of a 62-year-old deaf man (Everette Roy)[5] who was facing a charge of sexual interference with a minor. I was told that Mr. Roy could not hear, speak, read, write, or use American Sign Language (ASL).[6] Local sign language interpreters said they could not communicate with Mr. Roy, and the local deaf community in Nova Scotia agreed; they had no way of communicating with Mr. Roy.

Little did I know that this story would end up on national TV and appear on the front pages of many of the major newspapers in Canada (MacDougall, 1994). It seems the answer to the question "can a man who has no known mental disorder but who cannot hear, speak, use sign language, read, or write get a fair trial?" was a major story of national interest. The related question, of course, was, "can a deaf person who cannot communicate in court get away with any criminal behavior?"

After spending a week interviewing Everette Roy,[7] his family and friends, his employer, and many others including the psychiatrists at the Nova Scotia Hospital, I concluded that while Mr. Roy did not have a "standard" sign language such as ASL, he did have home sign—a communication system used to communicate in everyday life with family and friends in the community (Morford & Goldin-Meadow, 1997). The status of home sign as a formal linguistic entity remains under study with varying opinions from linguists (Carrigan & Coppola, 2017; Coppola & Newport, 2005; Goldin-Meadow, 2012). But from a practical point of view, this system of communication clearly could not be used in court—at least not in the short run. As far as mental status was concerned, although I did not administer any formal tests, I agreed completely with the six weeks of assessments done at the Nova Scotia Hospital. These assessments revealed no evidence of Mr. Roy having a known mental disorder.

Justice Kennedy accepted my assessment that Mr. Roy did not have a linguistic system that would allow for communication in all aspects of the justice system—mainly this was due to the absence of any interpreter who was acquainted with the communication system that Mr. Roy possessed. In my opinion, the fact that Mr. Roy did not have a "standard" communication system, either spoken, written, or signed, was not attributable to any known mental disorder, but rather due to the lack of exposure to a standard communication system—spoken or signed. Mr. Roy

5. R. v. Roy, [1994] NSJ No 82, 31 CR (4th) 388.

6. Or the minority local Maritime Sign Language. https://www.handspeak.com/study/index.php?id=165

7. Mr. Roy lived in Liverpool, Nova Scotia.

never attended a school for the deaf on a regular basis, never participated in any program designed for deaf people, and he did not participate in the local deaf community.

The judge granted Mr. Roy a Stay of Proceedings.[8] Mr. Roy walked out of the courtroom a free man. Justice Kennedy said that this stay was the "A bomb" of judgments—very problematic, but he stated he had no choice under the circumstances:

> . . . I find that the determination is so clear and predictable that it would be unfair to put the alleged victims, the children, through the trauma of testifying in this circumstance when I know that the trial will not be completed by this court.
>
> This is not a satisfactory conclusion of these matters. It is certainly not satisfactory for the alleged victims, the children and their families, who will not have their allegations heard by a court of law.
>
> It is certainly not satisfactory to the public of the Province of Nova Scotia. The public has an interest in these charges continuing to a conclusion. Certainly not satisfactory to Everette Roy who stands accused of serious offenses that he cannot defend himself against. Mr. Roy has spent several months in jail pending this determination. And, not satisfactory ultimately to this court.
>
> This court's function is to try cases and render decisions and frankly, the act of staying proceedings leaves a bad taste in my mouth. Not every problem allows for a satisfactory conclusion.
>
> We cannot try Everette Roy not because he is deaf. The deaf commonly participate in trials in this Province with little difficulty. This is not a problem. We cannot try Everette Roy because he has never been taught to communicate with us. We have not taught him to communicate with us. This is a social failure. Today, society is paying a price for it. I am staying the proceedings. Everette Roy is free to go.[9]

In my view, *Roy* was a classic case involving issues related to home sign. Clearly, Mr. Roy did not have ASL, and whatever sign system he did have allowed him to live normally in his community. I don't know what an intensive study of Mr. Roy's sign system would have revealed. Was it a "sophisticated" sign system, was it only a rudimentary sign system or was it just a "gesture system?" We will never know. My opinion at the time was that his communication system could not allow for communication in the justice system but I did say that based on my interactions with Mr. Roy, and with the assistance of his sister, I was able to determine that Mr. Roy in fact understood his charges and some of the necessary elements of the justice system, but not the more sophisticated aspects. Could he have been assessed, coached, and taught following the innovative techniques offered in the literature (Glickman, 2022; Glickman et al., 2020; Glickman et al., 2013; Glickman & Pollard Jr, 2013; O'Rourke et al., 2013)? My speculation is that, with a comprehensive approach, Mr. Roy could have developed a communication system that specially trained interpreters could have used to allow for a fair trial. Major accommodations would have been required.

---

8. A stay of proceedings is when a trial is stopped temporarily by the Crown attorney or ended by a judge. If the Crown issues a prosecutorial stay the trial has to resume within a year or the "proceedings shall be deemed never to have been commenced," as demanded by s. 579 (1) of the Criminal Code.

9. R. v. Roy, [1994] NSJ No 82, 31 CR (4th) 388.

The family of one of the alleged victims spoke out to the media - they felt that justice had not been served. However, others in the community spoke out publicly, saying that they felt Mr. Roy had been unjustly accused and was now suffering from an unwarranted stigma in this small community. The Nova Scotia and the larger Deaf community in Canada were disturbed by the impression that a deaf man could escape the justice system—innocent or guilty.

I subsequently attempted to become involved in the reformation of the Criminal Code that was occurring at that time in Canada, but the emphasis was on access to justice for persons with a disability who were victims of offenses such as sexual assault, and who were having difficulty getting their cases taken seriously by the justice system.[10] Most of the justice officials I talked to about the *Roy* case found it very interesting, but all agreed that it was probably unique and not worth challenging the fitness section of the criminal code that had just recently been reformed. A subsequent examination of the fitness section did not alter the code in any way.[11] Similarly, others involved with the justice system, including some members of the deaf community, felt that the *Roy* case was unique and the likelihood of such cases arising in the future was small. To be clear, these discussions took place some 30 years ago. In my view, what happened in the *Roy* case provides a clear rationale for reform of the Canadian Criminal Code to deal with this type of complex forensic situation involving deaf persons who don't use a "standard" form of sign language.

Signing in the Arctic—The Emergence of Inuit Sign Language (ISL)

The case of Bobby Suwarak (1999),[12] who lived in Baker Lake, Northwest Territories (NWT), now Nunavut, in Canada's Arctic, also turned out to be a high-profile case which caught the attention of both the print and broadcast media, locally and nationally.[13] Mr. Suwarak was a deaf Inuk[14] who was accused of sexual assault. Initially, a community member from Baker Lake, David Kautaq, provided interpretation in court using a form of sign language that Suwarak used in the community. This situation had obvious issues due to the potential conflict of interest and eventually, an ASL interpreter was called in. However, when it became obvious that the ASL interpreter could not communicate with Mr. Suwarak, a process was initiated to consult with me—most likely based on my experience with the *Roy* case.

After a non-conventional assessment which included observation of Mr. Suwarak communicating with a friend out on the tundra (MacDougall, 2000), I concluded that Mr. Suwarak most likely did have a viable communication system, which, after more extensive study in a

10. https://www.dawncanada.net/issues/women-with-disabilities-and-violence/

11. https://www.justice.gc.ca/eng/rp-pr/cp-pm/cr-rc/md-tm/defin.html. "The Committee recommends that the defence of "mental disorder" in section 16 and the definition in section 2 of the Criminal Code be retained in their present form." November 2002.

12. R. v. Suwarak, [2005] NuJ No 12, 2005 NUCJ 12, [2006] 2 WWR 151, 67 WCB (2d) 207, 2005 CarswellNun 12.

13. https://www.theglobeandmail.com/news/national/crown-stays-sex-charge-against-deaf-man/article668304/; https://nunatsiaq.com/stories/article/inuit_sign_language_could_open_courts_to_the_deaf/

14. The terms Inuit, Inuk, Nunavummiut are older terms than Eskimo, which is now considered to be pejorative except in certain local contexts.

community-based project supported by Justice Canada,[15] I later termed Inuit Sign Language (ISL). The *Suwarak* case was very complex involving many factors. Ultimately, in one of the court proceedings, the presiding judge mandated that the Nunavut Justice department undertake a special project to provide appropriate sign language interpretation for Mr. Suwarak in ISL so that he could meaningfully participate in a trial. The judge also suggested that I be consulted on this project.

The Nunavut Department of Justice offered support for this unique project for which I provided the expert consultation. This process was interrupted when Mr. Suwarak pled guilty to an additional offense and was sentenced to time in the Baffin Correctional facility in Iqaluit, the capital city of Nunavut. I remained involved with the case and joined forces with the local psychologist in the Baffin Correction Center. In a strange twist of fate, David Kautaq, from Baker Lake, became a guard at the correctional facility, thus providing a means for Mr. Suwarak to communicate with the corrections psychologist who was providing appropriate culture-based rehabilitation. Based on the success of that program, Mr. Suwarak became eligible for community placement at the adult training program at Arctic College. The success of that program, with David Kautaq providing interpretation and other support, was noted in the Legislative Assembly of Nunavut. There exists a strong tradition in Nunavut for recognizing Nunavummiut who have successfully engaged in rehabilitation programs.

Bobby Suwarak then got a job at the local hotel and was doing quite well, but the rules and policies in Nunavut were such that once the formal programs were completed, he needed to return to his home community. The housing situation in all of Nunavut is difficult and there are many reasons why this type of policy is in place.[16] However, in Mr. Suwarak's case, there were many good reasons from a risk point of view for him to remain in Iqaluit, but we were not successful in making our point regarding the high risk situation that he would encounter once back in the smaller community of Baker Lake. Soon thereafter, Mr. Suwarak was accused of violating his terms of release regarding the previous victim. Another trial was to be held and again I was consulted. After complex negotiations with all the stakeholders, the judge decided to continue with our original project to provide appropriate interpretation for Suwarak. The idea was to use a deaf Inuk from Rankin Inlet who knew both ASL[17] and what was now increasingly accepted as ISL (MacDougall, 2000) to serve as a Deaf Interpreter (DI) along with a hearing ASL interpreter.

The deaf Inuk was located in Rankin Inlet so the program of working out the logistics took place in Rankin Inlet, with the active participation of the defense lawyer who was from Cambridge Bay, Nunavut. One advantage of that location was that the local hotel also served as the location for court hearings and we were able to attend other court proceedings in order to familiarize everyone with the way the court functioned. It also gave us an opportunity to ensure that

---

15. MacDougall, J. C. (2000). *Access to justice for deaf persons in Nunavut. Focus on signed languages*. Prepared for the Research and Statistics Division. Department of Justice Canada. https://publications.gc.ca/site/archivee-archived.html?url=https://publications.gc.ca/collections/collection_2009/justice/J3-2-2000-17E.pdf

16. https://www.cbc.ca/news/canada/north/inuit-housing-crisis-1.6618940#:~:text=In%20March%202021%2C%20then%2DNunavut,Nunavut%20Housing%20Corporation%20is%20underfunded

17. Based on his experience in the south at a deaf residential school.

we had the needed vocabulary to function in a courtroom setting. We achieved good success with this approach; however, the defense decided that this situation caused an unacceptable delay under the Canadian Charter of Rights and Freedoms. The case was brought before the Supreme Court of Canada[18] which ruled as follows:

> Bobby Suwarak is an Inuit deaf mute who is facing trial on a charge of sexual assault. He applied for a stay of proceedings, alleging that his rights under s. 14 of the Charter of Rights and Freedom were violated because the Nunavut Court of Justice had not provided timely and satisfactory interpretation for his trial. The Crown brought a motion to have the Charter application dismissed on the basis that [it was necessary] to enable Suwarak and Inuit interpreters to be trained, so that Suwarak could fully participate in his trial. The Crown's motion was granted, rendering Suwarak' s motion moot. Suwarak seeks leave to appeal directly from the decision of the trial judge.
>
> Suwarak uses an Inuit sign language (ISL) that he and his family had developed to communicate. As in his previous involvements with the criminal justice system, one of Suwarak's relatives, David Kautaq,[19] acted as interpreter when he first appeared on these charges in March 2004. At this appearance, Suwarak was assisted by duty counsel, Tim Kavanagh, who asked that an American Sign Language (ASL) Interpreter be brought to the Baker Lake court for the next appearance. At the bail hearing, Kavanagh asked to appear as amicus curiae (amicus) as he could not communicate with Suwarak through the ASL interpreter.
>
> The amicus wrote to the Manager of Court Operations requesting an assessment of Suwarak's ability to communicate with an interpreter for his trial. The amicus suggested that Dr. James MacDougall perform the assessment, as MacDougall had twice assessed Suwarak's ability to communicate in two previous criminal proceedings.
>
> MacDougall found that Suwarak was capable of comprehension, and recommended that a training program be set up for Kautaq or Billy Suwarak, the applicant's brother. As an objective alternative, an ASL interpreter resident in Baker Lake could be trained to learn the ISL. The estimated training time was one to two years. The trial judge granted the Crown motion to have the Charter application dismissed.

The program to provide interpretation continued but in another unexpected development, the plaintiff in the case decided to withdraw the accusation and the Crown withdrew the charges. No explanation was ever provided. The result was that the interpretation paradigm was never tested in court. A few years later Mr. Suwarak was tried and convicted of unrelated charges[20] in a court proceeding that in my opinion did not provide appropriate interpretation. Mr. Suwarak was committed to a correctional institution outside of the Nunavut Territory. Mr. Suwarak served his time, and as far as I know is living without any further involvement in the justice system in a Canadian province.

---

18. https://www.scc-csc.ca/case-dossier/info/sum-som-eng.aspx?cas=31147
19. David Kautaq was a friend, not a relative of Bobby Suwarak.
20. https://nunatsiaq.com/stories/article/89789_nunavut_man_jailed_two_years_in_bizarre_graveyard_case/

I caution that the *Suwarak* case is very complex involving many aspects of the justice system. The events took place over a period of many years and this recounting of the case does not purport to be definitive in any way. The *Suwarak* case highlights the importance of consideration of Indigenous identity (MacDougall, 2013); Mr. Suwarak was an Inuk man from Nunavut (previously Northwest Territory) who never went to a school for the deaf, although he did at times attend the local community school. Contrary to many of his peers, he was not sent south to a residential school for the deaf and thus did not learn ASL, but used a sign language that was used in his community. There were other deaf people in Baker Lake, but Mr. Suwarak's main interactions were with his family and friends, not necessarily with other deaf people. This is a phenomenon seen elsewhere (MacDougall, 2013; MacDougall, 2015).

The main point that I wish to highlight is that the wheels of justice can be very different in diverse cultural and linguistic contexts. This is especially true of all matters relating to Indigenous justice (Adair, 2006; Ansloos et al., 2019; Bressan & Coady, 2017; Cunneen, 2006; MacDougall, 2001; Perdacher et al., 2019; Perlin, 2019; Rudin et al., 2022).

One positive outcome from the *Suwarak* case was the recognition of the existence of ISL (MacDougall, 2001; Schuit, 2012) and the support for official recognition of Indigenous sign languages as stated in the recently implemented Accessible Canada Act-Bill 81.[21] I believe that my involvement with the *Suwarak* case, along with the subsequent Nunavut-wide consultation with the deaf community in Nunavut and the formation of the Nunavut Deaf Society (NDS), played a major role in the inclusion of ISL in the Accessible Canada Act. There is at the present time a significant movement to recognize the sign languages of Indigenous people that have either been totally lost or exist in a vulnerable state (MacDougall, 2013; Nonaka, 2014; Schuit, 2012; Zeshan, 2010).

Section 14 of the Charter[22] states that a deaf person has the right to an interpreter, but who will be the interpreter? At the current time, as far as I know, there are no interpreter training programs in Canada directed at the issue of providing interpretation for Indigenous sign languages, including ISL. As important as it may be, this challenge cannot be met by simply adding the presence of a Deaf ASL Interpreter. The use of Indigenous Sign Languages calls for the involvement of an Indigenous interpreter, deaf and/or hearing. In the present environment in Canada with the Truth and Reconciliation Report[23] and in the more general Equity Diversity Inclusion (EDI) context worldwide, this is an issue that needs to be addressed on a priority basis (Fussell et al., 2021; Gano-Overway, 2021; Jimerson et al., 2021; Pollock, 2021; Ramos et al., 2021).

In this context, I note that I have had a number of other cases in First Nations[24] communities in various regions of Canada (Québec, Ontario, New Brunswick, and Nova Scotia) where Indigenous deaf people have had troubled backgrounds, and for various reasons, have suffered degrees of language and social deprivation, and now find themselves involved with the justice system. In these cases, cultural factors are paramount and, need to be taken into account. There is a high risk of misdiagnosis in these cases in terms of either underestimating or overestimating the effect of early linguistic/cultural experience.

21. Accessible Canada Act. https://laws-lois.justice.gc.ca/eng/acts/A-0.6/
22. https://www.justice.gc.ca/eng/csj-sjc/rfc-dlc/ccrf-ccdl/
23. https://www.rcaanc-cirnac.gc.ca/eng/1450124405592/1529106060525
24. https://www.rcaanc-cirnac.gc.ca/eng/1100100013785/1529102490303

A Brutal Murder in Ottawa—Issue of Bilingualism (ASL/LSQ)

Another high-profile case that came to my attention was the *Paré* (Jean-Marie Paré, 2002)[25] case in Ottawa which involved a Deaf man who brutally stabbed and murdered his estranged wife and her partner while they slept in his former home. This case revolved around the question of Mr. Paré's fitness to stand trial in view of his alleged severe cognitive and language deficits. After examination at the Royal Ottawa Hospital, Mr. Paré was diagnosed as unfit due to a mental disorder. According to the psychiatrist, the mental disorder was due to the inadequacy of Mr. Paré's use of sign language (ASL) to express or understand abstract concepts.

Mr. Paré spent 20 years under the jurisdiction of the Ontario Review Board (ORB) under the jurisdiction of the Forensic Hospital in Brockville Ontario.[26] Following the terms of the ORB, the fitness aspect had to be addressed on an annual basis. Each year Mr. Paré was declared unfit to stand trial due to a mental disorder.

As part of the hospital rehabilitation program, Mr. Paré was increasingly allowed to take part in community activities. He eventually found employment and engaged in other typical community activities. This "normal" behavior attracted the attention of some of the ORB members who began to question and even challenge the diagnosis of a mental disorder.

The media became aware of the situation and articles started to appear in the local papers raising the idea that a deaf person may be able to get away with murder. The media painted a picture of a deaf man who seemed to be able to function normally in the community but who nevertheless was deemed incompetent to stand trial, not allowing him to be held responsible for the crime that he freely admitted to committing. Eventually, the pressure became overwhelming and it was decided to hold a hearing in court concerning the fitness issue.

It was at that point that I was asked to become involved, most likely based on my involvement with the *Roy* and *Suwarak* cases. It is also worth mentioning again that in Canada, the diagnosis of fitness can only be made by a medical practitioner, most often a forensic psychiatrist, not a psychologist.[27] Ultimately, under Canadian law, fitness is a legal not a medical concept, which is decided by the judge or jury.[28] Fortunately, a forensic psychiatrist[29] in Toronto agreed to do a joint assessment of *Paré* with me. We subsequently carried out an extensive on-site assessment at the hospital in Brockville Ontario.

This case has many complexities and I do not have space to review all the aspects of the situation with *Paré*. I discovered that Mr. Paré was originally from Montreal and did attend a school for the deaf there but, at an early age, he was adopted due to family issues and moved to Gatineau,

---

25. R. v. Paré, [2002] OJ No 2004, [2002] OTC 351, 54 WCB (2d) 158.

26. https://www.theroyal.ca/

27. Efforts are currently underway in Canada to have psychologists certified to undertake fitness assessments. https://cpa.ca/fitness-to-stand-trial-and-criminal-responsibility-assessments-ongoing/

28. https://www.canada.ca/en/department-national-defence/corporate/policies-standards/legal-policies-directives/fitness-to-stand-trial-and-presence-of-a-mental-disorder-in-the-summary-trial-process.html

29. https://www.camh.ca/en/camh-news-and-stories/information-about-forensic-mental-health

Québec just across the border from Ottawa. Mr. Paré had a troubled background and from all indications, he suffered from a degree of early language deprivation associated with his situation. He made little use of speech and hearing. His primary language appeared to be Langue des Signes Québécoise (LSQ) (Parisot et al., 2015), but he also used ASL as he often crossed the border between Gatineau and Ottawa. Mr. Paré had some capacity with reading and writing in both English and French. Mr. Paré was assessed for cognitive capacity by qualified professionals from Québec who knew and used LSQ. They determined that his intellectual capacity was within the normal range.

Mr. Paré had been suffering from depression and related mental health issues shortly before he committed the crime. Although it was not completely clear, it appeared that he prematurely left the hospital where he was being treated before he proceeded to break into his former home through the garage, locate a hunting knife, and brutally murder his estranged wife and her partner while they were sleeping in bed. His two children were also in adjacent bedrooms nearby and became aware of the situation.

Given Mr. Paré's complex linguistic situation for the assessment, I recruited two highly qualified interpreters—one for LSQ and one for ASL. The LSQ interpreter was not only fluent in LSQ but had a good understanding of ASL as well. From the records, I determined that only ASL had been used to communicate with Mr. Paré for all of his fitness assessments. I began to think that this might be a critical issue for a deaf man who had LSQ as his primary language in the context of any language deprivation that he might have experienced because of his uneven education and personal experiences in his early years.

It became very clear during our assessment process that if the discussion centered on legal issues and questions related to fitness, Mr. Paré was most comfortable using ASL, but for more personal matters related to daily living, he was most comfortable using LSQ. In general, when the two interpreters worked together it was possible to improve Mr. Paré's understanding of the main elements related to fitness. On that basis the forensic psychiatrist was able to establish that Mr. Paré was, in his opinion (and in mine), fit to stand trial according to all the usual criteria. However, I added the opinion that Mr. Paré would not be able to follow the trial in real time unless special measures were taken involving, at minimum, an ASL and an LSQ interpreter, and possibly a Deaf interpreter and/or another linguistic expert. In essence, while the situation was very different, the result was the same as for the *Roy* case. However, contrary to *Roy*, due to Mr. Paré's existing knowledge of ASL and LSQ it would have been potentially possible to devise an interpreting situation that would accommodate his special situation.

After an extensive review of the case, I suggested that Mr. Paré may have been Not Criminally Responsible (NCR)[30] at the time of the offense. In the Canadian Criminal Code there is a section that deals with the concept of NCR. Contrary to the fitness provision which relates to the state of the accused at the time of the trial, NCR refers to their mental state at the time of the offense. I felt that a good case could be made to confirm that at the time of the offense, Mr. Paré was NCR

30. NCR. https://laws-lois.justice.gc.ca/eng/acts/C-46/section-16.html#:~:text=16%20(1)%20No%20person%20is,knowing%20that%20it%20was%20wrong

due to his mental health issues at the time. By his own account, he claims his mind was blank for the entire event. This idea provided some justification for Mr. Paré's involvement with the ORB and his time at the mental hospital being treated for a mental disorder.

Mr. Paré ultimately pled guilty by virtue of NCR, and this ended the uncertainty and angst that was associated with this situation for over 20 years. This case raised interesting questions regarding the degree of early language deprivation that would result in an inability to stand trial, especially in the context of Mr. Paré's bilingual status with LSQ and ASL. I want to stress that I have presented only highlights of the situation with the *Paré* case relevant to the issues that are the focus of the present article. For detailed legal aspects, readers are referred to the legal judgments.[31] The main point here is that, in the Canadian context where two "official" languages (English and French) are operative, issues of bilingualism involving ASL and LSQ in the context of potential early language deprivation deserve careful further study.

Unlike Mr. Roy, Mr. Paré did have some exposure to sign language[32] (LSQ) (albeit late in development) and, unlike Mr. Roy, he had a troubled family background. The other confounding factor was Mr. Paré's exposure to ASL during his late teen years at the Belleville school for the Deaf[33] and his living arrangements in Gatineau, Québec (a French-speaking area) and Ottawa (a primarily English-speaking area) with the result that he was to a degree bilingual (or quadrilingual) between ASL, LSQ, English, and French. Mr. Paré was declared unfit for over 20 years by forensic psychiatrists who repeatedly made the argument that sign language could not express abstract concepts, and then, the claim was made that Mr. Paré must have brain damage. This claim of brain damage was later shown to be unsubstantiated.

This case is important for many reasons. One reason is that it was heavily covered by the media who were proclaiming that a deaf person, by virtue of their deafness, could get away with murder. This had a terrible effect on the public perception of deafness in the community. The case also highlights the factor of official bilingualism in Canada—a significant number of deaf people travel back and forth between Québec, Ontario,[34] and other provinces. There are substantial numbers of deaf people who live in Ontario and New Brunswick[35] who use LSQ as their main means of communication and who are often bilingual as well. Should any of these deaf people become involved in the justice system it would be very important to keep these bilingual and bicultural realities in mind.

From Africa to the Canadian Winter—Languishing in the Canadian Justice System (2008)

The next case[36] involves a young deaf man who recently arrived from an African country and never attended a special program for deaf children, but who did attend his local village school. AB was

---

31. R. v. Paré, 2002 OJ No 2004, [2002] OTC 351, 54 WCB (2d) 158.
32. https://aqepa.org/courslsq/
33. https://asl.pdsbnet.ca/schools/sir-james-whitney-school-for-the-deaf/
34. https://www.aosf-ontario.ca/
35. http://www.nbdhhs.com/LSQProject.php
36. R. v. Isaac, 2009 ONCJ 662 (CanLII), 250 CCC (3d) 565.

accused of sexual assault in the recreation area associated with the apartment building in Toronto where he and his family lived. The local deaf service (at the time called the Canadian Hearing Society, CHS)[37] was contacted to help. Initially, the approach of the court was to accept the CHS recommendation that AB attend adult literacy classes for recent immigrants at Toronto's Bob Rumball Canadian Centre of Excellence for the Deaf (BRCCED)[38] mainly to help AB learn ASL. He attended the classes for a period but there were many logistical issues with transportation, and eventually he stopped attending the classes. He then allegedly reoffended (sexual assault) in a shopping mall near his home.

AB was admitted to the local correctional facility awaiting trial. However, because of the issues involved with sign language interpreting and uncertain mental status, I was called in to assist in the determination of fitness to stand trial. I worked with the CHS worker and visited AB in the correction facility and also interviewed his, mother, father, and sister. I determined that he arrived from Africa with his father to join his mother who had already immigrated to Canada. He arrived in the middle of a cold winter and evidently suffered trauma for many reasons including "weather shock" compared to the tropical weather at his original home in a small African village. My visits and assessments did not include any formal testing because of the complicated cultural and linguistic situation and the very restricted setting in the correctional facility. I did however make a video of the father showing the sign language that AB used in Africa with the family and in his village. Following extensive research on the situation for deaf persons in Africa, I was not able to determine if the form of sign language was in widespread use in his region of Africa but all indications were that this was a version of home sign (Goldin-Meadow, 2012; Morford & Goldin-Meadow, 1997; Witkin, 2015). I estimated at the time that AB's vocabulary was at the very least some 200-300 signs. None of the signs were similar in any way to ASL signs.

I offered the opinion that due to the general cultural factors along with the home sign of undetermined origin, it would be very difficult to do a valid assessment of a mental disorder in the context of fitness and, more importantly, I did not see any way that AB could participate in a trial at that time. The Crown pressed for a fitness hearing and this resulted in a fitness hearing being held in the special mental health court in Toronto. The judge ruled that a valid mental status assessment would be very difficult at this time and that fundamentally AB was suffering from educational deprivation—the extent of early linguistic deprivation could not be determined at this time due to a lack of detailed knowledge of his existing sign system. The recommendation was to have AB participate in ASL classes as originally recommended and then undertake further assessments as appropriate. However, because of the additional risk factors, this would have to be done in the context of the correctional facility, and as I pointed out, this would be virtually impossible under the present circumstances.

The Crown disagreed with the decision and kept advocating for a clear "not fit to stand trial by way of a mental disorder." That would put AB squarely into the Ontario Review Board system.

---

37. https://www.chs.ca/

38. Bob Rumball Canadian Centre of Excellence for the Deaf: https://www2.bobrumball.org/

Two issues arose as far as I was concerned. What is the "disease of the mind"[39] and how exactly would a valid assessment be carried out without significant additional resources and expertise that would take all the cultural and linguistic complexities into account? Eventually, the pressure mounted to have another fitness hearing. This time other forensic psychologists and psychiatrists, not necessarily specializing in deaf people, were brought in to do evaluations. The result was a consensus from those evaluations that AB was unfit to stand trial due to intellectual disability. I made my case in court that any such assessment would require more time and the application of additional expertise, but the judge accepted the opinion of the other psychologists. This decision by the court resulted in moving AB to the jurisdiction of the ORB who fortunately agreed that the conventional placement in a forensic ward would be very problematic for AB, and would not be conducive to my recommendation that AB be given a chance to learn ASL—for his own personal benefit as well as to allow the opportunity of a fair trial in the future.

Fortunately, I had kept up the involvement with the BRCCED[40] that was originally involved with the adult ASL classes for AB. Officials from BRCCED had visited him in the correctional facility and had met his family on a number of occasions. We then suggested to the ORB that placement in a secure group home at the BRCCED facility could be an alternative to meet this special situation. The ORB and the Centre for Addictions and Mental Health (CAMH)[41] (where AB remained after the evaluation) agreed with this approach. The issue was funding. Paradoxically, the chances of funding were much greater given AB's placement under the jurisdiction of the ORB due to the policies of funding for persons with significant developmental disabilities.

After a great deal of advocacy and excellent cooperation between CAMH, BRCCED, and the CHS,[42] the funding was obtained and AB was moved to a group home in rural Ontario. CAMH agreed to closely monitor the situation and provide psychiatric and social work consultation and backup. The staff at the BRCCED group home provided exemplary service in a very difficult and challenging situation. The family remained supportive despite transportation challenges and many other socio economic factors related to their status as newcomers to Canada. The defense

39. https://www.canada.ca/en/department-national-defence/corporate/policies-standards/legal-policies-directives/fitness-to-stand-trial-and-presence-of-a-mental-disorder-in-the-summary-trial-process.html

Unfit to stand trial means "unable on account of mental disorder to conduct a defence at any stage of the trial, and in particular, unable on account of mental disorder to understand the nature or object of the proceedings, understand the possible consequences of the proceedings, or communicate with counsel."

Mental disorder means "*a disease of the mind.*" The term "a disease of the mind" embraces any illness, disorder or abnormal condition which impairs the human mind and its functioning, excluding however, self-induced states caused by alcohol or drugs, as well as transitory mental states such as hysteria or concussion. It is a legal concept and it is therefore a question of law as to what mental conditions are included within the term.

40. https://www2.bobrumball.org/

41. Centre for Addiction and Mental Health: https://www.camh.ca/

42. Canadian Hearing Services: https://www.chs.ca/

lawyer went well above and beyond normal practice in order to navigate the complex legal situation. I remained involved for a number of years in regular review meetings. Slowly AB adjusted to the situation, and I am pleased to report that AB is now doing very well. He is learning ASL and engages in programs. Most recently, in view of the situation and in spite of many legal challenges, the Crown has finally dropped the charges. AB spent over 5 years in corrections or forensic wards and never participated in a trial where he could fairly address the charges.

The AB case raises many issues connected to the potential intersection of early language deprivation with diverse cultural/linguistic factors, as well as diagnoses of a mental disorder in the forensic context. Over the years I have been involved with a number of similar cases where a deaf person newly arrived in Canada through the "normal" immigration processes, as well as through the refugee process. Some arrive experiencing serious trauma from war-torn countries and related serious political upheavals in their home countries (Moers, 2017). All the cases are very different, but all call for a special approach to ensure that the realities of being deaf, in the context of very different and diverse cultural and linguistic situations, are taken into account in the forensic system.

Alleged Sexual Assault Victim from the Caribbean (2000)—Can't Use Her Language to Press Charges?

This final case is quite different since it involves a victim rather than an accused. I think it is important to present this perspective since I believe any reforms that we propose for the justice system need to be sensitive to both the victims and the accused, as well as to the witnesses and potential jurors (Olsen & Kermit, 2015; Russell et al., 2018).

This case involves a young deaf woman (LL) who immigrated from the Caribbean with her family to the Ottawa/Gatineau area. The accusation before the court was LL's claim that a person or persons who were part of a "group" in Gatineau sexually assaulted her. The issue that I was asked to consult on was related to the initial interaction that LL had at the police station when she first reported her accusation. LL at the time did not have standard ASL. She used the sign language she had acquired in the Caribbean (home sign or the Caribbean Sign language - not known). Interpretation at the police station was provided by LL's sister. In her initial appearance in court, no sign language interpreter was able to interpret for her. The judge ruled that the trial be postponed for a period during which LL could take sign language courses (ASL) and become proficient enough so that she could testify in court.

After two years of ASL classes, LL acquired a degree of sign language proficiency—at least adequate enough to participate in a trial with an ASL interpreter. However, the defense took the position that since the original evidence given to the police (involving her accusation of sexual assault), was not done in ASL, it could not be used as evidence, because an ASL interpreter could not "reliably" certify what she was saying with her sister acting as her interpreter. The original interview with the police was videotaped. I was called in to give an opinion on the status of the original interaction during the police interview. A highly qualified sign language interpreter was retained by the defense to review the video tape. That interpreter offered the opinion that the signs LL was using were not ASL and, in her opinion, could not be relied upon for admissible testimony.

On the other hand, after reviewing the tapes I concluded that there was little doubt concerning what LL was claiming regarding sexual assault and the identification of the time, place, and events that occurred. There was the possibility of bias in the interpretation by the sister, but this could be stated and weighed appropriately by the court. In my report, I pointed out the fact that LL was able to learn ASL in 2 years, indicated a high probability that the sign language she was using was most likely a form of Caribbean Sign Language[43]—or at the very least a sophisticated form of home sign (Coppola, 2020; Witkin, 2015).

Unfortunately, the trial took a strange twist when a technical problem with physical evidence and issues of consent arose. The judge finally ruled in favor of the defense. However, in his ruling, he did point out that he accepted my analysis of the situation and his ruling was independent of the issue concerning language in the original testimony.

This case involved an alleged victim of sexual assault. The defense in her case sought to dismiss charges because she used a communication system from the Caribbean, rather than ASL, that was interpreted by her sister in her original testimony to police. She later learned ASL and was able to participate in her trial. This case demonstrates the need for caution in declaring a home sign or village sign system as not being a viable language because there is no interpreter available for that specific linguistic system. In this case, it meant that potentially serious charges could not be laid by an alleged victim of sexual assault. This also illustrates a degree of systemic "audism" (Eckert & Rowley, 2013) in Section 14 of the Canadian Charter regarding sign language interpretation in the court. Section 14 assumes that for even the most obscure spoken language—somehow, somewhere, a speaker can be found to interpret in the court setting. This may be true for hearing persons, but there appears to be many barriers to such a provision for deaf persons.

The defense, in this case, claimed that whatever system of communication LL was using, it wasn't a "standard" language; therefore, it could not have any legitimacy in court. I disagreed and my opinion was upheld by the judge, but it was never reliably established what sign language was being used in her original testimony. LL did eventually learn ASL which is important to note. In this context, I believe the default position in the absence of any compelling evidence to the contrary is that when a person comes from another country and does not know ASL, we should assume that the sign system that the person uses may be sufficient to allow for communication in a court. Everyone should be given a reasonable chance to learn ASL. In the Canadian context offering the opportunity to learn LSQ is also very important.

I raise this case to highlight how issues of language and competence can affect victims as well as accused. If too much weight is put on a high level of "standard" language, there can be detrimental effects on victims' abilities to have their charges fairly addressed. In fact, this has also been an issue in matters related to persons with a developmental disability having charges of violence and other related issues being taken seriously by the courts (Hassan & Gordon, 2003).[44]

Discussion

I will now focus on the specific issues related to fitness and the Canadian Criminal Code that were raised in the cases I have presented in this article, namely, *Roy*, *Suwarak*, *Paré*, *AB*, and *LL*. Clearly the issues involved in the cases I presented are very complex and involve many different theoretical issues in various disciplines including psychology and the law. Most of these theoretical issues, such as the critical period hypothesis (Mayberry & Kluender, 2018; Mayberry & Lock,

43. https://sta.uwi.edu/rdifund/projects/ttel/sign_history.asp
44. https://archdisabilitylaw.ca/

2003) and home sign (Carrigan & Coppola, 2017; Coppola, 2020; Morford & Goldin-Meadow, 1997; Rissman et al., 2020), and decisions about best practices associated with these issues are far from resolved; therefore, the discussion that follows will only highlight certain aspects of these issues and cannot be considered definitive in any sense.

The recent book, *Deaf People in the Criminal Justice System* (Guthmann et al., 2021), provides a comprehensive review of issues, barriers and concrete recommendations faced by DHH people in the criminal justice system. Chapter 7, "Discourse, Sign Language Interpreters, and the Criminal Justice System: Implications for Communicating With Deaf People," by Teresa Smith is particularly relevant to the current chapter which focuses on issues of fitness for deaf people who do not have ready access to sign language interpretation for a variety of reasons.

In the case of deaf persons who suffer from language dysfluency, the book *Language Deprivation and Deaf Mental Health* (Glickman & Hall, 2019) and related articles (Gulati, 2018; Pollard & Fox, 2018; Ryan & Johnson, 2019; Wattman, 2018) are also relevant. In particular, the articles on forensic evaluation of deaf adults with language deprivation (Pollard & Berlinski, 2017; Pollard & Fox, 2018) offer a comprehensive and authoritative review of the situation with detailed recommendations based on research and their own clinical experience with clients in the forensic system. These recent books, chapters, and articles are a must read for anyone involved in the evaluation of deaf forensic clients.

Readers who seek additional information for the larger issues affecting all deaf people in the justice system can refer to the increasing number of articles and texts that deal with these more general issues (Dernevik et al., 2022; Gibbon & Doyle, 2011; Harry, 1986; Miller, 2001; Pollard Jr. & Berlinski, 2017; Pollard & Fox, 2018; Young et al., 2001; Young et al., 2000; Zidenberg et al., 2021). The classic papers by McCay Vernon and his associates are also highly recommended (Miller, 2004; Vernon & Miller, 2005). In the Canadian context see (Russell et al., 2018) as well as the Ontario Accessibility report.[45]

Other more recent papers outline many unmet issues and offer concrete suggestions for the management of a wide range of deaf persons who are caught up with many aspects of the justice or mental health system on an international basis (Chovaz et al., 2022; Crump & Glickman, 2011; Dernevik et al., 2022; Du Feu & Chovaz, 2014; Glickman, 2022; Glickman & Crump, 2013; Glickman et al., 2013; Harry, 1986; Liell et al., 2022; MacDougall, 2022; Miller, 2001; O'Rourke et al., 2013; O'Rourke & Grewer, 2005; Pollard & Fox, 2018; Vernon et al., 2001; Wattman, 2018; Wortzel, 2013; Young et al., 2001; Young et al., 2000; Zidenberg et al., 2021).

As noted earlier, my specific focus in this chapter is with Deaf persons who do not have a "standard" sign language, and who also do not have a known mental disorder. I acknowledge the importance of assessing the degree of interaction and intersection between all the diverse cultural/linguistic factors, and the very real possibility of the detrimental effects of early language deprivation in any modality (Glickman & Hall, 2019).

---

45. *Making Ontario's Courts Fully Accessible to Persons With Disabilities:* https://www.ontariocourts.ca/coa/about-the-court/publications-speeches/reports-courts-disabilities/

The question of deaf people who grew up in Indigenous communities is complicated as there appear to be cases where the community at large uses sign language (MacDougall, 2013). I do not think it is appropriate to make diagnoses about Language Deprivation Syndrome (LDS) (Glickman & Hall, 2018; Gulati, 2018) without the active and appropriate involvement of the relevant Indigenous communities. There are many elements of colonialism and white privilege that may be operative in this context (Bone et al., 2022; Rudin et al., 2022).

Similarly in the context of Black culture (Aramburo, 1989; Gebhard et al., 2022; James & Woll, 2000; Myers et al., 2010; Onyeador et al., 2021), given the history of segregation in the US and similar attitudes in Canada, it is important to be cautious in making statements concerning LDS and mental disorders generally without the active participation of those communities at all levels, including at the level of sign language interpretation, research, and professional intervention (Bernhardt, 2020; Crump & Glickman, 2011; Glickman & Crump, 2013; Glickman & Hall, 2019; Gulati, 2018; Marschark, 2005; O'rourke & Grewer, 2005; Perdacher et al., 2019; Pollard & Fox, 2018; Zaidman-Zait et al., 2017).

One of my main preoccupations and concerns is what happens to deaf people who pass through the justice system, especially those who are fairly convicted of serious criminal behaviors. In my practice, I remained heavily involved with a number of deaf persons well after experiences of initial assessment and court proceedings. It became very clear to me that both the corrections and forensic systems are not well suited for the management of deaf persons. I have interacted with a significant number of deaf persons in corrections in many areas of Canada, rural and urban. Contrary to the picture that is often presented concerning the corrections and the forensic systems, I found that for the most part, the officials and the frontline people, as well as other inmates were very concerned with the special needs of the deaf inmates.

I note that many of the cases I have been involved in were very high profile and, in others, I was only called in when the system was "stuck." So, I am not claiming my experiences are in any way representative of the larger picture. There exist many reports of vulnerable deaf inmates suffering abuse in the corrections system (Miller et al., 2005; Vernon et al., 1999). However, it did highlight for me that there was a high motivation on the part of most of the corrections, administrative, professional, and frontline personnel to meet the needs of these very special deaf clients. The issue was the system itself.

Perhaps the easiest way to summarize the situation is to invoke the concept of audism (Eckert & Rowley, 2013). Clearly, the Canadian justice system has evolved over many years to the point that most people can say it meets our highest ideals of fairness and justice for all while protecting the rights of the public at large. However, we know that in certain cases, especially involving traditionally marginalized groups, the justice system has been less than optimal, especially in view of reforms to the Charter of Rights that have been made over the years. The situation with Indigenous peoples is a special case with rulings such as *Gladue*[46] regarding special guidelines for sentencing and ideas such as sentencing circles (Rudin et al., 2022).

---

46. In section 718.2(e) of the Criminal Code, Parliament requires judges to consider all available sentences other than imprisonment that are reasonable in the circumstances and consistent with the harm done, for all offenders, and says judges must pay particular attention to the circumstances of Aboriginal offenders.

Apart from the implementation of Section 15 of the Charter[47] involving discrimination where deafness is included under disability, and the specific reference in Section 14[48] to the need for an interpreter if a person is deaf, nothing significant has been done to upgrade the justice, corrections, and forensic systems to catch up with knowledge and best practice based on research, especially as it relates to the fitness sections, which connect to mental health issues. The intersection of access to justice in the context of the historically troubled history of mental health issues with deaf persons has proved to be very complex and difficult to deal with at every level (Bernhardt, 2020; Glickman & Hall, 2019; Miller et al., 2005; Vernon & Miller, 2005).

In my view, based on my experience, it is the justice system itself that needs restructuring. Sophisticated accommodations involving innovative assessments and interpretation (including important aspects of Deaf interpretation, DI) can only go so far in addressing the fundamental issues.

The justice system clearly needs a revamp at all levels, and to reiterate, my specific focus here is on deaf people for whom an interpreter cannot be found under ordinary circumstances, and who do not have any clear mental disorder. At the moment, since Language Deprivation Syndrome (LDS) has not been fully established or accepted as a mental disorder (Gulati, 2018; Hall et al., 2017), I am not including that diagnosis as a mental disorder unless it is associated with a specified mental disorder. This may change as this area continues to develop at a rapid pace. For the moment, I wish to avoid the issue of whether LDS should be included in the DSM-5-TR[49] in the context of forensic issues. I note that there is existing controversy about the DSM-5-TR system itself that needs to be taken seriously, and the DSM-5-TR clearly states that the categorization system of mental disorders should be used with great caution in the forensic system (Frances, 2009; Frances & Halon, 2013; Wills & Gold, 2014; Wortzel, 2013). The DSM-5-TR was designed for the mental health system, not the forensic system. The details of this issue that are currently under debate, while relevant, are well beyond the scope of this chapter.

At the present time, LDS is not accepted in the DSM-5-TR and it is important that we deal with this reality. In this context, I believe there is nothing preventing practitioners from referring to this very real phenomenon in any clinical evaluation—especially in the context of the emerging literature and the number of prominent practitioners that are currently discussing this proposal (Glickman & Hall, 2019; Gulati, 2018; Hall et al., 2017). I have referred to and described this constellation of symptoms in many of my cases and in most, if not all cases, the presentation of these symptoms has been taken very seriously by both the mental health and the forensic legal systems.

---

47. Every individual is equal before and under the law and has the right to the equal protection and equal benefit of the law without discrimination and, in particular, without discrimination based on race, national or ethnic origin, colour, religion, sex, age or mental or physical disability.

48. A party or witness in any proceedings who does not understand or speak the language in which the proceedings are conducted or who is deaf has the right to the assistance of an interpreter.

49. *Diagnostic and Statistical Manual of Mental Disorders* (DSM-5-TR): https://www.psychiatry.org/psychiatrists/practice/dsm

Recommendations

1. Form a special subcommittee of the provincial review boards
   My suggestion is that the terms of the provincial Review Boards (e.g., Ontario Review Board)[50] be modified to establish a subcommittee to deal with deaf people who pose clear communication issues. This subcommittee could have representation from qualified professionals as well as defense and Crown counsel who have special training. Representatives from the Deaf community with an emphasis on issues of cultural and linguistic intersectionality would also be necessary. This committee would then make recommendations regarding appropriate assessment of language and mental status to the full board for review and the report would be made to the court in the ordinary way. Terms of bail and ancillary issues would be the same as for non-deaf persons.

2. Establish special protocols for forensic units
   The success of the approach involving the establishment of a special subcommittee would depend on the local forensic unit having a special protocol for DHH persons. This would involve access to specialized interpreters and other professionals and would be based on yearly training via Continuing Education (CE) courses given to the staff at the unit, independent of whether a deaf person was incarcerated at that particular time. As per common practice, the objective of the program in the forensic unit would be to establish whether the deaf person could participate in a trial with special communication and other accommodations. At the same time, efforts could be made to establish the issue of a mental disorder once the communication issues are settled.

3. Capitalize on virtual communications
   Clearly most forensic units, even with special accommodations, are not going to be able to engage in the programming that would be required along the lines suggested by Pollard (Pollard & Fox, 2018), Glickman (Glickman, 2022; Glickman & Hall, 2019), and others (Guthmann et al., 2021). The availability of specialists and funding would be an issue; however, with the increased use of virtual communication breaking down the state, provincial, and even international barriers to professional practice, I think many of these barriers could be overcome.

4. Establish special secure custodial units
   It is clear that in many cases where the assessment and programming may take a considerable period of time, there needs to be special custodial settings established, similar to the situation in the Toronto area at the BRCCED.[51] Over the years informal ad hoc arrangements have been made with the courts and the forensic and corrections systems to carry out assessments and programs such as those I have described above. The issue at present is the ad hoc nature of the programs, and the uncertainty of funding and sustainability. Joint partnerships where professionals work together between institutions such as CAMH[52] and BRCCED[53] have proved successful in the short term, but these are one-off programs

---

50. http://www.orb.on.ca/scripts/en/about.asp
51. https://www2.bobrumball.org
52. https://www.camh.ca/en/your-care/programs-and-services/forensic-general-units
53. https://www2.bobrumball.org/

that took an immense effort to establish and no formal protocols or systems have been established for future clients. Each time the wheel has to be reinvented.

5. Corrections facilities should maintain links to specialized deaf support services
In cases where there is no choice except for highly secure placement related to risk to the public, a deaf person will need to be incarcerated in a regular corrections facility. Connections with specialized services such as those offered by BRCCED could be established and maintained—such liaisons have already taken place previously (CHS and BRCCED), but again, nothing sustainable has evolved.

6. Reintegration into the community—the importance of active participation of the DHH community
Reintegration into the community needs to be considered. In this context, I think it is important for the Deaf community to become involved if the deaf person has been previously functioning as a part of that community. Many lessons and good ideas in this regard can be found in the context of Indigenous justice (Rudin et al., 2022) where community reintegration plays a huge role. Again, I have seen this happen especially in specific cases where the Deaf community in partnership with the local service agency and families of Deaf persons have worked together to ensure successful reintegration after rehabilitation.

7. Don't reinvent the wheel
All of my suggestions and examples given above require further elucidation and refinement (Cannon et al., 2022). Many of the programs are currently underway or have previously been tried in the US, the UK, and many other countries with varying degrees of success. These excellent examples of special programming need to be reviewed.[54] The extensive recommendations from previous studies in the Canadian as well as the international context need to be incorporated into recommendations for future development in this area (Bone et al., 2022; Byrne et al., 2021; Olsen & Kermit, 2015; Russell et al., 2018; Schwartz & Elder, 2018; Young et al., 2000).

8. Working together—the importance of intersectionality and EDI[55]
In my view, the Deaf community and associated stakeholders, families, professionals, and services providers cannot do this alone. We need the deaf and hearing anglophone and francophone communities to work together to demand reform of every aspect of the justice system. We also need the hearing and deaf Black community[56] and the hearing and deaf 2SLGBTQI+[57] communities, as well as all the other historically marginalized communities, to become involved in issues of DHH persons in the justice system (Cannon et al., 2016; Cannon et al., 2022; Foster & Kinuthia, 2003; Pavlenko & Blackledge, 2004; Pizzo & Chilvers, 2016; Wang et al., 2016).

54. https://www.nottinghamshirehealthcare.nhs.uk/national-high-secure-deaf-service

55. https://journal.equinoxpub.com/IJSLL/article/view/5819; https://www.abilities.ca/social-policy/deaf-culture-and-multi-culturalism/. The 1993 International Seminar on Youth and Development introduces the Deaf Participation Project.

56. https://globalnews.ca/news/7607371/basl-black-american-sign-language-canada/

57. https://www.facebook.com/oradeaf/

9. First Nation, Inuit, and Metis communities need to become engaged
In the present Canadian context we need to have the various Indigenous communities (First Nation, Inuit, and Metis)[58] highlight the needs and aspirations of DHH persons in their communities. In my view, Indigenous communities have many special insights to offer, especially in their historical connections to sign language and their strong value systems[59] (Adair, 2006; Baldry et al., 2016; Bone et al., 2022; Bressan & Coady, 2017; Cunneen, 2006; Kim et al., 2006; MacDougall, 2022; Perdacher et al., 2019; Perlin, 2019; Rudin et al., 2022).

10. DHH Multilingual Learners (DML) deserve a special approach: Emphasize the positive
The books by Cannon and Ladd (Cannon et al., 2022; Ladd, 2003) promote an approach for the field of deafness generally which stress positive abilities in order to not reinforce an overall negative picture of diverse deaf people, particularly those with significant language issues. The "Deaf Gain" perspective (Bauman & Murray, 2014) is particularly important in the context of deaf persons who are either in the forensic or the regular correction system and who are required to participate in rehabilitation programs. Many of the innovative approaches available in the literature are particularly applicable in this context (Cannon et al., 2016; Crump & Glickman, 2011; Glickman, 2009; Glickman & Hall, 2019; Glickman & Harvey, 2013; Ladd, 2003; Pollard & Fox, 2018). I believe that the changes suggested here will be of general benefit to the justice system as a whole (Bauman & Murray, 2014).

Summary and Conclusions

To summarize, in my view there remains a significant gap between the research, the practice, and the lived experience of deaf people in the justice system, particularly for deaf people who have diverse linguistic abilities and backgrounds. The determination of fitness presents formidable challenges that require a knowledge of not only the scientific theories concerning language development with deaf people, but also a sensitivity to intersectional variables involving sociocultural aspects, as well as the potential interaction of additional disabilities.

We are still in the early stages of understanding the complex interaction of all these variables, and we need to take the time to critically examine the biases and attitudes that we ourselves as practitioners bring to the situation. The one important consensus that does emerge is that each deaf individual that becomes involved with the criminal justice system presents as a unique case that requires the input of a team of professionals, as well as legal experts knowledgeable about the special situation for deaf people.

As stated earlier, I believe (at least in the Canadian justice system) there needs to be structural reform to the fitness section of the Canadian Criminal Code[60] to accommodate the special needs of linguistically and socioculturally diverse deaf people. The management of convicted deaf persons also needs radical restructuring. Special free-standing units need to be

---

58. https://www.rcaanc-cirnac.gc.ca/eng/1621447127773/1621447157184

59. For example, Inuit Qaujimajatuqangit, Inuit Societal Values: https://www.gov.nu.ca/information/inuit-societal-values

60. **672.22** (Canadian Criminal Code) An accused is presumed fit to stand trial unless the court is satisfied on the balance of probabilities that the accused is unfit to stand trial.

established to house offenders, where serious crimes are involved in the federal system, one or two model federal corrections facilities need to be established that can properly provide appropriate rehabilitation programs.

To some, these recommendations may seem unrealistic given the small numbers of cases and the overarching issues in the justice system at large—from policing to courts, to corrections, and special forensic units, but our system of justice and our Charter of Rights guarantees equal justice for all. At the present time, not only is that not the case for a small group of deaf people who have diverse linguistic and cultural experiences, but there remains a significant gap between our scientific knowledge, the lived experience of deaf people, and the actual practice in the justice system. Finally, it is extremely important for all our efforts to operate within the larger context of sensitivity in the current Equity, Diversity, and Inclusion (EDI) movement. This includes a significant aspect of self-reflection on the part of us all.

References

Adair, J. G. (2006). Creating indigenous psychologies. In U. Kim, K.-S. Yang, & K.-K. Hwang (Eds.), *Indigenous and cultural psychology: Understanding people in context* (pp. 467–485). Springer.

Ansloos, J., Stewart, S., Fellner, K., Goodwill, A., Graham, H., McCormick, R., Harder, H., & Mushquash, C. (2019). Indigenous peoples and professional training in psychology in Canada. *Canadian Psychology/Psychologie canadienne, 60*, 265–280. https://doi.org/10.1037/cap0000189

Aramburo, A. J. (1989). Sociolinguistic aspects of the Black Deaf community. In C. Lucas (Ed.), *The sociolinguistics of the deaf community* (pp. 103–119). Elsevier.

Baldry, E., McCausland, R., Dowse, L., McEntyre, E., & MacGillivray, P. (2016). 'It's just a big vicious cycle that swallows them up': Indigenous people with mental and cognitive disabilities in the criminal justice system. *Indigenous Law Bulletin, 8*(22), 10–16.

Bauman, H. D. L., & Murray, J. J. (2014). *Deaf gain: Raising the stakes for human diversity*. University of Minnesota Press.

Bernhardt, K. (2020). *Extending language deprivation to deaf education* [Review of *Language deprivation and deaf mental health* by N. Glickman & W. Hall. Oxford University Press.

Bone, T. A., Wilkinson, E., Ferndale, D., & Adams, R. (2022). Indigenous and deaf people and the implications of ongoing practices of colonization: A comparison of Australia and Canada. *Humanity & Society, 46*(3), 495–521.

Bressan, A., & Coady, K. (2017). *Guilty pleas among indigenous people in Canada*. Department of Justice Canada.

Byrne, B., Elder, B. C., & Schwartz, M. (2021). Enhancing deaf people's access to justice in Northern Ireland: Implementing Article 13 of the UN Convention on the Rights of Persons with Disabilities. *Scandinavian Journal of Disability Research, 23*, 74–84.

Cannon, J. E., Guardino, C., & Gallimore, E. (2016). A new kind of heterogeneity: What we can learn from d/Deaf and hard of hearing multilingual learners. *American Annals of the Deaf, 161*(1), 8–16.

Cannon, J. E., Guardino, C., & Paul, P. V. (2022). *Deaf and hard of hearing multilingual learners : foundations, strategies, and resources*. Routledge.

Carrigan, E. M., & Coppola, M. (2017). Successful communication does not drive language development: Evidence from adult homesign. *Cognition, 158*, 10–27.

Chovaz, C. J., Russell, D., & Daly, B. (2022). Lived experiences of deaf Canadians: What we want you to know! *Canadian Psychology/Psychologie canadienne, 63*(4), 651–666. https://doi.org/10.1037/cap0000313

Coppola, M. (2020). Gestures, homesign, sign language: Cultural and social factors driving lexical conventionalization. In O. Le Guen, J. Safar, & M. Coppola (Eds.), *Emerging sign languages of the Americas*, 349–390. De Gruyter.

Coppola, M., & Newport, E. L. (2005). Grammatical subjects in home sign: Abstract linguistic structure in adult primary gesture systems without linguistic input. *Proceedings of the National Academy of Sciences, 102*(52), 19249–19253.

Crump, C., & Glickman, N. (2011). Mental health interpreting with language dysfluent deaf clients. *Journal of Interpretation, 21*(1), 3.

Cunneen, C. (2006). Racism, discrimination and the over-representation of indigenous people in the criminal justice system: Some conceptual and explanatory issues. *Current Issues in Criminal Justice, 17*(3), 329–346.

Dernevik, M., Monteiro, B., Hough, L., & Kimber, E. (2022). Deaf people in forensic contexts. In G. C. Liell, M. J. Fisher, & L. F. Jones (Eds.), *Challenging bias in forensic psychological assessment and testing* (pp. 389–406). Routledge.

Du Feu, M., & Chovaz, C. (2014). *Mental health and deafness*. Oxford University Press.

Eckert, R. C., & Rowley, A. J. (2013). Audism: A theory and practice of audiocentric privilege. *Humanity & Society, 37*(2), 101–130. https://doi.org/10.1177/0160597613481731

Foster, S., & Kinuthia, W. (2003). Deaf persons of Asian American, Hispanic American, and African American backgrounds: A study of intraindividual diversity and identity. *Journal of Deaf Studies and Deaf Education, 8*(3), 271–290.

Frances, A. (2009). Whither DSM–V? *The British Journal of Psychiatry, 195*(5), 391–392. https://doi.org/10.1192/bjp.bp.109.073932

Frances, A., & Halon, R. (2013). The uses and misuses of the DSM in forensic settings. *Psychological Injury and Law, 6*, 336–344.

Fussell, G., Bianco, M., & Polkina, G. (2021). Fostering diversity, equity, and inclusion in online classes. In E. Langran & D. Rutledge (Eds.), *Proceedings of the SITE Interactive Conference* (pp. 15–19). Online. Association for the Advancement of Computing in Education. https://www.learntechlib.org/primary/p/220159/

Gano-Overway, L. (2021). Recognizing and expanding our commitment to diversity, equity, and inclusion. *Women in Sport and Physical Activity Journal, 29*(2), 83–86.

Gebhard, A., McLean, S., & St. Denis, V. (2022). *White benevolence : racism and colonial violence in the helping professions*. Fernwood Publishing.

Gibbon, S., & Doyle, C. (2011). The development and future of deaf forensic mental health services. *The British Journal of Forensic Practice, 13*(3), 191–196.

Glickman, N. S. (2009). *Cognitive-behavioral therapy for deaf and hearing persons with language and learning challenges*. Routledge.

Glickman, N. S. (2022). Book review: Deaf people in the criminal justice system: Selected topics on advocacy, incarceration, and social justice. *JADARA, 54*(3), 38.

Glickman, N. S., & Crump, C. (2013). Sign language dysfluency in some deaf persons: Implications for interpreters and clinicians working in mental health settings. In N. S. Glickman (Ed.), *Deaf mental health care* (pp. 125–155). Routledge

Glickman, N. S., Crump, C., & Hamerdinger, S. (2020). Language deprivation is a game changer for the clinical specialty of deaf mental health. *JADARA, 54*(1), 54.

Glickman, N. S., & Hall, W. C. (2019). *Language deprivation and deaf mental health*. Routledge/Taylor & Francis Group.

Glickman, N. S., & Harvey, M. A. (2013). *Culturally affirmative psychotherapy with deaf persons*. Routledge.

Glickman, N. S., Lemere, S., & Smith, C. M. (2013). Engaging deaf persons with language and learning challenges and sexual offending behaviors in sex offender-oriented mental health treatment. *JADARA, 47*(2).

Glickman, N. S., & Pollard Jr, R. Q. (2013). Deaf mental health research: Where we've been and where we hope to go. In N. S. Glickman (Ed.), *Deaf mental health care* (pp. 376–405). Routledge

Goldin-Meadow, S. (2012). Homesign: Gesture to language. In R. Pfau, M. Steinbach, & B. Woll (Eds.), *Sign language: An international handbook* (pp. 601–625). De Gruyter Mouton.

Gulati, S. (2018). Language deprivation syndrome. In N. S. Glickman & W. C. Hall (Eds.), *Language deprivation and deaf mental health* (pp. 24–53). Routledge.

Guthmann, D., Lomas, G. I., Paris, D. G., & Martin, G. A. (2021). *Deaf people in the criminal justice system: Selected topics on advocacy, incarceration, and social justice.* Gallaudet University Press.

Hall, W. C., Levin, L. L., & Anderson, M. L. (2017). Language deprivation syndrome: A possible neurodevelopmental disorder with sociocultural origins. *Social Psychiatry and Psychiatric Epidemiology, 52*, 761–776.

Harry, B. (1986). Interview, diagnostic, and legal aspects in the forensic psychiatric assessments of deaf persons. *Journal of the American Academy of Psychiatry and the Law Online, 14*(2), 147–162.

Hassan, S., & Gordon, R. M. (2003). *Developmental disability, crime, and criminal justice: A literature review.* Occasional Paper 01. Criminology Research Centre, Simon Fraser University. http://www.sfu.ca/crc/papers/hassangordon.pdf

James, M., & Woll, B. (2000). *Black deaf or deaf black.* [Unpublished doctoral dissertation]. City University, London.

Jimerson, S. R., Arora, P., Blake, J. J., Canivez, G. L., Espelage, D. L., Gonzalez, J. E., Graves, S. L., Huang, F. L., January, S.-A. A., & Renshaw, T. L. (2021). *Advancing diversity, equity, and inclusion in school psychology: Be the change.* Taylor & Francis.

Kim, U., Yang, K.-S., & Hwang, K.-K. (2006). Contributions to indigenous and cultural psychology. In U. Kim, K.-S. Yang, & K. K. Hwang (Eds.), *Indigenous and cultural psychology* (pp. 3–25). Springer.

Ladd, P. (2003). *Understanding deaf culture: In search of deafhood.* Multilingual Matters.

Liell, G. C., Fisher, M. J., & Jones, L. F. (2022). *Challenging bias in forensic psychological assessment and testing: Theoretical and Practical approaches to working with diverse populations.* Taylor & Francis.

MacDougall, J. (2000). *Access to justice for deaf persons in Nunavut: Focus on signed languages.* Department of Justice Canada.

MacDougall, J. C. (2001). Access to justice for deaf Inuit in Nunavut: The role of "Inuit sign language." *Canadian Psychology/Psychologie canadienne, 42*(1), 61–73. https://doi.org/10.1037/h0086880

MacDougall, J. C. (2022). Dialogue with the deaf: The future role of psychology. *Canadian Psychology/Psychologie canadienne, 63*(4), 637–650. https://doi.org/10.1037/cap0000341

MacDougall, J. C., Paterson, A.K. (1994, Janvier 18). Une personne incapable de communiquer peut-elle subir un process equitable? *La Presse.*

MacDougall, J. P. (2013). *Being deaf in a Yucatec Maya community: Communication and identity negotiation.* [Doctoral dissertation, McGill University]. escholarship@McGill. https://escholarship.mcgill.ca/concern/theses/qn59q786f

MacDougall, J. P. (2015). Deafness and sign language in a Yucatec Maya community: Emergent ethnographic practice. *Annals of Anthropological Practice, 39*(2), 150–175. https://doi.org/10.1111/napa.12077

Marschark, M. (2005). *Sign language interpreting and interpreter education: Directions for research and practice.* Oxford University Press.

Mayberry, R. I., & Kluender, R. (2018). Rethinking the critical period for language: New insights into an old question from American Sign Language. *Bilingualism: Language and Cognition, 21*(5), 886–905.

Mayberry, R. I., & Lock, E. (2003). Age constraints on first versus second language acquisition: Evidence for linguistic plasticity and epigenesis. *Brain and Language, 87*(3), 369–384.

Miller, K. R. (2001). *Forensic issues of deaf offenders.* Lamar University-Beaumont.

Miller, K. R. (2004). Linguistic diversity in a deaf prison population: Implications for due process. *Journal of Deaf Studies and Deaf Education, 9*(1), 112–119.

Miller, K. R., Vernon, M., & Capella, M. E. (2005). Violent offenders in a deaf prison population. *Journal of Deaf Studies and Deaf Education, 10*(4), 417–425.

Moers, P. W. (2017). From the world's trouble spots they arrive in our classrooms: Working with deaf refugees and immigrants. *Odyssey: New Directions in Deaf Education, 18*, 44–49.

Morford, J. P., & Goldin-Meadow, S. (1997). From here and now to there and then: the development of displaced reference in homesign and English. *Child Development, 68*(3), 420–435.

Myers, C., Clark, M. D., Musyoka, M. M., Anderson, M. L., Gilbert, G. L., Agyen, S., & Hauser, P. C. (2010). Black deaf individuals' reading skills: Influence of ASL, culture, family characteristics, reading experience, and education. *American Annals of the Deaf, 155*(4), 449–457.

Nonaka, A. M. (2014). (Almost) everyone here spoke Ban Khor Sign Language—Until they started using TSL: Language shift and endangerment of a Thai village sign language. *Language & Communication, 38*, 54–72.

O'Rourke, S., Glickman, N. S., & Austen, S. (2013). Deaf people in the criminal justice system: Is a culturally affirmative response possible or desirable? In N. S. Glickman (Ed.), *Deaf Mental Health Care* (pp. 341–375). Routledge.

O'Rourke, S., & Grewer, G. (2005). Assessment of Deaf people in forensic mental health settings: A risky business! *Journal of Forensic Psychiatry & Psychology, 16*(4), 671–684.

Olsen, T., & Kermit, P. (2015). Sign language, translation and rule of law—Deaf people's experiences from encounters with the Norwegian criminal justice system. *Scandinavian Journal of Disability Research, 17*(1), 23–41. https://doi.org/10.1080/15017419.2014.972448

Onyeador, I. N., Daumeyer, N. M., Rucker, J. M., Duker, A., Kraus, M. W., & Richeson, J. A. (2021). Disrupting beliefs in racial progress: Reminders of persistent racism alter perceptions of past, but not current, racial economic equality. *Personality and Social Psychology Bulletin, 47*(5), 753–765. https://doi.org/10.1177/0146167220942625

Parisot, A.-M., Rinfret, J., Villeneuve, S., & Voghel, A. (2015). Quebec Sign Language. In J. Bakken Jepsen, G. De Clerck, S. Lutalo-Kiingi, and W. B. McGregor (Eds.), *Sign languages of the world: A comparative handbook*, 701–728. De Gruyter Mouton.

Pavlenko, A., & Blackledge, A. (2004). *Negotiation of identities in multilingual contexts* (Vol. 45). Multilingual Matters.

Perdacher, E., Kavanagh, D., & Sheffield, J. (2019). Well-being and mental health interventions for Indigenous people in prison: systematic review. *BJPsych Open, 5*(6). https://doi.org/10.1192/bjo.2019.80

Perlin, D. (2019). Indigenous people and the criminal justice system: A practitioner's handbook. *Canadian Law Library Review, 44*, 22.

Pizzo, L., & Chilvers, A. (2016). Assessment and d/deaf and hard of hearing multilingual learners: considerations and promising practices. *American Annals of the Deaf, 161*(1), 56–66.

Pollard Jr., R. Q., & Berlinski, B. T. (2017). Forensic evaluation of deaf individuals: Challenges and strategies. *Journal of Social Work in Disability & Rehabilitation, 16*(3–4), 261–275.

Pollard, R. Q., & Fox, M. L. (2018). Forensic evaluation of deaf adults with language deprivation. In N. S. Glickman & W. C. Hall (Eds.), *Language deprivation and deaf mental health* (pp. 101–135). Routledge.

Pollock, S. (2021). *APA publishing's equity, diversity, and inclusion toolkit for journal editors.* APA. https://www.apa.org/pubs/authors/equity-diversity-inclusion-toolkit-journal-editors.pdf

Ramos, G., Ponting, C., Labao, J. P., & Sobowale, K. (2021). Considerations of diversity, equity, and inclusion in mental health apps: A scoping review of evaluation frameworks. *Behaviour Research and Therapy*, 103990.

Rissman, L., Horton, L., Flaherty, M., Senghas, A., Coppola, M., Brentari, D., & Goldin-Meadow, S. (2020). The communicative importance of agent-backgrounding: Evidence from homesign and Nicaraguan Sign Language. *Cognition, 203*, 104332.

Rudin, J., Greenspan, B. H., & Rondinelli, V. (2022). *Indigenous people and the criminal justice system* (2nd ed.). Emond.

Russell, D., Chovaz, D. C., Psych, D. C., & Boudreault, P. (2018). *Administration of justice: The experiences of Deaf, DeafBlind, and Deaf people with additional disabilities*. Canadian Association of the Deaf. https://cad.ca/wp-content/uploads/2019/07/CAD-Report-Final-April-26-2018.pdf

Ryan, C., & Johnson, P. (2019). Understanding language deprivation and its role in deaf mental health [Review of *Language Deprivation and Deaf Mental Health* by Neil S. Glickman & Wyatte C. Hall]. *American Annals of the Deaf, 164*(4), 519–522.

Schuit, J. (2012). Signing in the Arctic: External influences on Inuit Sign Language. In Z. Ulrike & V. Connie de (Eds.), *Sign languages in village communities: Anthropological and linguistic insights* (pp. 181–208). De Gruyter Mouton.

Schwartz, M. A., & Elder, B. C. (2018). Deaf access to justice in Northern Ireland: rethinking 'Reasonable Adjustment' in the Disability Discrimination Act. *Disability & Society, 33*(7), 1003–1024. https://doi.org/10.1080/09687599.2018.1478801

Vernon, M., & Miller, K. (2005). Obstacles faced by deaf people in the criminal justice system. *Am Ann Deaf, 150*(3), 283–291.

Vernon, M., Raifman, L. J., Greenberg, S. F., & Monteiro, B. (2001). Forensic pretrial police interviews of deaf suspects avoiding legal pitfalls. *International Journal of Law & Psychiatry, 24*(1), 45–59.

Vernon, M., Steinberg, A. G., & Montoya, L. A. (1999). Deaf murderers: Clinical and forensic issues. *Behavioral Sciences & the Law, 17*(4), 495–516.

Wang, Q., Andrews, J., Liu, H. T., & Liu, C. J. (2016). Case studies of multilingual/multicultural Asian Deaf adults: Strategies for success. *American Annals of the Deaf, 161*(1), 67–88.

Wattman, J. (2018). Interpreting for deaf people with dysfluent language in forensic settings: Application of the Integrated model of interpreting. In Neil S. Glickman & Wyatte C. Hall (Eds.), *Language deprivation and deaf mental health* (pp. 210–234). Routledge.

Wills, C. D., & Gold, L. H. (2014). Introduction to the special section on DSM-5 and forensic psychiatry. *Journal of the American Academy of Psychiatry and the Law Online, 42*(2), 132–135. https://jaapl.org/content/jaapl/42/2/132.full.pdf

Witkin, G. A. (2015). Clustering in lexical fluency tasks among deaf adults [Dissertation abstract]. *Dissertation Abstracts International: Section B: The Sciences and Engineering, 76*(2–B(E)).

Wortzel, H. S. (2013). The DSM-5 and forensic psychiatry. *Journal of Psychiatric Practice, 19*(3), 238–241. https://doi.org/10.1097/01.pra.0000430508.44768.9d

Young, A., Howarth, P., Ridgeway, S., & Monteiro, B. (2001). Forensic referrals to the three specialist psychiatric units for deaf people in the UK. *Journal of Forensic Psychiatry, 12*(1), 19–35.

Young, A., Monteiro, B., & Ridgeway, S. (2000). Deaf people with mental health needs in the criminal justice system: A review of the UK literature. *The Journal of Forensic Psychiatry, 11*(3), 556–570.

Zaidman-Zait, A., Curle, D., Jamieson, J. R., Chia, R., & Kozak, F. K. (2017). Health-related quality of life among young children with cochlear implants and developmental disabilities. *Ear and Hearing, 38*(4), 399–408.

Zeshan, U. (2010). Village sign languages: A commentary. In G. Mathur & D. J. Napoli (Eds.), *Deaf around the world: The impact of language* (pp. 221–230). Oxford University Press.

Zidenberg, A. M., Rine, S. S., & Olver, M. (2021). Correctional and forensic contexts of d/Deaf persons: implications for assessment and treatment. *Journal of Offender Rehabilitation, 60*(6), 375–394.

11

Palliative and End-of-Life Care of Deaf and Hard of Hearing Adults

Victor Maddalena and Myles K. Murphy

I was born deaf. Sound never existed in my life, and this is completely normal to me.

—*Nyle DiMarco*

Construct

In this chapter, we explore the challenges d/Deaf[1] people experience when accessing palliative, end-of-life care and bereavement care. Specifically, we discuss palliative care, accessing palliative care services, communications issues with health professionals including interpreter services, the role of family and community caregivers, symptom management, the physical environment in palliative care settings, and bereavement services. The audience for this chapter is clinicians and d/Deaf people and family members who are facing terminal illness and end of life.

Head-to-Head and Heart to Heart

The experiences of Deaf people at end of life remains a relatively unexplored area of research and yet, every Deaf person will experience death as a natural event. The power of research to bring to light issues, "giving voice" to Deaf people, is important to foster a dialogue among clinicians and family members. The challenge remains to bring lived experience to research and theory to practice. We begin by sharing the results of research we conducted in 2012 that examined palliative and end-of-life care in Newfoundland's Deaf community. We also present an illustrative case study that highlights some of the challenges d/Deaf people and their families face when accessing palliative care services.

Special thanks to the Newfoundland and Labrador Association of the Deaf for their support. The original research project (Maddalena et al., 2012) was funded by the Newfoundland and Labrador Centre for Health Research.

1. For literary ease, we use the term *d/Deaf* to encompass Deaf (as a cultural community), deaf and deafened (medical loss of hearing), and hard of hearing populations. The use of the capital "D" Deaf is a cultural designation. Small "d" deaf is a medical term referring to individuals with varying degrees of hearing loss and who do not necessarily identify with the Deaf community (CAD, 2015a).

Statements of Reflexivity

First Author: Victor Maddalena

My relationship with the Deaf community began in the early 1980s when I started learning sign language. A few very kind Deaf people took me under their wing and taught me sign language, and through these relationships, I learned about the vibrancy and diversity of the Deaf community and the richness of Deaf culture. I also learned about the day-to-day challenges and struggles faced by many Deaf people, especially when accessing health services. Over time and through my clinical nursing practice and academic research experience, I became interested in how vulnerable populations access health services. How vulnerable populations access health services has become the central theme of my academic research.

Second Author: Myles K. Murphy

Deafness is an integral part of my identity. I have spent my life living and working among the Deaf, and I have a deep respect and admiration for the diversity and resilience of the Deaf community. I have devoted much of my life to various leadership roles at the provincial and national level, advocating and promoting Deaf interests and Deaf culture. I have also been active in educating the public and interpreters in our beautiful sign language, a defining feature of our culture as Deaf people. It is how we communicate and how we identify as Deaf people. Participating in research has been a very rewarding experience. It is one way we, as Deaf people, can contribute to generating knowledge that can influence policy and improve the lives of Deaf people.

Recommendations

We conclude the chapter with recommendations for how the health system can better meet the needs of d/Deaf people and their families at end of life. Specifically, we explore strategies for improving end-of-life care for d/Deaf people and their families as well as professional providers of care. We also present an agenda for future research and how researchers can engage the d/Deaf community to identify research priorities and work toward policy change.

There is a very limited literature examining palliative and end-of-life care issues in the d/Deaf community. Indeed, in 2012, when we did our research project examining palliative and end-of-life care in Newfoundland's Deaf community, we were surprised to find our study was the first empirical research of its kind to examine the issue in any depth (Maddalena et al., 2012). As we started writing this chapter—12 years after we launched our initial study—we were surprised to find there was still a very limited literature exploring palliative and end-of-life care issues in the d/Deaf community. This is disappointing, considering d/Deaf people face more challenges than non-d/Deaf people at end of life and are more vulnerable to adverse health outcomes (Flaskerud & Winslow, 1998).

In 2012, we conducted a qualitative, participatory study examining the end-of-life experiences of Deaf people in Newfoundland. In this study, we interviewed seven participants (four men and three women), ranging in age from 40 to 65. We explored their experiences with death, dying, and accessing health services at end of life (Maddalena et al., 2012). We will refer to our findings from this study through this chapter, but it is worthwhile noting some of the highlights from the study:

- "Communication is a central feature of any effective care-provider/patient relationship. Paramount among our findings is that our participants felt that healthcare professionals must take into consideration the fact that Deaf patients and their Deaf caregivers communicate through sign language. This means that the services of trained American Sign Language (ASL) interpreters are needed in healthcare settings, as are other forms of visual communication; however, it is difficult to access ASL interpreters in non-urban settings, at night and on weekends. Moreover, health professionals must recognize that Deaf people have varying levels of ASL fluency, and thus a personalized approach to communication is needed." (Maddalena et al., 2012, p.110)
- "Many Deaf people live in isolation, separate from the hearing community. Thus, another study finding was that study participants had limited knowledge of the services, treatment, and symptom management options, and options for location of death (at home or in hospital) available to them; this, too, could have an adverse impact on the end-of-life journey of terminally ill Deaf people. Also, Deaf caregivers and family members lack appropriate access to bereavement support after the death of a loved one." (Maddalena et al., 2012, p. 110)

Kehl and Gartner (2010) conducted a qualitative study using a "death history" format with a key informant who was Deaf. They examined the challenges faced by one Deaf person as he encountered the death of family members. The researchers identified communication difficulties between and among the Deaf person, their family members, and health professionals. They also identified communication difficulties, physical challenges, financial barriers associated with accessing interpreters, a lack of cultural competence among health providers, and challenges with decision-making as being prominent concerns.

The Deaf Community

The Deaf comprise a unique cultural and linguistic community with a rich history and traditions (Cohen, 1994; Padden & Humphries, 2006). Unlike many communities defined by geography and place of residence, religion, or cultural values, inclusion in Deaf culture is defined by hearing loss, social bonds, common beliefs, and the use of sign language as the principal means of communication (CAD, 2015a). Tennant and Gluszak Brown (2010) observed,

> The Deaf community is not bound by geographical borders; instead, people elect to become members of the Deaf community by using American Sign Language (ASL) as their preferred mode of communication and by accepting the cultural identity of Deaf people. (p. 9)

The use of sign language is central to identity and inclusion in Deaf culture, since the use of sign language displays a willingness to conform to the belief that sign language is "normal" for Deaf people and that sign language is the principal means by which cultural identity is transmitted among members (Harris, 1995; Stebnicki & Coeling, 1999; Stokoe, 2005). While there has been no credible census of Deaf, deafened, and hard of hearing people in Canada, the Canadian Association of the Deaf (CAD) estimates (with strong disclaimers) there are 357,000 culturally Deaf Canadians and 3.21 million hard of hearing Canadians (CAD, 2015b).

Harris, in her exposition, *The Cultural Meaning of Deafness* (1995), highlights several distinguishing features that contribute to Deafness as a cultural identification. First, Deaf people view their Deafness as a constructive affirmation of their identity (as opposed to a disability), and the use of sign language is a unique characteristic of how Deaf people communicate with each other. This sets Deaf people apart from hearing people in a special way. This positive sense of identity is expressed when, for example, Deaf people do not experience regret when their children are born Deaf. Second, Harris (1995) identifies their shared experience of oppression and discrimination as embodied within the act of signing. She stated,

> The logic of this statement is that all signing Deaf people know that Deaf people face oppression and discrimination in contact situations with hearing people—therefore anyone seen signing must be similarly subject to the same forces of oppression and discrimination. (p. 167)

Many Deaf people experience discrimination and, in some cases, exploitation, violence, and exclusion from the benefits of mainstream society. As a result, interacting with institutions can be intimidating—even when accompanied by an interpreter—and these experiences often result in a weariness or mistrust of hearing people. All these features combine to create a strong sense of community and a strong reliance and identification with Deaf culture (Christensen & Delgado, 2000; Leigh & O'Brien, 2019; Stebnicki & Coeling, 1999; Padden & Humphries, 2006; Pollard & Listman, 2019; Malebranche et al., 2020).

Deaf people communicate using one of a variety of signed languages, the most common of which in North America is ASL or the French version, Langue des Signes du Québécois (LSQ). Allen and colleagues (2002) define ASL as, "... a nonlinear language using space, facial expressions and hand and body movements, fully exploiting the capacities of vision, spatial relations and visual-kinetic memory for storing and processing concurrent layers of information" (p. 200). ASL and LSQ are visual, gestural languages that make use of the individual's hands and facial and body movements to communicate ideas or concepts (Tennant & Gluszak Brown, 2010). There is a common misperception that ASL is merely a form of signed English. ASL must be interpreted (as opposed to translated) into English. ASL is its own language, with syntax and regional dialects. There are different versions of signed languages in countries around the world.

Hard of Hearing

The Canadian Hard of Hearing Association states that hearing loss ". . . is one of the fastest-growing health crises in Canada. Published in 2016, the Canadian Health Measures Survey (CHMS) found that 19% of Canadians experience a significant hearing loss that interferes with their ability to hear speech."[2]

---

2. Source: https://chha.ca/hearing-loss-101/ (Accessed October 6, 2025).

The causes of hearing loss are varied, including, for example, aging, prolonged exposure to loud noise, accident, illness, exposure to ototoxic drugs/chemicals, or genetics (Cunningham & Tucci, 2017). Cunningham and Tucci (2017) stated,

> The primary effect of adult hearing loss is impaired communication, which can adversely affect relationships with family and friends and create difficulties in the workplace. Untreated hearing loss in adults also has indirect health, psychosocial, and economic effects and leads to social isolation and a reduced quality of life. (p. 2465)

Hearing loss can vary from mild to profound, and strategies to address hearing loss should begin with an assessment of the type of hearing loss and determining whether it is conductive, sensorineural, or mixed. Most individuals with hearing loss still have the capacity to speak, and this aids in communication with health professionals. Their hearing deficit, however, must be carefully assessed and remedied with hearing aids, writing, or various forms of visual communication (Smith et al., 2015).

Effective communication is essential for providing quality health care. Elderly people or people with hearing loss should have their hearing status assessed on admission and appropriate assistive technology provided to them to aid in communication. Caregivers should seek input from patients regarding their preferred means of communication and attend to sound-related concerns in the clinic environment, for example, addressing issues such as poor audio-quality telephone communication and lengthy message menus (Lezzoni et al., 2004). Healthcare settings, especially acute or special-care units, for example, emergency rooms or intensive care units, are very difficult listening environments, and background noise can disrupt communication (Blustein et al., 2018).

In short, being d/Deaf can have a detrimental effect on your health (Alexander et al., 2012).

Health Issues in the Deaf Community

It is widely acknowledged that the history and present-day circumstances for many d/Deaf people is characterized by social exclusion and discrimination (Barnett et al., 2011; Brick, 2006; Cohen, 1994; Harris, 1995; Malebranche et al., 2020). Limited access to the benefits of society, including education and employment opportunities and access to appropriate health services, can lead to poor health status (AAP, 2022; Raphael, 2016). There are some factors, primarily related to the broad determinants of health that adversely affect the health status of Deaf people in both the American and Canadian context. (Brick, 2006; Evans et al., 1994).

The population health literature on the health status of Deaf Americans documents a strong relationship between social exclusion, limited educational and employment opportunities, limited access to health services, and poor health status, similar to other minority groups (Humphries & van Doorslaer, 2000; Kuenburg et al., 2016, Malebranche, et al., 2020; Marchand et al., 1998; Memon et al., 2002). Similar circumstances exist for Deaf people in Canada. Research demonstrates a strong relationship between poor health status, limited access to health services, and low socioeconomic status in minority populations (Evans et. al., 1994, Ouellette, 2006). A number of studies also document the prevalence of mental health issues in the Deaf community (Du Feu & Chovaz, 2014; Fellinger et al., 2012; Vernon & Leigh, 2007).

Margellos-Anast and colleagues (2005) state, "The special communication and cultural needs of Deaf individuals may lead to significant gaps in their knowledge of health, healthy living and how to properly act in a patient role within the health care system" (p. 388).

Unique cultural features of the Deaf community can also serve as barriers to accessing and utilizing health services. As noted above, the principal institutional barrier that hinders access for Deaf people is the limited access to health practitioners fluent in ASL. This includes health professionals who are fluent in ASL as well as those having access to ASL interpreters (Olson & Swabey, 2017). In this regard, many health professionals have limited knowledge of Deaf culture and limited means of communicating effectively with Deaf patients (Hoang et al., 2011; Meador & Zazove, 2005). An additional institutional barrier is the lack of institutional or health-related information available in ASL or another visual format. Moreover, Margellos-Anast also found many Deaf people are unfamiliar with medical terminology and basic health information (Margellos-Anast et al., 2005).

> ... [F]ocus[ing] on improving health care and health promotion efforts in the deaf/HOH community depends on improving communication, health literacy, and patient empowerment and involves holding health care organizations accountable for assuring adequate staffing of ASL interpreters and communication resources in order to reduce health disparities in this population. (Hommes et al., 2018, p. 956)

There is a growing body of research examining health issues in the Deaf community. When compared to the mainstream population, Deaf people have lower levels of formal education (Barnett & Franks, 2002), lower levels of English literacy (Barnett et al., 2011; NLAD, 2007), lower levels of income and employment (Barnett et al., 2011; Barnett & Franks, 2002; NLAD, 2007), and lower levels of health literacy (McKee et al., 2015; Naseribooriabadi et al., 2017; Pollard & Barnett, 2009). Lesch and colleagues (2019) report that older adults who are Deaf self-rated as less healthy as mainstream populations and identified increased risk of obesity, suicidal ideation, and intimate partner violence. Alexander et al. (2012) found in the United Kingdom that health status among the Deaf is poor compared to the mainstream population and the result of a combination of factors, stating,

> People from the Deaf community are at risk of poorer health because of a combination of poor-quality education, three-fold higher unemployment than in hearing individuals, increased mental ill health, and decreased availability and accessibility of health information. This risk is compounded by poorer access to primary and secondary health-care provision. (p. 980)

On many measures, d/Deaf people experience more health concerns and are vulnerable to poor health outcomes. They have limited access to preventive and diagnostic services, and many conditions go undetected or are poorly managed, for example, hypertension or diabetes (Du Feu, 2017).

A large national survey of Canadians with hearing loss, including Deaf people, showed a "... different and in some cases less favourable health status compared with Canadians without hearing problems" (Woodcock & Pole, 2007, p. 2140). McKee (2013) found older people who are d/Deaf are at high risk of breakdowns in communications with health providers and highlight the need to carefully assess patient hearing status and communication needs. They stated,

> ... [F]amily physicians must be cognizant of patients' communication and language needs. These patients should be identified by an easy-to-recognize sign or flag in the medical record to remind physicians and staff members of the need for potential accommodations. Individuals with significant hearing loss are heterogeneous in their degree of hearing loss, language and communication needs, and perceptions of their disabilities. (p. 360)

Communication breakdowns can also lead to medication error and misunderstandings around preventive or followup care (Olson & Swabey, 2017).

Regarding health status and access to the health system, research has shown that Deaf people generally self-assess their health status as being lower than mainstream populations (Zazove et al., 1993), and they tend to use the health system less often than hearing people (especially those who are prelingually Deaf). When they do access health services, they experience communication difficulties, fear, and frustration (Abou-Abdallah & Lamyman, 2021, Steinberg et al., 2006; Barnett et al., 2011; Parise, 1999).

Also, the recent COVID-19 pandemic highlighted the impact of widespread public health crises on high-risk, vulnerable populations, including d/Deaf people. Communicating public health guidelines or educating the public on the importance of vaccines and public health restrictions requires special attention to how the d/Deaf receive and understand this information (Correia & Ferreira, 2022). Skøt and colleagues (2017) interviewed d/Deaf people following natural disasters or traumatic events and found

> ... significant gaps in the provision of medical and psychosocial services for D/HH *[d/Deaf]* individuals following disasters and individual traumatic experiences. The difficulties reported by participants when accessing services are all centered on communication barriers. When communication barriers are present it is highly likely that D/HH individuals won't receive all the information they require. Recent research suggests that information deprivation has the potential to detrimentally impact D/HH individuals with trauma experiences. (p. 2474)

Heart-to-Heart: Clara and John

Clara and John live in rural Newfoundland.[3] Both are Deaf. They have family who live nearby who are hearing. John works in a local print shop and Clara works part-time in the kitchen at the nursing home. Two years ago, Clara noticed some specks of blood in her stool. She dismissed it as being caused by something she ate. Her husband noticed she was losing weight and complaining of fatigue. John encouraged Clara to go to the doctor, but she refused ,saying her experience with going to doctors and accessing the healthcare system in the past had been frustrating and less than

3. Please note that this is a fictitious case study.

positive. One day when Clara was at work, she passed out and was taken to the hospital. She was transferred to a regional hospital where she was diagnosed with terminal colorectal cancer with metastases to her liver and lungs.

Nancy, Clara's older sister—who is not Deaf—stepped in and immediately assumed the role of decision-maker. John and Nancy attended meetings with the doctor. The physician spoke to Nancy and not John. John felt excluded from decision-making regarding Clara's care. Without an interpreter present, Nancy would provide John with an abbreviated summary of what was discussed after the conversation with the doctor concluded. Nancy knew some basic sign language. John was very upset the doctors were communicating with Clara's sister, Nancy, instead of him, but neither Clara nor John wanted to make a fuss because they were afraid it would affect the care Clara was receiving.

Within days of being admitted to the regional hospital, they stopped Clara's treatment and transferred her to the palliative care unit. John did not understand why she was being moved to another unit. He did not understand what "palliative care" meant for Clara. John and Clara's experience in hospital was not positive, indeed it was fraught with problems. Some problems they encountered included the following:

- There was no ASL interpreter in the local area, and when Clara's sister was not present, John had to rely on writing his concerns on paper when interacting with the nurses and doctors. John's English literacy level was low, and he had difficulty explaining what he wanted to say. Some of the nurses and doctors relied on lipreading. Misunderstandings were common.
- To enter the palliative care unit, one has to interact with an audio-only intercom system. John frequently had difficulty accessing the unit because he couldn't hear the voice of the nurse who asked questions.
- Clara was experiencing many symptoms from her advanced cancer, and she had difficulty expressing the character of her pain and other symptoms.
- John and Clara did not want to strongly advocate for what they wanted. They were afraid if they did express their views, it would influence the care Clara was receiving.
- John and Clara did not own a car and traveling back and forth to the hospital was very difficult. John had to rely on friends and neighbors. Accommodation for John was also a problem. He often slept in a chair in Clara's room. While John's employer was understanding, John had to miss many days from his work, without pay. Their entire experience was a financial hardship.
- The lights in the hallway and Clara's room were very dim, and this made communicating in sign language very difficult.
- Clara did not want to die in the palliative care unit. She told John that she wanted to die in her own home. This was not raised with the doctors. They felt they did not have a choice in the matter.
- John did not know what to expect when Clara died. He was with her when she died, but he was confused about what her death would look like. He had never been with a dying person. In her final hours, John could not communicate with Clara because her eyes were closed. All he could do was hold her hand.
- When Clara died, John was grief-stricken. There was no grief support provided for John. He was provided with a brochure on grief support groups in his area. He didn't bother going because he knew he would feel out of place and there would be no ASL interpreter available. He went back home and tried to deal with his grief on his own. He felt very depressed and isolated.

Head-to-Head

John and Clara's experience with her terminal illness and death was very negative. There are many things that could have been done to improve Clara's end-of-life experience, including for example,

- Delays in attending to early warning signs of disease, for example, blood in stool can lead to poor health outcomes. Druel and colleagues (2018) found that colorectal cancer, prostate cancer, and melanoma tended to be diagnosed at a more advanced stage in the Deaf population than in the general population, and late diagnosis can lead to a poor prognosis. Many routine screening tests, such as a PAP test, a stool test for occult blood, and mammography are not well understood by many Deaf people. Tamaskar et al., (2000) found that Deaf people avoided seeking health care because of a lack of good communication and lack of interpreters.
- Efforts should have been made early in Clara's illness journey to secure a trained ASL interpreter so she could receive early diagnosis, treatment, and information regarding her disease, treatment options, and choice of place of death if warranted. If an interpreter could not be present locally, the use of assistive technology, for example, online ASL interpreter services, should have been employed (Maddalena et al., 2012).
- The use of family members for interpreter services is not ideal, unless the Deaf person requests it. Do not rely on lipreading and writing on paper for important decisions.
- Providing John and Clara with pre-printed cards with basic statements may have aided communication with the doctors and nurses when Clara was experiencing symptoms (e.g., "NAUSEA," "PAIN," "HUNGRY," "WATER," etc.).
- The principles of voluntary informed consent should always be followed. Decisions around treatment, palliation, and place of death should be discussed openly with the patient and her family. Clara, and ideally John, should have been involved in decisions regarding her treatment, palliative care, and place of death.
- Palliative care units need to be mindful of the physical environment when Deaf patients are admitted, including adequate lighting to facilitate communicating in sign language. (Maddalena et al., 2012). Social workers should have been involved to assist John, who did not have the means to travel. Patient care units that have locked access and intercoms should be aware that Deaf people may be unable to access the unit because they can't hear the speaker.
- When the palliative care unit knew they were admitting a Deaf patient, they should have reached out to a local Deaf association for assistance and guidance on how to meet Clara and John's needs.
- Grief therapy groups are typically designed for hearing people. While Deaf people may attend such services with an interpreter, they often feel out of place. Other arrangements for grief therapy should have been explored.
- If patient-centered care is the gold standard for care, then Clara and John's needs should have been assessed and addressed.

Death and Dying

It is axiomatic that every person alive today will experience death at some point. This is best captured by the quote attributed to Benjamin Franklin, one of the Founding Fathers of the United States, when he said, "The only two certainties in life are death and taxes" (Sparks, 1856, p. 410)

The trajectory toward death among individuals varies from long and slow to abrupt, and whether a "good death"[4] or a traumatic, stressful, painful one, the outcome remains the same. How people experience illness and death will vary considerably, and their experience will be shaped by a wide range of factors (some within their control and others outside of their control), including for example, cultural or spiritual perceptions of death, the cause of death, and demographic factors such as age, gender, sexual orientation, income, dis/ability status, family and social status, among others (Davies, 2005; Marchand et al., 1998; Memon et al., 2002). The social and economic determinants of health as well as the political and historical context and geographic location of their death also figure prominently in a person's experience with illness and death (Evans et al., 1994). This highlights the need to be mindful of the Deaf person's experience at end of life (Salladay & San Agustin, 1984).

Death is a biological function simply defined as, "a permanent cessation of all vital functions: the end of life,"[5] but death is more complex than the simple cessation of life. It occurs in a particular cultural, social, and historical context (Davies, 2005). Experience with death varies among individuals. Healthcare professionals deal with death, in some instances, on a daily basis; others less frequently. Some people or families have minimal or limited experience with death (Munro-Ludders, 1992). This is particularly true in the Deaf community.

> Study participants reported that they had limited experience with death. Many Deaf people feel isolated from the hearing community, and even from their own hearing family members. Participants described situations in which family members were terminally ill and expressed that they felt excluded from family discussions about diagnosis, prognosis, and treatment options. They felt marginalized in terms of family decision making; they were often left out of discussions between family members and health professionals. (Maddalena et al., 2012, p.108)

Many d/Deaf people, especially older generations, may have spent their formative years in residential education programs, and as a result, may have had limited exposure to death among family members. Munro-Ludders (1992) stated,

> The deaf child who resides throughout the school years in a residential program of a deaf school would, by the very nature and process of residential placements, become limited in their understandings of the day-to-day dealings of life at home. (p. 36)

---

4. According to a study by Field and Cassell (as cited in Gustafson, 2007) a "good death" is defined as one that is, ". . . free from avoidable death and suffering for patients, families and caregivers in general accordance with the patients' and families' wishes." The original source of the quote is Institute of Medicine (US) Committee on Care at the End of Life; M. J. Field & C. K. Cassell (Eds.), (1997). *Approaching death: Improving care at the end of life* (p. 1). National Academies Press. Available from https://www.ncbi.nlm.nih.gov/books/NBK233600/

5. https://www.merriam-webster.com/dictionary/death

Even when raised in hearing families, many Deaf children are sheltered from the experiences of home life.

> The deaf youngster in a family of non-signers may in fact only have an inkling, or perhaps no clue at all as to the rationale and significance behind all that is happening around him or her, such as the grieving and funerary events when Aunt Mary has "kicked the bucket," or when Daddy has "gone to Jesus." Thus, as it were, it would not be unlikely for the deaf child to wonder where the "bucket" is that Aunt Mary has kicked, or when will Daddy come back home after visiting Jesus? The issue is emotionally, developmentally, and educationally complex and often paradoxical. (Munro-Ludder, 1992, p. 37)

Our cultural experience of death has changed over time. My great-grandparents and their contemporaries in the late 1800s and early 1900s lived in rural, multigenerational, close-knit family units where the death of children under the age of 5 was not uncommon and the death of elderly family members typically occurred within the home.[6] Postdeath rituals such as wakes or vigils often occurred in the home as well. Our modern lives and everchanging family units brought about by changing social and cultural beliefs have changed how and where we experience terminal illness and death. End of life and death have become more institutionalized than in the past. Whereas at one time home deaths were common, now many deaths, including post-death funeral rituals, occur in institutionalized settings.

> Canada continues to have a hospital-centric care system for those who are dying, despite the preference of most individuals to die in their community and other home-like settings. In 2015, 58% of decedents in Canada were hospitalized more than once in their last year of life and 61% of Canadians died in hospital. (Hsu & Garner, 2020)

Historically, medical practice and how it cared for people with terminal and life-threatening illnesses and death evolved in the context of social and technological change, as well as changes in public policy and opinion. While care for the sick and dying has existed since humans walked on the earth, the creation of palliative care and hospices evolved out of a growing awareness of the need to provide comfort care to the dying. Milligan and Potts (2009) stated,

> The word palliative derives from the Latin *pallium*, meaning cloak or covering—reflected in the Middle Eastern blessing, "may you be wrapped in tenderness, you my brother, as in a cloak." The original

---

6. Aaron O'Neill states, ". . . one third of all children born in 1830 did not make it to their fifth birthday. Child mortality remained above 25 percent for the remainder of the nineteenth century, before falling at a much faster rate throughout the 1900s. By the year 2020, Canada's child mortality rate is expected to be just five deaths per thousand births" (Source: https://www.statista.com/statistics/1041751/canada-all-time-child-mortality-rate/#:~:text=Child%20mortality%20in%20Canada%2C%201830%2D2020&text=This%20means%20that%20one%20third,faster%20rate%20throughout%20the%201900s)

> meaning of the word "hospice" was not derived, as many assume, from "hospital," but was a term familiar to those on pilgrimages, meaning "a resting place for weary travellers." (pp. 5–6)

Palliative care was recognized as a medical specialty in 1987; however, the principals of palliative care have been in existence for centuries, and religious orders were often involved with care for the dying, first in homes and later in institutional settings (Milligan & Potts, 2009).

Palliative care is often a misunderstood term. Many associate being referred to a palliative care service as "the end is near," or care delivered before dying; however, this is not always the case. The World Health Organization (2020) defined palliative care as

> . . . an approach that improves the quality of life of patients (adults and children) and their families who are facing problems associated with life-threatening illness. It prevents and relieves suffering through the early identification, correct assessment and treatment of pain and other problems, whether physical, psychosocial or spiritual.[7]

In ASL, there is no single sign for palliative care. The way palliative care can be signed is "comfort care—person—close to dying." This captures the essence of what palliative care is, and what it does. If you Google any number of vulnerable social groups—and I use this term specifically for social groups, not individuals—for example, individuals who identify as 2SLGBTQI+,[8] people with disabilities, various cultural or ethnic groups, the elderly, children, immigrants, and refugees, among others, you will find a considerable literature examining how these groups experience end of life and palliative care. As noted earlier, the literature on the d/Deaf (and Deaf in particular), however, remains limited. It is important to remember as well that the d/Deaf community is very diverse, and many d/Deaf people identify with more than one social, gender group, religious, dis-ability, and cultural group, among others.

Communication

There are three basic categories of people with hearing loss that experience communication difficulties: (a) people with varying degrees of hearing loss (i.e., hard of hearing people), (b) deaf people who are able to speak and use various approaches to communicating (e.g., writing), and (c) Deaf people who rely primarily on the use of sign language for communication (Barnett, 2002).

For many Deaf people, ASL is their first language, and for many, English is considered their second language. Many people who were born Deaf have never heard spoken English, and therefore English literacy levels among Deaf people vary, depending on education, exposure to hearing culture, and family relationships. Generally, English literacy levels are lower than the mainstream population (NLAD, 2007). The Newfoundland and Labrador Association of the Deaf conducted a study in 2007 entitled, *Employment and Employability in the Deaf Community: An*

---

7. World Health Organization—*Palliative Care* (https://www.who.int/news-room/fact-sheets/detail/palliative-care).

8. Two-Spirit, lesbian, gay, bisexual, transgender, queer, intersex, and additional sexually and gender diverse people.

Employability Strategy for Deaf people within the Northeast Avalon Region. In this study, they commented on the use of English language among the Deaf, saying,

> The English language is considered a second language of the Deaf community in Newfoundland and Labrador. The majority of people who are Deaf do not easily understand spoken and written English. One of the primary causes of this difficulty with English literacy is that English is a language that Deaf people have not heard or have heard only in a limited way. (NLAD, 2007, p. 18)

The English language uses many idioms, metaphors, slang, and common expressions in day-to-day conversations that are not well understood by Deaf people, thus highlighting the need for an ASL interpreter or Deaf interpreter (DI) to facilitate effective communication between the d/Deaf person and health professionals (Kuenberg et al., 2016). Also, in the healthcare setting, the use of medical terminology can present challenges for hearing and d/Deaf people alike.

For those who are hard of hearing, it may be helpful to use written English to communicate, assuming visual and manual dexterity are not impeded, since English is likely to be their primary language, particularly for those who communicate orally. However, in the case of communicating health education materials, health professionals should carefully assess literacy skills because literacy levels in the general population tend to be low (Jamieson, 2006) and lower in the d/Deaf community (NLAD, 2007).

It is often assumed that someone who is d/Deaf can lipread. However, it is generally understood among Deaf people that lipreading is not a reliable form of communication. Many Deaf people can lipread to a limited extent for common conversational topics; however, it is not a reliable form of communication to use when discussing complex matters related to health, illness, treatment options, and making serious decisions, among others. It is not uncommon for Deaf people, when in conversation with a nonsigning, hearing person, to nod their heads in agreement when spoken to, even though they may not fully understand what is being said (Kritzinger, et al., 2013). It is often easier for them to agree than it is to struggle to find a common way to communicate. Relying on lipreading in clinical settings can lead to poor health outcomes (Maddalena et al., 2012).

Health literacy is an important concept when communicating with patients (Sørensen et al., 2015). The emphasis is not only on effective communication but also taking into consideration how the patient and their families understand what is being communicated. Naseribooriabadi and colleagues (2017) define health literacy as, ". . . the knowledge, motivation, and a set of abilities required to access, understand, process, evaluate, and use health information to make judgments regarded to three-fold health domains as health care, dis-ease prevention, and health promotion" (p. 1465).

In their review of research related to health literacy in the d/Deaf population, Malebranche et al. (2020) found it was clear that many d/Deaf individuals had low levels of health literacy primarily due to a lack of tailored information on health matters and limited access to mass media health information due to communication and language barriers. For this reason, it is important for health professionals to assess the health literacy of their d/Deaf patients and tailor communication appropriately (Naseribooriabadi et al., 2017). In a similar vein, it is important, therefore, to develop training on Deaf culture for health professionals and training for health educators to help them develop health education that is culturally appropriate for Deaf people (Hoang, 2011).

Interpreter Services

The ASL interpreter and the DI play an important role in bridging the gap between the hearing and Deaf person. A DI is defined as,

> . . . a specialist who provides interpreting services in American Sign Language, langues des signes québécoise (LSQ), and other visual and tactual communication forms used by individuals who are Deaf, hard of hearing, and deafblind. As a Deaf person, the Deaf Interpreter starts with a distinct set of formative linguistic, cultural, and life experiences that enables nuanced comprehension and interaction in a wide range of visual language and communication forms influenced by region, culture, age, literacy, education, class, and physical, cognitive, and mental health. These experiences coupled with professional training give the Deaf interpreter the ability to effect successful communication across all types of interpreted interactions, both routine and high risk (Canadian Hearing Services, 2023)

The role of the ASL interpreter or DI is dynamic and complex, involving many assessment, adaptive, and perceptual skills, including, ". . . demonstrating cultural adaptability, situation assessment, solving problems creatively, language and interpreting, and managing the discourse" (Olson & Swabey, 2017, p. 195).

The availability of interpreter services is an important consideration for the Deaf patient when accessing culturally appropriate health services. Indeed, effective communication is central to the patient–provider interaction, and a lack of interpreter services can jeopardize the Deaf patient's well-being. Olson and Swabey (2017) state, "The lack of consistent provision of quality interpreting for deaf patients is a communication barrier adversely affecting healthcare treatment and outcomes for deaf Americans" (p. 192).

There is a dearth of healthcare providers who are fluent in ASL; therefore, there is a need to engage the services of an ASL interpreter in patient encounters (Hommes et al., 2018). In larger urban settings, it is usually possible to secure the services of an ASL interpreter. The more rural and remote areas present challenges when trying to obtain the services of a trained ASL interpreter, especially on evenings or weekends. Some Deaf people may choose to rely on family members or close friends to provide interpreter services, though this is not optimal, given that family members or friends can be biased in their understanding of the Deaf person's intentions (Barnett, 2002). In some instances, for example, when a Deaf person's ASL fluency is low or in special circumstances, it may be preferable to employ the services of a DI.

As noted above, Deaf people's encounters with the healthcare system are often characterized by frustration and anxiety. The reasons for this are numerous and primarily related to communication difficulties, limited health literacy, and health professionals' limited understanding of Deaf culture and the challenges Deaf people encounter (Hoang, et al., 2011; Lezzoni et al., 2004).

Health organizations are busy, chaotic places with accepted codes of conduct, behaviors, and norms. Deaf people may have limited exposure to illness and death and thus may not be familiar or comfortable with the norms associated with health institutions or services. Deaf people are often very sensitive to not offend others and can be timid in terms of being assertive and asking questions. In situations where a health professional understands sign language, the communication between care provider and patient or caregiver is greatly enhanced. In most cases, however, a trained ASL interpreter or DI is preferable and will lead to a more effective patient–provider interaction (Barnett, 2002; Hoang, et al., 2011; Lezzoni et al., 2004; Maddalena et al., 2012).

Managing Symptoms

Assessing pain in the hearing population is challenging because pain is a uniquely subjective experience. Wideman et al. (2019) stated,

> Pain is an enigmatic phenomenon that is challenging to treat and study. One challenging attribute is its subjective nature. Pain is defined as a subjective experience, which means that it cannot be directly observed by those who are not experiencing it. Yet, clinicians and researchers rely upon observations and measures to assess and infer the pain experienced by other people. (p. 212)

One of the issues that was raised by participants in our study (Maddalena et al., 2012) was that the expression of pain and symptom management was a concern. One participant stated,

> Common descriptors of pain—such as "stabbing," "throbbing," "dull," or "sharp"—are not helpful, as Deaf people do not typically characterize pain in this manner. It is easier for them to communicate the intensity and location of their pain (Maddalena et al., 2012, p. 109).

As one Deaf participant explained,

> Deaf have a really hard time explaining what kind of pain they have . . . for example, stabbing—they ask if it's a stabbing pain, and the Deaf person is, like, "Stabbing?" Pain doesn't look like stabbing. It doesn't look like pinching. It's really hard to get a Deaf person to explain the feeling for the word (Maddalena et al., 2012, p. 109).

Assessing someone's pain when they are unable to communicate is particularly challenging. As noted above, the Deaf have a particularly hard time describing the quality of their pain. Identifying the location of their pain and intensity is relatively easy. Even ASL interpreters note the challenges in communicating pain (Lefort et al., 2014). In sign language, there is one sign for pain, and additional descriptors are added to describe location, intensity, and character.

There is a very limited literature specifically examining the assessment of pain in the Deaf population (Palese et al., 2011). ASL is a visual language, therefore, common descriptors of the intensity and quality of pain lean toward visual descriptions rather than expressions of how the pain feels. As an outcome of our 2012 palliative care study, the researchers identified the need to development effective pain assessment and management tools specifically for Deaf people.

One study in Italy examined the use of one-dimensional pain scales to assess pain for Deaf people (Palese, et al., 2011). The principal aim of this study was to explore the preferred pain evaluation scale and method of administration when evaluating Deaf patients' pain. In this study, four one-dimensional pain scales were identified as ones they used in practice with Deaf clients:

- Numerical Pain Rating Scale (NRS): Usually a horizontal 0 to 10 rank order scale with 0 being "no pain" and 10 being the "worst pain."
- Visual Analogue Scale (VAS): Usually a 10 cm horizontal line with two anchors that delineates "no pain" and "worst imaginable pain."

- Faces Pain Scale (FPS): Originally developed as pediatric pain scale, it depicts six faces that progress from a "smiley" face, meaning "no hurt," to a tearful face with a downturned, frowning mouth, meaning "hurt worst."
- Iowa Pain Thermometer (IPT): Consists of seven pain descriptors for different levels of pain ("no pain" to "most intense pain imaginable") that are aligned with a vertical pain thermometer.

In this study, participants preferred the IPT scale for its simplicity of concept and its vertical orientation. They found the horizontal orientation of the NRS and VAS to be confusing, and participants reported that they did not understand the relationship between the FPS faces and pain. Participants noted that measuring pain using a one-dimensional measure of intensity is not enough, and other characteristics of the pain experience are also important.

In a review article, Allen et al. (2002) focused mainly on end-of-life care for Deaf seniors, examining key challenges that researchers and clinicians may face when working with Deaf patients/individuals, including the assessment of pain. As noted earlier, ASL is described as a nonlinear language which uses space, facial expressions, and hand and body movements. The authors highlighted how facial expressions convey meaning without which assessing pain would be difficult. For example, although there is a sign for pain, facial expressions can also convey the intensity and variations of pain. The location where the sign is made often denotes the location of the pain.

Allen et al. (2002) discussed two one-dimensional pain assessment scales that were also studied in the Palese et al. (2011) paper: the FPS and the NRS. They noted that the use of raised and lowered eyebrows in the faces depicted in the FPS have no linguistic association with ASL. Rather, the FPS facial expressions are components of ASL signs for happy, glad, surprised, etc., which may explain the confusion about meaning. The NRS uses ranked numbers along a horizontal continuum (often 0 to 5 or 0 to 10), with 0 as "no pain" and the highest number as "worst pain." The authors again note how ASL is nonlinear language and consequently "the spatial importance of the scalar zero point and end points must be explained to Deaf persons if a horizontal scale is used" (p. 201). The authors noted that their previous research indicated that vertical scales may be more easily understood by the Deaf population.

Bhalotra and Kakkar (2017) highlighted the importance of conducting a proper assessment of the patient's ability to communicate and involving an interpreter where possible. They stated,

> A language specialist [interpreter] can help to elicit an optimum history, assist with the preoperative evaluation, explain the importance of, and techniques associated with, postoperative interventions (e.g., the use of deep breathing exercises and lung expansion maneuvers by incentive spirometry), and train the patient to quantify postoperative pain by explaining simple pain scoring systems like the visual analog scale. (p. 654)

They go on to state the importance of postoperative management of pain and symptoms, highlighting the potential for serious negative consequences of poorly managed pain.

> This can cause increases in heart rate and blood pressure; delayed gastric emptying leading to nausea, vomiting, and paralytic ileus; and hyperglycemia with delayed wound healing. Failure to cough and take deep breaths predisposes to the development of chest infections, while movement restriction

> and hypercoagulability predispose to deep vein thrombosis. These factors further result in delayed mobilization and prolonged hospitalization and have financial implications. Pain and separation from family members may precipitate confusion, fear, and postoperative psychosis. (p. 654)

In summary, there is limited research in the area of pain assessment in the Deaf population. Palese et al. (2011) and others suggest this is because Deaf persons are excluded from studies of reliability and validity of pain measurement tools, even though a great deal of work has been done with various other cultural linguistic groups and populations to validate these tools. The challenge of assessing pain experienced by Deaf people is compounded by the need for ASL interpreters (if they are available).

While the study by Maddalena et al. (2012) identified pain assessment and management as an important issue for Deaf people in the palliative care setting at end of life, it is worth noting that the issue of assessing pain has broader implications as Deaf people seek routine health services for other ailments, including, for example, cardiac pain, acute abdominal pain, or headaches among others.

From the perspective of the health professional—and the Deaf person—it is important to have access to tools to assist with the assessment of pain, since pain is often one of the symptoms that brings people to seek medical care. This has particular importance for health professionals who encounter Deaf people in the clinical setting. Assessing the character, intensity, and duration of pain are all important considerations when assessing pain, developing a treatment plan, and monitoring its effectiveness.

Caregivers: Family and Community

For many Deaf people, the concept of family extends beyond biological family member and includes close friends and other Deaf community members. The Deaf community typically is a close-knit social network where individual members rely on each other and provide support to each other, especially in times of difficulty. When facing terminal illness and end of life, it is not unusual to find caregivers who are close friends and community members (Maddalena et al., 2012). Being attentive to the physical environment at end of life is important for d/Deaf patients and their families. Kehl and Gartner (2010) stated,

> Attention to details, such as maximizing mobility of the hands and obtaining competent interpreters when direct communication is no longer possible or when communicating with a Deaf family, will help ensure that Deaf people and their families can receive the very best care at the end of their lives. (p. 92)

Ensuring access to space where there is good lighting can also facilitate participation of family members being involved in their care.

Recommendations

- If a Deaf patient has been admitted to a palliative care unit or is receiving home palliative care services, seek assistance from a local Deaf association to receive education on how to best attend to the needs of a Deaf person and their family.

- Effective communication with the patient and their family is very important. This will typically involve the services of a trained ASL interpreter or DI. If there are no ASL interpreters available, then alternatives such as video ASL interpreting services should be explored (Du Feu, 2017; Ebert & Heckerling, 1995; Maddalena et al. 2012; McEwan & Anton-Culver, 1988). Relying on family members for interpreting is also not optimal, unless the Deaf person specifically expresses a preference for a family member.
- Lipreading or writing notes are not effective means of communication with a Deaf person and are not a reliable alternative to the services of a trained ASL interpreter.
- Voluntary and informed consent is the foundation upon which an effective patient–provider relationship should be established. Communication with a Deaf person about the nature of their illness, prognosis, treatment options, and options for home or hospital death are important.
- Health professionals need to determine the health literacy level of both the patient and their family and communicate information using the most effective and appropriate methods means of communication (Naseribooriabadi et al., 2017; Zazove, 1993)
- When a d/Deaf patient is admitted to a palliative care service, clearly identify the personnel who will be involved in their care and seek consistency in care providers. (Maddalena et al, 2012)
- Including ASL interpreters in the educational and primary care setting will improve health outcomes and improve patient satisfaction (MacKinney et al., 1995).

Bereavement Support

Losing a loved one is a painful and often traumatic experience. In most instances, the bereavement period following the death of a loved one is temporary, and the sense of loss diminishes over time. The renowned grief expert Rabbi Earl Grollman once said, "Grief is not a disorder, a disease or a sign of weakness. It is an emotional, physical and spiritual necessity, the price you pay for love. The only cure for grief is to grieve."[9]

To grieve is normal, and indeed there is reason to believe that the availability of opportunities to grieve either privately or publicly is important to those who have lost someone they love.

> As such, bereavement can be viewed as a normal, natural human experience, one which most people manage to come to terms with over the course of time. Nevertheless, it is associated with a period of intense suffering for most individuals, with an increased risk of developing mental and physical health problems. Adjustment can take months or even years and is subject to substantial variation between individuals and across cultures. (Stroebe et al., 2007, p. 1960)

Unresolved grief can be associated with an increased risk of physical and mental illness and mortality from many causes, including suicide (Strobe et al. 2007, p. 1962).

In our 2012 research, we found there were limited opportunities for Deaf people to participate in grief support groups, primarily because most grief support groups are designed for hearing people and either the d/Deaf person or the group may not feel comfortable sharing experiences through an interpreter.

---

9. Earl A. Grollman famous quotes: https://www.inspiringquotes.us/author/2322-earl-a-grollman

> Most Deaf people feel isolated from the hearing community and receive supportive care and comfort from family or community members. Participants in this study acknowledged that sharing their feelings on the subject of death is uncomfortable for them. (Maddalena et al., 2012, p. 110)

As noted above, grieving the death of a loved one is normal and with the passage of time there is reason for hope. Many d/Deaf people live in families and communities where they can avail of support. Funeral rituals, religious ceremonies, and sharing their feelings with their close friends are all part of the grieving process. In larger urban centers, there may be groups or one-on-one bereavement supports for Deaf people and their families. In rural areas, accessing such services may require assistive technologies. It is worthwhile searching for these types of services while their loved one is dying rather than after death has occurred.

> The bereaved individual stands between two forces: on the one hand the biological facts of life present death as decay with the implication that life simply ends—it is a tale that is told; on the other hand, the cultural facts of life present death as a potent with its own significance. For the great majority of individuals, society triumphs and the bereaved comes to live an ongoing life of some purpose and fulfilment. (Davies, 2005, p. 13)

Assistive Technologies and Education

Advances in technology have opened new possibilities for education and communication for Deaf people and their families. The "smart phone" and the ability to text has greatly improved the ability to communicate for Deaf people. Assistive technology such as Skype or various remote interpreting services may be helpful if the community has appropriate internet access and physical capabilities. This is assuming internet services allow for the data transfer requirements of video conferencing. Access to remote ASL interpreting services may also reduce the need for travel to access health services or consultation. Online, real-time video interpreter services are available and not bound by geographical limitations or restrictions.

Our team developed YouTube video education series entitled, *Palliative Care Guide for the Deaf Community*. The six-part series includes the following: Introduction, Part 1: Getting the Diagnosis, Part 2: Treatment of Illness, Part 3: Palliative Care, Part 4: As You Get Close to Dying, and Part 5: After Death. The video can be found on YouTube by keying "deaf palliative care" in the YouTube search engine window.

Much of our health education materials are in written English and therefore may not be the most effective way to communicate information to people with low literacy levels. The growth in online video education on platforms such as YouTube are making health-related education in sign language more accessible to Deaf people. There is no substitute for face-to-face education with people who are knowledgeable about Deaf culture and signed languages. Palliative care services and clinicians who have patients who are d/Deaf should seek information and education on how to effectively serve their needs.

A Future Research Agenda

Research is a powerful tool to improve health equity for individuals and populations. Engaging d/Deaf people in the research process to improve their health or the health of their community is also empowering. Participating in research as an active partner and "owning" the process and outcomes also promotes agency and autonomy. Working with the d/Deaf community in partnership to examine issues of concern is desirable, and indeed necessary, to achieve meaningful results.

Given the unique characteristics and needs in the d/Deaf community and the limited body of research examining the issue of end-of-life and palliative care, an important question emerges: Why are researchers not doing more research in this area? There are Deaf academics researching many aspects of the Deaf experience, but few non-Deaf academic researchers. Potential reasons researchers are not involved in research in the Deaf community are varied and may include, for example, a lack of interest in end-of-life and palliative care as a subject area, a general lack of understanding of Deaf culture, or not knowing how to "connect" or engage with the community. It may also be the case that such research does not happen unless there is a personal connection between the researcher and the Deaf community. Many researchers may be intimidated by the language barrier, in much the same way as an English-speaking researcher may be reluctant to engage with communities that speak a different language, or who may be from a different culture. Improving health equity for d/Deaf people is important, and this can be achieved by involving d/Deaf people in the research process to achieve this aim (Morisod et al., 2021).

Regarding research on end-of-life and palliative care for the d/Deaf, the following are just a few topics that warrant more research:

- It is important to understand how d/Deaf people interact with the health system and vice versa; how do we overcome the communication barriers that exist?
- How do we accommodate the needs of d/Deaf people when they, for example, experience a new or life-threatening diagnosis?
- How do we communicate the complexities of health care to Deaf people when, in many instances, there are no signs (in ASL) to adequately explain technical terms or procedures? How do we ensure they have access to patient-centered care?
- How can health inequities be minimized for the d/Deaf?
- There is a need to develop and test new tools for assessing pain (and other symptoms) that are culturally appropriate for people with hearing loss.
- How can we redesign palliative care units to accommodate the needs of a d/Deaf patient and their family?
- What constitutes meaningful and culturally appropriate bereavement care for Deaf caregivers and family members, especially in rural areas?
- What is the most effective way to communicate health education material to the d/Deaf?

It is important to engage the Deaf community in setting a research agenda to ensure that the research is meaningful to their lives and has the potential to influence policy and improve their health.

References

Abou-Abdallah, M., & Lamyman, A. (2021). Exploring communication difficulties with deaf patients. *Clinical Medicine*, *21*(4), e380–e383. https://doi.org/10.7861/clinmed.2021-0111

Alexander, A., Ladd, P., & Powell, S. (2012). Deafness might damage your health, *The Lancet*, *379*(9820): 979–981. https://doi.org/10.1016/S0140-6736(11)61670-X

Allen, B., Meyers, N., Sullivan, J., & Sullivan, M. (2002). American Sign Language and end-of-life care: Research in the deaf community. *HEC Forum: An Interdisciplinary Journal on Hospitals' Ethical and Legal Issues, 14*(3), 197–208. https://doi.org/10.1023/a:1020508511133

American Academy of Pediatrics (AAP). (2022). *Pediatric collections: Social determinants of health: Part 1: Underserved communities* (1st ed.). https://www.aap.org/Pediatric-Collections-Social-Determinants-of-Health-Part-1-Underserved-Communities-Paperback?srsltid=AfmBOoriVxOpbED-KIdovTwl1iKKZaXpak-e_QbN4Mp3X_eXtP1biIDLs

Barnett S. (2002). Communication with deaf and hard-of-hearing people: A guide for medical education. *Academic Medicine: Journal of the Association of American Medical Colleges, 77*(7), 694–700. https://doi.org/10.1097/00001888-200207000-00009

Barnett, S., & Franks, P. (2002). Health care utilization and adults who are deaf: Relationship with age at onset of deafness. *Health Services Research, 37*(1), 103–118. https://doi.org/10.1111/1475-6773.99106

Barnett, S., Klein, J. D., Pollard, R. Q., Jr., Samar, V., Schlehofer, D., Starr, M., Sutter, E., Yang, H., & Pearson, T. A. (2011). Community participatory research with deaf sign language users to identify health inequities. *American Journal of Public Health, 101*(12), 2235–2238. https://doi.org/10.2105/AJPH.2011.300247

Barnett S., McKee M., Smith S. R., & Pearson, T. A. (2011). Deaf sign language users, health inequities, and public health: Opportunity for social justice. *Preventing Chronic Disease: Public Health Research, Practice and Policy*, 8(2), Article A45. http://cdc.gov/pcd/issues/2011/mar/10_0065.htm

Bhalotra, A. R., & Kakkar, B. (2017). Anesthesia for the deaf and mute. *Korean Journal of Anesthesiology, 70*(6): 654–655 https://doi.org/10.4097/kjae.2017.70.6.654

Blustein, J., Weinstein, B. E., & Chodosh, J. (2018). Tackling hearing loss to improve the care of older adults. *BMJ (Clinical research ed.), 360*, Article k21. https://doi.org/10.1136/bmj.k21

Brick, K. (2006). Our civil rights movements: A guide for all. In H. Goodstein (Ed.), *The deaf way II reader: Perspectives from the Second International Conference on Deaf Culture* (pp. 199–204). Gallaudet University Press.

Canadian Association of the Deaf (CAD). (July 3, 2015a). *Deaf culture versus medicalization.* http://cad.ca/issues-positions/deaf-culture-vs-medicalization/

Canadian Association of the Deaf (CAD). (July 3, 2015b). *Statistics on deaf Canadians.* http://cad.ca/issues-positions/statistics-on-deaf-canadians/

Canadian Hearing Services. (2023). *About deaf interpreting.* https://www.chs.ca/service/about-deaf-interpreting

Christensen, K. M., & Delgado, G. L. (2000). *Deaf plus: A multicultural perspective.* DawnSignPress.

Cohen, L. H. (1994). *Train go sorry: Inside a deaf world.* Houghton Mifflin Company.

Correia, L. P. F., & Ferreira, M.A. (2022). Health care of deaf persons during coronavirus pandemics. *Revista Brasileira de Enfermagen, 75*(Suppl 1), Article e20201036.

Cunningham, L. L., & Tucci, D. L. (2017). Hearing loss in adults. *The New England Journal of Medicine, 377*(25), 2465–2473. https://doi.org/10.1056/NEJMra1616601

Davies, D. J. (2005). *A Brief History of Death.* Blackwell Publishing.

Druel, V., Hayet, H., Esman, L., Clavel, M., & Rougé Bugat, M.-E. (2018). Assessment of cancers' diagnostic stage in a Deaf community—Survey about 4363 Deaf patients recorded in French units. *BMC Cancer, 18*(1), 93. https://doi.org/10.1186/s12885-017-3972-3

Du Feu, M. (2017). Deaf people: What every clinician needs to know. *British Journal of Psychiatric Advances, 23*(2), 89–94 https://doi.org/10.1192/apt.bp.116.016154

Du Feu, M., & Chovaz, C. (2014). *Mental health and deafness.* Oxford University Press.

Ebert, D. A., & Heckerling, P. S. (1995). Communicating with deaf patients: Knowledge, beliefs, and practice of physicians. *Journal of the American Medical Association, 273*(3), 227–229.

Evans, R. G., Barer, M. L., & Marmor, T. R. (Eds.). (1994). *Why are some people healthy and others Not? The determinants of health of populations.* De Gruyter. https://doi.org/10.1515/9783112421628

Fellinger, J., Holzinger, D., & Pollard, R. (2012). Mental health of deaf people. *Lancet, 379*, 1037–1044.

Flaskerud, J., & Winslow, B. (1998). Conceptualizing vulnerable populations in health related research. *Nursing Research, 47*(2), 69–78.

Gustafson, D. H. (2007). A good death. *Journal of Medical Internet Research, 9*(1), Article e6.

Harris, J. (1995). *The cultural meaning of Deafness: Language, identity and power relations*. Avebury.

Hoang, L., LaHousse, S. F., Nakaji, M. C., & Sadler, G. R. (2011). Assessing deaf cultural competency of physicians and medical students. *Journal of Cancer Education: The Official Journal of the American Association for Cancer Education, 26*(1), 175–182. https://doi.org/10.1007/s13187-010-0144-4

Hommes, R. E., Borash, A. I., Hartwig, K., & DeGraciai, D. (2018). American Sign Language interpreters perceptions of barriers to healthcare communication in deaf and hard of hearing patients. *Journal of Community Health, 43*, 956–961 https://doi.org/10.1007/s10900-018-0511-3

Hsu, A. T., & Garner, R. E. (2020). Associations between the receipt of inpatient palliative care and acute care outcomes: A retrospective study. *Health Reports, 31*(10), 3–13.

Humphries, K. H., and van Doorslaer, E. (2000). Income-related health inequality in Canada. *Social Science and Medicine, 50*(5), 663–671.

Jamieson, D. G. (2006) Literacy in Canada. *Paediatric and Child Health, 11*(9), 573–574. https://doi.org/10.1093/pch/11.9.573

Kehl, K. A., & Gartner, C. M. (2010). Can you hear me now? The experience of a deaf family member surrounding the death of loved ones. *Palliative Medicine, 24*(1) 88–93.

Kuenburg, A., Fellinger, P., & Fellinger, J. (2016). Health care access among deaf people. *Journal of Deaf Studies and Deaf Education, 21*(1), 1–10. https://doi.org/10.1093/deafed/env042

Kritzinger, J. Schneider, M., Swartz, L., & Braathen, S. H. (2013). "I just answer 'yes' to everything they say": Access to health care for deaf people in Worcester, South Africa and the politics of exclusion. *Patient Education and Counseling, 94*, 379–383.

LeFort, S., Maddalena, V., & Murphy, M. (2014). *Assessing pain: The deaf community's experience (part 2)* [Poster presentation]. Canadian Pain Society 35th Scientific Meeting, May 20–22, 2014, Quebec City, Quebec.

Leigh, I. W., & O'Brien, C. A. (Eds.). (2019). *Deaf identities: Exploring new frontiers*. Oxford University Press.

Lesch, H., Burcher, K., Wharton, T., Chapple, R., & Chapple, K. (2019). Barriers to healthcare services and supports for signing deaf older adults. *Rehabilitation Psychology, 64*(2), 237–244.

Lezzoni, L. I., O'Day, B. L., Killeen, M., & Harker, H. (2004). Communicating about health care: Observations from persons who are Deaf or hard of hearing. *Annals of Internal Medicine, 140*, 356–362.

MacKinney, T. G., Walters, D., Bird, G. L., & Nattinger, A. B. (1995). Improvements in preventive care and communications for deaf patients: Results of a novel primary health care program. *Journal of General Internal Medicine, 10*(3), 133–137.

Maddalena, V., O'Shea, F., & Murphy, M. (2012). Palliative and end of life care in Newfoundland's Deaf community. *Journal of Palliative Care, 28*(2), 105–112.

Malebranche, M., Morisod, K., & Bodenmann, P. (December 14, 2020). Deaf culture and health care. *Canadian Medical Association Journal, 14*(192), Article E1809. http://doi.org/10.1503/cmaj.200772

Marchand, S., Wikler, D., & Landesman, B. (1998). Class, health and justice. *The Milbank Quarterly, 76*(3), 449–467.

Margellos-Anast, H., Hedding, T., Perlman, T., Miller, L., Rogers, R., Kivland, L., DeGutis, D., Giloth, B., & Whitman, S. (2005). Developing a standardized comprehensive health survey for use with Deaf adults. *American Annals of the Deaf, 150*(4), 388–396.

McEwan, E., Anton-Culver, H. (1988). The medical communication of Deaf patients. *The Journal of Family Practice, 26*(3), 289–291.

McKee, M. M. (2013). Caring for older patients who have significant hearing loss. *American Family Physician, 87*(5), 360–366.

McKee, M. M., Paasche-Orlow, M. K., Winters, P. C., Fiscella, K., Zazove, P., Sen, A., & Pearson, T. (2015). Assessing health literacy in deaf American Sign Language users. *Journal of Health Communication, 20* Suppl 2(0 2), 92–100. http://doi.org/10.1080/10810730.2015.1066468

Meador, H. E., & Zazove, P. (2005). Health care interactions with deaf culture. *Journal of the American Board of Family Medicine, 18*(3), 218–222.

Memon, M., Abbas, F., Khaonolakar, M. Dixon, J., & Singh, I. (June 2002). Health issues in ethnic minorities: Awareness and action. *Journal of the Royal Society of Medicine, 95*(6), 293–295.

Milligan, S., & Potts, S. (2009). The history of palliative care. In E. Stevens, S. Jackson and S. Milligan, Palliative nursing: Across the spectrum of care (pp. 5–16). Wiley-Blackwell.

Morisod, K., Malebranche, M. Marti, J., Spycher, J., Grazioli, V. S., & Bodenmann, P. (2021). Interventions aimed at improving healthcare and health education equity for d/Deaf patients: A systematic review. *European Journal of Public Health, 32*(4), 548–556.

Munro-Ludders, B. (1992). Deaf and dying: Deaf people and the process of dying. *Journal of the American Deafness and Rehabilitation Assocation, 26*(1), 31–41.

Naseribooriabadi, T., Sadoughi, F., & Sheikhtaheri, A. (2017). Barriers and facilitators of health literacy among D/deaf. *Iran Journal of Public Health, 46*(11), 1465–1474.

Newfoundland and Labrador Association of the Deaf (NLAD). (2007). *Employment and employability in the deaf community: An employability strategy for deaf people within the northeast Avalon region*. https://www.nlad.org/

Olson, A. M., & Swabey, L. (2017). Communication access for deaf people in healthcare settings: Understanding the work of American Sign Language interpreters. *Journal for Healthcare Quality, 39*(4), 191–199.

O'Neill, A. (2024). *Child mortality rate (under five years old) in Canada, from 1830 to 2020*. Statista. https://www.statista.com/statistics/1041751/canada-all-time-child-mortality-rate/#:~:text=Child%20mortality%20in%20Canada%2C%201830%2D2020&text=This%20means%20that%20one%20third,faster%20rate%20throughout%20the%201900s

Ouellette, S. E. (2006). Reconstructing deafness: A solution-focused approach to mental health. In H. Goodstein (Ed.), *The deaf way II reader: Perspectives from the Second International Conference on Deaf Culture* (pp. 181–188). Gallaudet University Press.

Padden, C. A., & Humphries, T. L. (2006). *Inside deaf culture.* Harvard University Press.

Palese, A., Salvador, L., & Cozzi, D. (2011). One-dimensional scales for pain evaluation adopted in Italian nursing practice: Giving preference to deaf patients. *Journal of Nursing Measurement, 19*(2), 91–104.

Parise, N. (1999). *Breaking cultural barriers to health care: The voice of the deaf* [Master's thesis], eScholarhip@McGill. https://escholarship.mcgill.ca/concern/theses/z890rw61b.

Pollard, R. Q, Jr., & Barnett, S. (2009). Health-related vocabulary knowledge among deaf adults. *Rehabilitation Psychology, 54*(2), 182–185. https://doi.org/10.1037/a0015771.

Pollard, R. Q, Jr., & Listman, J. (2019). Deaf culture. In J. S. Damico & M. J. Bell (Eds.), *The Sage encyclopedia of human communication sciences and disorders* (pp. 544–548).

Raphael, D. (2016). *Social determinants of health: Canadian perspectives* (3d ed.). Canadian Scholars' Press.

Salladay, S., & San Agustin, T. (1984). Special needs of the deaf dying patient. *Death education, 8*(4), 257–269. https://doi.org/10.1080/07481188408252464

Skøt, L., Jeppesen, T., Mellentin, A. I., & Elklit, A. (2017). Accessibility of medical and psychosocial services following disasters and other traumatic events: Experiences of deaf and hard-of-hearing individuals in Denmark. *Disability and Rehabilitation, 39*(24), 2468–2476. https://doi.org/10.1080/09638288.2016.1236154

Smith, A. K., Jain, N., & Wallhagen, M. L. (2015). Hearing loss in palliative care. *Journal of Palliative Medicine, 18*(6), 559–562. https://doi.org/10.1089/jpm.2014.0367

Sørensen, K., Pelikan, J. M., Röthlin, F., Ganahl, K., Slonska, Z., Doyle, G., Fullam, J., Kondilis, B., Agrafiotis, D., Uiters, E., Falcon, M., Mensing, M., Tchamov, K., van den Broucke, S., Brand, H., & HLS-EU

Consortium (2015). Health literacy in Europe: Comparative results of the European Health Literacy Survey (HLS-EU). *European Journal of Public Health, 25*(6), 1053–1058. https://doi.org/10.1093/eurpub/ckv043

Sparks, J. (1856). *The writings of Benjamin Franklin, Vol. X (1789–1790).* Macmillan.

Stebnicki, J. A. M., & Coeling H. V. (1999). The culture of the deaf. *Journal of Transcultural Nursing, 10*(4), 350–357. http://doi.org/10.1177/104365969901000413

Steinberg, A. G., Barnett, S., Meador, H. E., Wiggins, E. A., & Zazove, P. (2006). Health care system accessibility. Experiences and perceptions of deaf people. *Journal of General Internal Medicine, 21*(3), 260–266. https://doi.org/10.1111/j.1525-1497.2006.00340.x

Stroebe, M., Schut, H., & Stroebe, W. (2007). Health outcomes of bereavement. *Lancet (London, England), 370*(9603), 1960–1973. https://doi.org/10.1016/S0140-6736(07)61816-9.

Stokoe, W. C., Jr. (2005). Sign language structure: An outline of the visual communication systems of the American deaf. *Journal of Deaf Studies and Deaf Education, 10*(1), 3–37. https://doi.org/10.1093/deafed/eni001

Tamaskar, P., Malia, T., Stern, C., Gorenflo, D., Meador, H., & Zazove, P. (2000). Preventive attitudes and beliefs of deaf and hard-of-hearing individuals. *Archives of Family Medicine, 9*(6), 518–526. https://doi.org/10.1001/archfami.9.6.518

Tennant, R. A., & Gluszak Brown, M. (2010). *The American Sign Language handshape dictionary.* Gallaudet University Press.

Vernon, M., & Leigh, I. W. (2007). Mental health services for people who are deaf. *American Annals of the Deaf, 152*(4), 374–381. https://doi.org/10.1353/aad.2008.0005

Wideman, T. H., Edwards, R. R., Walton, D. M., Martel, M. O., Hudon, A., & Seminowicz, D. A. (2019). The multimodal assessment model of pain: A novel framework for further integrating the subjective pain experience within research and practice. *The Clinical Journal of Pain, 35*(3), 212–221. https://doi.org/10.1097/AJP.0000000000000670

Woodcock, K., & Pole, J. D. (2007). Health profile of deaf Canadians: Analysis of the Canada Community Health Survey. *Canadian Family Physician, 53*(12), 2140–2141.

World Health Organization. (2020). *Palliative care.* https://www.who.int/news-room/fact-sheets/detail/palliative-care

Zazove, P., Niemann, L. C., Gorenflo, D. W., Carmack, C., Mehr, D., Coyne, J. C., & Antonucci, T. (1993). The health status and health care utilization of deaf and hard-of-hearing persons. *Archives of Family Medicine, 2*(7), 745–752. https://doi.org/10.1001/archfami.2.7.745

Index